Rick Steves

SNAPSHOT

Kraków, Warsaw & Gdańsk

CONTENTS

INTRODUCTION

This Snapshot guide, excerpted from my guidebook *Rick Steves Eastern Europe*, introduces you to a trio of grand Polish cities: historic Kraków, thriving Warsaw, and gorgeous Gdańsk. Covering the best of Poland, this book offers an enjoyable cross-section of this proud nation.

Poland's historical capital, Kraków, clusters around one of Europe's biggest and most inviting market squares. Explore Kraków's picture-perfect Old Town—filled with museums, restaurants, university life, and Old World charm—and head to the Kazimierz neighborhood to learn about Poland's Jewish story. Side-trip to the world's most powerful memorial to the victims of the Holocaust at Auschwitz-Birkenau concentration camp.

For a look at today's Poland, visit Warsaw—leveled in World War II, rebuilt soon after, and now rapidly gentrifying. Stroll through Warsaw's reconstructed Old Town, promenade along newly spiffed-up boulevards, gape up at the communist-style Palace of Culture and Science, and dip into engaging museums on WWII history, native son Fryderyk Chopin, Polish painters, and much more.

On the Baltic Coast, Gdańsk offers a vibrantly colorful main drag fronted by opulent old Hanseatic facades, plus inspiring tales from the toppling of communism at the shipyard where the Solidarity trade union was born. Nearby in Pomerania is a pair of medieval red-brick sights: the imposing Gothic headquarters of the Teutonic Knights, Malbork Castle; and the appealing, gingerbread-scented town of Toruń.

To help you have the best trip possible, I've included the following topics in this book:

• **Planning Your Time,** with advice on how to make the most of your limited time

• **Orientation,** including tourist information (abbreviated as TI), tips on public transportation, local tour options, and helpful hints

• **Sights** with ratings:

▲▲▲—Don't miss

▲▲—Try hard to see

▲—Worthwhile if you can make it

No rating—Worth knowing about

• **Sleeping and Eating,** with good-value recommendations in every price range

• **Connections,** with tips on trains, buses, and boats

Practicalities, near the end of this book, has information on money, phoning, making hotel reservations, eating, transportation, and more, plus Polish survival phrases.

To travel smartly, read this little book in its entirety before you go. It's my hope that this guide will make your trip more meaningful and rewarding. Traveling like a temporary local, you'll get the absolute most out of every mile, minute, and dollar.

Szczęśliwej podróży—happy travels!

Rick Steves

POLAND

POLAND

Polska

Americans who think of Poland as run-down—full of rusting factories, smoggy cities, and gloomy natives—are speechless when they step into Kraków's vibrant main square, Gdańsk's colorful Royal Way, or Warsaw's lively Old Town. While parts of the country are still cleaning up the industrial mess left by the Soviets, Poland also has some breathtaking medieval cities that show off its kindhearted people, dynamic history, and unique cultural fabric.

The Poles are a proud people—as moved by their spectacular failures as by their successes. Their quiet elegance has been tempered by generations of abuse by foreign powers. The Poles place a lot of importance on honor, and you'll find fewer scams and con artists here than in other Eastern European countries.

In a way, there are two Polands: lively, cosmopolitan urban centers, and countless tiny farm villages in the countryside. City-dwellers often talk about the "simple people" of Poland—those descended from generations of farmers, working the same plots for centuries and living an uncomplicated, agrarian lifestyle. This large contingent of salt-of-the-earth folks—who like things the way they are—is a major reason why Poland was hesitant to join the European Union and remains fiercely "Euroskeptic."

Poland is arguably Europe's most devoutly Catholic country. Catholicism has long defined these people, holding them together through times when they had little else. Squeezed between Protestant Germany (originally Prussia) and Eastern Orthodox Russia, Poland wasn't even a country for genera-

tions (1795-1918). Its Catholicism helped keep its spirit alive. In the last century, while "under communism" (as that age is referred to), Poles once again found their religion a source of strength as well as rebellion—they could express dissent against the atheistic regime

by going to church. Some of Poland's best sights are churches, usually filled with locals praying silently. While these church interiors are worth a visit, be careful to show the proper respect: Maintain silence, keep a low profile, and if you want to snap pictures, do so discreetly.

Visitors are sometimes surprised at how much of Poland's story is a Jewish story. Before World War II, 80 percent of Europe's Jews lived in Poland. Warsaw was the world's second-largest Jewish city (after New York), with 380,000 Jews (out of a total population of 1.2 million). Poland was a magnet for Jewish refugees because of its relatively welcoming policies. Still, Jews were forbidden from owning land; that's why they settled mostly in the cities. But the Holocaust (and a later Soviet policy of sending "troublemaking" Jews to Israel) decimated the Jewish population. This tragic chapter, combined with postwar border shifts and population movements, made Poland one of Europe's most ethnically homogeneous countries. Today, virtually everyone in the country is an ethnic Pole, and only a few thousand Polish Jews remain.

Poland has long been extremely pro-America. Of course, their big neighbors (Russia and Germany) have been their historic enemies. And when Hitler invaded in 1939, the Poles felt let down by their supposed European friends (France and Britain), who declared war on Germany but provided virtually no military support to the Polish resistance. America, meanwhile, has been regarded as the big ally from across the ocean—and the home of the largest population of Poles outside of Poland. In 1989, when Poland finally won its freedom, many Poles only half-joked that they should apply to become the 51st state of the US.

POLAND

Poland Almanac

Official Name: Rzeczpospolita Polska (Republic of Poland), or Polska for short.

Snapshot History: This thousand-year-old country has been dominated by foreigners for much of the past two centuries, finally achieving true independence (from the Soviet Union) in 1989.

Population: Nearly 38.5 million people, slightly more than California. About 97 percent are ethnic Poles who speak Polish (though English is also widely spoken). Three out of every four Poles are practicing Catholics. The population is younger than most European countries, with an average age of 39 (Germany's is 46).

Latitude and Longitude: 52°N and 20°E (similar latitude to Berlin, London, and Edmonton, Alberta).

Area: 121,000 square miles, the same as New Mexico (or Illinois and Iowa put together).

Geography: Because of its overall flatness, Poland has been a corridor for invading armies since its infancy. The Vistula River (650 miles) runs south-to-north up the middle of the country, passing through Kraków and Warsaw, and emptying into the Baltic Sea at Gdańsk. Poland's climate is generally cool and rainy—40,000 storks love it.

Biggest Cities: Warsaw (the capital, 1.7 million), Kraków (757,000), and Łódź (747,000).

Economy: The Gross Domestic Product is $814 billion, with a GDP per capita of $21,100. The 1990s saw an aggressive and successful transition from state-run socialism to privately owned capitalism. Still, Poland's traditional potato-and-pig-farming society is behind the times, with 16 percent of the country's workers producing less than 3 percent of its GDP. About one in ten Poles is unemployed, and nearly one in five lives in poverty. And yet, perhaps because its economy is so primitive, Poland fared especially well through the recent economic downturn.

Currency: 1 złoty (zł, or PLN) = 100 groszy (gr) = about 30 cents; 3 zł = about $1.

On my first visit to Poland, I had a poor impression of Poles, who seemed brusque and often elbowed ahead of me in line. I've since learned that all it takes is a smile and a cheerful greeting—preferably in Polish—to break through the thick skin that helped these kind people survive the difficult communist times. With a friendly *Dzień dobry!*, you'll turn any grouch into an ally. It may help to know that, because of the distinct cadence of Polish, Poles speaking English sometimes sound more impatient, gruff, or irritated than they actually are. Part of the Poles' charm is that they're not as slick and self-assured as many Europeans: They're

Real Estate: A typical one-bedroom apartment in Warsaw (250 square feet) rents for roughly $600 a month.

Government: Poland's mostly figurehead president selects the prime minister and cabinet, with legislators' approval. They govern along with a two-house legislature (Sejm and Senat) of 560 seats. Since late 2014, the prime minister has been Ewa Kopacz, of the centrist Civic Platform. President Bronisław Komorowski, also of the Civic Platform, is up for re-election in 2015. (For more on Polish politics, see page 14.)

Flag: The upper half is white, and the lower half is red—the traditional colors of Poland. Poetic Poles claim the white represents honor, and the red represents the enormous amounts of blood spilled by the Poles to honor their nation. The flag sometimes includes a coat of arms with a crowned eagle (representing Polish sovereignty). Under Poland's many oppressors (including the Soviets), the crown was removed from the emblem, and its talons were trimmed. On regaining its independence, Poland coronated its eagle once more.

The Average Pole: In spite of its tumultuous history, Poland is a relatively upbeat nation: 74 percent of all Poles report they are "quite happy." Three-quarters use the Internet, and the average Pole will live to about age 77. The average Polish woman gets married at age 26 and will have 1.3 children.

Not-so-Average Poles: Poland's three big airports offer a rundown of just a few of the country's biggest names: St. John Paul II (in Kraków), Fryderyk Chopin (in Warsaw), and Lech Wałęsa (in Gdańsk). And, despite the many "Polack jokes" you've heard (and maybe repeated), you're already familiar with many other famous Polish intellectuals—you just don't realize they're Polish. The "Dumb Polack" Hall of Fame includes Mikołaj Kopernik **(Nicolas Copernicus),** scientist **Marie Curie** (née Skłodowska), writer Teodor Józef Korzeniowski (better known as **Joseph Conrad,** author of *Heart of Darkness*), filmmaker **Roman Polański** (*Chinatown, The Pianist*), **Daniel Libeskind** (the master architect for redeveloping the 9/11 site in New York City)...and one of this book's co-authors.

kind, soft-spoken, and quite shy. On a recent train trip in Poland, I offered my Polish seatmate a snack—and spent the rest of trip enjoying a delightful conversation with a new friend.

HELPFUL HINTS

Restroom Signage: To confuse tourists, the Poles have devised a secret way of marking their WCs. You'll see doors marked with *męska* (men) and *damska* (women)—but even more often, you'll simply see a triangle (for men) or a circle (for women). A sign with a triangle, a circle, and an arrow is directing you to

POLAND

Top 10 Dates That Changed Poland

A.D. 966—The Polish king, Mieszko I, is baptized a Christian, symbolically uniting the Polish people and founding the nation.

1385—The Polish queen (called a "king" by sexist aristocrats of the time) marries a Lithuanian duke, starting the two-century reign of the Jagiełło family.

1410—Poland defeats the Teutonic Knights at the Battle of Grunwald, part of a Golden Age of territorial expansion and cultural achievement.

1572—The last Jagiellonian king dies, soon replaced by bickering nobles and foreign kings. Poland declines.

1795—In the last of three Partitions, the country is divvied up by its more-powerful neighbors: Russia, Prussia, and Austria.

1918—Following World War I, Poland gets back its land and sovereignty.

1939—The Free City of Gdańsk (then called Danzig) is invaded by Nazi Germany, starting World War II. At war's end, the country is "liberated" (i.e., occupied) by the Soviet Union.

1980—Lech Wałęsa leads a successful strike, demanding more freedom from the communist regime.

1989—Poland gains independence under its first president—Lech Wałęsa. Fifteen years later, Poland joins the European Union.

2010—President Lech Kaczyński and 95 other high-level government officials are killed in a plane crash in Russia.

the closest WCs.

Pay to Pee: Many Polish bathrooms charge a small fee (around 1 zł). You may even be charged at a restaurant where you're paying to dine.

Train Station Lingo: "PKP" is the abbreviation for Polish National Railways ("PKS" is for buses). In larger towns with several train stations, you'll normally use the one called Główny (meaning "Main"—except in Warsaw, where it's Centralna). *Dworzec główny* means "main train station." Most stations have several platforms *(peron)*, each of which has two tracks *(tor)*. Departures are generally listed by the *peron*, so keep your eye on both tracks for your train. Arrivals are *przyjazdy*, and departures are *odjazdy*. Left-luggage counters or lockers are marked *przechowalnia bagażu. Kasy* are ticket windows. These can be marked (sometimes only in Polish) for specific needs—domestic tickets, international tickets, and so on; ask fellow travelers to be sure you select the right line. The line you choose will invariably be the slowest one—leave plenty of time to buy your ticket before your train departs (or, if you're running out of time, buy it on board for 10 zł extra).

Larger stations have customer service centers where you may have to wait longer (take a number), but you're more likely to encounter English-speaking staff. For longer and/or express journeys, you'll likely be given two separate tickets: one for the trip itself, and the other for your seat assignment. On arriving at a station, to get into town, follow signs for *wyjście (sometimes followed by do centrum or do miasta)*. Ongoing construction to improve Poland's rail lines may make some of your train journeys take much longer than normal, and delays are common.

Museum Tips: Most museums in Poland are closed on Monday, and the ticket office typically closes a half-hour before the museum's closing time. Poland's museums tend to frequently tweak their opening times—try to confirm hours locally if you have your heart set on a particular place.

Polish Artists: Though Poland has produced world-renowned scientists, musicians, and writers, the country isn't known for its artists. Polish museums greet foreign visitors with fine artwork by unfamiliar names. If you're planning to visit any museums in Poland, two artists in particular are worth remembering: **Jan Matejko,** a 19th-century positivist who painted grand historical epics; and one of his students, **Stanisław Wyspiański,** a painter and playwright who led the charge of the Młoda Polska movement—the Polish answer to Art Nouveau—in the early 1900s.

Telephones: Remember these Polish prefixes: 800 is toll-free, and 70 is expensive (like phone sex). Many Poles use mobile phones (which come with the prefix 50, 51, 53, 60, 66, 69, 72, 78, 79, or 88).

POLISH HISTORY

Poland is flat. Take a look at a topographical map of Europe, and you'll immediately appreciate the Poles' historical dilemma: The path of least resistance from northern Europe to Russia leads right through Poland. Over the years, many invaders—from Genghis Khan to Napoleon to Hitler—have taken advantage of Poland's

strategic location. The country is nicknamed "God's playground" for the many wars that have rumbled through its territory. Poland has been invaded by Soviets, Nazis, French, Austrians, Russians, Prussians, Swedes, Teutonic Knights, Tatars, Bohemians, Magyars—and, about 1,300 years ago, Poles.

POLAND

Medieval Greatness

The first Poles were the Polonians ("people of the plains"), a Slavic band that arrived here in the eighth century. In 966, Mieszko I, Duke of the Polonian tribe, adopted Christianity and founded the Piast dynasty (which would last for more than 400 years). Centuries before Germany, Italy, or Spain first united, Poland was born.

Poland struggled against two different invaders in the 13th century: the Tatars (Mongols who ravaged the south) and the Teutonic Knights (Germans who conquered the north). But despite these challenges, Poland persevered. The last king of the Piast dynasty was also the greatest: Kazimierz the Great, who famously "found a Poland made of wood and left one made of brick and stone," bringing Poland (and its capital, Kraków) to international prominence. The progressive Kazimierz also invited Europe's much-persecuted Jews to settle here, establishing Poland as a haven for the Jewish people, which it would remain until the Nazis arrived.

Kazimierz the Great died at the end of the 14th century without a male heir. His grand-niece, Princess Jadwiga, became "king" (the Poles weren't ready for a "queen") and married Lithuanian Prince Władysław Jagiełło, uniting their countries against a common enemy, the Teutonic Knights. Their marriage marked the beginning of the Jagiellonian dynasty and set the stage for Poland's Golden Age. During this time, Poland expanded its territory, the Polish nobility began to acquire more political might, Italy's Renaissance (and its architectural styles) became popular, and the Toruń-born astronomer Nicholas Copernicus shook up the scientific world with his bold new heliocentric theory. Up on the Baltic coast, the port city of Gdańsk took advantage of its Hanseatic League trading partnership to become one of Europe's most prosperous cities.

Foreign Kings and Partitions

When the Jagiellonians died out in 1572, political power shifted to the nobility. Poland became a republic of nobles governed by its wealthiest 10 percent—the *szlachta,* who elected a series of foreign kings. In the 16th and 17th centuries—with its territory spanning from the Baltic Sea to the Black Sea—the Polish-Lithuanian Commonwealth was the largest state in Europe.

But over time, many of the elected kings made poor diplomatic decisions and squandered the country's resources. To make matters worse, the nobles' parliament (Sejm) introduced the concept of *liberum veto* (literally "I freely forbid"), whereby any measure could be vetoed by a single member of parliament. This policy, which effectively demanded unanimous approval for any law to be passed, paralyzed the Sejm's waning power. Sensing the Commonwealth's weakness, in the mid-17th century forces from Sweden rampaged through Polish and Lithuanian lands in the devastating "Swedish Deluge." While Poland eventually reclaimed its territory, a third of its population was dead. The Commonwealth continued to import self-serving foreign kings, including Saxony's Augustus the Strong and his son, who drained Polish wealth to finance vanity projects in their hometown of Dresden.

By the late 18th century, Poland was floundering and surrounded by three land-hungry empires (Russia, Prussia, and Austria). The Poles were unaware that these neighbors had entered into an agreement now dubbed the "Alliance of the Three Black Eagles" (since all three of those countries, coincidentally, used that bird as their symbol); they began to circle Poland's white eagle like vultures. Stanisław August Poniatowski, elected king with Russian support in 1764, would prove to be Poland's last.

Over the course of less than 25 years, Russia, Prussia, and Austria divided Poland's territory among themselves in a series of three Partitions. In 1772 and again in 1790, Poland was forced into ceding large chunks of its territory to its neighbors. Desperate to reform their government, Poles enacted Europe's first democratic constitution (and the world's second, after the US Constitution) on May 3, 1791—still celebrated as a national holiday. This visionary document protected the peasants, dispensed with both *liberum veto* and the election of the king, and set up something resembling a modern nation. But the constitution alarmed Poland's neighbors, who swept in soon after with the third and final Partition in 1795. "Poland" disappeared from Europe's maps, not to return until 1918.

Even though Poland was gone, the Poles wouldn't go quietly. As the Partitions were taking place, Polish soldier Tadeusz Kościuszko (also a hero of the American Revolution) returned home to lead an unsuccessful military resistance against the Russians in 1794.

Napoleon offered a brief glimmer of hope to the Poles in the early 19th century, when he marched eastward through Europe and set up the semi-independent "Duchy of Warsaw" in Polish lands. But that fleeting taste of freedom lasted only eight years; with Napoleon's defeat, Polish hopes were dashed. The Congress of Vienna, which redistributed Polish territory to Prussia, Russia, and Austria, is sometimes called (by Poles) the "Fourth Partition." In a classic case of "my enemy's enemy is my friend," the Poles still have great affection for Napoleon for how fiercely he fought against their mutual foes.

The Napoleonic connection also established France as a safe haven for refugee Poles. After another failed uprising against

Russia in 1830, many of Poland's top artists and writers fled to Paris—including pianist Fryderyk Chopin and Romantic poet Adam Mickiewicz (whose statue adorns Kraków's main square and Warsaw's Royal Way). These Polish artists tried to preserve the nation's spirit with music and words; those who remained in Poland continued to fight with swords and fists. By the end of the 19th century, the image of the Pole as a tireless, idealistic insurgent emerged. During this time, some Romantics—with typically melodramatic flair—dubbed Poland "the Christ of nations" for the way it was misunderstood and persecuted by the world, despite its inherent nobility.

Poles didn't just flock to France during the Partitions. Untold numbers of Polish people uprooted their lives to pursue a better future in the New World. About 10 million Americans have Polish ancestry, and most of them came stateside from the mid-19th to early 20th centuries. Because the sophisticated and educated tended to remain in Poland, these new arrivals were mostly poor farmers who were (at first) unschooled and didn't speak English, placing them on a bottom rung of American society. It was during this time that the tradition of insulting "Polack jokes" emerged. Some claim these originated in Chicago, which was both a national trendsetter in humor and a magnet for Polish immigrants. Others suggest that German immigrants to America imported insulting stereotypes of their Polish neighbors from the Old World. Either way, the jokes only became more vicious through the 20th century, until the Polish government actually lobbied the US State Department to put a stop to them.

As the map of Europe was redrawn following World War I, Poland emerged as a reborn nation, under the war hero-turned-head of state, Marshal Józef Piłsudski. The newly reformed "Second Polish Republic," which patched together the bits and pieces of territory that had been under foreign rule for decades, enjoyed a diverse ethnic mix—including Germans, Russians, Ukrainians, Lithuanians, and an enormous Jewish minority. A third of Poland spoke no Polish. The historic Baltic port city of Gdańsk—which was bicultural (German and Polish)—was granted the special "Free City of Danzig" status to avoid dealing with the prickly issue of whether to assign it to Germany or Poland. But the peace was not to last.

World War II
On September 1, 1939, Adolf Hitler began World War II by attacking Danzig to bring it into the German fold. Before the month was out, Hitler's forces had overrun Poland, and the Soviets had taken over a swath of eastern Poland (today still part of Ukraine, Belarus, and Lithuania).

The Nazis considered the Poles *slawische Untermenschen,* "Slavic sub-humans" who were useful only for manual labor. Remember that Poland was also home to a huge population of another group the Nazis hated, Jews. Nazi Germany annexed Polish regions that it claimed historic ties to, while the rest (including "Warschau" and "Krakau") became a puppet state ruled by the *Generalgouvernement* and Hitler's handpicked governor, Hans Frank. The Nazis considered this area *Lebensraum*—"living space" that wasn't nice enough to actually incorporate into Germany, but served perfectly as extra territory for building things that Germans didn't want in their backyards...such as Auschwitz-Birkenau, the notorious death camp that functioned as a factory for the mass-production of murder.

The Poles anxiously awaited the promised military aid of France and Britain; when help failed to arrive, they took matters into their own hands, forming a ragtag "Polish Home Army" and staging incredibly courageous but lopsided battles against their powerful German overlords (such as the Warsaw Uprising). Throughout the spring of 1945, as the Nazis retreated from their failed invasion of the Soviet Union, the Red Army gradually "liberated" Poland from Nazi oppression, guaranteeing it another four decades of oppression under another regime.

With six million deaths over six years—including both Polish Jews and ethnic Poles—Poland suffered the worst per-capita WWII losses of any nation. By the war's end, one out of every five Polish citizens was dead—and 90 percent of those killed were civilians. While the human and infrastructure loss of World War II was incalculable, that war's cultural losses were also devastating—some 60,000 paintings were lost.

At the war's end, the victorious Allies shifted Poland's borders significantly westward—folding historically German areas into Polish territory and appropriating previously Polish areas for the USSR. This prompted a massive movement of populations—which today we'd decry as "ethnic cleansing"—as Germans were forcibly removed from western Poland, and Poles from newly Soviet territory were transplanted to Poland proper. Entire cities were repopulated (such as the formerly German metropolis of Breslau, which was renamed Wrocław and filled with refugee Poles from Lwów, now Lviv, in Ukraine). After millions died in the war, millions more were displaced from their ancestral homes. When the dust settled, Poland was in rubble, and almost exclusively populated by Poles.

Saddle on a Cow: Poland Under Communism
Poland suffered horribly under the communists. A postwar intimidation regime was designed to frighten people "on board"

POLAND

The Heritage of Communism

Poland has been free, democratic, and capitalist since 1989, but some adults carry lots of psychological baggage from living under communism. While the vast majority of Poles much prefer the current system to the old one, even the gloomiest memories are tinged with nostalgia. A friend who was 13 in 1989 recalled those days this way:

"My childhood is filled with happy memories. Under communism, life was family-oriented. Careers didn't matter. There was no way to get rich, no reason to rush, so we had time. People always had time.

"But there were also shortages—many things were 'in deficit.' We stood in line not knowing what would be for sale. We'd buy whatever shoes were available and then trade. At grocery stores, vinegar and mustard were always on the shelf, along with plastic cheese to make it seem less empty. Milk and bread were very low quality—it wasn't unusual to find a cigarette butt in your loaf. We had to carry ration coupons, which we'd present when buying a staple that was in short supply. They'd snip a corner

off the coupon after making the sale. We didn't necessarily buy what we needed—just anything that could be bartered on the black market. I remember my mother and father had to

and coincided with government seizure of private property, rationing, and food shortages. The country enjoyed a relatively open society under Premier Władysław Gomułka in the 1960s, but the impractical, centrally planned economy began to unravel in the 1970s. Stores were marked by long lines stretching around the block.

The little absurdities of communist life—which today seem almost comical—made every day a struggle. For years, every elderly woman in Poland had hair the same strange magenta color. There was only one color of dye available, so if you had dyed hair, the choice was simple: Let your hair grow out (and look clownishly half red and half white), or line up and go red.

During these difficult times, the Poles often rose up—staging major protests in 1956, 1968, 1970, and 1976. Stalin famously noted that introducing communism to the Poles was like putting a saddle on a cow.

When an anti-communist Polish cardinal named Karol Wojtyła was elected pope in 1978, then visited his homeland in 1979, it was a sign to his countrymen that change was in the air.

'organize' for special events...somehow find a good sausage and some Coca-Cola.

"Instead of a tidy roll of toilet paper, bathrooms came with a wad of old newspapers. Sometimes my uncle would bring us several toilet paper rolls, held together with a string—absolutely the best gift anyone could give.

"Boys in my neighborhood collected pop cans. Since drinks were very limited in Poland, cans from other countries represented a world of opportunities beyond our borders. Parents could buy their children these cans on the black market, and the few families who were allowed to travel returned home with a treasure trove of cans. One boy up the street from me went to Italy, and proudly brought home a Pepsi can. All of the boys in the neighborhood wanted to see it—it was a huge status symbol. But a month later, communism ended, you could buy whatever you wanted, and everyone's can collections were worthless.

"We had real chocolate only for Christmas. The rest of the year, for treats we got something called 'chocolate-like product,' which was sweet, dark, and smelled vaguely of chocolate. And we had oranges from Cuba for Christmas, too. Everybody was excited when the newspapers announced, 'The boat with the oranges from Cuba is just five days from Poland.' We waited with excitement all year for chocolate and those oranges. The smell of Christmas was so special. Now we have that smell every day. Still, my happiest Christmases were under communism."

In 1980, Lech Wałęsa, an electrician at the shipyards in Gdańsk, became the leader of the Solidarity movement, the first workers' union in communist Eastern Europe. After an initial 18-day strike at the Gdańsk shipyards, the communist regime gave in, legalizing Solidarity.

But the union grew too powerful, and the communists felt their control slipping away. On Sunday, December 13, 1981, Poland's head of state, General Wojciech Jaruzelski, declared martial law in order to "forestall Soviet intervention." (Whether the Soviets actually would have intervened remains a hotly debated issue.) Tanks ominously rolled through the streets of Poland on that snowy December morning, and the Poles were terrified.

Martial law lasted until 1983. Each Pole has his or her own chilling memories of this frightening time. During riots, the people would flock into churches—the only place they could be safe from the ZOMO (riot police). People would go for their evening walks during the 19:30 government-sanctioned national news as a sign of protest. But Solidarity struggled on, going underground and becoming a united movement of all demographics, 10 million members strong (more than a quarter of the population).

In July of 1989, the ruling Communist Party agreed to hold open elections (reserving 65 percent of representatives for themselves). Their goal was to appease Solidarity, but the plan backfired: Communists didn't win a single contested seat. These elections helped spark the chain reaction across Eastern Europe that eventually tore down the Iron Curtain. Lech Wałęsa became Poland's first post-communist president.

Poland in the 21st Century

When 10 new countries joined the European Union in May 2004, Poland was the most ambivalent of the bunch. After centuries of being under other empires' authority, the Poles were hardly eager to relinquish some of their hard-fought autonomy to Brussels. Many Poles thought that EU membership would make things worse (higher prices, a loss of traditional lifestyles) before they got better. But most people agreed that their country had to join to survive in today's Europe. Today most Poles begrudgingly acknowledge that the benefits of EU membership have outweighed the drawbacks.

The most obvious initial impact of EU membership was the tremendous migration of young Poles seeking work in other EU countries (mostly Britain, Ireland, and Sweden, which were the first to waive visa requirements for Eastern European workers). Many found employment at hotels and restaurants. Visitors to London and Dublin noticed a surprising language barrier at hotel front desks, and Polish-language expat newspapers joined British gossip rags on newsstands. Those who remained in Poland were concerned about the "brain drain" of bright young people flocking out of their country. But with the recent global recession, quite a few Polish expats returned home.

Poland is by far the most populous of the recent EU members, with nearly 39 million people (about the same as Spain, or about half the size of Germany). This makes Poland the sixth-largest of the 27 EU member states—giving it serious political clout, which it has already asserted...sometimes to the dismay of the EU's more established powers.

On the American political spectrum, Poland may be the most "conservative" country in Europe. Poles are phobic when it comes to "big government"—likely because they've been subjugated and manipulated by so many foreign oppressors over the centuries. For most of the 2000s, the country's right wing was represented by a pair of twin brothers, Lech and Jarosław Kaczyński. (The Kaczyński brothers were child actors who appeared in several popular movies together.) Their conservative Law and Justice Party is

Polish Jokes

Through the dreary communist times, the Poles managed to keep their sense of humor. A popular target of jokes was the riot police, called the ZOMO. Here are just a few of the things Poles said about these unpopular cops:

- It's better to have a sister who's a whore than a brother in the ZOMO.
- ZOMO police are hired based on the 90-90 principle: They have to weigh at least 90 kilograms (200 pounds), and their I.Q. must be less than 90.
- ZOMO are dispatched in teams of three: one who can read, one who can write, and a third to protect those other two smart guys.
- A ZOMO policeman was sitting on the curb, crying. Someone came up to him and asked what was wrong. "I lost my dog!" he said. "No matter," the person replied. "He's a smart police dog. I'm sure he can find his way back to the station." "Yes," the ZOMO said. "But without him, I can't!"

The communists gave their people no options at elections: If you voted, you voted for the regime. Poles liked to joke that in some ways, this made communists like God—who created Eve, then said to Adam, "Now choose a wife." It was said that communists could run a pig as a candidate, and it would still win; a popular symbol of dissent became a pig painted with the words "Vote Red."

There were even jokes about jokes. Under communism, Poles noted that there was a government-sponsored prize for the funniest political joke: 15 years in prison.

pro-tax cuts, fiercely Euroskeptic (anti-EU), and very Catholic. In the 2005 presidential election, Lech Kaczyński emerged as the victor; several months later, he took the controversial step of appointing his identical twin brother Jarosław as Poland's prime minister.

The political pendulum swung back toward the center in October of 2007, when the Kaczyński brothers' main political rival, the pro-EU Donald Tusk, led his Civic Platform Party to victory in the parliamentary elections. The name Kaczyński loosely means "duck"—so the Poles quipped that they were led by "Donald and the Ducks."

Tragically, the levity wasn't to last. On April 10, 2010, a plane carrying President Lech Kaczyński crashed in a thick fog near the city of Smolensk, Russia. All 96 people on board—including top government, military, and business officials, high-ranking clergy, and others—were killed, plunging the nation into a period of stunned mourning. Poles wondered why, yet again, an

POLAND

Bar Mleczny (Milk Bar)

When you see a "bar" in Poland, it doesn't mean alcohol—it means cheap grub. Eating at a *bar mleczny* (bar MLECH-neh)

is an essential Polish sightseeing experience. These cafeterias, which you'll see all over the country, are an incredibly cheap way to get a good meal...and, with the right attitude, a fun cultural experience.

In the communist era, the government subsidized the food at milk bars, allowing workers to enjoy a meal out. The tradition continues today, as milk-bar prices remain astoundingly low: My bill for a filling meal usually comes to about $5. And, while communist-era fare was gross, today's milk-bar cuisine is usually quite tasty.

Milk bars usually offer many of the traditional tastes listed in the "Polish Food" section. Common items are soups (like *żurek* and *barszcz*), a variety of cabbage-based salads, *kotlet* (fried pork chops), pierogi (like ravioli, with various fillings), and *naleśniki* (pancakes). You'll see glasses of juice and (of course) milk, but most milk bars also stock bottles of water and Coke.

There are two types of milk bars: updated, modern cafeterias that cater to tourists (English menus), add some modern twists to their traditional fare, and charge about 50 percent more; and time-machine dives that haven't changed for decades. At truly traditional milk bars, the service is aimed at locals, which means no English menu and a confusing ordering system.

Every milk bar is a little different, but here's the general procedure: Head to the counter, wait to be acknowledged, and point to what you want. Handy vocabulary: *to* (sounds like "toe") means "this"; *i* (pronounced "ee") means "and."

If the milk-bar lady asks you any questions, you have three options: nod stupidly until she just gives you something; repeat one of the things she just said (assuming she's asked you to choose between two options, like meat or cheese in your pierogi); or hope that a kindly English-speaking Pole in line will leap to your rescue. If nothing else, ordering at a milk bar is an adventure in gestures. Smiling seems to slightly extend the patience of milk-bar staffers.

Once your tray is all loaded up, pay the cashier, do a double-take when you realize how cheap your bill is, then find a table. After the meal, bus your own dishes to the little window.

unprecedented tragedy had befallen their nation. (Ironically, the group's trip was intended to put a painful chapter of Poland's history to rest: a commemoration of the Polish officers and enlisted men killed in the Soviet massacre at Katyń.)

The ensuing presidential election pitted the deceased president's brother, Jarosław Kaczyński, against Donald Tusk's Civic Platform compatriot, Bronisław Komorowski. Komorowski's victory—and Donald Tusk's re-election as prime minister in 2011 (the first re-election of a PM since the end of communism)—have given the centrist Civic Platform the reins of Poland for the foreseeable future.

Meanwhile, Poland's economy has kept chugging along, even as the rest of Europe and much of the world were bogged down by an economic downturn. More than a quarter of Poland's trade is with neighboring Germany—another of Europe's healthiest economies—and Poland was the only European Union country that didn't have a recession in 2009. When I asked some Polish friends about this, they replied—cynically, but not without a hint of truth—"Well, when you have a backwards, agrarian economy, you're pretty resistant to international market fluctuations." Poland is a big, self-sustaining, insular economy. In recent years, Poland's relatively weak currency ("cheaper" than the euro, yet also shielded from euro volatility) and robust economy are luring foreign investment, paradoxically threatening the very autonomy that has buffered it so far. As Europe struggles to deal with its debt crisis and flagging economic might, it will be interesting to see the role that Poland plays.

In 2014, in a move indicative of Poland's importance on the European stage, Donald Tusk left his post as prime minister to become the president of the European Council—the top job of the entire European Union. As Tusk moved to Brussels to assume his post, his successor (and fellow Civic Platform member), Ewa Kopacz, became prime minster—and, one would hope, will continue to spur Poland's evolution.

POLISH FOOD

Polish food is hearty and tasty. Because Poland is north of the

Carpathian Mountains, its weather tends to be chilly, which limits the kinds of fruits and vegetables that flourish here. As in other northern European countries (such as Russia or Scandinavia), dominant staples include potatoes, dill, berries, beets, and rye. Much of what you might think of as "Jewish cuisine" turns up on Polish menus (gefilte fish, potato pancakes, chicken soup, and so forth)—which makes sense, given that Poles and Jews lived in the same area for centuries under the same climatic and culinary influences.

Polish soups are a highlight. The most typical are *żurek* and *barszcz*. *Żurek* (often translated as "sour soup" on menus) is a light-colored soup made from a sourdough base, usually containing a hard-boiled egg and pieces of *kiełbasa* (sausage). *Barszcz*, better known to Americans as borscht, is a savory beet soup that you'll see in several varieties: *Barszcz czerwony* (red borscht) is a thin, flavorful broth with a deep red color, sometimes containing dumplings or a hard-boiled egg. *Barszcz ukraiński* (Ukrainian borscht) is similar, but has vegetables mixed in (usually cabbage, beans, and carrots). In summer, try the "Polish gazpacho"—*chłodnik*, a cream soup with beets, onions, and radishes that's served cold. I never met a Polish soup I didn't like...until I was introduced to *flaki* (sometimes *flaczki*)—tripe soup.

Another familiar Polish dish is pierogi. These ravioli-like dumplings come with various fillings. The most traditional are minced meat, sauerkraut, mushroom, cheese, and blueberry; many restaurants also experiment with more exotic fillings. Pierogi are often served with specks of fatty bacon to add flavor. Pierogi are a budget traveler's dream: Restaurants serving them are everywhere, and they're generally cheap, tasty, and very filling.

Bigos is a rich and delicious sauerkraut stew cooked with meat, mushrooms, and whatever's in the pantry. *Gołąbki* is a dish of cabbage leaves stuffed with minced meat and rice in a tomato or mushroom sauce. *Kotlet schabowy* (fried pork chop)—once painfully scarce in communist Poland—remains a local favorite to this day. *Kaczka* (duck) is popular, as is freshwater fish: Look for *pstrąg* (trout), *karp* (carp, beware of bones), and *węgorz* (eel). On the Baltic Coast (such as in Gdańsk), you'll also see *łosoś* (salmon), *śledź* (herring), and *dorsz* (cod). Poles eat lots of potatoes, which are served with nearly every meal.

For a snack on the go, Poles love *zapiekanki* (singular *zapiekanek*): a toasted baguette with melted cheese, garlic, ketchup or other sauces, rubbery mushrooms from a can, and sometimes onions or other toppings. It's like the poor cousin of a French-bread pizza, and is a favorite late-night snack for bar-hopping young people. The bagel-like rings you'll see sold on the street, *obwarzanki* (singular *obwarzanek*), are also cheap, and usually fresh and tasty.

Poland has good pastries. A *piekarnia* is a bakery specializing in breads. But if you really want something special, look for a *cukiernia* (pastry shop). The classic Polish treat is *pączki*, glazed jelly doughnuts. They can have different fillings, but most typical

POLAND

is a wild-rose jam. *Szarlotka* is apple cake—sometimes made with chunks of apples (especially in season), sometimes with apple filling. *Sernik* is cheesecake, and *makowiec* is poppy-seed cake. *Winebreda* is an especially gooey Danish. *Babeczka* is like a cupcake filled with pudding. You may see *jabłko w cieście*—slices of apple cooked in dough, then glazed. *Napoleonka* is a French-style treat with layers of crispy wafers and custard.

Lody (ice cream) is popular. The tall, skinny cones of soft-serve ice cream are called *świderki,* sometimes translated as "American ice cream." The most beloved traditional candy is *ptasie mleczko* (birds' milk), which is like a semi-sour marshmallow covered with chocolate. E. Wedel is the country's top brand of chocolate, with outlets in all the big cities.

Thirsty? *Woda* is water, *woda mineralna* is bottled water (*gazowana* is with gas, *niegazowana* is without), *kawa* is coffee, *herbata* is tea, *sok* is juice, and *mleko* is milk. Żywiec, Okocim, and Lech are the best-known brands of *piwo* (beer).

Wódka (vodka) is a Polish staple—the word means, roughly, "precious little water." Żubrówka, the most famous brand of vodka, comes with a blade of grass from the bison reserves in eastern Poland (look for the bottle with the bison). The bison "flavor" the grass...then the grass flavors the vodka. Poles often mix Żubrówka with apple juice, and call this cocktail *szarlotka* ("apple cake"); it also goes by the name *tatanka* (a Native American word for "bison"). For "Cheers!" say, *"Na zdrowie!"* (nah ZDROH-vyeh).

Unusual drinks to try if you have the chance are *kwas* (a cold, fizzy, Ukrainian-style nonalcoholic beverage made from day-old rye bread) and *kompot* (a hot drink made from stewed berries). Poles are unusually fond of carrot juice (often cut with fruit juice); Kubuś is the most popular brand.

"Bon appétit" *is* "*Smacznego*" (smatch-NEH-goh). To pay, ask for the *rachunek* (rah-KHOO-nehk).

POLISH LANGUAGE

Polish is closely related to its neighboring Slavic languages (Slovak and Czech), with the biggest difference being that Polish has lots of fricatives (hissing sounds—"sh" and "ch"—often in close proximity). Consider the opening line of Poland's most famous tongue-twisting nursery rhyme: *W Szczebrzeszynie chrzaszcz brzmi w trzcinie* ("In Szczebrzeszyn, a beetle is heard in the reeds"—pronounced vuh shih-chehb-zheh-shee-nyeh khzhahshch bzh-mee vuh tzhuh-cheen-yeh...or something like that).

Polish intimidates Americans with long, difficult-to-pronounce words. But if you take your time and sound things out, you'll quickly develop an ear for it. One rule of thumb to help you out: The stress is always on the next-to-last syllable.

Polish has some letters that don't appear in English, and some letters and combinations are pronounced differently than in English:

ć, ci, and cz all sound like "ch" as in "church"
ś, si, and sz all sound like "sh" as in "short"
ż, ź, zi, and rz all sound like "zh" as in "leisure"
dż and dź both sound like the "dj" sound in "jeans"
ń and ni sound like "ny" as in "canyon"
ę and ą are pronounced nasally, as in French: "en" and "an"
c sounds like "ts" as in "cats"
ch sounds like "kh" as in the Scottish "loch"
j sounds like "y" as in "yellow"
w sounds like "v" as in "Victor"
ł sounds like "w" as in "with"

So to Poles, "Lech Wałęsa" isn't pronounced "lehk wah-LEH-sah," as Americans tend to say—but "lehkh vah-WEHN-sah."

The Polish people you meet will be impressed and flattered if you take the time to learn a little of their language. To get started, check out the selection of Polish survival phrases on the following pages.

As you're tracking down addresses, these words will help: *miasto* (mee-AH-stoh, town), *plac* (plahts, square), *rynek* (REE-nehk, big market square), *ulica* (OO-leet-sah, road), *aleja* (ah-LAY-yah, avenue), and *most* (mohst, bridge).

Polish Survival Phrases

Keep in mind a few Polish pronunciation tips: **w** sounds like "v,"
ł sounds like "w," **ch** is a back-of-your-throat "kh" sound (as in the Scottish
"loch"), and **rz** sounds like the "zh" sound in "pleasure." The vowels with a
tail (**ą** and **ę**) have a slight nasal "n" sound at the end, similar to French.

English	Polish	Pronunciation
Hello. (formal)	*Dzień dobry.*	jehn **doh**-brih
Hi. / Bye. (informal)	*Cześć.*	cheshch
Do you speak English? (asked of a man)	*Czy Pan mówi po angielsku?*	chih pahn **moo**-vee poh ahn-**gyehl**-skoo
Do you speak English? (asked of a woman)	*Czy Pani mówi po angielsku?*	chih **pah**-nee **moo**-vee poh ahn-**gyehl**-skoo
Yes. / No.	*Tak. / Nie.*	tahk / nyeh
I (don't) understand.	*(Nie) rozumiem.*	(nyeh) roh-**zoo**-myehm
Please. / You're welcome. / Can I help you?	*Proszę.*	**proh**-sheh
Thank you (very much).	*Dziękuję (bardzo).*	jehn-**koo**-yeh (**bard**-zoh)
Excuse me. / I'm sorry.	*Przepraszam.*	psheh-**prah**-shahm
(No) problem.	*(Żaden) problem.*	(**zhah**-dehn) **proh**-blehm
Good.	*Dobrze.*	**dohb**-zheh
Goodbye.	*Do widzenia.*	doh veed-**zay**-nyah
one / two / three	*jeden / dwa / trzy*	**yeh**-dehn / dvah / tzhih
four / five / six	*cztery / pięć / sześć*	**chteh**-rih / pyench / sheshch
seven / eight	*siedem / osiem*	**shyeh**-dehm / **oh**-shehm
nine / ten	*dziewięć / dziesięć*	**jeh**-vyench / **jeh**-shench
hundred / thousand	*sto / tysiąc*	stoh / **tih**-shants
How much?	*Ile?*	**ee**-leh
local currency	*złoty (zł)*	**zwoh**-tih
Write it.	*Napisz to.*	**nah**-peesh toh
Is it free?	*Czy to jest za darmo?*	chih toh yehst zah **dar**-moh
Is it included?	*Czy jest to wliczone?*	chih yehst toh vlee-**choh**-neh
Where can I find / buy...?	*Gdzie mogę dostać / kupić...?*	guh-**dyeh moh**-geh **doh**-statch / **koo**-peech
I'd like... (said by a man)	*Chciałbym...*	**khchaw**-beem
I'd like... (said by a woman)	*Chciałabym...*	**khchah**-wah-beem
We'd like...	*Chcielibyśmy...*	**khchehl**-ee-bish-mih
...a room.	*...pokój.*	**poh**-kooey
...a ticket to ___.	*...bilet do ___.*	**bee**-leht doh ___
Is it possible?	*Czy jest to możliwe?*	chih yehst toh mohzh-**lee**-veh
Where is...?	*Gdzie jest...?*	guh-**dyeh** yehst
...the train station	*...dworzec kolejowy*	**dvoh**-zhehts koh-leh-**yoh**-vih
...the bus station	*...dworzec autobusowy*	**dvoh**-zhehts ow-toh-boos-**oh**-vih
...the tourist information office	*...informacja turystyczna*	een-for-**maht**-syah too-ris-**titch**-nah
...the toilet	*...toaleta*	toh-ah-**leh**-tah
men / women	*męska / damska*	**mehn**-skah / **dahm**-skah
left / right / straight	*lewo / prawo / prosto*	**leh**-voh / **prah**-voh / **proh**-stoh
At what time...?	*O której godzinie...?*	oh kuh-**too**-ray gohd-**zhee**-nyeh
...does this open / close	*...będzie otwarte / zamknięte*	**bend**-zheh oht-**vahr**-teh / zahm-**knyehn**-teh
Just a moment.	*Chwileczkę.*	khvee-**letch**-keh
now / soon / later	*eraz / niedługo / później*	**teh**-rahz / nyed-**woo**-goh / **poozh**-nyey
today / tomorrow	*dzisiaj / jutro*	**jee**-shigh / **yoo**-troh

POLAND

In a Polish Restaurant

English	Polish	Pronunciation
I'd like to reserve... (said by a man)	Chciałbym zarezerwować...	**khchaw**-beem zah-reh-zehr-**voh**-vahch
I'd like to reserve... (said by a woman)	Chciałabym zarezerwować...	**khchah**-wah-beem zah-reh-zehr-**voh**-vahch
We'd like to reserve...	Chcielibyśmy zarezerwować...	**khchehl**-ee-bish-mih zah-reh-zehr-**voh**-vahch
...a table for one person / two people.	...stolik na jedną osobę / dwie osoby.	**stoh**-leek nah **yehd**-now oh-**soh**-beh / dvyeh oh-**soh**-bih
Is this table free?	Czy ten stolik jest wolny?	chih tehn **stoh**-leek yehst **vohl**-nih
Can I help you?	W czym mogę pomóc?	vchim **moh**-geh **poh**-moots
The menu (in English), please.	Menu (po angielsku), proszę.	**meh**-noo (poh ahn-**gyehl**-skoo) **proh**-sheh
service (not) included	usługa (nie) wliczona	oos-**woo**-gah (nyeh) **vlee**-choh-nah
cover charge	wstęp	vstenp
"to go"	na wynos	nah **vih**-nohs
with / without	z / bez	z / behz
and / or	i / lub	ee / loob
milk bar (cheap cafeteria)	bar mleczny	bar **mletch**-nih
fixed-price meal (of the day)	zestaw (dnia)	**zehs**-tahv (dih-**nyah**)
specialty of the house	specjalność zakładu	speht-**syahl**-nohshch zah-**kwah**-doo
half portion	pół porcji	poow **ports**-yee
daily special	danie dnia	**dah**-nyeh dih-**nyah**
appetizers	przystawki	pshih-**stahv**-kee
bread	chleb	khlehb
cheese	ser	sehr
sandwich	kanapka	kah-**nahp**-kah
soup	zupa	**zoo**-pah
salad	sałatka	sah-**waht**-kah
meat / poultry	mięso / drób	**myehn**-soh / droob
fish / seafood	ryba / owoce morza	**rih**-bah / oh-**voht**-seh **moh**-zhah
fruit / vegetables	owoce / warzywa	oh-**voht**-seh / vah-**zhih**-vah
dessert	deser	**deh**-sehr
(tap) water	woda (z kranu)	**voh**-dah (**skrah**-noo)
mineral water	woda mineralna	**voh**-dah mee-neh-**rahl**-nah
carbonated / not carbonated	gazowana / niegazowana	gah-zoh-**vah**-nah / **nyeh**-gah-zoh-vah-nah
milk	mleko	**mleh**-koh
(orange) juice	sok (pomarańczowy)	sohk (poh-mah-rayn-**choh**-vih)
coffee / tea	kawa / herbata	**kah**-vah / hehr-**bah**-tah
wine	wino	**vee**-noh
red / white	czerwone / białe	chehr-**voh**-neh / bee-**ah**-weh
sweet / dry / semi-dry	słodkie / wytrawne / półwytrawne	**swoht**-kyeh / vih-**trahv**-neh / poow-vih-**trahv**-neh
glass / bottle	szklanka / butelka	**shklahn**-kah / boo-**tehl**-kah
beer	piwo	**pee**-voh
vodka	wódka	**vood**-kah
Cheers!	Na zdrowie!	nah **zdroh**-vyeh
Enjoy your meal.	Smacznego.	smatch-**neh**-goh
More. / Another.	Więcej. / Inny.	**vyehnt**-say / **ee**-nih-nih
The same.	Taki sam.	**tah**-kee sahm
the bill	rachunek	rah-**khoo**-nehk
I'll pay.	Ja płacę.	yah **pwaht**-seh
tip	napiwek	nah-**pee**-vehk
Delicious!	Pyszne!	**pish**-neh

KRAKÓW

Kraków is easily Poland's best destination: a beautiful, old-fashioned city buzzing with history, enjoyable sights, tourists, and college students. Even though the country's capital moved from here to Warsaw 400 years ago, Kraków remains Poland's cultural and intellectual center. Of all of the Eastern European cities laying claim to the boast "the next Prague," Kraków is for real.

Kraków grew wealthy from trade in the late 10th and early 11th centuries. Traders who passed through were required to stop here for a few days and sell their wares at a reduced cost. Local merchants turned around and sold those goods with big price hikes...and Kraków thrived. In 1038, it became Poland's capital.

Tatars invaded in 1241, leaving the city in ruins. Krakovians took this opportunity to rebuild their streets in a near-perfect grid, a striking contrast to the narrow, mazelike lanes of most medieval towns. The destruction also paved the way for the spectacular Main Market Square—still Kraków's best attraction.

King Kazimierz the Great sparked Kraków's Golden Age in the 14th century. In 1364, he established the university that still defines the city (and counts Copernicus and St. John Paul II among its alumni).

But Kraków's power waned as Poland's political center shifted to Warsaw. In 1596, the capital officially moved north. At the end of the 18th century, three neighboring powers—Russia, Prussia, and Austria—partitioned Poland, annexing all of its territory and dividing it among themselves. Warsaw ended up as a satellite of oppressive Moscow, and Kraków became a poor provincial backwater of Vienna. After Napoleon briefly reshuffled the map of

Kraków Essentials

English	Polish	Pronounced
Main Train Station	*Kraków Główny*	KROCK-oof GWOHV-nee
Old Town	*Stare Miasto*	STAH-reh mee-AH-stoh
Main Market Square	*Rynek Główny*	REE-nehk GWOHV-nee
Cloth Hall	*Sukiennice*	soo-kyeh-NEET-seh
Floriańska Street	*Ulica Floriańska*	OOH-leet-suh floh-ree-AHN-skah
Park around the Old Town	*Planty*	PLAHN-tee
Castle Hill	*Wawel*	VAH-vehl
Jewish Quarter	*Kazimierz*	kah-ZHEE-mehzh
Vistula River	*Wisła*	VEES-wah
Salt Mine	*Wieliczka*	vee-LEECH-kah
Planned Communist Suburb	*Nowa Huta*	NOH-vah HOO-tah

Europe in the early 19th century, Kraków was granted the status of a semi-independent city-state for about 30 years. The feisty Free City of Kraków, a tiny sliver wedged between three of Europe's mightiest empires, enjoyed an economic boom that saw the creation of the Planty park, the arrival of gas lighting and trams, and the construction of upscale suburbs outside the Old Town. Only after the unsuccessful Kraków Uprising of 1846 was Kraków forcefully brought back into the Austrian fold. But despite Kraków's reduced prominence, Austria's comparatively liberal climate allowed the city to become a haven for intellectuals and progressives (including a young revolutionary thinker from Russia named Vladimir Lenin).

The Nazis overran Poland in September of 1939, installing a ruling body called the *Generalgouvernement*, headed by former attorney Hans Frank. Germany wanted to quickly develop "Krakau" (as they called it) into the German capital of the nation. They renamed the Main Market Square "Adolf-Hitler-Platz," tore down statues of Polish figures (including the Adam Mickiewicz statue that dominates the Main Market Square today), and invested heavily in construction and industrialization (opening the door for Oskar Schindler to come and take over a factory from its

Jewish owners). The German overlords imposed a "New Order" that included seizing businesses, rationing, and a strict curfew for Poles and Jews alike. A special set of "Jewish laws" targeted, then decimated, Poland's huge Jewish population.

Kraków's cityscape—if not its people—emerged from World War II virtually unscathed. But when the communists took over, they decided to give intellectual (and potentially dissident) Kraków an injection of good Soviet values—in the form of heavy industry. They built Nowa Huta, an enormous steelworks and planned town for workers, on Kraków's outskirts, thereby dooming the city to decades of smog. Thankfully, Kraków is now much cleaner than it was 20 years ago.

St. John Paul II was born (as Karol Wojtyła) in nearby Wadowice and served as archbishop of Kraków before being called to Rome. Today, the hometown boy-turned-saint draws lots of pilgrims and is, for many, a big part of the city's attraction. Saintly ties aside, Kraków might be the most Catholic town in Europe's most Catholic country; be sure to visit a few of its many churches.

University life, small but thought-provoking museums, great restaurants, sprawling parks, and Jewish history round out the city's appeal. Over the last generation, Kraków has become the darling of Polish tourism. Today, with hundreds of creative places to eat and drink within its Old Town walls, and with more than its share of sights, it lures an estimated 7 million visitors a year.

PLANNING YOUR TIME

Don't skimp on your time in Kraków. It takes a minimum of two days to experience the city, and a third or fourth day lets you dig in and consider a world of fascinating side-trips. More than just good for sightseeing, Kraków is simply charming; more than any town in Europe, it seems made for aimless strolling.

Almost everyone coming to Kraków also visits the Auschwitz-Birkenau Concentration Camp Memorial—and should—which is about an hour and a half away. This demands the better part of a day to fully appreciate (either as a round-trip from Kraków, or en route to or from another destination), and also requires an online reservation. Auschwitz is covered in detail in the next chapter.

If you have only two full days (the "express plan"), start off with my self-guided walk through the Old Town and a quick stroll up to Wawel Castle, then wind down your day in Kazimierz (the Jewish and nightlife district). Your second day is for a side-trip to Auschwitz, and another evening in Kraków. This plan gives you an enticing once-over-lightly, but leaves almost no time for entering the sights.

More time buys you the chance to relax, enjoy, and lin-ger: Tackle the Old Town and Wawel Castle on the first day,

KRAKÓW

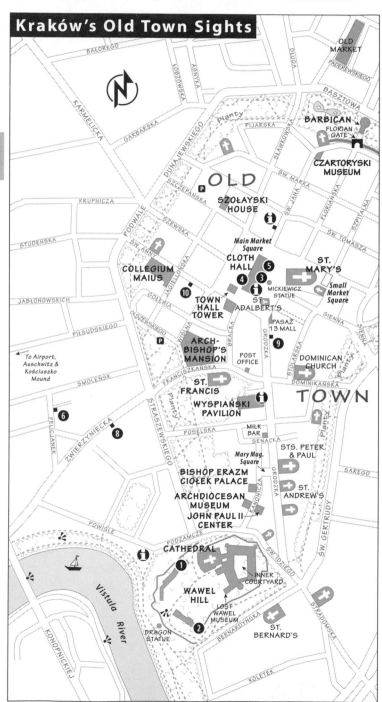

Kraków's Old Town Sights

OLD MARKET

BAŁOREGO

ŁOZOWSKA

BASZTOWA

DŁUGA

PADEREWSKIEGO

KARMELICKA

GARBARSKA

AŚNYKA

Planty

PIJARSKA

BARBICAN

FLORIAN GATE

SŁAWKOWSKA

CZARTORYSKI MUSEUM

KRUPNICZA

DUNAJEWSKIEGO

SW. MARKA

OLD

SW. JANA

FLORIAŃSKA

SW. TOMASZA

STUDENSKA

SZCZEPAŃSKA

SW. ANNY

SZEWSKA

SZOŁAYSKI HOUSE

Main Market Square

CLOTH HALL **5**

ST. MARY'S

4 **3**

Small Market Square

COLLEGIUM MAIUS

MICKIEWICZ STATUE

JABŁONOWSKICH

JAGIELLOŃSKA

10

TOWN HALL TOWER

ST. ADALBERT'S

SIENNA

SIENNA

PIŁSUDSKIEGO

GOŁĘBIA

PASAŻ 13 MALL

OLSZEWSKIEGO

WIŚLNA

BRACKA

9

P

ARCH-BISHOP'S MANSION

GRODZKA

STOLARSKA

DOMINICAN CHURCH

To Airport, Auschwitz & Kościuszko Mound

POST OFFICE

SMOLEŃSK

FRANCISZKAŃSKA

DOMINIKAŃSKA

ST. FRANCIS

WYSPIAŃSKI PAVILION

TOWN

6

STRASZEWSKIEGO

Planty

MILK BAR

8

ZWIERZYNIECKA

POSELSKA

SENACKA

Mary Mag. Square

STS. PETER & PAUL

FELICJANEK

BISHOP ERAZM CIOŁEK PALACE

GRODZKA

KANONICZA

SAREGO

ST. ANDREW'S

ARCHDIOCESAN MUSEUM

JOHN PAUL II CENTER

SW. GERTRUDY

POWIŚLE

PODZAMCZE

CATHEDRAL

1

INNER COURTYARD

Planty

ŚWIDZIŃSKIEGO

Vistula River

WAWEL HILL

LOST WAWEL MUSEUM

STRADOMSKA

2

DRAGON STATUE

BERNARDYŃSKA

ST. BERNARD'S

KONOPNICKIEJ

KOLETEK

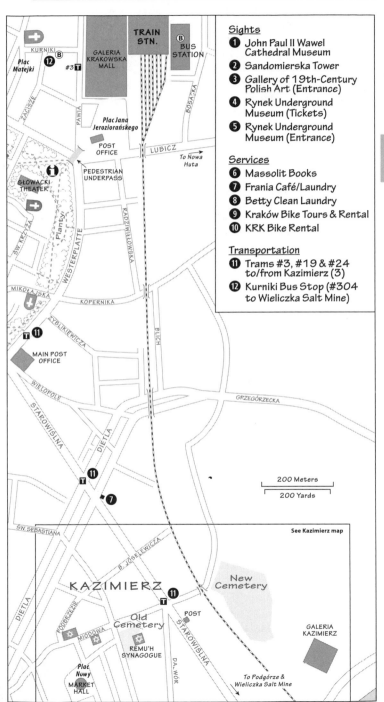

Sights

1. John Paul II Wawel Cathedral Museum
2. Sandomierska Tower
3. Gallery of 19th-Century Polish Art (Entrance)
4. Rynek Underground Museum (Tickets)
5. Rynek Underground Museum (Entrance)

Services

6. Massolit Books
7. Frania Café/Laundry
8. Betty Clean Laundry
9. Kraków Bike Tours & Rental
10. KRK Bike Rental

Transportation

11. Trams #3, #19 & #24 to/from Kazimierz (3)
12. Kurniki Bus Stop (#304 to Wieliczka Salt Mine)

KRAKÓW

Kazimierz and museums of your choice on the second day, and Auschwitz (and other side-trips) with additional days. If you have a special interest, you could side-trip to Wieliczka Salt Mine, St. John Paul II pilgrimage sites on the outskirts of town, or the communist architecture of the Nowa Huta suburb.

Regardless of how long you stay, your evening choices are many and varied: Savor the Main Market Square over dinner or a drink, take in a jazz show, do a pub crawl through the city's many youthful bars and clubs, or enjoy traditional Jewish music and cuisine in Kazimierz.

Orientation to Kraków

Kraków (Poles say KROCK-oof, but you can say KRACK-cow; it's sometimes spelled "Cracow" in English) is mercifully compact, flat, and easy to navigate. While the urban sprawl is big (with 757,000 people), the tourist's Kraków feels small. You can walk from the northern edge of the Old Town to the southern edge (Wawel Hill) in about 15 minutes.

Most sights—and almost all recommended hotels and restaurants—are in the Old Town (Stare Miasto), which is surrounded by a greenbelt called the Planty. In the center of the Old Town lies the Main Market Square (Rynek Główny, a.k.a. "the Square"). From the Main Market Square, the main train station is a 15-minute walk to the northeast; Kazimierz (the Jewish and nightlife quarter) is a 20-minute walk to the southeast; and Wawel Hill (with a historic castle, museums, and Poland's national church) is a 10-minute walk south. Just beyond Wawel is the Vistula River. Taxis are easy, and cabbies are generally honest; you can get just about anywhere in a snap for 10-15 zł.

TOURIST INFORMATION

Kraków has many helpful TIs, called InfoKraków (www.infokrakow.pl). Five branches are in or near the Old Town (all open daily May-Sept 9:00-19:00, Oct-April 9:00-17:00, unless otherwise noted):

• In the **Planty** park, between the main train station and Main Market Square (in round kiosk at ulica Szpitalna 25, tel. 12-432-0110)

• On **ulica Św. Jana,** just north of the Main Market Square (specializes in concert tickets, at #2, tel. 12-421-7787)

• In the **Cloth Hall** right on the Main Market Square (tel. 12-433-7310)

• In the **Wyspiański Pavilion,** just south of the Square on ulica Grodzka (daily 9:00-17:00, plac Wszystkich Świętych 3, not at the window but inside the building, tel. 12-616-1886)

• Just west of **Wawel Hill** (also covers the entire region, Powiśle 11, mobile 513-099-688)

Other TI branches are in **Kazimierz** (daily 9:00-17:00, ulica Józefa 7, tel. 12-422-0471) and the **airport** (daily 9:00-19:00, tel. 12-285-5341).

At any TI, ask what's new in fast-changing Kraków, browse the brochures, and pick up the free map and the *Kraków Tourist Information Compendium* booklet. The TIs also offer a free room-finding service and sell tickets for bus tours and walking tours (though only for one walking-tour company, See Kraków; for other options, see "Tours in Kraków," later).

Sightseeing Pass: The TI's **Kraków Tourist Card** isn't a good value for most visitors. It covers public transportation, includes admission to several city museums (basically everything except the Wawel Hill sights and Wieliczka Salt Mine), and offers discounts to outlying sights and tours—but Kraków's museums are already cheap, and public transportation is mostly unnecessary (75 zł/2 days, 95 zł/3 days).

Warning: Many private travel agencies, room-booking services, and tour operators masquerade as TIs, with deceptive blue-and-white *i* signs. If I haven't listed them in this section, they're not a real TI.

ARRIVAL IN KRAKÓW

By Train: Kraków's slick, new main train station (called "Kraków Główny"), just northeast of the Old Town, is very user-friendly. The main concourse has all of the amenities, and then some: ATMs, lockers (under the big schedule board between the ticket windows), WCs, takeaway coffee, a handy Biedronka mini-supermarket, giant informational touchscreens, and a complete mini-shopping mall. The main concourse has a long row of numbered ticket windows (some for domestic tickets only, others for domestic and international—check signs before you line up). Consider booking your ticket at the Passenger Service Center (in the middle of the row of ticket windows, between #11 and #12)—it may have a longer wait, but they're more likely to speak English and can be helpful if you have a complicated request (no extra fee, daily 8:00-19:40). From the ticket area, numbered escalators lead directly up to the platforms above.

The halls of the train station flow into the vast, modern Galeria Krakowska shopping mall—a glittering gauntlet of consumerism. To find anything in this confusing complex, follow the English signs (*Station Hall* is for tickets). The mall and the station face a broad plaza (plac Dworcowy), across the ring road from the Planty park and Old Town.

Taxis from the station are cheap and easy: From the tracks, take the elevator or stairs to the rooftop above you, where you'll find a giant parking lot where taxis wait. Be sure to use a taxi clearly marked with a company name and telephone number. Additional taxis wait outside both ends of the station. The usual metered rate to downtown is a reasonable 10-15 zł.

Most hotels are within easy **walking** distance of the station. It's about a 15-minute stroll to the Main Market Square. Just follow *Exit to the City* and *Old Town* signs, and you'll be routed directly into, and through, the Galeria Krakowska mall. At the far end of the mall, you can either turn left and continue to follow signs for the Old Town; or, if you're headed to Kazimierz, go out the doors straight ahead to hop on tram #3. If you head to the Old Town, you'll pop out into plac Dworcowy; continue straight ahead to take the broad ramp down into a pedestrian underpass beneath the busy ring road. Emerging into the Planty on the other side, the Main Market Square is straight ahead (you'll see the twin spires of St. Mary's Church).

By Bus: The bus station is directly behind the main train station. When arriving by bus, it's easiest to get into town by first heading into the train station, then continuing through it, following the above directions.

To get *to* the bus station from the Old Town (such as to catch a bus to Auschwitz), first head to the main train station (go through the Planty park and use the underpass). Once in the station, head all the way through to the far end (past platform 5, exit marked for *bus station*). Exiting the train station, escalate up to the bus terminal (marked *MDA Dworzec Autobusowy*). Inside are the standard amenities (lockers and WCs), domestic and international ticket windows, and an electronic board showing the next several departures. Some bus departures, marked on the board with a green *G,* leave from the upper *(gorna)* stalls, which you can see out the window. Other bus departures, marked with a red *D,* leave from the lower *(dolna)* stalls; to find these, use the stairs or the elevator right in the middle of the bus terminal. Note that some minibuses, such as those to Auschwitz, also leave from, or near, this station (though the buses and minibuses that go to the Wieliczka Salt Mine leave from the opposite end of the station/mall complex).

By Car: *Centrum* signs lead you into the Old Town—you'll know you're there when you hit the ring road that surrounds the Planty park. Parking garages surround the Old Town. Your hotelier can advise you on directions and parking.

By Plane: The small, modern **John Paul II Kraków-Balice Airport** is about 10 miles west of the center, with separate international and domestic terminals (airport code: KRK, airport info: tel. 12-295-5800, www.krakowairport.pl). To get to downtown

Kraków, you can take a speedy train, a slower public bus, or a taxi.

The handy train is the fastest choice (unless it's closed for maintenance)—it zips you from the terminal straight to the main train station's platform 1 (10 zł, buy ticket from machine or from conductor on train, 2/hour, 18 minutes; see train arrival instructions earlier).

To get from the airport to Kraków's main bus station by **public bus,** catch bus #208, #292, or (at night) #902 in front of the airport (4 zł, 50-minute trip depending on traffic, see bus arrival instructions earlier).

For door-to-door service, hop in a **cab** at the taxi stand in front of the terminal (ask about the fare up front—should be around 70-80 zł, more expensive at night, about 30 minutes). You can also arrange a taxi transfer in advance (such as with recommended driver Andrew Durman, listed later, under "Tours in Kraków"). Various shuttle services also operate for a slightly lower price; ask your hotelier.

Note that many budget flights—including those on Wizz Air and Ryanair—use the **International Airport Katowice in Pyrzowice** (Międzynarodowy Port Lotniczy Katowice w Pyrzowicach, airport code: KTW, www.katowice-airport.com). This airport is about 18 miles from the city of Katowice, which is about 50 miles west of Kraków. Direct buses run sporadically between Katowice Airport and Kraków's main train station (50 zł, trip takes 1.75 hours, generally scheduled to meet incoming flights). You can also take the bus from Katowice Airport to Katowice's train station (hourly, 50 minutes), then take the train to Kraków (hourly, 1.5 hours). Wizz Air's website is useful for figuring out your connection: www.wizzair.com.

HELPFUL HINTS

Sightseeing Schedules: Some sights are closed on Monday (including the Gallery of 19th-Century Polish Art, Szołayski House, and a few museums in Kazimierz), but many sights are open (including the churches and Jagiellonian University Museum, and in Kazimierz, all of the Jewish-themed sights). On Saturday, most of Kazimierz's Jewish-themed sights are closed. Also be aware of days that certain sights are free: On Sunday, the National Museum branches (including the Gallery of 19th-Century Polish Art in the Cloth Hall) are free, but some are open limited hours. And on Monday, Schindler's Factory Museum is free (and crowded), as well as two of the sights at Wawel Castle (but open only in the morning).

Post Office: The main post office (Poczta Główna) is at the intersection of Starowiślna and the Westerplatte ring road, a few blocks east of the Main Market Square (Mon-Fri 7:30-20:30, Sat 8:00-14:00, closed Sun).

Bookstore: For an impressive selection of new and used English books, try **Massolit Books,** just west of the Old Town. They also have a café with drinks and light snacks, and a good children's section (Sun-Thu 10:00-20:00, Fri-Sat 10:00-21:00, ulica Felicjanek 4, tel. 12-432-4150, www.massolit.com).

Laundry: Frania Café is a dream come true for a traveler with dirty laundry. Halfway between the Old Town and Kazimierz, this inviting café/pub has ample washers and dryers, relaxing ambience, free Wi-Fi and a loaner laptop, a full bar serving up espresso drinks and laundry-themed hard drinks, very long hours, and a friendly staff. Those in search of a mellow hangout might want to come here even if they don't need to wash clothes (16 zł/load self-service, 26 zł for them to do it for you in 2 hours—consider dropping it off on your way to Kazimierz and picking it up on the way back, likely open daily 10:30-24:00, ulica Starowiślna 26, mobile 783-945-021, www.laundromat.pl).

Betty Clean is a full-service laundry that's closer to the Old Town, but pricey (about 13 zł/shirt, 22 zł/pants, takes 24 hours, 50 percent more for express 3-hour service, Mon-Fri 7:30-19:30, Sat 8:00-15:30, closed Sun, just outside the Planty park at ulica Zwierzyniecka 6, tel. 12-423-0848).

GETTING AROUND KRAKÓW

Kraków's top sights and best hotels are easily accessible by foot. You'll need wheels only if you're going to the Kazimierz Jewish quarter or the Nowa Huta suburb.

By Public Transit: Trams and buses zip around Kraków's urban sprawl. The same tickets work system-wide and can be purchased at most kiosks or at the machines (accepting coins and small bills) at most stops. You can also buy tickets on board—some trams have machines on board, which take only coins and cost the same; otherwise, you'll buy your ticket from the driver and pay a bit more.

A *bilet jednoprzejazdowy,* which covers any single journey (including transfers) costs 3.80 zł. However, many journeys you're likely to take—such as between the Old Town and Kazimierz—are likely to be brief, so you'll save a bit by buying a 20-minute ticket *(20-minutowy)* for 2.80 zł. You can also get longer-term tickets for 24 hours (15 zł), 48 hours (24 zł), and 72 hours (36 zł)—though unless your accommodations are a tram ride away from the sights, you're unlikely to need these. These prices are for a "one-zone" ticket, which covers almost everything of interest in Kraków (including Nowa Huta, the St. John Paul II pilgrimage sites, and the Kościuszko Mound)—unless you're headed for the airport or Wieliczka Salt Mine, which are beyond the city limits and require a slightly more expensive *aglomeracyjny* ticket (4 zł for a single journey). Always validate your ticket when you board the bus or tram (24-, 48-, and 72-hour tickets must be validated only the first time you use them).

By Taxi: Just as in other Eastern European cities, only take cabs that are clearly marked with a company logo and telephone number. Kraków taxis start at 7 zł and charge about 3 zł per kilometer. Rides are usually very short and generally cost less than 20 zł; however, due to the Old Town's many traffic restrictions and pedestrian zones, a "short ride across town" may require looping all the way around the center. You're more likely to get the fair metered rate by calling or hailing a cab, rather than taking one waiting at tourist spots. To call a cab, try **Radio Taxi** (tel. 19191).

By Bike: The riverfront bike path is enticing on a nice day; the Planty park, while inviting, can be a bit crowded for biking. **Kraków Bike Tours** rents a wide variety of new, good-quality bikes (10 zł/first hour, cheaper per hour for longer rentals, 50 zł/day, 60 zł/24 hours, daily 9:30-19:00, just off the Square at Grodzka 2; see listing later, under "Tours in Kraków"). Nearby, **KRK Bike Rental** rents cheaper bikes (8 zł/hour, 45 zł/24 hours, April-Oct daily 9:00-21:00, less in bad weather, closed Nov-March, ulica Św. Anny 4, mobile 509-267-733, www.krkbikerental.pl).

Tours in Kraków

Local Guides

Hiring a guide in Kraków is fun and affordable, and makes a huge difference in your experience. I've enjoyed working with three in particular, any of whom can show you the sights in Kraków and also have cars for day-tripping into the countryside: **Marta Chmielowska** (350 zł/4 hours, 500 zł/day, same prices by foot or car, can be more for larger groups and for long-distance trips, mobile 603-668-008, martachm7@gmail.com); **Tomasz Klimek** (250 zł/half-day, 400 zł/day, slightly more with a car, mobile 605-231-923, www.krakow.tourism.pl, tomasz.klimek@interia.pl); and **Anna Bakowska** (same prices as Marta, mobile 604-151-293, www.leadertour.eu, leadertour@wp.pl). I wouldn't bother hiring a guide for the trip to Auschwitz (which generally costs 600-700 zł)—only official Auschwitz guides can legally give tours onsite, so you'll wind up joining one of the tours once there. While there's still a benefit to hiring a guide to take you to Auschwitz—door-to-door service and commentary en route—it's a better value to hire a driver (like Andrew, listed next).

Kraków at a Glance

▲▲▲**Main Market Square** Stunning heart of Kraków and a people magnet any time of day. **Hours:** Always open. See page 44.

▲▲▲**Schindler's Factory Museum** Historic building where Oskar Schindler saved more than 1,000 Jewish workers, now filled with engaging exhibit about Kraków's WWII experience. **Hours:** April-Oct Mon 10:00-16:00 (closes at 14:00 first Mon of month), Tue-Sun 10:00-20:00; Nov-March Mon 10:00-14:00, Tue-Sun 10:00-18:00. See page 90.

▲▲**Planty** Once a moat, now a scenic park encircling the city. **Hours:** Always open. See page 38.

▲▲**St. Mary's Church** Landmark church with extraordinary wood-carved Gothic altarpiece. **Hours:** Mon-Sat 11:45-17:45, Sun 14:00-17:45. See page 41.

▲▲**Cloth Hall** Fourteenth-century market hall with 21st-century souvenirs. **Hours:** Summer Mon-Fri 9:00-18:00, Sat-Sun 9:00-15:00, sometimes later; winter Mon-Fri 9:00-16:00, Sat-Sun 9:00-15:00. See page 46.

▲▲**St. Francis Basilica** Lovely Gothic church with some of Poland's best Art Nouveau. **Hours:** Daily 6:00-19:45. See page 48.

▲▲**Wawel Cathedral** Poland's splendid national church, with tons of tombs, a crypt, and a climbable tower. **Hours:** April-Sept Mon-Sat 9:00-17:00, Sun 12:30-17:00; Oct-March Mon-Sat 9:00-16:00, Sun 12:30-16:00. See page 55.

▲▲**Wawel Castle Grounds** Historic hilltop with views, castle, cathedral, courtyard with chakras, and a passel of museums. **Hours:** Grounds open daily 6:00 until dusk, but many of the museums closed Mon, and Sun in winter. See page 59.

▲▲**Gallery of 19th-Century Polish Art** Worthwhile collection of paintings by should-be-famous artists, upstairs in the Cloth Hall. **Hours:** Tue-Sun 10:00-18:00, closed Mon. See page 66.

▲▲**Rynek Underground Museum** Super-modern exhibit on medieval Kraków filling excavated cellars beneath the Main

Market Square. **Hours:** Mon 10:00-20:00, Tue 10:00-16:00 (closed first Tue of month), Wed-Sun 10:00-22:00, shorter hours in winter. See page 73.

▲▲**Old Jewish Cemetery** Poignant burial site in Kazimierz, with graves from 1552 to 1800. **Hours:** Sun-Fri 9:00-16:00, sometimes until 18:00 May-Sept, closes earlier in winter and by sundown on Fri, closed Sat. See page 82.

▲**Czartoryski Museum** Varied collection, with European paintings and Polish armor, handicrafts, and decorative arts. **Hours:** Likely closed for restoration, otherwise Tue-Sun 10:00-16:00, closed Mon. See page 71.

▲**Jagiellonian University Museum: Collegium Maius** Proud collection of historic university, surrounding a tranquil courtyard where medieval professors lived. **Hours:** Entry by guided tour; 30-minute version—Mon-Sat 10:00-15:00, until 18:00 Tue and Thu in April-Oct, no tours Sun; one-hour version in English—usually Mon-Fri at 13:00, no tours Sat-Sun. See page 74.

▲**New Jewish Cemetery** Graveyard with tombs from after 1800, partly restored after Nazi desecration. **Hours:** Sun-Fri 8:00-18:00, until 16:00 in winter, closed Sat. See page 84.

▲**Ethnographic Museum** Traditional rural Polish life on display. **Hours:** Tue-Sat 11:00-19:00, Thu until 21:00, Sun 11:00-15:00, closed Mon. See page 88.

▲**Pharmacy Under the Eagle** Small Podgórze exhibit about the Holocaust in Kraków, including three evocative historic films. **Hours:** April-Oct Mon 10:00-14:00, Tue-Sun 9:00-17:00; Nov-March Mon 10:00-14:00, Tue-Thu and Sat 9:00-17:00, Fri 10:00-17:00, closed Sun and the second Tue of each month. See page 89.

▲**Museum of Contemporary Art in Kraków** Today's thought-provoking art, displayed in renovated old warehouses behind Schindler's Factory Museum. **Hours:** Tue-Sun 11:00-19:00, closed Mon. See page 95.

KRAKÓW

Drivers

Since Kraków is such a useful home base for day trips, it can be handy to splurge on a private driver for door-to-door service. **Andrew (Andrzej) Durman,** a Pole who lived in Chicago and speaks fluent English, is a gregarious driver, translator, miracle worker, and all-around great guy. While not an officially licensed tour guide, Andrew is an eager conversationalist and loves to provide lively commentary while you roll. Although you can hire Andrew for a simple airport transfer or an Auschwitz day trip, he also enjoys tackling more ambitious itineraries, from helping you track down your Polish roots to taking you on multiple-day journeys around Poland and beyond (prices are for up to 4 people if you book direct: 400 zł to Auschwitz, 250 zł to Wieliczka Salt Mine, 80 zł for transfer from Kraków-Balice Airport, 500 zł for transfer from Katowice Airport, 600 zł for an all-day trip into the countryside—such as into the High Tatras or to track down your Polish roots near Kraków, more to cover gas costs for trips longer than 100 km one-way; long-distance transfers for up to 4 people to Prague, Budapest, Vienna, or Berlin for 1,800 zł; also available for multiday trips—price negotiable, all prices higher for bigger van, tel. 12-411-5630, mobile 602-243-306, www.tour-service.pl, andrew@tour-service.pl).

Local guide Marta Chmielowska's husband, **Czesław** (a.k.a. Chester), can also drive you to nearby locations (300 zł for all-day trip to Auschwitz for 1-2 people, 350 zł for 3-8 people; 220 zł to Wieliczka Salt Mine, including waiting time, or a very long day combining Wieliczka and Auschwitz for 550 zł; to book, see Marta's contact information, earlier).

Walking Tours

Various companies run daily city walking tours in English in summer. Most do a three-hour tour of the Old Town as well as a three-hour tour of Kazimierz, the Jewish district (most charge about 50 zł per tour, depending on company). Another option is to combine the Old Town and Kazimierz into a single, four-hour tour (130 zł). Because the scene is continually evolving, it's best to pick up local fliers (the TI works exclusively with one company, See Kraków, but hotel reception desks generally have more options), then choose the one that fits your interests and schedule. Three people can hire their own great local guide for about the same amount of money.

Crazy Guides

This irreverent company offers tours to the communist suburb of Nowa Huta and other outlying sights.

Bike and Segway Tours

Kraków Bike Tours is a well-established operation that runs daily three-hour bike tours in English in summer. The tours make 25 stops in the Old Town, Kazimierz, and Podgórze (90 zł, includes loaner bike, May-Sept daily at 10:00 and 15:00, spring and fall only 1/day at 12:00, confirm schedule and meet tour at their office down the passage at Grodzka 2—right at the bottom of the Square, tel. 12-430-2034, mobile 788-800-231, www.krakowbiketour.com, krakowbiketour@gmail.com). They also offer Segway tours (call to arrange, mobile 510-394-657).

Bus Tours
As Kraków is so easily seen on foot, taking a bus tour doesn't make much sense here. But they can be handy for reaching outlying sights. Various tour companies run bus-plus-walking itineraries (each of them around 100-130 zł), including Auschwitz (6 hours), Wieliczka Salt Mine (4 hours), and other regional side-trips. Look for fliers around town.

Buggy Tours
Romantic, horse-drawn buggies trot around Kraków from the Main Market Square. The going rate is a hefty 100 zł for a 30-minute tour.

Golf-Cart Tours
Several outfits around town (including on the Square) offer tours on a golf cart with recorded commentary. Given the limits on car traffic in the old center, this can be a handy way to connect the sights for those with limited mobility. Generally you'll pay about 160 zł for a 45-minute tour around the Old Town; add another 160 zł to extend the trip to Kazimierz, and another 160 zł if you want to continue all the way to the Podgórze former Jewish ghetto and Schindler's Factory Museum (this price is for the entire golf cart, up to 4 people; they also do point-to-point transfers within town for 50 zł).

Kraków's Royal Way Walk

Most of Kraków's major sights are conveniently connected by this self-guided walk. This route is known as the "Royal Way" because the king used to follow this same path when he returned to Kraków after a journey. After the capital moved to Warsaw, most kings still used Wawel Cathedral for important events. In fact, from 1320 to 1795, nearly every Polish king traversed Kraków's Royal Way at least twice: on the day he was crowned and on the day he was buried. You could sprint through this walk in about an hour and a half (less than a mile altogether), but it's much more fun if you take it like the kings did...slowly.

• *Begin just outside the main gate at the north end of the Old Town.*

▲Barbican (Barbakan) and City Walls

Tatars (mysterious and terrifying invaders from Central Asia) attacked Kraków three times in the 13th century. After the first attack destroyed the city in 1241, Krakovians built this wall. The original rampart had 47 watchtowers and eight gates. The big, round defensive fort standing outside the wall is a barbican—built to fortify the defenses after the Tatars had overrun Central and Eastern Europe. Structures like this pro-

vided extra fortification to weak sections—namely, the gates. Imagine how it looked in 1500, when this barbican stood outside the town moat with a long bridge leading to the Florian Gate— the city's main entryway. Today you can pay to scramble along the passages and fortifications of the barbican, though there's little to see inside, other than a small but good exhibit giving you a sense of how the walls were designed. The same ticket also lets you climb up onto the surviving stretch of Old Town walls flanking the Florian Gate (entry from inside walls).

Cost and Hours: 8 zł, April-Oct daily 10:30-18:00, last entry 30 minutes before closing, closed Nov-March.

• *The greenbelt in which the Barbican sits is called the...*

▲▲Planty

By the 19th century, Kraków's no-longer-necessary city wall had fallen into disrepair. As Austrians were doing all over their

empire, they decided to tear down what remained, fill in the moat, and plant trees. (The name comes not from the English "plant," but from the Polish *plantovac*, or "flat"—because they flattened out this area to create it.) Today, the Planty is a beautiful park that stretches 2.5 miles around the entire perimeter of Kraków's Old Town. To give your Kraków visit an extra dimension, consider a quick bike ride around the Planty (best early in the morning, when it's less crowded) with a side-trip along the parklike riverbank near Wawel Castle; you'll see bike-rental places around the Old Town.

Circle around the left side of the Barbican. On your left, keep an eye out for a unique monument depicting an elderly, bearded man in the corner of a huge frame. This honors **Jan Matejko,** arguably Poland's most beloved painter, who specialized in giant-scale epic historical scenes that would easily fill this frame. We'll hear Matejko's name several more times on this walk.

As you continue around the Barbican, look down to see the much lower ground level around its base—making it easy to imagine that the Planty was once anything but flat.

• Across the busy street from the Barbican, standing in the middle of the long park, is the...

KRAKÓW

Grunwald Monument

This memorial honors one of the most important battles in the history of a nation that has seen more than its share: the Battle of Grunwald on July 15, 1410, when Polish and Lithuanian forces banded together to finally defeat the Teutonic Knights, who had been running roughshod over the lands along the Baltic. Lying dramatically slain at the base of this monument, like a toppled Goliath, is the defeated Grand Master of the Teutonic Knights—German crusaders who had originally been brought to Poland as mercenaries. It's easy to see this vanquished statue as a thinly veiled metaphor for one of Poland's powerful, often domineering, neighbors that the Poles stood up to—and defeated. When the Nazis took power here, this statue was one of the first things they tore down. When they left, it was one of the first things the Poles put back up.

• If you'd like to see a slice of Krakovian life, side-trip one block to the left of the monument, to the local farmers market.

The Old Market (Stary Kleparz)

The colorful Old Market offers a refreshing dash of today's Kraków that has nothing to do with history or tourism. It's just lots of hardscrabble people selling what they grow or knit, and lots of others buying. Wander around as if on a cultural scavenger hunt. Find the freshest doughnuts *(pączki),* the most popular bakery, the villager selling slippers she knitted, and the old man with the smoked cheese.

Hours: Mon-Sat 7:00-18:00—but busiest and most interesting in the morning, closed Sun.

• Now retrace your steps to the Barbican, and enter the Old Town by walking through the...

Florian Gate (Brama Floriańska)

As you approach the gate, look up at the **white eagle**—representing courage and freedom—the historic symbol of the Polish people.

Inside the gate, notice the little chapel on the right with a replica of the famous **Black Madonna of Częstochowa,** probably the

most important religious symbol among Polish Catholics. The original, located in Częstochowa (70 miles north of Kraków), is an Eastern Orthodox-style icon of mysterious origin with several mystical legends attached to it. After the icon's believed role in protecting a monastery from Swedish invaders in the mid-17th century, it was named "Queen and Protector of Poland."

Once through the gate, look back at it. High above is **St. Florian,** patron of the fire brigade. As fire was a big concern for a wooden city of the 15th century, Florian gets a place of honor.

• *You're standing at the head of Kraków's historic (and now touristic) gamut...*

▲Floriańska Street (Ulica Floriańska)

Hanging on the inside of the city wall in both directions is a makeshift **art gallery,** where—traditionally—starving students hawk the works they've painted at the Academy of Fine Arts (across the busy street from the barbican). These days, the art is so kitschy, this stretch of the town's fortification is nicknamed "The Wailing Wall."

If you were to detour along the gallery (to the right with your back to the gate), in a block you'd arrive at another fine collection—the eclectic **Czartoryski Museum.** This museum, which may be closed for renovation during your visit, is home to a rare Leonardo da Vinci oil painting.

Standing at the top of Floriańska street, you can't miss two restaurant chains: **Coffee Heaven** (the local Starbucks) and **McDonald's.** When renovating the McDonald's building, a Gothic cellar was discovered—so it was excavated and seating was added. Today, you can super-size your ambience by dining on a Big Mac and fries under a medieval McVault.

About halfway down the long block, on the left (at #45, round green sign), look for **Jama Michalika** ("Michael's Cave"). This dark, atmospheric café, popular with locals for its coffee and pastries, began in 1895 as a simple bakery in a claustrophobic back room. Around the turn of the 20th century, this was a hangout of the Młoda Polska (Young Poland) movement—the Polish answer to Art Nouveau. The walls are papered with sketches from poor artists—local bohemians who couldn't pay their tabs. In 1915, this was home to the first Polish cabaret. Today that stage is used by a folk troupe that performs traditional music and dance with dinner many evenings (pick up the flier, and see the description of **Jama Michalika** later, under "Entertainment in Kraków"). Poke around inside this circa-1900 time warp and appreciate this unique art gallery. Consider having coffee and dessert here, or a cigar in the charming smokers' bar in front (daily 9:00-22:00).

About a block farther down, at #20 (on the right), **Staropolskie Trunki** ("Old Polish Drinks") offers an education in vodka—with as much tasting as you'd like. It's a friendly little place with a long bar and countless local vodkas and liquors—all open and ready to be tasted. Best of all, there's a cheery local barista to talk you through the experience (five tastes for 10 zł with a fun explanation that amounts to a private tour, buy a bottle and the tastes are free, daily 10:00-24:00).

Continue strolling down Floriańska street. Notice that all over town, storefronts advertising themselves as "tourist information" offices are actually tourist sales agencies. And money-exchange counters can be thieves with an address. (Do the arithmetic—the buying and selling rates should be within 6 percent or so, and there should be no fee.) Along with the fast-food joints, also notice some uniquely Polish snacks. The various pizza and kebab windows also sell *zapiekanki*—a toasted baguette with toppings, similar to a French bread pizza. Or, for an even quicker bite, buy an *obwarzanek* (ring-shaped, bagel-like roll, typically fresh) from a street vendor; many still use their old-fashioned blue carts.

Another block ahead on the left (at #3, 50 yards before the big church), you'll see **Jazz Club u Muniaka.** In the 1960s, Janusz Muniak was one of the first Polish jazzmen. Since 1994, he's run this place, and jams regularly here in a cool cellar surrounded by jazzy art. If you hang around the bar before the show, you might find yourself sitting next to Janusz himself as he smokes his pipe...and gets ready to smoke on the saxophone (for details, see "Entertainment in Kraków," later).

• *Continue into the Main Market Square, where you'll run into...*

▲▲St. Mary's Church (Kościół Mariacki)

A church has stood on this spot for 800 years. The original church was destroyed by the first Tatar invasion in 1241, but all subsequent versions—including the current one—have been built on the same foundation. You can look down the sides to see how the Main Market Square has risen about seven feet over the centuries.

How many church towers does St. Mary's have? Technically,

KRAKÓW

the answer is one. The shorter tower belongs to the church; the taller one is a municipal watchtower, from which you'll hear a bugler playing the hourly *hejnał* song. According to Kraków's favorite legend, during that first Tatar invasion, a town watchman saw the enemy approaching and sounded the alarm. Before he could finish the tune, an arrow pierced his throat—which is why, even today, the *hejnał* stops suddenly partway through. Today's buglers—12 in all—are firemen first, musicians second. Each one works a 24-hour shift up there, playing the *hejnał* on the hour, every hour (broadcast on national Polish radio at noon). Be sure to catch one of these tiny, hourly, broken performances.

To see one of the most finely crafted Gothic altarpieces anywhere, it's worth paying admission to enter the church. The front door is open 14 hours a day and is free to those who come to pray, but tourists use the door around the right side (buy your ticket across the little square from this door).

Cost and Hours: 10 zł, Mon-Sat 11:45-17:45, Sun 14:00-17:45 (these are last-entry times). The famous wooden altarpiece is open between noon and 18:00; try to be here by 11:50 for the ceremonial opening (Mon-Sat) or at 18:00 for the closing (except on Sat, when it's left open for the service on Sun).

Visiting the Church: Inside, you're struck by the lavish decor. This was the church of the everyday townspeople, built out of a spirit of competition with the royal high church at Wawel Castle. At the altar is one of the best medieval woodcarvings in existence—the exquisite, three-part **altarpiece** by German Veit Stoss (Wit Stwosz in Polish). Carved in 12 years and completed in 1489, it's packed with emotion rare in Gothic art. Get as close as you can and study the remarkable

details. Stoss used oak for the structural parts and linden trunks for the figures. When the altar doors are closed, you see scenes from the lives of Mary and Jesus. The open altar depicts the Dormition (death—or, if splitting theological hairs, heavenly sleep) of the Virgin. The artist catches the apostles around Mary, reacting in the seconds after she collapses. Mary is depicted in three stages:

Kazimierz the Great (1333-1370)

Out of the many centuries of Polish kings, only one earned the nickname "great," and he's the only one worth remembering: Kazimierz the Great.

K. the G., who ruled Poland from Kraków in the 14th century, was one of those larger-than-life medieval kings who left his mark on all fronts—from war to diplomacy, art patronage to womanizing. His scribes bragged that Kazimierz "found a Poland made of wood, and left one made of brick and stone." He put Kraków on the map as a major European capital. He founded many villages (some of which still bear his name) and replaced wooden structures with stone ones (such as Kraków's Cloth Hall). Kazimierz also established the Kraków Academy (today's Jagiellonian University), the second-oldest university in Central Europe. And to protect all these new building projects, he heavily fortified Poland by building a series of imposing forts and walls around its perimeter.

Most of all, Kazimierz is remembered as a progressive, tolerant king. In the 14th century, other nations were deporting—or even interning—their Jewish subjects, who were commonly scapegoated for anything that went wrong. But the enlightened Kazimierz created policies that granted Jews more opportunities (often related to banking and trade) and allowed them a chance for higher social standing—establishing the country as a safe haven for Jews in Europe.

Kazimierz the Great was the last of Poland's long-lived Piast dynasty. Although he left no male heir—at least, no legitimate one—Kazimierz's advances set the stage for Poland's Golden Age (14th-16th centuries). After his death, Poland united with Lithuania (against the common threat of the Teutonic Knights), the Jagiellonian dynasty was born, and Poland became one of Europe's mightiest medieval powers.

life leaving her earthly body, being escorted to heaven by Jesus, and (at the very top) being crowned in heaven. The six scenes on the sides are the Annunciation, birth of Jesus, visit by the Three Magi, Jesus' Resurrection, his Ascension, and Mary becoming the mother of the apostles at Pentecost.

There's more to St. Mary's than the altar. While you're admiring this church's art, notice the flowery Neo-Gothic painting covering the choir walls. Stare up into the starry, starry blue ceiling. As you wander around, consider that the church was renovated a century ago by three Polish geniuses from two very different artistic generations: the venerable positivist Jan Matejko and his Art Nouveau students, Stanisław Wyspiański and Józef Mehoffer (we'll learn more about these two later on our walk). The huge silver bird under the organ loft in back is a crowned white eagle, the symbol of Poland.

Tower Climb: In the summer, you may be able to climb up the 239 stairs to the top of the taller tower to visit the *hejnał* fireman. While it's a huff—with some claustrophobic stone stairs, followed by some steep, acrophobic wooden ones—the view up top is the best you'll find of the Square. However, in recent years the city and the church have been wrangling over whose job it is to renovate the rickety tower, so it may be closed during your visit. To see if it's open, look for the little door just to the left of the main entrance, which faces the Square.

• *Leaving the church, notice the neck clamps dangling from the exterior walls near the side door. If you were leaving Mass in centuries past, there would be locals chained here for public humiliation. You'd spit on them before turning right and stepping into one of the biggest market squares anywhere.*

▲▲▲Main Market Square (Rynek Główny), a.k.a. "The Square"

Kraków's marvelous Square, one of Europe's most gasp-worthy public spaces, bustles with street musicians, colorful flower stalls, cotton-candy vendors, loitering teenagers, breakdancing tweens, businesspeople commuting by foot, gawking tourists, and the lusty coos of pigeons. This Square is where Kraków lives. It's often filled with various special events, markets, and festivals. The biggest are the seasonal markets  before Easter and Christmas, but you're also likely to stumble on something special going on here anytime between June and August.

The Square was established in the 13th century, when the city had to be rebuilt after being flattened by the Tatars. At the time, it was the biggest square in medieval Europe. It was illegal to sell anything on the street, so everything had to be sold here on the Main Market Square. It was divided into smaller markets, such as the butcher stalls, the ironworkers' tents, and the still-standing Cloth Hall (described later).

Notice the modern **fountain** with the glass pyramid at this end of the Square. A major excavation of the surrounding area created a museum of Kraków's medieval history that literally sprawls beneath the Square.

The statue in the middle of the Square is a traditional meeting place for Krakovians. It depicts Romantic poet **Adam Mickiewicz** (1789-1855), who's considered the "Polish Shakespeare." His epic

The Młoda Polska (Young Poland) Art Movement

Polish art in the late 19th century was ruled by positivism, a school with a very literal, straightforward focus on Polish his-

tory (Jan Matejko led the charge; see page 186). But when the new generation of Kraków's artists came into their own in the early 1900s, they decided that the old school was exactly that. Though moved by the same spirit and goals as the previous generation—evoking Polish patriotism at a time when their country was being occupied—these new artists used

very different methods. They were inspired by a renewed appreciation of folklore and peasant life. Rather than being earnest and literal (an 18th-century Polish war hero on horseback), the new art was playful and highly symbolic (the artist frolicking in a magical garden in the idyllic Polish countryside). This movement became known as Młoda Polska (Young Poland)—Art Nouveau with a Polish accent.

Stanisław Wyspiański (vees-PAYN-skee, 1869-1907) was the leader of Młoda Polska. He produced beautiful artwork, from simple drawings to the stirring stained-glass images in Kraków's St. Francis Basilica. Wyspiański was an expert at capturing human faces with realistic detail, emotion, and personality. The versatile Wyspiański was also an accomplished stage designer and writer. His patriotic play *The Wedding*—about the nuptials of a big-city artist and a peasant girl—is regarded as one of Poland's finest dramas. You'll find excellent examples of Wyspiański's art in Kraków's St. Francis Basilica and Szołayski House, and in Warsaw's National Museum.

Józef Mehoffer (may-HOH-fehr), Wyspiański's good friend and rival, was another great Młoda Polska artist. Mehoffer's style is more expressionistic and abstract than Wyspiański's, often creating an otherworldly effect. See Mehoffer's work in Kraków's St. Francis Basilica and at the artist's former residence (see the Józef Mehoffer House, page 291); and in Warsaw, at the National Museum.

Other names to look for include **Jacek Malczewski** (mahl-CHEHV-skee), who specialized in self-portraits, and **Olga Boznańska** (bohz-NAHN-skah), the movement's only prominent female artist. Both are featured in Warsaw's National Museum; Malczewski's works also appear in Kraków's Gallery of 19th-Century Polish Art.

masterpiece, *Pan Tadeusz,* is still regarded as one of the greatest works in Polish literature. A wistful, nostalgic tale of Polish-Lithuanian nobility, *Pan Tadeusz* stirred patriotism in a Poland that had been dismantled by surrounding empires. If you survey the Square from here, you'll notice that the Old Town was spared the bombs of World War II. The Nazis considered Kraków a city with Germanic roots and wanted it saved. But they were quick to destroy any symbols of Polish culture or pride. The statue of Adam Mickiewicz, for example, was pulled down immediately after occupation.

Near the end of the Square, you'll see the tiny, copper-domed **Church of St. Adalbert,** one of the oldest churches in Kraków (10th century). This Romanesque structure predates the Square. Like St. Mary's (described earlier), it seems to be at an angle because it's aligned east-west, as was the custom when it was built. (In other words, the churches aren't crooked—the Square is. Any other "crooked" building you see around town predates the 13th-century grid created during the rebuilding of Kraków.)

Drinks are reasonably priced at cafés on the Square (most around 10-15 zł). Find a spot where you like the view and the chairs, then sit and sip. Order a coffee, Polish *piwo* (beer, such as Żywiec, Okocim, or Lech), or a shot of *wódka* (Żubrówka is a good brand). For a higher vantage point, the Cloth Hall's **Café Szał terrace,** overlooking the Square and St. Mary's Church, offers one of the nicest views in town (open daily until 24:00; terrace costs 2 zł to enter except free on Sun-Mon, after 20:00, and with art gallery ticket; 10-15-zł drinks, some light meals, enter through Gallery of 19th-Century Polish Art entrance).

As the Square buzzes around you, imagine this place before 1989. There were no outdoor cafés, no touristy souvenir stands, and no salesmen hawking cotton candy or neon-lit whirligigs. The communist government shut down all but a handful of the businesses. They didn't want people to congregate here—they should be at home, resting, because "a rested worker is a productive worker." The buildings were covered with soot from the nearby Lenin Steelworks in Nowa Huta. The communists denied the pollution, and when the student "Green Brigades" staged a demonstration in this Square to raise awareness in the 1970s, they were immediately arrested. How things have changed.

• *The huge, yellow building right in the middle of the Square is the...*

▲▲Cloth Hall (Sukiennice)

In the Middle Ages, this was the place where cloth-sellers had their market stalls. Kazimierz the Great turned the Cloth Hall into a permanent structure in the 14th century. In 1555, it burned

down and was replaced by the current building. The crowned letter *S* (at the top of the gable above the entryway) stands for King Sigismund the Old, who commissioned this version of the hall. As Sigismund fancied all things Italian (including women—he married an Italian princess), this structure is in the Italianate Renaissance style. Sigismund kicked off a nationwide trend, and you'll still see Renaissance-style buildings like this one all over the country, making the style as typically Polish as it is typically Italian. We'll see more works by Sigismund's imported Italian architects at Wawel Castle.

Recently restored and gleaming, the Cloth Hall is still a func-

tioning market—selling mostly souvenirs, including wood carvings, chess sets, jewelry (especially amber), painted boxes, and trinkets (summer Mon-Fri 9:00-18:00, Sat-Sun 9:00-15:00, sometimes later; winter Mon-Fri 9:00-16:00, Sat-Sun 9:00-15:00). Cloth Hall prices are slightly inflated, but still cheap by American standards. You're paying a little extra for the convenience and the atmosphere, but you'll see locals buying gifts here, too.

WCs are at each end of the Cloth Hall. The upstairs of the Cloth Hall is home to the excellent **Gallery of 19th-Century Polish Art** (enter behind the statue of Adam).

• *Browse through the Cloth Hall passageway. As you emerge into the other half of the Square, the big tower on your left is the...*

Town Hall Tower

This is all that remains of a town hall building from the 14th century—when Kraków was the powerful capital of Poland. After the 18th-century Partitions of Poland, Kraków's prominence took a nosedive. By the 19th century, Kraków was Nowheresville. As the town's importance crumbled, so did its town hall. It was cheaper to tear down the building than to repair it, and all that was left standing was this nearly 200-foot-tall tower. In summer, you can climb the tower, stopping along the way to poke around an exhibit on Kraków history, but the views from up top are disappointing. Still you can step into the entryway to see a model of an earlier version of the church, with a fanciful, Prague-style, multispired tower.

Cost and Hours: 7 zł, April-Oct daily 10:30-18:00, last entry 30 minutes before closing, closed Nov-March.

Nearby: The **gigantic head** at the base of the Town Hall Tower is a sculpture by contemporary artist Igor Mitoraj, who studied here in Kraków. Typical of Mitoraj's works, the head is an empty shell that appears to be wrapped in cloth. While some locals enjoy having a work by their fellow Krakovian in such a prominent place, others disapprove of its sharp contrast with the Square's genteel Old World ambience. Tourists enjoy playing peek-a-boo with the head's eyes—a fun photo op.

• *When you're finished on the Square, we'll head toward Wawel Hill. But we'll take a one-block detour from the Royal Way to introduce you to one of Kraków's best churches. Leave on the street called ulica Bracka, in the middle of the bottom of the Square (next to the Deutsche Bank, straight ahead from the end of the Cloth Hall). Follow this one long block (and across the busy Franciszkańska street) directly to the low-key side door of a big red-brick church. Go ye.*

▲▲St. Francis Basilica (Bazylika Św. Franciszka)

This beautiful Gothic church, which was St. John Paul II's home

church while he was archbishop of Kraków, features some of Poland's best Art Nouveau in situ (in the setting for which it was intended). After an 1850 fire, it was redecorated by the two leading members of the Młoda Polska (Young Poland) movement: Stanisław Wyspiański and Józef Mehoffer. These two talented and fiercely competitive Krakovians were friends who apprenticed together under Poland's greatest painter, Jan Matejko. The glorious decorations of this church are the result of their great rivalry run amok.

Cost and Hours: Free, daily 6:00-19:45—but frequent services, so be discreet.

◯ Self-Guided Tour: Before entering, notice the board to the right of the door displaying death announcements for community members.

Entering through this door, turn left into the altar area to enjoy the paintings and stained-glass windows by **Stanisław Wyspiański.** The windows flanking the high altar represent the Blessed Salomea (left, the church's founder, buried in a side chapel) and St. Francis (right, the church's namesake). Salomea was a medieval Polish woman who became queen of Hungary, but later returned to Poland and entered a convent after her husband's death. Notice she's dropping a crown—repudiating the earthly world

KRAKÓW

and giving herself over to the simple, stop-and-smell-God's-roses lifestyle of St. Francis. Notice also the Mucha-like paintings by Wyspiański on the pilasters between the windows.

As you face the back of the church, look at the window in the rear of the nave: *God the Father Let It Be,* Wyspiański's greatest masterpiece. The colors beneath the Creator change from yellows and oranges (fire) to soothing blues (water), depending on the light. Wyspiański was supposedly inspired by Michelangelo's vision of God in the Sistine Chapel, though he used a street beggar to model God's specific features. Wyspiański also painted the delightful floral designs decorating the walls of the nave—fitting for a church dedicated to a saint so famous for his spiritual connection to nature.

Walk up the nave toward the door under that window. The chapel on the right side, after the transept, contains some evocative Stations of the Cross. This is **Józef Mehoffer**'s response to Wyspiański's work. The centerpiece of the room is a replica of the Shroud of Turin—which, since it touched the original shroud, is also considered a holy relic.

Back out in the nave, the modern painting (with an orange-and-blue background, midway up the nave on

Karol Wojtyła (1920-2005): The Greatest Pole

The man who became St. John Paul II began his life as Karol Wojtyła, born to a humble family in the town of Wadowice near Kraków on May 18, 1920. Karol's mother died when he was a young boy. When he was a teenager, he moved with his father to Kraków to study philosophy and drama at Jagiellonian University. Young Karol was gregarious and athletic—an avid skier, hiker, swimmer, and soccer goalie. During the Nazi occupation in World War II, he was forced to work in a quarry. In defiance of the Nazis, he secretly studied theology and appeared in illegal underground theatrical productions. When the war ended, he resumed his studies, now at the theology faculty.

After graduating in 1947, Wojtyła swiftly rose through the ranks of the Catholic Church hierarchy. By 1964, he was arch-bishop of Kraków, and just three years later, he became the youngest cardinal ever. Throughout the 1960s, he fought an ongoing battle with the regime when they refused to allow the construction of a church in the Kraków suburb of Nowa Huta. After years of saying Mass for huge crowds in open fields, Wojtyła finally convinced the communists to allow the construc-tion of the Lord's Ark Church in 1977. A year later, Karol Wojtyła was called to the papacy—the first non-Italian pope in more than four centuries. In 1979, he paid a visit to his native Poland. In a series of cautiously provocative speeches, he demonstrated to his countrymen the potential for mass opposition to communism.

Imagine you're Polish in the 1970s. Your country was dev-astated by World War II and has struggled under an oppressive regime ever since. Food shortages are epidemic. Lines stretch around the block even to buy a measly scrap of bread. Life is bleak, oppressive, and hopeless. Then someone who speaks your language—someone you've admired your entire life, and one of the only people you've seen successfully stand up to the regime—becomes one of the world's most influential people. A Pole like you is the leader of a billion Catholics. He makes you believe that

the left) depicts **St. Maksymilian Kolbe,** the Catholic priest who sacrificed his own life to save a fellow inmate at Auschwitz in 1941 (notice the *16670*—his concentration camp number—etched into the background). Kolbe is particularly beloved here, as he actually served at this church.

Just before going out the back door (below Wyspiański's stained-glass window), find the **silver plate** labeled "Jan Paweł II" on the second pew from the last (on right); this was St. John Paul II's favorite place to pray when he lived in the Archbishop's Palace across the street.

• *Stepping outside (through the back door), look to the right. The light-yellow building across the street is the...*

the impossible can happen. He says to you again and again: *"Nie lękajcie się"*—"Have no fear." And you begin to believe it.

From his bully pulpit, the Pope had a knack for cleverly challenging the communists—just firmly enough to get his point across, but stopping short of jeopardizing the stature of the Church in Poland. Gentle but pointed wordplay was his specialty. The inspirational role he played in the lives of Lech Wałęsa and the other leaders of Solidarity emboldened them to rise up; it's no coincidence that the first successful trade-union strikes in the Soviet Bloc took place shortly after John Paul II became pope (for more on Solidarity, see page 246). Many people (including Mikhail Gorbachev) credit John Paul II for the collapse of Eastern European communism.

Even as John Paul II's easy charisma attracted new worshippers to the Church (especially young people), his conservatism on issues such as birth control, homosexuality, and female priests pushed away many Catholics. Under his watch, the Church struggled with pedophilia scandals. Many still fault him for turning a blind eye and not putting a stop to these abuses much earlier. By the end of his papacy, John Paul II's failing health and conservatism had caused him to lose stature in worldwide public opinion.

And yet, approval of the Pope never waned in Poland. His countrymen—even the relatively few atheists and agnostics—saw John Paul II both as the greatest hero of their people...and as a member of the family, like a kindly grandfather. When Pope John Paul II died on April 2, 2005, the mourning in his homeland was particularly deep and sustained. Musical performances of all kinds were canceled, and the irreverent MTV-style music channel simply went off the air out of respect.

A speedy nine years after his death, Karol Wojtyła became St. John Paul II in April of 2014. Out of 265 popes, only two have been given the title "great." There's already talk in Rome of increasing that number to three. Someday soon we may speak of this man as "St. John Paul the Great." His countrymen already do.

Archbishop's Palace

This building (specifically, the window over the stone entryway) was St. John Paul II's residence when he was the archbishop of Kraków. When he became Pope, it remained his home-away-from-Rome for visits to his hometown. After a long day of saying formal Mass during his visits to Kraków, he'd wind up here. Weary as he was, before going to bed he'd stand in the window for hours, chatting casually with the people assembled below—about religion, but also about sports, current events, and whatever was on their minds. In 2005, when the Pope's health deteriorated, this street filled with his supporters, even though he was in Rome. For days, somber locals focused their vigil on

this same window, their eyes fixed on a black crucifix that had been placed here. At 21:37 on the night of April 2, 2005, the Pope passed away in Rome. Ten thousand Krakovians were on this street, under this window, listening to a Mass broadcast on loudspeakers from the church. When the priest announced the Pope's death, every single person simultaneously fell to their knees in silence. For the next several days, thousands of the faithful continued to stand on this street, staring intently at the window where they last saw the man they considered to be the greatest Pole.

• *Now turn right, walk along the side of the church, pass a few monuments and a tram stop, and turn right again down busy...*

Grodzka Street

Now you're back on the Royal Way proper. At the corner of Grodzka street stands the modern, copper-colored **Wyspiański Pavilion.** Step inside (daily 9:00-17:00), past the little TI, to see three new stained-glass windows based on designs Wyspiański once submitted for a contest to redecorate Wawel Cathedral. Although these designs were rejected back then, they were finally realized on the hundredth anniversary of his death (in 2007). Visible from inside the building during the day, and gloriously illuminated to be seen outside the building at night, they represent three Polish historical figures: the gaunt St. Stanisław (Poland's first saint), the skeletal Kazimierz the Great (in the middle), and the swooning King Henry the Pious.

Now continue down Grodzka street. This lively thoroughfare, connecting the Square with Wawel, is teeming with shops—and some of Kraków's best restaurants (see "Eating in Kraków," later). Survey your options now, and choose (and maybe reserve) your favorite for dinner tonight. This street is also characterized by its fine arcades over the sidewalks. While this might seem like a charming Renaissance feature, the arcades were actually added by the Nazis after they invaded in 1939; they wanted to convert Kraków into a city befitting its status as the capital of their Polish puppet state.

This is also a good street to find some of Kraków's **milk bars.** The most traditional one is about two blocks down, on the right (at #45), with a simple *Bar Mleczny* sign. These government-subsidized cafeterias are the locals' choice for a quick, cheap, filling, lowbrow lunch. Prices are deliriously cheap (soup costs about a dollar), and the food isn't bad.

• *One more block ahead, the small square on your right is...*

Mary Magdalene Square (Plac Św. Marii Magdaleny)

Back when Kraków was just a village, this was its main square. Today, it offers a great visual example of Kraków's deeply religious character. In the Middle Ages, Kraków was known as "Small Rome" for its many churches. Today, there are 142 churches and monasteries within the city limits (32 in the Old Town alone)—more per square mile than anywhere outside of Rome. You can see several of them from this spot: The nearest, with the picturesque white facade and row of saints out front, is the **Church of Saints Peter and Paul** (Poland's first Baroque church, and a popular tourist concert venue). The statues lining this church's facade are the 11 apostles (minus Judas), plus Mary Magdalene, the square's namesake. The next church to the right, with the twin towers, is the Romanesque **St. Andrew's** (now with a Baroque interior). This is the oldest church in town, from the 11th century, and was designed to double as a place of last refuge—notice the arrow slits around the impassable lower floor. According to legend, a spring inside this church provided water to citizens who holed up here during the Tatar invasions. The church was saved, but that didn't save the rest of Kraków from being overrun by marauding armies. Imagine this stone fortress of God being the only building standing amid a smoldering and flattened Kraków after the 13th-century destruction.

If you look farther down the street, you can see three more churches. And even the square next to you used to be a church, too—it burned in 1855, and only its footprint survives.

• *Go through the square and turn left down...*

Kanonicza Street (Ulica Kanonicza)

With so many churches around here, the clergy had to live somewhere. Many lived on this well-preserved street—supposedly the oldest street in Kraków. As you walk, look for the cardinal hats over three different doorways. The **Hotel Copernicus,** on the left at #16, is named for a famous guest who stayed here five centuries ago. Directly across the street at #17, the **Bishop Erazm Ciołek Palace** hosts a good exhibit of medieval art and Orthodox icons. Next door, the yellow house at #19 is where Karol Wojtyła lived for 10 years after World War II—long before he became St. John Paul II. Today this building houses the **Archdiocesan Museum,** which features a few sparse exhibits about Kraków's favorite son. Across the street is the **John Paul II Center,** which has another modest exhibit about the late pontiff and saint, and also provides information about the new Sanctuary of St. John Paul II on Kraków's outskirts. All three of these sights are described later, under "Sights

KRAKÓW

in Kraków."

• *We're at the end of Kanonicza street, and our self-guided walk is finished. But there's still much more to see. Across the busy street, a ramp leads up to the most important piece of ground in all of Poland: Wawel.*

Sights in Kraków

WAWEL HILL: THE HEART AND SOUL OF POLAND

KRAKÓW

Wawel (VAH-vehl), a symbol of Polish royalty and independence, is sacred territory to every Polish person. A castle has stood here since the beginning of Poland's recorded history. Today, Wawel— awash in tourists—is the most visited sight in the country. Crowds and an overly complex admissions system for the hill's many historic sights can be exasperating. Thankfully, a stroll through the cathedral and around the castle grounds requires no tickets, and—with the help of the following  commentary—is enough. I've described these sights in the order of a handy self-guided walk. The many museums on Wawel (all described in this section) are mildly interesting, but can be skipped (grounds open daily from 6:00 until dusk, inner courtyard closes 30 minutes earlier). In June, it's mobbed with students, as it's a required field trip for Polish school kids.

Wawel Sights: The sights you'll enter at Wawel are divided into two institutions: church and castle, each with separate tickets. Tickets for the castle sights are sold at two points (at the long line at the top of the ramp, or with no line at the top of the hill, across the central square). The most important church sight—the cathedral—is mostly free, but to enter the paid sights inside (or the museum), get a ticket at the office across from the cathedral entrance.

• *From Kanonicza street—where my self-guided walk ends—head up the long ramp to the castle entry.*

Entry Ramp

Huffing up this ramp, it's easy to imagine how this location—rising above the otherwise flat plains around Kraków—was both strategic and easy to defend. When Kraków was part of the Habsburg Empire in the 19th century, the Austrians turned this castle complex into a fortress, destroying much of its delicate beauty. When Poland regained its independence after World War I, the castle was returned to its former glory. The bricks you see on your left as you climb the ramp bear the names of Poles from around the world who donated to the cause.

The jaunty equestrian statue ahead is **Tadeusz Kościuszko** (1746-1817), a familiar name to many Americans. Kościuszko was a hero of the American Revolution and helped design West Point. When he returned to Poland, he fought bravely but unsuccessfully against the Russians (during the Partitions that would divide Poland's territory among three neighboring powers). Kościuszko also gave his name to several American towns, a county in Indiana, a brand of mustard from Illinois, and the tallest mountain in Australia.

• *Hiking through the Heraldic Gate next to Kościuszko, you pass the ticket office (if you'll be going into the museums, use the other ticket office, with shorter lines, on the top of the hill—see "Tickets and Reservations," later). As you crest the hill and pass through the stone gate, on your left is...*

▲▲Wawel Cathedral

Poland's national church is its Westminster Abbey. While the history buried here is pretty murky to most Americans, to Poles, this

church is *the* national mausoleum. It holds the tombs of nearly all of Poland's most important rulers and greatest historical figures.

Cost and Hours: It's usually free to walk around the main part of the church. You must buy a 12-zł ticket to climb up the tallest tower; visit the crypt, the royal tombs, and some of the lesser cha-

pels; and tour the John Paul II Wawel Cathedral Museum. Buy this ticket at the house across from the cathedral entry, where you can also rent an audioguide (7 zł). The cathedral is open April-Sept Mon-Sat 9:00-17:00, Sun 12:30-17:00, closes one hour earlier Oct-March, last entry 30 minutes before closing (tel. 12-429-9516, www.katedra-wawelska.pl). Note that the cathedral's museum (described later) is closed on Sunday.

Cathedral Exterior

Go around to the far side of the cathedral to take in its profile. This uniquely eclectic church is the product of centuries of haphazard additions...yet somehow, it works. It began as a simple, stripped-down Romanesque church in the 12th century. (The white base of the nearest tower is original. Anything at Wawel that's made of white limestone like this was probably part of the earliest Romanesque structures.) Kazimierz the Great and his predecessors gradually surrounded the cathedral with some 20 chapels,

KRAKÓW

KRAKÓW

which were further modified over the centuries, making this beautiful church a happy hodgepodge of styles. To give you a sense of the historical sweep, scan the chapels from left to right: 14th-century Gothic, 12th-century Romanesque (the base of the tower), 17th-century Baroque (the inside is Baroque, though the exterior is a copy of its Renaissance neighbor), 16th-century Renaissance, and 18th- and 19th-century Neoclassical. (This variety in styles is even more evident in the chapels' interiors, which we'll see soon.)

Pay attention to the two particularly interesting domed chapels to the right of the tall tower. The gold one is the Sigismund Chapel, housing memorials to the Jagiellonian kings—including Sigismund the Old, who was responsible for Kraków's Renaissance renovation in the 16th century. The Jagiellonian Dynasty was a high point in Polish history. During that golden 16th century, Poland was triple the size it is today, stretching all the way to the Ottoman Empire and the Black Sea. Poles consider the Sigismund Chapel, made with 80 pounds of gold, to be the finest Renaissance chapel north of the Alps. The copper-domed chapel next to it, home to the Swedish Waza dynasty, resembles its neighbor (but it's a copy built 150 years later, and without all that gold).

Go back around and face the church's **front entry** for more architectonic extravagance. The tallest tower, called the Sigismund Tower, has a clock with only an hour hand. Climbing a few steps into the entry, you see Gothic chapels (with pointy windows) flanking the door, a Renaissance ceiling, lavish Baroque decoration over the door, and some big bones (a simple whale rib, but thought to have been the bones of the mythic Wawel dragon in medieval times—and put here as an oddity to be viewed by the public). (Back then, there were no museums, so notable items like these were used to lure

people to the church.) It's said that as long as the bones hang here, the cathedral will stand. The door is the original from the 14th century, with fine wrought-iron work. The *K* with the crown stands for Kazimierz the Great. The black marble frame is made of Kraków stone from nearby quarries.

Cathedral Interior

The cathedral interior is slathered in Baroque memorials and tombs, decorated with tapestries, and soaked in Polish history. The ensemble was designed to help keep Polish identity strong through the ages. It has...and it still does.

⊘ **Self-Guided Tour:** After you step inside, you'll follow the one-way, clockwise route that leads you through the around the back of the apse, then back to the entry.

At the entry, look straight ahead to see the silver tomb **canopy,** inspired by the one in St. Peter's Basilica at the Vat contains the remains of the first Polish saint, Stanisław (fro 11th century). In front of the canopy, look for a metallic reliqu that's shaped like a book with its pages being ruffled by the win The glass capsule in the reliquary holds a drop of St. John Pau II's blood. It takes this shape because of what believers consider a highly significant moment during his memorial service: Before a crowd of thousands on St. Peter's Square in Rome, a book was placed on John Paul II's simple wooden coffin. As the service processed, its pages were ruffled back and forth by the wind, until they were finally slammed shut...as if the Holy Spirit were "closing the book" on his life.

Go behind this canopy into the ornately carved **choir** area. For 200 years, the colorful chair to the right of the high altar has been the seat of Kraków's archbishops, including Karol Wojtyła, who served here for 14 years before becoming pope. It's here that coronations took place.

Now you'll continue into the left aisle. From here, if you have a ticket, you can enter two of the optional attractions: Seventy claustrophobic wooden stairs lead up to the 11-ton **Sigismund Bell** and pleasant views of the steeples and spires of Kraków. Then, to the left (closer to where you entered), descend into the little **crypt** (with a rare purely Romanesque interior), which houses the remains of Adam Mickiewicz, the Romantic poet whose statue dominates the Main Market Square. You'll also find a white marble monument to Fryderyk Chopin (who's buried in Paris), put here on the 200th anniversary of his birth in 2010.

Now continue around the apse (behind the main altar). After curving around to the right, look for the red-marble tomb (on

the right) of The Great One— **Kazimierz,** of course. Look for *Kazimierz Wielki*—at his feet you can see a little beaver. This is an allusion to a famous saying about Kazimierz, the nation-builder: He found a Poland made of wood, and left one made of brick and stone.

...may notice that there's one VIP (Very Important Pole) ...ssing...Karol Wojtyła, a.k.a. John Paul II. Even so, a ...e steps toward the entrance, on the left, is the **Chapel ...ohn Paul II.** The late pontiff left no specific requests for ...ody, and the Vatican controversially (to Poles, at least) chose ...ntomb him in Vatican City, instead of sending him back ...me to Wawel. While Karol Wojtyła's remains are in St. Peter's ...asilica, this chapel was recently converted to honor him—with a plaque in the floor and an altar with his picture. Someday, Poles hope, he may be moved here (but, the Vatican says, don't hold your breath).

Ten steps farther, on the right, is the white sarcophagus of **St. Jadwiga** (with a dog at her feet). This 14th-century "king" of Poland advanced the fortunes of her realm by partnering with the king of Lithuania. The resulting Jagiellonian dynasty fought off the Teutonic Knights, helped Christianize Lithuania, and oversaw a high-water mark in Polish history. (Despite the queen's many contributions, the sexism of the age meant that she was considered a "king" rather than a "queen.") All the flowers here demonstrate how popular she remains among Poles today; she was sainted by Pope John Paul II in 1997. Across from Jadwiga, peek into the gorgeous 16th-century **Sigismund Chapel,** with its silver altar (this is the gold-roofed chapel you just saw from outside). Locals consider this the "Pearl of the Polish Renaissance" and the finest Renaissance building outside Italy.

Just beyond is a door leading back outside. If you don't have a ticket, your tour is finished—head out here. But those with a ticket can keep circling around.

Next, look into the **Waza Chapel:** Remember that its exterior matches the restrained, Renaissance style of the Sigismund Chapel, but the interior is clearly Baroque, slathered with gold and silver—quite a contrast.

To the left of the main door, take a look at the Gothic **Holy Cross Chapel,** with its seemingly Orthodox-style 14th-century frescoes.

In the back corner of the church is the entrance to the **royal tombs** (you'll exit outside the church, so be sure you're done in here first). The first big room, an original Romanesque space called St. Leonard's Crypt, houses Poland's greatest war heroes: Kościuszko (of American Revolution fame), Jan III Sobieski (who successfully defended Vienna from the Ottomans; he's in the simple black coffin with the gold inscription *J III S*), Sikorski, Poniatowski, and so on. Poles consider this room highly significant as the place where St. John Paul II celebrated his first Mass after becoming a priest (in November of 1946). Then you'll wander through several rooms of second-tier Polish kings, queens, and their kids. Head down more stairs to find the plaque honoring the Polish victims of the Katyń massacre in the USSR during World War II. Stepping into the next room, you'll see the cathedral's two newest tombs: President Lech Kaczyński and his wife Helena, who were among the 96 Polish politicians killed in a tragic 2010 plane crash—which was delivering those diplomats to a ceremony memorializing the Katyń massacre. Up a few stairs is the final grave, belonging to Marshal Józef Piłsudski, the WWI hero who seized power and ruled Poland from 1926 to 1935. His tomb was moved here so the rowdy soldiers who came to pay their respects wouldn't disturb the others.

KRAKÓW

• *Nearby (and covered by the same ticket as the tower and crypt) is the cathedral's museum.*

John Paul II Wawel Cathedral Museum

This small museum, up the little staircase across from the cathedral

entry, was recently spiffed up and re-dedicated to Kraków's favorite archbishop. It fills four rooms with artifacts relating to both the cathedral and St. John Paul II.

Downstairs is the Royal Room, with vestments, swords, regalia, holy robes, and items that were once buried with the kings, as well as early treasury items (from the 11th through 16th centuries). Upstairs are a later treasury collection (17th through 20th centuries) and a "Papal Room" with items from St. John Paul II's life: his armchair, vestments, and miter (pointy pope hat—notice how the golden decorations on this one incorporate the Black Madonna of Częstochowa), plus souvenirs from his travels.

Admission to this museum is included with your ticket to the cathedral's special options (Sigismund Bell tower, plus crypt and royal tombs), and its collection is worth a quick look, especially if you're interested in St. John Paul II (April-Sept Mon-Sat 9:00-17:00, Oct-March Mon-Sat 9:00-16:00, closed Sun year-round; pick up free brochure at entrance, tel. 12-429-3321).

• *When you're finished with the cathedral sights, stroll around the...*

▲▲Wawel Castle Grounds

In the rest of the castle, you'll uncover more fragments of Kraków's history and have the opportunity to visit several museums. I consider the museums skippable, but if you want to visit them, buy tickets before you enter the inner courtyard.

◐ Self-Guided Walk: This tour, which doesn't enter any of the admission-charging attractions, is plenty for most visitors.

• *Behind the cathedral, a grand green-and-pink entryway leads into the palace's dramatically Renaissance-style...*

Inner Courtyard: If this space seems to have echoes of Florence, that's because it was designed and built by young Florentines after Kazimierz's original castle burned down. Notice the three distinct levels: The ground

floor housed the private apartments of the higher nobility (governors and castle administrators); the middle level held the private apartments of the king; and the top floor—much taller, to allow more light to fill its large spaces—were the public state rooms of the king. The ivy-covered wing to the right of where you entered is Fascist in style, built as the headquarters of the notorious Nazi governor of German-occupied Poland, Hans Frank. (He was tried and executed in Nürnberg after the war.) At the far end of the courtyard is a false wall, designed to create a pleasant Renaissance symmetry, and also to give the illusion that the castle is bigger than it is. Looking through the windows, notice that there's nothing but air on the other side. When foreign dignitaries visited, these windows could be covered to complete the illusion. The entrances to most Wawel museums are around this courtyard, and some believe that you'll find something even more special: chakra.

Adherents to the Hindu concept of **chakra** believe that a powerful energy field connects all living things. Some believe that, mirroring the seven chakra points on the body (from head to groin), there are seven points on the surface of the earth where this energy is most concentrated: Delhi, Delphi, Jerusalem, Mecca, Rome, Velehrad...and Wawel Hill—specifically over there in the corner (immediately to your left as you enter the courtyard—the stretches of wall flanking the door to the baggage-check room). Look for peaceful people (here or elsewhere on the castle grounds) with their eyes closed. One thing's for sure: They're not thinking of Kazimierz the Great. The smudge marks on the wall are from people pressing up against this corner, trying to absorb some good vibes from this chakra spot.

The Wawel administration seems creeped out by all this. They've done what they can to discourage this ritual (such as putting up information boards right where the power is supposedly most focused), but believers still gravitate from far and wide to hug the wall. Give it a try...and let the Force be with you. (Just for fun, ask a Wawel tour guide about the chakra, and watch her squirm—they're forbidden to talk about it.)

• *If you want to visit some of the* **castle museums** *(you can enter four of the five from this courtyard), you'll first need to buy tickets elsewhere. Stick with me for a little longer to finish our tour of the grounds, and we'll wind up near a ticket office.*

Head back out to the side of the cathedral to survey the...

Field of History: This hilltop has seen lots of changes over the years. Kazimierz the Great turned a small fortress into a mighty Gothic castle in the 14th century. Today, you'll see the cathedral and a castle complex, but little remains of Kazimierz's grand fortress (which burned to the ground in 1499) other than the white stones around the restaurant on the square. In the grassy field across from the cathedral, you'll see the **foundations** of two Gothic churches that were destroyed when the Austrians took over Wawel in the 19th century and needed a parade ground for their troops. (They built the red-brick hospital building beyond the field, now used by the Wawel administration.)

• *Head downhill through the square, across to the gap in the buildings beyond the field, to the...*

Viewpoint over the Vistula: Belly up to the wall and enjoy the panorama over the **Vistula River** and Kraków's outskirts. The "Polish Mississippi"—which runs its entire course in Polish lands—is the nation's artery for trade and cultural connection. It stretches 650 miles from the foothills of the Tatra Mountains in southern Poland, through most of the country's major cities (Kraków, Warsaw, Toruń), before emptying into the Baltic Sea in Gdańsk.

From this viewpoint, you can see some unusual landmarks, including the odd wavy-roofed building just across the river (which houses the Manggha Japanese art gallery) and the biggest conference center in Poland (opened in 2015, to the left of the wavy building). The ball to the left of that is the balloon that tourists ride for a vast view. To the right, the symmetrical little bulge that tops the highest hill on the horizon is the **Kościuszko Mound**. And on a particularly crisp day, far in the distance (beyond the wavy building), you can see the Tatra Mountains marking the border of Slovakia.

Now look directly below you, along the riverbank, to find a fire-belching monument to the **dragon** that was instrumental in the founding of Kraków. Once upon a time, a prince named Krak founded a town on Wawel Hill. It was the perfect location—except for the fire-breathing dragon who lived in the caves under the hill and terrorized the town. Prince Krak had to feed the dragon all of the town's livestock to keep the monster from going after the townspeople. But Krak, with the help of a clever shoemaker, came up with a plan. They stuffed a sheep's skin with sulfur and left it outside the dragon's cave. The dragon swallowed it, and before long, developed a terrible case of heartburn. To put the fire out, the dragon started drinking water from the Vistula. He kept drinking and drinking until he finally exploded. The town was saved, and Kraków thrived. Today visitors enjoy watching the dragon blow fire into the air (about every four minutes, but can vary from a big plume to a tiny puff).

If you want to head down to see the Vistula and the dragon close up, take a shortcut through the nearby **Dragon's Den** (Smocza Jama, enter at the little copper-roofed brick building, at the far right of this viewpoint plaza). It's just a 135-step spiral staircase and a few underground caverns—worthwhile only as a quick way to get from the top of Wawel down to the banks of the Vistula 3 zł, pay at machine—coins only, April-Oct daily 10:00-17:00, July-Aug until 18:00, closed Nov-March).

If you'd like a higher viewpoint on the riverfront, you can pay 4 zł to climb 137 stairs to the top of **Sandomierska Tower** (at the far end of the hill, past the visitors center, no elevator). But I'd skip it—disappointingly, the view from up top is only through small windows (May-Sept daily 10:00-18:00, June-Aug until 19:00, Oct Sat-Sun only 10:00-17:00, closed Nov-April).

• *Our Wawel tour is finished. If you'd like to explore some of the museums, you can buy your tickets in the nearby visitors center (head back into the main Wawel complex—with the empty field—and turn right); here you'll also find WCs, a café, a gift shop, and other amenities. Or go down to the riverfront park: Walk downhill (through the Dragon's Den, or use the main ramp and simply circle around the base of the hill) to reach the park—one of the most delightful places in Kraków to simply relax, with beautiful views back on the castle complex.*

Wawel Castle Museums

There are five museums and exhibits in Wawel Castle (not including the cathedral and Cathedral Museum, the Dragon's Den, or Sandomierska Tower—all described above). A sixth exhibit, featuring Leonardo da Vinci's masterful painting *Lady with an*

Ermine, will likely be on display at least through 2015.

Remember: While the following sights are fascinating to Poles, casual visitors often find that the best visit is simply to enjoy the exteriors and the cathedral (following my self-guided tour, described earlier); the only ticket really worth considering is for the Leonardo. Each venue has its own admission and slightly different hours (tel. 12-422-5155, ext. 219, www.wawel.krakow.pl). English descriptions are posted, and you can rent an audioguide for 20 zł that covers some of the sights (State Rooms, Crown Treasury and Armory, and Oriental Art; get this at the ticket office on the courtyard). If you're visiting all of the sights, start with the Royal State Rooms and/or Royal Private Apartments (which share an entrance), then—on your way back down—see the Leonardo exhibit, the Oriental Art exhibit, and the Crown Treasury and Armory. Then head back out into the outer courtyard for the Lost Wawel exhibit.

Tickets and Reservations: Each sight has separate tickets (prices listed below), which you'll buy at one of two ticket windows. Most people line up at the top of the entry ramp, but it's faster to buy tickets at the visitors center at the far corner of the castle grounds (across the field from the cathedral, near the café). You generally can't buy tickets at the door of each sight (except for—sometimes—Lost Wawel), so decide in advance which ones you want to see and buy all your tickets at the start of your visit. A limited number of tickets are sold for each sight; boards count down the number of tickets available for each one on the day you're there. Tickets come with an assigned entry time (though you can usually sneak in before your scheduled appointment). In the summer, ticket lines can be long, and sights can sell out by midmorning. You can make a free reservation for some of the sights (tel. 12-422-1697, extra fee applies), but frankly, the sights aren't worth all the fuss—if they're sold out, you're not missing much.

Hours: Unless otherwise noted, the museums are open April-Oct Tue-Fri 9:30-17:00, Sat-Sun 11:00-17:00, closed Mon; Nov-March Tue-Sat 9:30-16:00, closed Sun-Mon; last entry one hour before closing.

Exceptions: In summer (April-Oct), Lost Wawel and the Crown Treasury and Armory are free and open on Mondays (9:30-13:00). Off-season (Nov-March), everything closes on Monday, but Lost Wawel, the Royal State Rooms, and the Leonardo exhibit (Jan-March only) remain open on Sunday.

Eating: Various light eateries circle the castle courtyard, but if you just want a drink, it's hard to beat the affordable self-service café next to the Lost Wawel entrance, with fine views across to the cathedral.

▲Royal State Rooms (Komnaty Królewskie)

While precious to Poles, these rooms are mediocre by European standards. Still, this is the best of the Wawel museums. First, climb up to the top floor and wander through some ho-hum halls with paintings and antique furniture. Along the way, you'll walk along the outdoor gallery (enjoying views down into the courtyard). Finally, you'll reach the Throne Room, with 30 carved heads in the ceiling. According to

legend, one of these heads got mouthy when the king was trying to pass judgment—so its mouth has been covered to keep it quiet. Continue into some of the palace's finest rooms, with 16th-century Brussels tapestries (140 of the original series of 300 survive), remarkably decorated wooden ceilings, and gorgeous leather-tooled walls. Wandering these halls (with their period furnishings), you get a feeling for the 16th- and 17th-century glory days of Poland, when it was a leading power in Eastern Europe. The Senate Room, with its throne and elaborate tapestries, is the climax.

Cost and Hours: 18 zł, see hours listed earlier, plus Nov-March also open—and free—Sun 10:00-16:00, enter through courtyard.

Royal Private Apartments (Prywatne Apartamenty Królewskie)

The rooms, which look similar to the State Rooms, can only be visited with a guided (and included) tour. As spaces are strictly limited, these tend to sell out the fastest (on busy days, they may already be booked up by around 10:00).

Cost and Hours: 25 zł, request English tour when buying your ticket—they depart 3/hour, see hours listed earlier, enter through courtyard.

Oriental Art (Sztuka Wschodu)

Though small, this exhibit displays swords, carpets, banners, vases, and other items dating from the 1683 Battle of Vienna, in which the Ottoman army attempted to capture the Austrian capital. These are trophies of Jan III Sobieski, the Polish king who led a pan-European army to victory in that battle.

Cost and Hours: 8 zł, see hours listed earlier, enter through courtyard; don't miss entry on your way back downstairs from Royal State Rooms.

KRAKÓW

Crown Treasury and Armory (Skarbiec i Zbrojownia)

This is a decent collection of swords, saddles, and shields; ornately decorated muskets, crossbows, and axes; and cannons in the basement. Off in a smaller side room are some of the most precious items. Look for the regalia given to Jan III Sobieski as thanks for his defeat of the Ottoman invaders in the Battle of Vienna: giant swords consecrated by the pope and the mantle (robe) of the Order of the Holy Ghost from France's King Louis XIV. Nearby is the 13th-century coronation sword of the Polish kings and some gorgeously inlaid rifles.

Cost and Hours: 18 zł, see hours listed earlier, plus April-Oct also open—and free—Mon 9:30-13:00, enter through courtyard.

▲▲Leonardo da Vinci's *Lady with an Ermine*

The single best and most famous painting in Kraków is normally displayed at the Czartoryski Museum. But while that space is closed for renovation (likely through 2015, and possibly longer), you'll most likely find the canvas at Wawel Castle. It's well worth the price of entry to view this rare, small (21 x 16 inches), but magnificently executed portrait of a teenage girl—a rare surviving work by one of history's greatest minds. (If you have your heart set on seeing this painting, make sure it's here before making the trip—it may be on loan or in storage.)

Cost and Hours: 10 zł, see hours listed earlier, plus Jan-March also open Sun 10:00-16:00, enter through courtyard.

Visiting the Museum: Spend some time lingering over the canvas (dating from 1489 or 1490). The girl is likely Cecilia Gallerani, the young mistress of Ludovico Sforza, the duke of Milan and Leonardo's employer. The ermine (white during winter) suggests chastity (thus bolstering Cecilia's questioned virtue), but is also a naughty reference to the duke's nickname, Ermellino—notice that his mistress is sensually, um, "stroking the ermine."

Painted before the *Mona Lisa*, the portrait was immediately recognized as revolutionary. Cecilia turns to look at someone, her gaze directed to the side. Leonardo catches this unguarded, informal moment, an unheard-of gesture in the days of the posed, front-facing formal portrait. Her simple body language and faraway gaze speak volumes about her inner thoughts and personality. Leonardo tweaks the generic Renaissance "pyramid" composition, turning it to a three-quarters angle, and softens it with curved lines that trace from Cecilia's eyes and down her cheek and sloping shoulders before doubling back across her folded arms. The background—once gray and blue—was painted black in the 19th century.

Lady with an Ermine is one of only three surviving oil paintings by Leonardo. It's better preserved than her famous cousin in

Paris *(Mona Lisa)*, and—many think—simply more beautiful. Can we be sure it's really by the enigmatic Leonardo? Yep—the master's fingerprints were found literally pressed into the paint (he was known to work areas of paint directly with his fingertips).

▲Lost Wawel (Wawel Zaginiony)

This exhibit traces the history of the hill and its various churches and castles. Begin by viewing the model of the entire castle complex in the 18th century (pre-Austrian razing). From here, the one-way route leads through scarcely explained excavations of a 10th-century church. The collection includes models of the cathedral at various historical stages (originally Romanesque—much simpler, before all the colorful, bulbous domes, chapels, and towers were added—then Gothic, and so on). Circling back to the entrance, find the display of fascinating decorative tiles from 16th-century stoves that once heated the place.

Cost and Hours: 10 zł, see hours listed earlier, plus April-Oct also open—and free—Mon 9:30-13:00; Nov-March also open—and free—Sun 9:30-13:00; enter near snack bar across from side of cathedral.

NATIONAL MUSEUM BRANCHES

Kraków's National Museum (Muzeum Narodowe) is made up of a series of small but interesting collections scattered throughout the city (www.muzeum.krakow.pl). I've listed the best of the National Museum's branches below. A 35-zł combo-ticket covers all of these museums (good for your entire stay), so consider that option if you'll be visiting more than three of them. National Museum branches are free to enter on Sunday (but some have reduced hours on that day, and only some exhibits at Szołayski House are free).

▲▲Gallery of 19th-Century Polish Art (Galeria Sztuki Polskiej XIX Wieku)

This small and surprisingly enjoyable collection of works by obscure Polish artists fills the upper level of the Cloth Hall. While you probably won't recognize any of the Polish names in here—and this collection isn't quite as impressive as Warsaw's National Gallery—many of these paintings are just plain delightful. It's worth a visit to see some Polish canvases in their native land, and to enjoy views over the Square from the hall's upper terraces.

Cost and Hours: 14 zł, free on Sun, Tue-Sun 10:00-18:00, closed Mon, last entry 30 minutes before closing, dry 7-zł audioguide, entrance on side of Cloth Hall facing Adam Mickiewicz statue, tel. 12-424-4600.

Background: Keep in mind that during the 19th century—when every piece of art in this museum was created—there was no "Poland." The country had been split up among its powerful neighbors in a series of three Partitions, and would not appear again on the map of Europe until after World War I. Meanwhile, the 19th century was a period of national revival throughout Europe, when various previously marginalized ethnic groups began to take pride in what made them different from their neighbors. So the artists you see represented here were grappling with trying to forge a national identity at a time when they didn't even have a nation. You'll sense a pessimism that comes from a country that feels abused by foreign powers, mingled with a resolute spirit of national pride.

◐ Self-Guided Tour: The collection fills just four rooms: Two small rooms in the center and two big halls on either side. On a quick visit, focus on the highlights in the big halls I mention here.

Entering the Cloth Hall, buy your ticket and head up the stairs—pausing on the first floor to peek out onto the inviting

café terrace (your museum ticket gets you in) for a fine view of the Square and St. Mary's. Then continue up to the main exhibit, on the second floor.

The first two small rooms don't feature much of interest. You enter **Room I** (Bacciarelli Room), with works from the Enlightenment; straight ahead is **Room II** (Michałowski Room), featuring Romantic works from 1822 to 1863. The larger, twin halls on either side merit a linger.

Siemiradzki Room (Room III, on the right): This features art of the Academy—that is, "conformist" art embraced by the art critics of the day. Entering the room, turn right and survey the canvases counterclockwise. The space is dominated by the works of Jan Matejko, a remarkably productive painter who specialized in epic historical scenes that he presented in such a way as to comment on his own era.

• *Circling the room, look for these paintings. The first two paintings you see are worth examining.*

1. Jan Matejko—*Wenyhora:* The first big canvas is Matejko's depiction of Wenyhora, a late-18th-century Ukrainian soothsayer who, according to legend, foretold Poland's hardships—the three Partitions, Poland's pact with Napoleon, and its difficulties regaining nationhood. Like many Poles of the era, Matejko was preoccupied with Poland's tragic fate, imbuing this scene with an air of inevitable tragedy.

2. Jacek Malcezewski—*Death of Ellenai:* A similar gloominess is reflected in this canvas. The main characters in a Polish

Romantic poem, Ellenai and Anhelli, have been exiled to a remote cabin in Siberia (in Russia, one of the great powers occupying Poland). Just when they think things can't get worse, Ellenai dies. Anhelli sits immobilized by grief.

• *Dominating the right side of the hall is...*

   3. Jan Matejko—*Tadeusz Kościuszko:* One of the heroes of the American Revolution, now back in his native Poland fight-

ing the Russians, doffs his hat after his unlikely victory at the battle at Racławice. In this battle (which ulti-mately had little bearing on Russia's drive to overtake Poland), a ragtag army of Polish peasants defeated the Russian forces. Kościuszko is clad in an American uniform, sym-bolizing Matejko's respect for the American ideals of democracy and self-determination.

• *Dominating the far wall is...*

   4. Henryk Siemiradzki—*Nero's Torches:* On the left, Roman citizens eagerly gather to watch Christians being burned at the

stake. The symbolism is clear: The meek and down-trodden (whether Christians in the time of Rome, or Poles in the heyday of Russia and Austria) may be perse-cuted now, but we have faith that their noble ideals will ultimately prevail.

• *On the next wall, find...*

   5. Pantaleon Szyndler—*Bathing Girl:* This piece evokes the orientalism popular in 19th-century Europe, when romanticized European notions of the Orient (such as harem slave girls) were popular artistic themes. Already voyeuristic, the painting was originally downright lewd until Szyndler painted over a man leer-ing at the woman from the left side of the canvas.

• *The huge canvas on this wall is...*

   6. Jan Matejko—*The Prussian Homage:* The last Grand Master of the fearsome Teutonic Knights swears allegiance to the Polish king in 1525. This historic ceremony took place in the Main Market Square in Kraków, the capital at the time. Notice the Cloth Hall and the spires of St. Mary's Church in the background. Matejko has painted his own face on one of his favorite historical figures, the jester Stańczyk at the foot of the throne.

• *Continue the rest of the way around the room. Keep an eye out for Tadeusz Ajdukiewicz's portrait of Helena Modrzejewska, a popular actress of the time, attending a party in this very building. Finally, backtrack through Room I and continue into the...*

Chełmoński Room (Room IV): Featuring works of the late 19th century, this section includes Realism and the first inklings of Symbolism and Impressionism. Just as elsewhere in Europe (including Paris, where many of these artists trained), artists were beginning to throw off the conventions of the Academy and embrace their own muse.

• *As you proceed counterclockwise through the room, the first stretch of canvases features landscapes and genre paintings. Tune in to a couple of appealing nature scenes: Józef Chełmoński's small, misty Cranes, and...*

1. Wladyslaw Malecki—*A Gathering of Storks:* The majestic birds stand under big willows in front of the setting sun. Even seemingly innocent wildlife paintings have a political message: Storks are particularly numerous in Poland, making them a subtle patriotic symbol.

• *A few canvases down, find...*

2. Józef Brandt—*A Meeting on the Bridge:* This dramatic painting shows soldiers and aristocrats pushing a farmer into a ditch—a comment on the state of the Polish people at that time. Just to the right, see Brandt's *Fight for a Turkish Standard.* This artist specialized in battle scenes, frequently involving a foe from the East—as was often the reality here along Europe's buffer zone with Asia.

• *Just to the left of Brandt's works is...*

3. Samuel Hirszenberg—*School of Talmudists:* Young Jewish students pore over the Talmud. One of them, deeply lost in thought, may be pondering more than ancient Jewish law. This canvas suggests the inclusion of Jews in Poland's cultural tapestry during this age. While still subject to pervasive bigotry here, many Jewish refugees found Poland to be a relatively welcoming, tolerant place to settle on a typically hostile continent.

• *Dominating the end of the room is...*

4. Józef Chełmoński—*Four-in-Hand:* In this intersection of worlds, a Ukrainian horseman gives a lift to a pipe-smoking noble-man. Feel the thrilling energy as the horses charge directly at you through splashing puddles.

• *Heading back toward the entrance, on the right wall, watch for...*

5. Witold Pruszkowski—*Water Nymphs:* Based on Slavic legends (and wearing traditional Ukrainian costumes), these mischievous, siren-like beings have just taken one victim (see his hand in the foreground) and are about to descend on another (seen faintly in the upper-right corner). Beyond this painting are some travel pictures from Italy and France (including some that are very Impressionistic, suggesting a Parisian influence).

• *Flanking the entrance/exit door are two of this room's best works. First, on the right, is...*

6. Władysław Podkowiński—*Frenzy:* This gripping painting's title *(Szał),* tellingly, has been translated as either *Ecstasy* or *Insanity.* A pale, sensuous woman—possibly based on a socialite for whom the artist fostered a desperate but unrequited love—clutches an all-fired-up black stallion, who's frothing at the mouth. This sexually charged painting caused a frenzy indeed at its 1894 unveiling, leading the unbalanced artist to attack his own creation with a knife (you can still see the slash marks in the canvas).

• *On the other side of the door is...*

7. Jacek Malczewski—*Introduction:* A young painter's apprentice on a bench contemplates his future. Surrounded by nature and with his painter's tools beside him, it's easy to imagine this as a self-portrait of the artist as a young man... wondering if he's choosing the correct path. Malczewski was an extremely talented Młoda Polska artist who tends to be overshadowed by his contemporary, Wyspiański. Viewing this canvas—and others by him—makes me feel grateful that he decided to stick with painting.

▲Szołayski House (Kamienica Szołayskich)

This restored mansion, just one block from the Main Market Square, features high-quality temporary exhibits, most often showcasing Art Nouveau works by the Młoda Polska movement. If you're lucky, you may see the excellent "Forever Young! Poland and Its Art Around 1900" exhibit (likely on display at least through 2015), which offers a concise overview of this period of artistic flourishing. This exhibit collects the works of a variety of turn-of-the-20th-century artists around themes (scenery of Kraków—see Wyspiański's hauntingly beautiful *Planty Overlooking Wawel*; portraits; and some fine Art Nouveau posters and books). Whatever exhibits are on display, they typically feature some masterpieces by the movement's founder, Stanisław Wyspiański, though many of these are currently in restoration and/or storage (but you can still see his works inside St. Francis Basilica).

Cost and Hours: 11 zł, some exhibits free on Sun, open Tue-Sat 10:00-18:00, Sun 10:00-16:00, closed Mon, last entry 30 minutes before closing, 1 block northwest of the Square at plac Szczepański 9, tel. 12-292-8183.

Nearby: The charming, recently restored square that Szołayski House faces, **plac Szczepański,** is a hub for youthful, cutting-edge, artistic types. Tucked in a corner of the Old Town, just away from the Square, it's a strange and wonderful little oasis of urban sophistication holding out against the rising tide of tacky tourism. In addition to Szołayski House itself, the square has several bohemian cafés (including the recommended Charlotte). If you follow Szczepańska street one more block out to the Planty, then turn left, you'll find **Bunker Sztuki,** an art gallery that fills an unfortunate communist-era building that really does feel like a bunker. But this conformist architecture is filled with quite the opposite: changing exhibitions of contemporary art (some exhibits free, others require a ticket, Tue-Sun 12:00-20:00, closed Mon, http://ha.art.pl). The gallery's fine café, under a delightfully airy canopy facing the Planty, has an almost Parisian ambience—a great place to escape the crowds (see "Eating in Kraków," later).

Bishop Erazm Ciołek Palace (Pałac Biskupa Erazma Ciołka)

This branch of the National Museum features two separate art collections. Upstairs, the extensive "Art of Old Poland" section shows off works from the 12th through the 18th centuries, with room after room of altarpieces, sculptures, paintings, and more. The "Orthodox Art of the Old Polish Republic" section on the ground floor offers a taste of the remote Eastern reaches of Poland, with icons and other ecclesiastical art from the Orthodox faith. You'll see a sizeable section of the iconostasis (wall of icons) from the town of Lipovec. Both collections are covered by the same ticket and are very well-presented in a modern facility. Items are labeled in English, but there's not much description.

Cost and Hours: 12 zł, free on Sun, audioguide-5 zł, Tue-Sat 10:00-18:00, Sun 10:00-16:00, closed Mon, Kanonicza 17, tel. 12-424-9371.

▲Czartoryski Museum (Muzeum Czartoryskich)

This eclectic collection, displaying armor, handicrafts, decorative arts, and paintings, is one of Kraków's best-known (and most overrated) museums. It's wrapping up a multi-year renovation; during your visit, some or all of its collection may already be open again. But the painting gallery—with its top pieces (a Leonardo and a Rembrandt)—may take longer to reopen. Likely through at least 2015, its undisputed highlight, Leonardo's *Lady with an Ermine*, will be displayed instead at Wawel Castle. Before visiting this museum, get the latest from a TI about how much is open.

Background: The museum's collection came about, in part, thanks to Poland's 1791 constitution (Europe's first), which inspired Princess Izabela Czartoryska to begin gathering bits of Polish history and culture. She fled with the collection to Paris after the 1830 insurrection, and 45 years later, her grandson returned it to its present Kraków location. When he ran out of space, he bought part of the monastery across the street, joining the buildings with a fancy passageway. The Nazis took the collection to Germany, and although most of it has been returned, some pieces are still missing.

The museum owns two undisputed masterpieces, which are in varying states of accessibility. Art lovers will want to ask around for the scoop on their latest locations. While the museum is closed, its top painting—**Leonardo da Vinci's *Lady with an Ermine***— can likely be found at Kraków's Wawel Castle (described earlier). **Rembrandt van Rijn's *Landscape with the Good Samaritan*** (1638) may be on display in another city (or possibly in Kraków). The museum technically owns a third masterpiece, **Raphael's *Portrait of a Young Man*,** but its whereabouts are unknown. Arguably one of the most famous and most valuable stolen paintings of all time, it's quite likely a self-portrait (but possibly a portrait of Raphael by another artist), depicting a Renaissance dandy, clad in a fur coat, with a self-satisfied smirk. Painted (perhaps) by the Renaissance master in 1513 or 1514, and purchased by a Czartoryski prince around the turn of the 19th century, the work was seized by the occupying Nazis during World War II. Along with the paintings by Leonardo and Rembrandt, this Raphael decorated the Wawel Castle residence of Nazi governor Hans Frank. But when Frank and the Nazis fled the invading Red Army at the end of the war, many of their pilfered artworks were lost—including the Raphael. For decades, this canvas was synonymous with art theft—the (literal) poster boy for Nazi crimes against culture. Then, dramatically, a Polish news site announced in 2012 that the priceless painting had been found, safe and sound (in a bank vault in an undisclosed location). Unfortunately, this was a misinterpretation of remarks made by government officials. But authorities are still hopeful the painting "will surface sooner or later" and that the "Czartoryski Raphael," as it's called, will be returned to this museum.

Cost and Hours: If museum is open—around 12 zł, free on Sun, open Tue-Sun 10:00-16:00 or possibly until 18:00, closed

Mon, last entry 30 minutes before closing, 2 blocks north of the Main Market Square at ulica Św. Jana 19, tel. 12-422-5566, www.czartoryski.org.

Visiting the Museum: If the museum is open, you'll wander through rooms of ornate armor (including a ceremonial Turkish tent from the 1683 siege of Vienna, plus feathered Hussar armor), tapestries, treasury items, majolica pottery, and Meissen porcelain figures. Rounding out the exhibits are painting galleries (including Italian, French, and Dutch High Renaissance and Baroque, as well as Czartoryski family portraits) and ancient art (mostly sculptures and vases).

More National Museum Branches

While less interesting than the branches listed above, the National Museum's **Main Branch** (Gmach Główny) is worth a visit for museum completists. It features 20th-century Polish art and temporary exhibits (10 zł, west of the Main Market Square at aleja 3 Maja 1). The new **Europeum** collection, housed in a restored granary, features works by European masters, including Breughel and Veneziano, along with a range of lesser-known artists (just west of the Old Town at plac Sikorskiego 6). You can also check out the museum of Wyspiański's friend and rival, the **Józef Mehoffer House** (Dom Józefa Mehoffera, 6 zł, ulica Krupnicza 26, tel. 12-421-1143), and the former residence of their mentor, the **Jan Matejko House** (Dom Jana Matejki, 8 zł, ulica Floriańska 41, tel. 12-422-5926).

OTHER ATTRACTIONS

▲▲Rynek Underground Museum (Podziemia Rynku)

Recent work to renovate the Square's pavement unearthed a wealth of remains from previous structures. Now you can do some urban

spelunking with a visit to this high-tech medieval-history museum, which is literally underground—beneath all the photo-snapping tourists on the Square above.

Cost and Hours: 19 zł, free on Tue, open Mon 10:00-20:00, Tue 10:00-16:00 (but closed first Tue of each month), Wed-Sun 10:00-22:00, shorter hours in winter; last entry 1.25 hours before closing, enter at north end of Cloth Hall near the fountain, Rynek Główny 1, tel. 12-426-5060, www.podziemiarynku.com.

Visiting the Museum: You'll enter through a door near the north end of the Cloth Hall (close to the fountain, facing St.

Mary's). Climb down a flight of stairs, buy your ticket, then follow the numbered panels—1 to 70—through the exhibit (all in English). Cutting-edge museum technology illuminates life and times in medieval Kraków: Touchscreens let you delve into topics that intrigue you, 3-D virtual holograms resurrect old buildings, and video clips illustrate everyday life on unexpected surfaces (such as a curtain of fog).

All of this is wrapped around large chunks of early structures that still survive beneath the Square; several "witness columns" of rock and dirt are accompanied by diagrams helping you trace the layers of history. Interactive maps emphasize Kraków's Europe-wide importance as an intersection of major trade routes, and several models, maps, and digital reconstructions give you a good look at Kraków during the Middle Ages—when the Old Town looked barely different from today. You'll see a replica of a blacksmith's shop and learn how "vampire prevention burials" were used to ensure that the suspected undead wouldn't return from the grave. In the middle of the complex, look up through the glass of the Square's fountain to see the towers of St. Mary's above. Under the skylight is a model of medieval Kraków. While it looks much the same as today, notice a few key changes: the moat ringing the Old Town, where the Planty is today; and the several smaller market halls out on the Square.

Deeper in the exhibit, explore the long corridors of ruined buildings that once ran alongside the length of the Cloth Hall. There are many intriguing cases showing artifacts that shops would have sold (jewelry, tools, amber figurines, and so on). Also in this area, you'll find a corridor with images of the Square all torn up for the recent renovation, plus a series of five modern brick rooms, each showing a brief, excellent film outlining a different period of Kraków's history. These "Kraków Chronicles" provide a big-picture context to what otherwise seems like a loose collection of cool museum gizmos, and also help you better appreciate what you'll see outside the museum's doors.

▲Jagiellonian University Museum: Collegium Maius

Kraków had the second university in Central Europe (founded in 1364, after Prague's), boasting such illustrious grads over the centuries as Copernicus and St. John Paul II. With around 150,000 students (including 500 Norwegian med students), this city is still very much a university town, and Jagiellonian University proudly offers tours of its historic oldest building, the 15th-century Collegium Maius (one block west of the Main Market Square at ulica Jagiellońska 15). In the Middle Ages, professors were completely devoted to their scholarly pursuits. They were unmarried and lived, ate, and slept here in an almost monastic environment. They taught downstairs and lived upstairs. In many ways, this building feels more like a monastery than a university.

The university also comes with some chilling history. On November 6, 1939, the occupying Nazis called all professors together for a meeting. With 183 gathered unknowingly in a hall, they were suddenly loaded into trucks and sent to their deaths in concentration camps. You decapitate a culture when you kill its intelligentsia.

Tours: Student guides lead visitors through the musty and mildly interesting interior of the complex. You'll choose between two different guided tours: 30 minutes (very popular) or one hour. It's smart to call ahead to find out when the shorter tour is scheduled in English, and to reserve for either tour (tel. 12-663-1307 for advance reservations, or tel. 12-663-1521 for same day, www.maius. uj.edu.pl).

The **30-minute tour** covers the "main exhibition" route: the library, refectory (with a gorgeously carved Baroque staircase), treasury (including Polish filmmaker Andrzej Wajda's honorary Oscar), assembly hall, and some old scientific instruments (12 zł, a few tours per day in English, 20 people maximum, leaves every 20 minutes Mon-Sat 10:00-15:00, until 18:00 Tue and Thu in April-Oct, last tour departs 40 minutes before closing, no tours Sun). On Tuesday afternoons, the tour is free (runs 15:00-18:00, shorter hours in winter, last tour departs 40 minutes before closing). Be aware that these tours can book up—especially the free Tuesday afternoon departures.

The **one-hour tour** adds some more interiors, room after room of more old scientific instruments, medieval art (mostly church sculptures), a Rubens, a small landscape from the shop of Rembrandt, and Chopin's piano (16 zł, usually in English Mon-Fri at 13:00, no tours Sat-Sun).

Before you leave, enjoy a cup of hot chocolate at the chocolate shop (down the stairs near the entrance)—widely regarded as the best in town.

Dominican Church, a.k.a. Holy Trinity Church (Bazylika Trójcy Świętej)

Sitting in the middle of town, facing St. Francis Basilica from a couple of blocks away, this may not be Kraków's finest church, but it's still worth a peek. Inside, you'll find a Neo-Gothic space that was rebuilt after a devastating 1850 fire. You may be approached

and offered an audioguide to tour the church, in exchange for a donation; it's a good little tour and worth doing, if you have the time. Or, for a quick visit, tune in to just a few details: The unique metal chandeliers are one of many modern flourishes added during the late-19th-century restoration of the church. Climb the staircase in the left aisle to reach the chapel of St. Hyacinth. Locally known as St. Jacek, this early Dominican leader—called the "Apostle of the North"—is also the patron saint of pierogi (stuffed dough, similar to ravioli). During a famine, St. Jacek supposedly invented pierogi and—in a loaves-and-fishes-type miracle—produced plateful after plateful, feeding the desperate locals. His image adorns Kraków's annual Pierogi Cup contest, and to this day, when old-fashioned Poles are surprised, they might exclaim, *"Święty Jacek z pierogami!"* ("St. Hyacinth and his pierogi!"). Back down in the main part of the church, stroll slowly past the gorgeously carved wooden seats of the choir area (behind the altar); then, at the main altar, identify the three parts of the trinity: Jesus (short beard), God (long beard), and Holy Spirit (beardless dove).

Cost and Hours: Free but donation requested, daily 6:30-13:00 & 16:00-20:00, facing plac Dominikański at Stolarska 12.

Archdiocesan Museum (Muzeum Archidiecezjalne)

This museum, in a building where St. John Paul II lived both as a priest and as a bishop, consists of several parts: the underwhelming ground-floor collection of sacral art (with altars, paintings, and vestments); various temporary exhibits; and the top-floor museum devoted to St. John Paul II. Wandering past the scores of paintings and photographs, the late pontiff's cult of personality is almost palpable. Unfortunately, because the collection mostly consists of elaborate gifts received by the Holy Father from around the world, it offers little intimacy or insight into the man himself. Still, admirers of St. John Paul II will appreciate it. This museum shares a collection with the St. John Paul II Sanctuary (part of the John Paul II Center) on the outskirts of town; visit here only if you won't be going to the more interesting collection at the museum there.

Cost and Hours: 5 zł, Tue-Fri 10:00-16:00, Sat-Sun 10:00-15:00, closed Mon, Kanonicza 19-21, tel. 12-421-8963, www.muzeumkra.diecezja.pl.

John Paul II Center Exhibition

This modest exhibition space, across the street from the Archdiocesan Museum, is the headquarters for the construction of the sprawling John Paul II Center (described later). If you can't make it out to the actual center, stop in here to learn more about it—with photographs, artifacts, and films relating to the late pontiff.

Cost and Hours: Free, daily 10:00-16:00, Kanonicza 18, tel. 12-429-6471, www.janpawel2.pl.

KRAKÓW

KAZIMIERZ (JEWISH QUARTER)

The neighborhood of Kazimierz (kah-ZHEE-mezh), 20 minutes by foot southeast of Kraków's Old Town, is the historic heart of Kraków's once-thriving Jewish community. After years of neglect, the district was rediscovered by Krakovians and tourists alike in the mid-2000s. Even so, visitors expecting a polished, touristy scene like Prague's Jewish Quarter will be surprised...and maybe disappointed. This is basically a local-feeling, slightly run-down neighborhood with a handful of Jewish cemeteries, synagogues, and restaurants, and often a few pensive Israeli tour groups wandering the streets. It's also the city's edgy, hipster culture center, jammed with colorful, creative bars and designer boutiques—sometimes oddly juxtaposed with a somber reverence for Judaism. But for many, this is where you'll find the true soul of the European Jewish experience.

Try to visit any day except Saturday, when most Jewish-themed sights are closed (except the Old Synagogue, High Synagogue, and Galicia Jewish Museum). Monday comes with a few closures: the Ethnographic Museum, Museum of Contemporary Art in Kraków, and Museum of Municipal Engineering. On Monday, the Schindler's Factory Museum is free, but it's also open shorter hours and is more crowded than usual.

Note that it's respectful for men to cover their heads while visiting a Jewish cemetery or synagogue. While some of these sights offer loaner yarmulkes, it's easiest to bring your own hat.

Getting to Kazimierz: From the Old Town, it's about a 20-minute **walk,** which gets you out of the fairy-tale tourist zone and into the real, soot-stained, workaday Kraków (that's a good thing). From the Main Market Square, walk down ulica Sienna (near St. Mary's Church). At the fork, bear right through the Planty park. At the intersection with the busy Westerplatte ring road, you'll continue straight ahead (bear right at fork, then continue straight across the busy ring road) down Starowiślna for 15 more minutes. To hop the **tram,** go to the stop on the left-hand side of ulica Sienna (at the intersection with Westerplatte, across

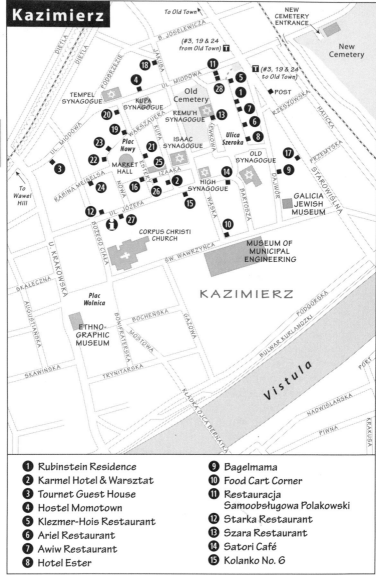

Kazimierz

❶ Rubinstein Residence
❷ Karmel Hotel & Warsztat
❸ Tournet Guest House
❹ Hostel Momotown
❺ Klezmer-Hois Restaurant
❻ Ariel Restaurant
❼ Awiw Restaurant
❽ Hotel Ester
❾ Bagelmama
❿ Food Cart Corner
⓫ Restauracja Samoobsługowa Polakowski
⓬ Starka Restaurant
⓭ Szara Restaurant
⓮ Satori Café
⓯ Kolanko No. 6

the street from the Poczta Główna, or main post office). Catch tram #3, #19, or #24 and go two stops to Miodowa. Walking or by tram, at the intersection of Starowiślna and Miodowa, you'll see a small park across the street and to the right. To reach the heart of Kazimierz—ulica Szeroka—cut through this park. You can also take this tram from near the train station (see "Arrival in Kraków,"

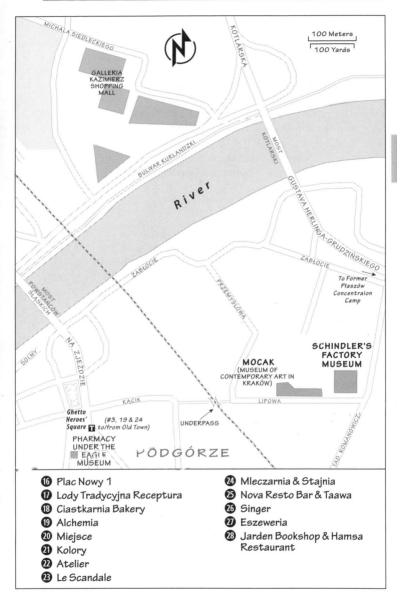

KRAKÓW

16 Plac Nowy 1
17 Lody Tradycyjna Receptura
18 Ciastkarnia Bakery
19 Alchemia
20 Miejsce
21 Kolory
22 Atelier
23 Le Scandale

24 Mleczarnia & Stajnia
25 Nova Resto Bar & Taawa
26 Singer
27 Eszeweria
28 Jarden Bookshop & Hamsa
   Restaurant

earlier). To return to the Old Town, catch tram #3, #19, or #24 from the intersection of Starowiślna and Miodowa (kitty-corner from where you got off the tram), and go two stops back to the Poczta Główna stop.

Information: An official **TI** is just a few blocks off the bottom of ulica Szeroka, at ulica Józefa 7 (daily 9:00-17:00, tel.

12-422-0471).

Tours: As Kazimierz's sights are spread out and not presented in a unified way, it's a good place to hire a **local guide**. **Jarden Bookshop** (listed later) runs several tours (prices based on the number of people; I've listed the price per person for 2 people): Jewish Kazimierz overview (70 zł, 2 hours, walking tour), Kazimierz and the WWII ghetto (90 zł, 3 hours, walking, the best overview), *Schindler's List* sights (120 zł, 2 hours, by car), and Auschwitz-Birkenau (190 zł, 6-7 hours, by car). Call to reserve ahead, as tours are by appointment only. Pairs or singles may be able to join an already scheduled tour (which lowers the price for everybody).

Central Kazimierz

Ulica Szeroka is the core of Kazimierz; within a few blocks of here, you'll find two cemeteries (quite different and both worth a visit), six synagogues, and three museums, as well as the lively market square called plac Nowy. The various sights in this area operate independently and can be seen in any order.

Ulica Szeroka

Begin your visit by getting oriented on the neighborhood's hub, **ulica Szeroka ("Broad Street").** More of a long, parking-lot square than a street, this strip is surrounded by Jewish-themed restaurants, hotels, and synagogues.

The **Jarden Bookshop** at the top of the square is worth a stop. While there are many new bookstores in Kazimierz (mostly inside the various museums and synagogues), this is the original. It serves as an unofficial information point for the neighborhood and sells a wide variety of fairly priced books on Kazimierz and Jewish culture in the region, including a good 5-zł Kraków map of Jewish monuments and the well-illustrated 18-zł *Jewish Kraków* guidebook (Mon-Fri 9:00-18:00, Sat-Sun 10:00-18:00, ulica Szeroka 2, tel. 12-429-1374, www.jarden.pl, jarden@jarden.pl).

Circling around the left side of the building that houses Jarden and the recommended Hamsa restaurant, you'll find where a local entrepreneur has restored a row of rustic old Jewish **shop fronts,** as they would have appeared in Kazimierz's pre-Holocaust prime. This lane leads to **Miodowa street,** which you can follow left to reach two of Kazimierz's lesser-known synagogues (Tempel and Kupa, both described later). In the opposite direction, Miodowa crosses busy Starowiślna, then goes under a train tunnel to reach the New Cemetery (also described later).

Back on ulica Szeroka, circle around to the downhill side of the little **park** to find a low-profile monument honoring the "65 thousand Polish citizens of Jewish nationality from Kraków and its environs" who were murdered by the Nazis during the Holocaust. Tragically, this piece of Kraków's history was all but lost during the communist period. After 1989, interest in Kazimierz's unique Jewish history was faintly rekindled. But it was only when Steven Spielberg chose to film *Schindler's List* here in 1993 that the world took renewed interest in Kazimierz. (A local once winked to me, "They ought to build a statue to Spielberg on that square.")

Turn 180 degrees, facing the bottom end of ulica Szeroka, to get your bearings. On your left is a strip of hotels and restaurants, many of them offering live traditional Jewish **klezmer music** nightly in summer. The Ester Hotel near the bottom of the square often has outdoor klezmer music in good weather—allowing you to get a taste of this unique musical form before committing to a full meal.

Halfway down this side of the square, the green house at #14 is where **Helena Rubinstein** was born in 1870. At age 31, she emigrated to Australia, where she parlayed her grandmother's traditional formula for hand cream into a cosmetics empire. Many cosmetics still used by people worldwide today were invented by Rubinstein, who died at age 92 in New York City as one of the most successful businesswomen of all time—just one of many illustrious Jewish residents of Kazimierz.

On the right side of the square, near the top, is the entrance to the **Rem'uh Synagogue and Old Cemetery.** Partway down this side, little Lewkowa lane zigzags through the heart of the district to **Isaac Synagogue** and the **plac Nowy market.** All of these are described later. Exploring these streets, you may see some dilapidated buildings that are typical of this district. Kazimierz is so ramshackle, in part, because many of the buildings are still under state control; during World War II, the Nazis seized Jewish-owned property, which was later nationalized by the communists, and therefore lacks clear ownership today.

Next, head down to the bottom end of ulica Szeroka, which dead-ends at the **Old Synagogue** (now a good museum, and perhaps Kazimierz's most worthwhile synagogue to enter—described later). The bit of white stone wall and rampart to the left of the Old Synagogue is a reconstruction of the original Kazimierz town wall from the 14th century.

Find the big **map of Kazimierz** directly in front of the synagogue, and use it for a historical orientation—reading the district's past into its current street plan. What are now Starowiślna and Dietla streets—which frame off Kazimierz in a triangle of land hemmed in by the riverbank—were once canals, meaning that Kazimierz was built on an island. When King Kazimierz the Great—who reportedly didn't care much for Krakovians—founded this district in 1335, he envisioned it as a separate town to rival Kraków. (If you have a 50-zł note, take a look at it: That's Kazimierz the Great on the front, and on the back you'll see his capital, Cracovia, and the most important town he founded, Casmirus.) Examining the map, notice plac Wolnica, the big market square to rival Kraków's, and Corpus Christi Church, which was intentionally built to compete for attention with St. Mary's. After Jews began to settle here in the early 16th century, a wall along Jakuba street (directly behind the Old Cemetery) separated Jewish Kazimierz (where we are now) from Christian Kraków (around the market squares and big church, to the west). But by 1800, the dense Jewish population spilled over those boundaries and filled the entire district.

For much of Kazimierz's history, Jews and Christians lived in relative harmony, side-by-side. As an example of this, notice the intersection just west of plac Nowy, where ulica Bożego Ciała ("Corpus Christi Street") crosses ulica Meiselsa ("Rabbi Meisel Street"). Also notice the district called Podgórze, directly across the river from Kazimierz. This is where the Nazis ultimately forced Kazimierz's Jewish residents into a ghetto. It contains several powerful sights, including the **Pharmacy Under the Eagle** and the **Schindler's Factory Museum** (both described later).

While Kazimierz's Jewish story is powerful, don't miss its other, more recent claim to fame—its youthful counterculture. As you face the Old Synagogue, the street to the right, **ulica Józefa,** leads past the **High Synagogue,** then a stretch of engaging designer boutiques. This area is the best place in Kraków to spot up-and-coming fashion and design.

▲▲Old Jewish Cemetery (Stary Cmentarz)

This small cemetery was used to bury members of the Jewish community from 1552 to 1800. With more than a hundred of the top Jewish intellectuals of that age buried here, this is considered one of the most important Jewish cemeteries in Europe. It has been renovated—so in a way, it actually feels newer than the

New Cemetery. After the New Cemetery (described next) was opened in 1800, this one gradually fell into disrepair. What remained was further desecrated by the Nazis during World War II. In the 1950s, it was discovered, excavated, and put back together as you see here. Shattered gravestones form a mosaic wall around

Jewish Kraków

In the 14th century, King Kazimierz the Great created policies that encouraged Jews fleeing other kingdoms to settle in Poland. Kraków's Jewish community—which was originally concentrated in the university district—clashed with the students, and when a destructive fire broke out in 1495, the Jews were blamed. The king at the time forced all of Kraków's Jews to move to Kazimierz (which was then a separate town).

After several centuries as a town divided by a wall into Christian (west) and Jewish (east) neighborhoods, Kazimierz was integrated as part of Kraków around 1800, and the Jewish community flourished. Around that same time, Polish lands had the biggest Jewish population in the world (about 4 million)—and Kraków was a center of Jewish culture.

By the start of World War II, 65,000 Jews lived in Kraków (mostly in Kazimierz)—making up more than a quarter of the city's population. When the Nazis arrived, they immediately sent most of Kraków's Jews to the ghetto in the eastern Polish city of Lublin. Soon after, they forced Kraków's remaining 15,000 Jews into a walled ghetto at Podgórze, across the river. The Jews' cemeteries were defiled, their buildings ransacked and destroyed. In 1942, the Nazis began transporting Kraków's Jews to death camps (including Płaszów, just on Kraków's outskirts, and Auschwitz). Many others were worked to death in the Podgórze ghetto. Only a few thousand Kraków Jews survived the war. During World War II, occupied Poland had the strictest laws in the Nazi realm: This was the only place where, if you were caught trying to help Jews escape, your entire family could be executed. And yet, many Poles risked their lives to help escapees.

Today's Kraków has only about 200 Jewish residents. During the communist era, this waning population was ignored or mistreated. But in recent years, Kazimierz has enjoyed a renaissance of Jewish culture—thanks largely to the popularity of *Schindler's List* (which was partly filmed here). Look for handwritten letters from Steven Spielberg and the cast in local restaurants (such as Ariel) and hotels. While few Jews live here now, the spirit of the Jewish tradition lives on in the many synagogues, as well as in the soulful cemeteries.

the perimeter. As in all Jewish cemeteries, you'll see many small stones stacked on the graves. The tradition comes from placing stones—representing prayers—over desert graves to cover the body and prevent animals from disturbing it. Behind the little synagogue to the left, the tallest tombstone next to the tree belonged to Moses Isserles (a.k.a. Remu'h), an important 16th-century rabbi. He is believed to have been a miracle worker, and his grave was one of the only ones that remained standing after World War II. Notice the written prayers crammed into the cracks and crevices of the tombstone.

KRAKÓW

Cost and Hours: 5 zł, also includes entry to attached Remu'h Synagogue—described later; very sporadic hours according to demand—especially outside peak season—but generally open Sun-Fri 9:00-16:00, can be open until 18:00 May-Sept, closes earlier off-season and by sundown on Fri, always closed Sat, enter through Remu'h Synagogue at ulica Szeroka 40.

▲New Jewish Cemetery (Nowy Cmentarz)

This much larger site has graves of those who died after 1800. Nazis also vandalized this cemetery, selling many of its gravestones to stonecutters and using others as pavement in their concentration camps. Many of the gravestones have since been cemented back in their original positions. Other headstones could not be replaced and were used to create the moving mosaic wall and Holocaust monument (on the right as you enter). Most gravestones are in one of four languages: Hebrew (generally the oldest, especially if there's no other language, though some are  newer "retro" tombstones); Yiddish (sounds like a mix of German and Hebrew and uses the Hebrew alphabet); Polish (Jews who assimilated into the Polish community); and German (Jews who assimilated into the German community). The earliest graves are simple stones, while later ones imitate graves in Polish Catholic cemeteries—larger, more elaborate, and with a long stone jutting out to cover the body. Notice that some new-looking graves have old dates. These were most likely put here well after the Holocaust (or even after the communist era) by relatives of the dead.

Cost and Hours: Free, Sun-Fri 8:00-18:00, until 16:00 in winter, closed Sat. It's tricky to find: Go under the railway tunnel at the east end of ulica Miodowa, and jog left as you emerge. The cemetery is to your right (enter through gate with small *cmentarz* *żydowski* sign).

Synagogues

Six different synagogues in Kazimierz welcome visitors. Some synagogues have been converted into museums, while others are still used for services. The first two synagogues listed below are on Kazimierz's main square, ulica Szeroka; the next four are all within three blocks to the west.

Remu'h Synagogue, which is tight, cozy, and dates from 1553, has been carefully renovated and is fully active. Notice the original 16th-century frescoed walls and ceilings, and the money-box at the door (included in 5-zł entry fee for Old Cemetery, same unpredictable hours as Old Cemetery, ulica Szeroka 40).

The **Old Synagogue** (Stara Synagoga), the oldest surviving Jewish building in Poland, is now a good three-room museum on local Jewish culture, with informative English descriptions. Most of the exhibits are displayed in the impressive main

prayer hall. The synagogue is eight steps down from street level because Jewish buildings weren't allowed to be taller than Christian ones. In order to have the proper proportion for the building, the ground floor needed to be lower (9 zł, free on Mon; April-Oct Mon 10:00-14:00, Tue-Sun 9:00-17:00; Nov-March Mon 10:00-14:00, Tue-Wed and Sat-Sun 9:00-16:00, Fri 10:00-17:00; good 50-stop audioguide-10 zł; ulica Szeroka 24, tel. 12-422-0962).

The **High Synagogue**—so called because its prayer room is upstairs—displays changing exhibits, most of which focus on the people who lived here before the Holocaust (9 zł, daily 9:00-20:00, shorter hours in winter, just around the corner from the Old Synagogue at ulica Józefa 38, tel. 12-430-6889).

Isaac Synagogue (Synagoga Izaaka), one of Kraków's biggest, was built in the 17th century. On the walls in the prayer hall are giant paintings of prayers for worshippers who couldn't afford to buy books (with translations posted below). The synagogue also serves as the local center for the Hasidic Jewish group Chabad, with a kosher restaurant and a library (7 zł, 5 zł extra to borrow descriptions; April-Oct Sun-Thu 8:30-20:00, Fri 8:30-14:30, closed Sat; Nov-March Sun-Thu 8:30-18:00, Fri 8:30-13:30, closed Sat; a block west of ulica Szeroka at ulica Kupa 18, tel. 12-430-2222). In addition to its Sabbath services, this is Kraków's only synagogue that has daily prayers (at 8:30). They also host klezmer

The Synagogue

A synagogue is a place of public worship, where Jews gather to pray, sing, and read from the Torah. Most synagogues have similar features, though they vary depending on the congregation.

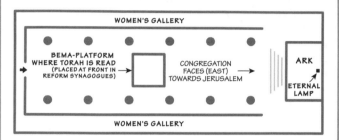

The synagogue generally faces toward Jerusalem (so in Kraków, worshippers face east). At the east end is an alcove called the **ark,** which holds the Torah. These scriptures (the first five books of the Old Testament) are written in Hebrew on scrolls wrapped in luxuriant cloth. The other main element of the synagogue is the **bema,** an elevated platform from which the Torah is read aloud (the equivalent of a pulpit in a Christian church). In traditional Orthodox synagogues, the bema is near the center of the hall, and the reader stands facing the same direction as the congregation. In other branches of Judaism, the bema is at the front, and the reader faces the worshippers. Orthodox synagogues have separate worship areas for men and women, usually with women in the balcony.

The synagogue walls might be decorated with elaborate patterns of vines or geometric designs, but never statues of people, as that might be seen as idol worship. A lamp above the ark is always kept lit, as it was in the ancient temple of Jerusalem, and candelabras called menorahs also recall the temple. Other common symbols are the two tablets of the Ten Commandments given to Moses, or a Star of David, representing the Jewish king's shield.

At a typical service, the congregation arrives at the start of Sabbath (Friday evening). As a sign of respect toward God, men don yarmulkes (small round caps). As the cantor leads songs and prayers, worshippers follow along in a book of weekly readings. At the heart of the service, everyone stands as the Torah is ceremoniously paraded, unwrapped, and placed on the bema. Someone—the rabbi, the cantor, or a congregant—reads the words aloud. The rabbi ("teacher") might give a commentary on the Torah passage.

music concerts many evenings at 18:00 (60 zł).

Tempel Synagogue (Synagoga Templu) has the grandest interior—big and dark, with elaborately decorated, gilded ceilings and balconies—and the most lived-in feel of the bunch (5 zł, Sun-Fri 10:00-16:00, sometimes until 18:00, closed Sat, corner of ulica Miodowa and ulica Podbrzezie).

The smaller **Kupa Synagogue** (Synagoga Kupa), clean and brightly decorated, sometimes hosts temporary exhibits (5 zł, Sun-Fri 10:00-17:00, closed Sat, Miodowa 27).

▲Galicia Jewish Museum (Galicja Muzeum)

This museum focuses on the present rather than the past. With a series of photographs displayed around a restored Jewish furniture factory, the permanent "Traces of Memory" exhibit shows today's remnants of yesterday's Judaism in the area around Kraków (a region known as "Galicia"). From forgotten synagogues to old Jewish gravestones flipped over and used as doorsteps, these giant postcards of Jewish artifacts (with good English descriptions) ensure that an important part of this region's heritage won't be forgotten. Good temporary exhibits complement this permanent collection.

Cost and Hours: 15 zł, daily 10:00-18:00, 1 block east of ulica Szeroka at ulica Dajwór 18, tel. 12-421-6842, www.galicia jewishmuseum.org. The museum also serves as a sort of cultural center, with a good bookstore and café.

Kazimierz Market Square (Plac Nowy)

While tourists have overrun the historic buildings of the Jewish quarter, and throngs of young clubbers clog the Kazimierz streets after dark, the market square retains the gritty flavor of the district before tourism and gentrification. The circular brick building in the center is a slaughterhouse where the animals were properly killed—kosher-style—so Jewish butchers could sell the meat. It's surrounded by busy market stalls and grazing locals. This is a welcome real-world contrast to Kraków's touristy Main Market Square (stalls open Tue-Sun 6:00-14:00, a few also open later, closed Mon). Consider dropping by here for some shopping, people-watching, or a quick, cheap, and local lunch. For dessert, buy some fruit from a vendor. There's a fun antique shop at #3. This square also has the highest concentration of nightlife in town, and several fun and funky spots are open during the day as stay-awhile cafés (see "Entertainment in Kraków," later). On Sunday mornings, the square is filled with flea-market stalls (see the stall numbers painted onto the pavement).

Museum of Municipal Engineering
(Muzeum Inżynierii Miejskiej)

This pleasant museum fills the immaculately restored red-brick buildings of an old tram depot in a quiet part of Kazimierz. Exhibits include a history of the town's public-transit system (including several antique trams), old Polish-made cars and motorcycles (among them the tiny commie-era Polski Fiat), typography and historical printing presses, and a hands-on area for kids called "Around the Circle."

Cost and Hours: 10 zł, family ticket-29 zł, includes English audioguide, free on Tue; open Tue-Sun 10:00-16:00, until 18:00 on Tue and Thu June-Sept, closed Mon, Św. Wawrzyńca 15, tel. 12-421-1242.

▲Ethnographic Museum (Muzeum Etnograficzne)

This clever, refreshingly good museum hides a few blocks west of the Jewish area of Kazimierz, in the former town hall. It sits on plac Wolnica, which was Kazimierz's primary market square and was once almost as big as Kraków's. On the ground floor, you'll find models of traditional rural Polish homes, as well as musty replicas of the interiors (like an open-air folk museum moved inside). The exhibit continues upstairs, where each in a long lineup of traditional Polish folk costumes is identified by specific region. You'll see exhibits on village lifestyles, rustic tools, and musical instruments (including a Polish bagpipe). A highlight is the explanation of traditional holiday celebrations—from elaborate crèche scenes at Christmas, to a wall of remarkably painted Easter eggs. Some items are labeled in English, but it's mostly in Polish. The top floor features temporary exhibits.

Cost and Hours: 13 zł, free on Sun, open Tue-Sat 11:00-19:00, Thu until 21:00, Sun 11:00-15:00, closed Mon, ulica Krakowska 46, tel. 12-430-6023, www.etnomuzeum.eu.

Nearby: From plac Wolnica, Mostowa street stretches two blocks south to the river and a newly built, modern, padlock-studded **pedestrian bridge** (called Kładka Ojca Bernatka) that crosses the Vistula to the Podgórze neighborhood described next. The bridge itself is a fun way to connect to Podgórze without hiking back to the main drag to catch a tram, and it comes with a nice look at the local side of Kazimierz: Mostowa street has become a popular place for trendy cafés and eateries, and the river embankment park near the bridge hosts some inviting cafés.

Near Kazimierz: Podgórze

The neighborhood called Podgórze (POD-goo-zheh), directly across the Vistula from Kazimierz, has one of Kraków's most famous sights: Schindler's Factory Museum.

KRAKÓW

Background: This is the neighborhood where the Nazis forced Kraków's Jews into a ghetto in early 1941. (*Schindler's List* and the films in the Pharmacy Under the Eagle museum depict the sad scene of the Jews loading their belongings onto carts and trudging over the bridge into Podgórze.) Non-Jews who had lived here were displaced to make way for the new arrivals. The ghetto was surrounded by a wall with a fringe along the top that resembled Jewish gravestones—a chilling premonition of what was to come. A short section of this wall still stands along Lwowska street. The tram continued to run through the middle of Podgórze, without stopping—giving Krakovians a chilling glimpse at the horrifying conditions inside the ghetto.

Getting There: To get to Ghetto Heroes' Square, continue through Kazimierz on tram #3, #19, or #24 (described earlier, under "Getting to Kazimierz") to the stop called plac Bohaterow Getta. You can also simply continue walking along Starowiślna, about 10 minutes past the other Kazimierz sights—it's just across the bridge. If you're coming from plac Wolnica (the big square with the Ethnographic Museum), be sure to take the recently opened, modern footbridge, which gives you a more interesting look at Kazimierz (see earlier).

Ghetto Heroes' Square (Plac Bohaterow Getta)

This unassuming square is the focal point of the visitor's Podgórze. Today the square is filled with a monument consisting of 68

empty metal chairs—representing the 68,000 people deported from here. This is intended to remind viewers that the Jews of Kazimierz were forced to carry all of their belongings—including furniture—to the ghetto on this side of the river. It was also here that many Jews waited to be sent to extermination camps. The small, gray building at the river end of Ghetto Heroes' Square feels like a train car inside, evocative of the wagons that carried people from here to certain death.

▲Pharmacy Under the Eagle (Apteka pod Orłem)

This small but newly modernized and excellent museum, on Ghetto Heroes' Square, tells the story of Tadeusz Pankiewicz, a Polish Catholic pharmacist who chose to remain in Podgórze when it became a Jewish ghetto. During this time, the pharmacy was an important meeting point for the ghetto residents, and Pankiewicz and his staff heroically aided and hid Jewish victims of the Nazis. (Pankiewicz survived the war and was later acknowledged by Israel as one of the "Righteous Among the Nations"—non-Jews

KRAKÓW

who risked their lives to help the Nazis' victims during World War II. You'll see his medal on display in the white memorial room at the end of the museum.) Today the pharmacy hosts an exhibit about the Jewish ghetto. You'll enter into the re-created pharmacy, where the "windows" are actually screens that show footage from the era. Push buttons, pull out drawers, answer the phone—it's full of interactive opportunities to better understand what ghetto life was like. You'll learn about people who worked in the pharmacy (including riveting interviews with eyewitnesses—some in English, others subtitled) and hear Pankiewicz telling stories about that tense time. You'll also learn a bit about the pharmacy business from that period.

Cost and Hours: 10 zł; if you're also going to the Schindler's Factory Museum, buy the 23-zł combo-ticket, free on Mon; April-Oct Mon 10:00-14:00, Tue-Sun 9:00-17:00; Nov-March Mon 10:00-14:00, Tue-Thu and Sat 9:00-17:00, Fri 10:00-17:00; closed Sun and the second Tue of each month; plac Bohaterow Getta 18, tel. 12-656-5625, www.mhk.pl/branches/eagle-pharmacy.

▲▲▲Schindler's Factory Museum (Fabryka Emalia Oskara Schindlera)

One of Europe's best museums about the Nazi occupation fills some of the factory buildings where Oskar Schindler and his

Jewish employees worked. While the museum tells the story of Schindler and his workers, it broadens its perspective to take in the full experience of all of Kraków during the painful era of Nazi rule—making it the top WWII museum in this country so profoundly affected by that war. It's loaded with in-depth information (all in English), and touchscreens invite you to learn more and watch eyewitness interviews. Scattered randomly between the exhibits are replicas of everyday places from the age—a photographer's shop, a tram car, a hairdresser's salon—designed to give you a taste of 1940s Kraków. Throughout the museum are calendar pages outlining wartime events and giving a sense of chronology. Note that you'll see nothing of the actual factory or equipment, as the threat of the advancing Red Army forced Schindler to move his operation lock, stock, and barrel to Nazi-occupied Czechoslovakia in 1944.

Cost and Hours: 19 zł, 22-zł combo-ticket with next-door Museum of Contemporary Art, 23-zł "Memory Trail" combo-ticket with Pharmacy Under the Eagle; free on Mon; open April-Oct Mon 10:00-16:00 (except closes at 14:00 first Mon of month),

Tue-Sun 10:00-20:00; Nov-March Mon 10:00-14:00, Tue-Sun 10:00-18:00; last entry 1.5 hours before closing, tel. 12-257-1017, www.mhk.pl/branches/oskar-schindlers-factory. The museum limits the number of visitors, but it's rarely a problem except on particularly busy Mondays (when you might want to book ahead on their website).

Getting There: It's in a gloomy industrial area a five-minute walk from Ghetto Heroes' Square (plac Bohaterow Getta): Head up Kącik street (use the pedestrian underpass, then head to the left of the big, glass skyscraper), go under the railroad underpass marked *Kraków-Zabłocie,* and continue two blocks, past MOCAK (the Museum of Contemporary Art in Kraków, described later) to the second big building on the left (ulica Lipowa 4). Look for signs to *Emalia.*

◑ Self-Guided Tour: You'll begin on the ground floor, where you'll buy your ticket and have the chance to tour the special exhibits. There's also a "film café" (interesting for fans of the movie) with refreshments. Then head upstairs to the first floor.

First Floor: The 35-minute **film,** called *Lipowa 4* (this building's address), sets the stage with interviews of both Jews

and non-Jews describing their wartime experience (find it just off of the museum's first, circular room; subtitled in English, it runs continuously 10:15-15:50). From here, the one-way route winds through the permanent exhibit, called "Kraków Under Nazi Occupation 1939-1945." "Stereoscopic" (primitive 3-D) photos of prewar Kraków capture an idyllic age when culture flourished and the city's Jews (more than one-quarter of the population) blended more or less smoothly with their Catholic-Pole neighbors. A video explains the Nazi invasion of Poland in early September of 1939: It took them only a few weeks to overrun the country (which desperately awaited the promised-for help of their British and French allies, who never arrived). Watch the film clip of SS soldiers marching through the Main Market Square—renamed "Adolf-Hitler-Platz"—and read stories about how the Nazis' *Generalgouvernement* attempted to reshape the life of its new capital, "Krakau." (Look for the decapitated head of the Grunwald monument, which had been a powerful symbol of a Polish military victory over German forces.) You'll see the story of a newly German-owned shop selling Nazi propaganda and learn how professors at Kraków's Jagiellonian University were arrested to prevent them from fomenting rebellion among their students. During this time, Polish secondary

KRAKÓW

Oskar Schindler (1908-1974) and His List

Steven Spielberg's instant-classic, Oscar-winning 1993 film, *Schindler's List*, brought the world's attention to the inspiring story of Oskar Schindler, the compassionate German business-man who did his creative best to save the lives of the Jewish workers at his factory in Kraków. Spielberg chose to film the story right here in Kazimierz, where the historical events actually unfolded. Today the Schindler's Factory Museum gives visitors the chance to learn not just about the man and his workers, but about the historical context of their story: the Nazi occupation of Poland.

Oskar Schindler was born in 1908 in the Sudetenland (cur-rently part of the Czech Republic, then predominantly German). Early on, he displayed an idiosyncratic interpretation of ethics that earned him both wealth and enemies. As Nazi aggressions escalated, Schindler (who was very much a Nazi) carried out espionage against Poland; when Germany invaded the coun-try in 1939, Schindler smelled a business opportunity. Early in the Nazi occupation of Poland, Schindler came to Kraków and lived in an apartment at ulica Straszewskiego 7 (a block from Wawel Castle, but unmarked and not available for tours). He took over the formerly Jewish-owned Emalia factory at ulica Lipowa 4, which produced metal pots and pans that were dipped into protective enamel; later the factory also began producing arma-ments for the Nazi war effort. The factory was staffed by about 1,000 Jews from the nearby Płaszów Concentration Camp, which was managed by the ruthless SS officer Amon Göth (depicted in *Schindler's List*—based on real events—shooting at camp inmates for sport from his balcony).

At a certain point, Schindler began to sympathize with his Jewish workers, and gradually did what he could to protect them and offer them better lives. Schindler fed them far better than most concentration-camp inmates and allowed them to sell some of the pots and pans they made on the black market to

schools were closed—effectively prohibiting learning among Poles, whom the Nazis considered inferior. But Polish students continued to meet clandestinely with their teachers. You'll also see images of Hans Frank—the hated puppet ruler of Poland—moving into the country's most important symbol of sovereignty, Wawel Castle. The exhibit also details how early Nazi policies targeted Jews, with roundups, torture, and execution. (Down the staircase is an eerie simulation of a cellar prison.) As the Nazis ratcheted up their genocidal activities, troops swept through Kraków on March 3, 1941, forcing all the remaining Jews in town to squeeze into the newly created Podgórze ghetto. At the bottom of the stairs, look for the huge pile of plunder—Jewish wealth stolen by the Nazis.

make money. After he saw many of his employees and friends murdered during an SS raid in 1943, he ramped up these efforts. He would come up with bogus paperwork to classify those threatened with deportation as "essential" to the workings of the factory—even if they were unskilled. He sought and was granted permission to build a "concentration camp" barracks for his workers on the factory grounds, where they lived in far better conditions than those at Płaszów. These lucky few became known as *Schindlerjuden*—"Schindler's Jews."

As the Soviet army encroached on Kraków in October of 1944, word came that the factory would need to be relocated west, farther from the front line. While Schindler could easily have simply turned his workers over to the concentration-camp system and certain death—as most other industrialists did—he decided to bring them with him to his new factory at Brünnlitz (Brněnec, in today's Czech Republic). He assembled a list of 700 men and 300 women who worked with him, along with 200 other Jewish inmates, and at great personal expense, moved them to Brünnlitz. At the new factory, Schindler and the 1,200 people he had saved produced grenades and rocket parts—virtually all of them, the workers later claimed, mysteriously defective.

After the war, Schindler—who had spent much of his fortune protecting his Jewish workers—hopped around Germany and Argentina, repeatedly attempting but failing to break back into business (often with funding from Jewish donors). He died in poverty in 1974. In accordance with his final wishes, he was buried in Jerusalem, and today his grave is piled high with small stones left there by appreciative Jewish visitors. He has since been named one of the "Righteous Among the Nations" for his efforts to save Jews from the Holocaust. Thomas Keneally's 1982 book *Schindler's Ark* brought the industrialist's tale to a wide audience that included Steven Spielberg, who vaulted Schindler to the ranks of a pop-culture icon.

Second Floor: Climb upstairs using the long **staircase,** which was immortalized in a powerful scene in *Schindler's List*. At the top of the stairs on the right is a small room that served as "Schindler's office" for the film; more recently, it's been determined that his actual office was elsewhere (we'll see it soon).

You'll walk through a corridor lined by a replica of the wall that enclosed the **Podgórze ghetto** and see poignant exhibits about the horrific conditions there (including a replica of the cramped living quarters). The Nazis claimed that Jews had to be segregated here, away from the general population, because they "carried diseases."

Continue into the office of Schindler's secretary, with exhibits about Schindler's life and video touchscreens that play testimonial

KRAKÓW

footage of Schindler's grateful employees. Then proceed into the actual **Schindler's office.** The big map (with German names for cities) was uncovered only in recent years when the factory was being restored. Because Schindler's short tenure here was the only time in the factory's history that these Polish place names would appear in German, it's believed that this map was hung over his desk. Facing the map is a giant monument of enamel pots and pans, like those that were made in this factory. There are 1,200 pots—one for each Jewish worker that Schindler saved. Inside the monument, the walls are lined with the names on Schindler's famous list. The creaky floorboards are intentional: a reminder that the Nazis knew every step you took.

Proceeding through the exhibit, you'll learn more about everyday life—both for ghetto dwellers and for everyday non-Jewish Krakovians, including the Polish resistance (see the Home Army's underground print shop). More eyewitness accounts relate the terrifying days of March 13 and 14, 1943, when the Podgórze ghetto was liquidated, sending survivors to the nearby Płaszów

Concentration Camp. The replica of the Płaszów quarry, where inmates were forced to work in unimaginably difficult conditions, provides a poignant memorial for those who weren't fortunate enough to wind up on Schindler's list.

Now head all the way back down to the ground floor.

Ground Floor: Exhibits here capture the uncertain days near the end of the war in the summer of 1944, when Nazis arrested between 6,000 and 8,000 suspected saboteurs after the Warsaw Uprising, and sent them to Płaszów (see the replica of a basement hideout for 10 Jews who had escaped the ghetto); and later, when many Nazis had fled Kraków, leaving residents to await the Soviet Union's Red Army (see the replica air-raid shelters). The Red Army arrived here on January 18, 1945—at long last, the five years, four months, and twelve days of Nazi rule were over. The Soviets caused their own share of damage to the city before beginning a whole new occupation that would last for generations...but that's a different museum.

Finally, walk along the squishy floor—evoking how life for

anyone was unstable and unpredictable during the Nazi occupation—into the **Hall of Choices.** The six rotating pillars tell the stories of people who chose to act—or not to act—when they witnessed atrocities. Think about the ramifications of the choices they made...and what you would have done in their shoes. The final room holds two books: a white book listing those who tried to help, and a black book listing Nazi collaborators. Exiting the museum, notice the portraits of Oscar Schindler's workers who lived long and happy lives after the war.

Before heading back to downtown Kraków, consider paying a visit to the superb—and very different—museum that fills the buildings on the factory grounds, behind this main building.

▲Museum of Contemporary Art in Kraków (Muzeum Sztuki Współczesnej w Krakowie)

Called "MOCAK" for short, this museum exhibits a changing array of innovative and thought-provoking works by contemporary

artists, often with heavy themes tied to the surrounding sites. With the slogan *Kunst macht frei* ("Art will set you free"—a pointed spin on the Nazis' *Arbeit macht frei* concentration-camp motto), the museum occupies warehouse buildings once filled

by Schindler's workers. Now converted to wide-open, bright-white halls, the buildings house many temporary exhibits as well as two permanent ones (the MOCAK Collection in the basement, and the library in the smaller side building). Pick up the floor plan as you enter. It's all well-described in English, and engaging even for non-art lovers.

Cost and Hours: 10 zł, free on Tue, open Tue-Sun 11:00-19:00, closed Mon, Lipowa 4, tel. 12-263-4001, www.mocak.pl.

Sights Outside of Kraków

Along with the new St. John Paul II pilgrimage sights (best suited for believers), there are other interesting sights outside of town— an impressive salt mine, a purpose-built communist town, and an unusual earthwork. All require a bus or tram ride to reach.

ST. JOHN PAUL II AND PILGRIMAGE SITES

Pilgrims coming to Kraków eager to walk in the footsteps of St. John Paul II are sometimes disappointed by the lack of actual museums relating to the man in the city center (though the churches affiliated with him are dazzling). However, there are worthwhile sites outside the city: the John Paul II Center and Sanctuary on the outskirts of Kraków, and the John Paul II Family Home Museum in the town of Wadowice, an hour's drive away (and covered later).

The two biggest, most impressive JPII destinations are about four miles south of Kraków's Old Town. While the main attraction here for pilgrims is the John Paul II Center and Sanctuary, historically and geographically you'll come first to the Divine Mercy Sanctuary—so I've covered that first. As they're separated by a pensive 20-minute walk (on adjacent hilltops, so you'll hike down, then back up), it makes sense to combine them in a single visit unless your time is limited.

The sites aren't worth the trek for the merely curious, but they offer a glimpse of the powerful reverence and deep faith that characterizes the Polish character. If you're a pilgrim—or think you might be one—visiting these sites can be worthwhile; to make the most of your time, consider hiring a driver or a local guide with a car.

Getting to the John Paul II Center and Sanctuaries: Public transportation from central Kraków is workable, but not ideal. The easiest public-transit route is to take **tram #8** (which loops around the Old Town, including stops next to St. Francis Basilica at plac Wszystkich Świętych, and near Wawel Castle) to the Divine Mercy Sanctuary (Sanktuarium Bożego Miłosierdzia stop)—about 30 minutes. From the tram stop, you'll huff uphill along the wall to find the entrance to the complex. After touring the Divine Mercy sights, you can walk to the St. John Paul II Sanctuary. (As the JPII Center approaches completion, better transportation connections may be added—ask at the TI before making the trip.) A **taxi** from downtown costs around 30-40 zł one-way and takes 20-30 minutes (or hire a local guide for an easy round-trip). Another option is to take the **Papa Bus,** a minibus that parks across the street from JPII's Kraków window, next to St. Francis Basilica. You can pay 10 zł one-way for the ride to the center, or (better) pay 20 zł round-trip for a loop that includes both the center and the Divine Mercy complex, with waiting time at both and a little commentary en route (though English may be limited...or nonexistent). They'll leave when enough people show up (2 people minimum, though they may prefer to hold out for more), so you may have to wait.

Divine Mercy Sanctuary
(Sanktuarium Bożego Miłosierdzia)
This complex, built around a humble red-brick convent, honors the important 20th-century St. Faustina. From an early age, Faustina Kowalska (1905-1938) felt a deep connection to the stories of Jesus

Christ. Despite her generally frail health, she became a nun at age 20. One cold and blustery evening in 1931, a young beggar rang the bell at the convent door and asked for some food. Faustina rustled around the kitchen, found some soup, and brought it to the man—who, upon eating it, revealed his true nature to Faustina: A figure of Jesus Christ clad in a white robe, with one hand raised in blessing, and the other touching his chest. Emanating from his chest were twin beams of light: red (representing blood, the life of souls) and white (water, which through baptism washes souls righteously clean). Transformed by her experience, Faustina worked with an artist to create a painted version of the image—called the Divine Mercy—which has been embraced by Polish Catholics as one of the most important symbols of their faith. She died at 33—the same age as Jesus. The story of Faustina deeply moved a young Karol Wojtyła, who came to study in Kraków the same year Faustina passed away. When he became pope, he dedicated the first Sunday after Easter as the day of Divine Mercy worldwide. In 2000, he made his fellow Krakovian the first Catholic saint of the third millennium. To properly revere the newly important St. Faustina, a bold, futuristic church and visitors center was built alongside her original convent.

Today, pilgrims from around the world come here to revere the relics both of Faustina and of John Paul II, and to learn more about her story from the convent's present-day sisters—many of whom speak English. While some pilgrimage sites can quickly be overtaken by tacky commercialism, the Divine Mercy complex retains a dignified and reverent air.

While strolling the campus, visitors can see three parts: the smaller original chapel; a replica of Faustina's cell; and the huge, modern church, with its soaring bell tower. All of them are free to enter, but donations are happily accepted; each one has slightly different hours.

Original Chapel: Entering the complex through the side gate, you'll come up a walkway with flags from around the world, and plaques translating the Divine Mercy's message—"Jesus, I trust in you"—in dozens of languages. Just before entering, look up and to the right—the window with the flowers marks the cell where Faustina died. Inside the chapel (daily 6:00-21:15), the altar to the left of the main altar displays an early copy of the famous painting of Faustina's Divine Mercy vision. Her relics are in the white case just below the painting; in the white kneeler just in front of the chapel, notice the little reliquary holding one of her bones (which worshippers can embrace as they pray).

Leaving the chapel, turn left and go to the far end of the accommodations building; enter the door on the right (follow signs for *Cela Św. Siostry Faustyny* and *Noclegi/Accommodations*) to find the...

Replica of Faustina's Cell: While this is a newer building, here they've re-created Faustina's convent cell, including many of her personal effects. Drop a coin in the slot for an evocative headphone description of these items, and of the vision of Jesus that put her convent on the map (usually open daily 8:30-18:00).

Dominating the campus—and oddly juxtaposed with the old buildings—is the futuristic, glass-and-steel...

Main Church: Consecrated by Pope John Paul II on his final visit to Poland in 2002, this building has several parts (daily 7:00-

20:00). The **lower level** has a variety of small chapels, each one donated by Catholic worshippers in a different country (Germany, Hungary, Slovakia, and so on)—and each with a dramatically different style. The central chapel on this level has a modern altar and another bone of St. Faustina. Upstairs, the **main sanctuary** is a sleek cylindrical space with wooden sunbeams sharply radiating from the altar area. That altar—framed by the gnarled limbs of windblown trees, representing the suffering of human existence—contains a replica of the Divine Mercy painting, flanked by the woman who saw the vision (Faustina, on the right) and the Polish pope who made it a worldwide phenomenon (John Paul II, on the left). Look back to the grand stained-glass window over the door—a sun sets low behind an illuminated cross, over the water.

Head back out to the terrace surrounding the church. The bold **tower**—as tall as St. Mary's on Main Market Square, and with a statue of John Paul II at the bottom—has an elevator that you can ride up to a glassed-in viewpoint offering panoramas over the Divine Mercy campus, the adjacent John Paul II Center, and—on the distant horizon—the spires of Wawel Cathedral and Kraków's Old Town. Near the base of the tower is a **canopy** where Mass is said on Divine Mercy Sunday each year, before a crowd of 100,000 who fill the fields below.

John Paul II Center (Centrum Jana Pawła II) and Sanctuary

This work-in-progress complex, funded entirely by private donors, celebrates the life and sainthood of Kraków's favorite son.

Construction is ongoing, but for now there are at least two sections of the complex worth visiting: the sanctuary (free, daily 7:30-19:00) and the museum (7 zł, Tue-Sun 10:00-16:00, closed Mon).

The **Sanctuary of St. John Paul II,** consecrated in 2013, is big and splendid. In the **downstairs** area, the central chapel features paintings of JPII's papal visits to various pilgrimage sites, both in Poland (Częstochowa) and abroad (Fátima, Lourdes). Most of the chapels ringing the outside have different depictions of the Virgin Mary. Find the chapel that's a replica of the St. Leonard's Crypt under Wawel Cathedral—the first place where John Paul II celebrated Mass as a young priestling—which contains JPII's actual papal tomb from the crypt beneath St. Peter's Basilica at the Vatican. (When he became a saint, his remains—which, controversially, are kept in Rome rather than his homeland—were moved up into the main part of the church, and this simple grave marker was donated to this church.) You'll also see a reliquary in the shape of a book with fluttering pages, holding a small amount of John Paul II's blood. This blood was kept in secret by JPII's personal secretary, only revealed after his death, when it was given to a select few churches. In another chapel, you'll find the tombs of a few recent cardinals; as they're running out of space below Wawel Cathedral, this chapel is poised to handle the overflow. And in yet another chapel, you'll see finely executed reliefs in rock salt, in the style of Wieliczka Salt Mine.

Head upstairs to the **main sanctuary,** with its sleek modern style. The concrete structure supports large white walls, which will

eventually be filled with dynamic mosaics of Bible stories (several of these are already in place). Above the main altar, in the middle, you'll see the Three Kings delivering their gifts to the Baby Jesus and the Virgin Mary—with St. John Paul II serenely overlooking the scene. In the back-left corner, a smaller chapel focuses on a painting of St. John Paul II; in the hazy background, you can see the dome of St. Peter's at the Vatican (left) and the twin spires of St. Mary's in Kraków (right)—driving home the point that although John Paul II belonged to the world, first and foremost he's considered a son of Kraków and of Poland.

The adjacent **St. John Paul II Museum** is filled with the many gifts bestowed on him (African carved masks and ivory tusks; Latin American tapestries; the key to the city of Long Branch, New Jersey; and a pair of glass doves of peace given to him—perhaps with a touch of irony—by US Vice President Dick Cheney); ornate worship aids (chalices, crosses, and so on); and modern art

KRAKÓW

that celebrates the modern pope and his life's work. There are also personal items, from his papal ski gear to the place settings from his Vatican dinner table to his stylish red leather shoes. You'll also see the throne from his last visit to Poland in 2002, and a replica of the humble room across the street from St. Francis Basilica where he stayed on visits back to his homeland.

John Paul II Sights in Wadowice

Karol Wojtyła was born and lived up until age 18 in Wadowice (VAH-doh-veet-seh), about 30 miles (a one-hour drive) southwest of Kraków. As it's roughly in the same direction as Auschwitz, a local guide or driver can help you connect both places for one busy day of contrasts. Visiting by public bus is possible; ask the TI for details.

The lovely town of Wadowice (about 20,000 people) has a quaint and beautifully restored main square with a pretty Baroque steeple. John Paul II pilgrims find it worth a visit to see the area's best museum on the man, which fills four floors of the tenement building where his family lived through his adolescence, right across the street from the town church. The **John Paul II Family Home Museum** offers visitors a multimedia overview of the life and times of one of the Catholic Church's newest saints. You'll see rooms of the family home, a collection of clothing and other articles that belonged to JPII, photographs and video clips of his life and of the tumultuous period in which he lived, and plenty of interactive displays to bring the entire story to life. Admission is limited, and you'll be accompanied the entire time. Ideally, time your visit to go with an English guide (typically 2/day, likely at 11:00 and 14:00—but confirm online or by phone); otherwise, you'll join the Polish tour. Either way, the tour can be a bit rushed, with less time to linger over the exhibits than you might like (18 zł with a Polish guide, or 25 zł with English guide, free and crowded on Tue; open daily May-Sept 9:00-19:00, April and Oct 9:00-18:00, Nov-March 9:00-16:00, closed the last Tue of each month, last entrance 1.5 hours before closing, ulica Kościelna 7, tel. 33-823-2662, www.domjp2.pl).

MORE SIGHTS OUTSIDE OF KRAKÓW
▲▲Wieliczka Salt Mine (Kopalnia Soli Wieliczka)

Wieliczka (veel-EECH-kah), a salt mine 10 miles southeast of Kraków, is beloved by Poles. Deep beneath the ground, the mine is filled with sculptures that miners have lovingly carved out of the salt. You'll explore this unique gallery—learning both about the art and about medieval mining techniques—on a required tour. Though the sight is a bit overrated, it's unique and practically obligatory if you're in Kraków for a few days. In my experience with tour groups, about half the people love Wieliczka, while half feel it's a waste of time—but it can be hard to predict which half you're in. Read the description here carefully before you decide. And expect a lot of walking.

KRAKÓW

Cost and Hours: The standard "tourist route" costs 79 zł and is by guided tour only. English tours are offered daily year-round (June-Sept every half-hour 8:30-18:00, Oct-May every hour 9:00-17:00), with the exception of a few holidays when the mine is closed. If you miss the English-language tour (or decide to just show up and take whatever's going next), you can rent an audioguide for an extra 10 zł. They also have a more in-depth, interactive "Miner's Route" where visitors wear coveralls and helmets and actually operate some of the old equipment (details on website). The mine is in the town of Wieliczka at ulica Daniłowicza 10 (tel. 12-278-7302, www.kopalnia.pl).

You'll pay an extra 10 zł for permission to use your camera—but be warned that flash photos often don't turn out, thanks to the irregular reflection of the salt crystals. Dress warmly—the mine is a constant 57 degrees Fahrenheit.

Your ticket includes a dull **mine museum** at the end of the tour. It adds an hour to the mine tour and is discouraged by locals ("1.5 miles more walking, colder, more of the same"). Make it clear when you buy your ticket that you're not interested in the museum.

Getting There: The salt mine, 10 miles from Kraków, can be reached a variety of ways: by **train** (take it to the Wieliczka Rynek Kopalnia station, about a five-minute walk from the mine; 4 zł, about hourly, less Sat-Sun, departs from main train station); by **bus #304** (4-zł *aglomeracyjny* ticket, 3/hour, 40-minute trip, catch bus at Kurniki stop across from church near Galeria Krakowska mall, get off at stop called Wieliczka Kopalnia Soli); by **minibus** (2.50 zł, 4/hour or with demand, *Wieliczka Soli* sign in window, 30-40 minutes, generally departs from across Pawia street from the Galeria Krakowska mall); or by **private driver**.

Background: Wieliczka Salt Mine has been producing salt since at least the 13th century. Under Kazimierz the Great, one-third of Poland's income came from these precious deposits. Wieliczka miners spent much of their lives underground, leaving for work before daybreak and returning after sundown, rarely emerging into daylight. To pass the time, and to immortalize their national pride and religiosity in art, 19th-century miners began to carve figures, chandeliers, and eventually even an elaborate chapel out of the salt. Until a few years ago, the mine still produced salt. Today's miners—about 400 of them—primarily work on maintaining the 200 miles of chambers. This entire network is supported by wooden beams (because metal would rust).

Visiting the Mine: From the lobby, your guide leads you 380 steps down a winding staircase. From this spot you begin a 1.5-mile stroll, generally downhill (more than 800 steps down altogether), past 20 of the mine's 2,000 chambers (with signs explaining when they were dug), finishing 443 feet below the surface. When you're done, an elevator beams you back up.

The tour shows how the miners lived and worked, using horses who spent their whole adult lives without ever seeing the light of

day. It takes you through vast underground caverns, past subterranean lakes, and introduces you to some of the mine's many sculptures (including one of Copernicus—who actually visited here in the 15th century—as well as an army of salt elves, and this region's favorite son, St. John Paul II). Your jaw will drop as you enter the enormous **Chapel of St. Kinga,** carved over three decades in the early 20th century. Look for the salt-relief carving of the Last Supper (its 3-D details are astonishing, considering it's just six inches deep). You'll end your visit with a five-minute multimedia show.

While advertised as two hours, your tour finishes in a deep-down shopping zone 1.5 hours after you started (they hope you'll hang out and shop). Note when the next elevator departs (just 3/hour), and you can be outta there on the next lift. Zip through the shopping zone in two minutes, or step over the rope and be immediately in line for the great escape (you'll be escorted quite some distance to the elevator, into which you'll be packed like mine workers).

▲Nowa Huta

Nowa Huta (NOH-vah HOO-tah, "New Steel Works"), an enormous planned workers' town, offers a glimpse into the stark, grand-scale aesthetics of the communists. Because it's five miles east of central Kraków and a little tricky to see on your own, skip it unless you're determined. But architects and communist sympathizers may want to make a pilgrimage here.

Getting There: Tram #4 goes from near Kraków's Old Town (catch the tram on the ring road near Kraków's main train station, at the Basztowa stop) along Pope John Paul II Avenue (aleja Jana Pawła II) to Nowa Huta's main square, plac Centralny (about 30 minutes total), then continues a few minutes farther to the main gate of the Tadeusz Sendzimir Steelworks—the end of the line. From there it returns to plac Centralny and back to Kraków.

Lunch in Nowa Huta: Plan on munching a cheap, drab lunch in the no-name milk bar on Nowa Huta's plac Centralny (Mon-Sat 7:00-20:00, closed Sun, at #1 next to a grocery store under an arcade, about 100 yards from the tram stop for sector C).

Tours: True to its name, Mike Ostrowski's **Crazy Guides** is a loosely run operation that takes tourists to Nowa Huta in genuine communist-era vehicles (mostly Trabants and Polski Fiats). While the content is good, Mike and his comrades are laid-back, very informal, and sometimes crude. If you're offended by a foul-mouthed hipster guide, or if you don't like the idea of careening down the streets of Kraków in a car that feels like a cardboard box with a lawnmower engine, skip this tour. For the rest of us, it's a fun and convenient way to experience Nowa Huta (139 zł/person for 2.5-hour "communism tour" of Nowa Huta; 179 zł/person for 4-hour "communism deluxe" tour that also includes lunch at a milk bar and a visit to their period-decorated communist apartment; 169 zł/person for 4-hour Real Kraków tour that covers the basic Nowa Huta trip plus outlying sights; other crazy experiences also available, cash only, reserve ahead and they'll pick you up at your hotel, mobile 500-091-200, www.crazyguides.com, info@crazyguides.com). If you're already hiring a **local guide** in Kraków, consider paying a little extra to add a couple of hours for a short side-trip by car to Nowa Huta.

Background: Nowa Huta was the communists' idea of paradise. It's one of only three towns outside the Soviet Union that were custom-built to show-case socialist ideals. (The others are Dunáujváros—once called Sztálin-város—south of Budapest, Hungary; and Eisenhüttenstadt—once called Stalinstadt—near Brandenburg, Germany.) Completed in just 10 years (1949-1959), Nowa Huta was built primarily because the Soviets felt that smart and sassy Kraków needed a taste of heavy industry. Farmers and villagers were imported to live and work in Nowa Huta. Many of

the new residents, who weren't accustomed to city living, brought along their livestock (which grazed in the fields around unfinished buildings). For commies, it was downright idyllic: Dad would cheerily ride the tram into the steel factory, mom would dutifully keep house, and the kids could splash around at the man-made beach and learn how to cut perfect red stars out of construction paper. But Krakovians had the last laugh: Nowa Huta, along with Lech Wałęsa's shipyard in Gdańsk, was one of the home bases of the Solidarity strikes that eventually brought down the regime. Now, with the communists long gone, Nowa Huta remains a sooty suburb of Poland's cultural capital, with a whopping 200,000 residents.

Touring Nowa Huta: Nowa Huta's focal point used to be known simply as **Central Square** (plac Centralny), but in a fit of poetic justice, it was recently renamed for the anti-communist Ronald Reagan. This square is the heart of the planned town. A map of Nowa Huta looks like a clamshell: a semi-circular design radiating from Central/Reagan Square. Numbered streets fan out like spokes on a wheel, and trolleys zip workers directly to the immense factory.

Believe it or not, the inspiration for Nowa Huta was the Renaissance (which, thanks to the textbook Renaissance design of the Cloth Hall and other landmarks, Soviet architects considered typically Polish). Notice the elegantly predictable arches and galleries that would make Michelangelo proud. The settlement was loosely planned on the gardens of Versailles (comparing aerial views of those two very different sites—both with axes radiating from a central hub—this becomes clear). When first built (before it was layered with grime), Nowa Huta was delightfully orderly, primly painted, impeccably maintained, and downright beautiful... if a little boring. It was practical, too: Each of the huge apartment blocks is a self-contained unit, with its own grassy inner courtyard, school, and shops. Driveways (which appear to dead-end at underground garage doors) lead to vast fallout shelters.

Today's Nowa Huta is a far cry from its glory days. Wander around. Poke into the courtyards. Reflect on what it would be like to live here. It may not be as bad as you imagine. Ugly as they seem from the outside, these buildings are packed with happy little apartments filled with color, light, and warmth.

The wide boulevard running northeast of Central/Reagan Square, now called Solidarity Avenue (aleja Solidarności, lined with tracks for tram #4), leads to the **Tadeusz Sendzimir Steelworks.** Originally named for Lenin, this factory was supposedly built using plans stolen from a Pittsburgh plant. It was designed to be a cog in the communist machine—reliant on iron ore from Ukraine, and therefore worthless unless Poland remained in the Soviet Bloc. Down from as many as 40,000 workers at its peak, the steelworks now employs only about 10,000. Today there's little to see other than the big sign, stern administration buildings, and smokestacks in the distance. Examine the twin offices flanking the sign—topped with turrets and a decorative frieze inspired by Italian palazzos, these continue the Renaissance theme of the housing districts.

Another worthwhile sight in Nowa Huta is the **Lord's Ark Church** (Arka Pana, several blocks northwest of Central/Reagan Square on ulica Obrońców Krzyża). Back when he was archbishop of Kraków, Karol Wojtyła fought for years to build a church in this most communist of communist towns. When the regime refused, he insisted on conducting open-air Masses before crowds in fields—until the communists finally capitulated.

Consecrated on May 15, 1977, the Lord's Ark Church has a Le Corbusier–esque design that looks like a fat, exhausted Noah's Ark resting on Mount Ararat—encouraging Poles to persevere through the floods of communism. While architecturally interesting, the church is mostly significant as a symbol of an early victory of Catholicism over communism.

▲Kościuszko Mound (Kopiec Kościuszki)

On a sunny day, the parklands west of the Old Town are a fine place to get out of the city and commune with Krakovians at play. On the outskirts of town is the Kościuszko Mound, a nearly perfectly conical hill erected in 1823 to honor Polish and American military hero Tadeusz Kościuszko. The mound incorporates soil that was brought here from battlefields where the famous general fought, both in Poland and in the American Revolution. Later, under Habsburg rule, a citadel with a chapel was built around the mound, which provided a fine lookout over this otherwise flat terrain. And more recently, the hill was reinforced with steel and cement to prevent it from eroding away. You'll pay to enter the walls and walk to the top—up a curlicue path that makes the mound resemble a giant soft-serve cone—and inside you'll find a modest Kościuszko museum. While not too exciting, this is a pleasant place for an excursion on a nice day.

Cost and Hours: 12 zł, includes museum, mound open daily 9:00-dusk, until 23:00 Fri-Sun, museum open daily 9:30-16:30, café, tel. 12-425-1116, www.kopieckosciuszki.pl.

Getting There: Ride tram #1 or #6 (from in front of the Wyspiański Pavilion or the main post office) to the end of the line, called Salvator, then follow the well-marked path uphill for 20 minutes.

Shopping in Kraków

Two of the most popular Polish souvenirs—amber and pottery—come from areas far from Kraków. You won't find any great bargains on those items here, but several shops specializing in them are listed below. Somewhat more local are the many wood carvings you'll see.

The **Cloth Hall,** smack-dab in the center of the Main Market Square, is the most convenient place to pick up any Polish souvenirs. It has a great selection, respectable prices, and the city's highest concentration of pickpockets (summer Mon-Fri 9:00-18:00, Sat-Sun 9:00-15:00, sometimes later; winter Mon-Fri 9:00-16:00, Sat-Sun 9:00-15:00).

Here are some other souvenir ideas, and neighborhoods or streets that are particularly enjoyable for browsing.

JEWELRY

The popular **amber** *(bursztyn)* you'll see sold around town is found on northern Baltic shores; if you're also heading to Gdańsk, wait until you get there. One unique alternative that's a bit more local is **"striped flint"** *(krzemień pasiasty),* a stratified stone that's polished to a high shine. It's mined in a very specific subregion near Kraków, and has become popular recently among Hollywood celebrities. Each piece has its own unique wavy, sandy patterns.

Jewelry shops abound in the Old Town. For a good selection of striped flint, amber, and other jewelry, try the no-name shop on **plac Mariacki,** the little square facing the side entrance of St. Mary's Church; they also have a selection of Polish folk costumes in the basement (at #9). A few more jewelry and design shops cluster along Sławkowska street, which runs north from the Main Market Square. At #23, stop in at **Galeria Kreko,** with modern works mostly by Polish artists; the shop next door has more jewelry, plus hand-carved and painted wooden figures. **Galeria Skarbiec** ("Treasury"), two blocks south of the Main Market Square, is another good choice, with a more stylish, upscale vibe (Grodzka 35).

POLISH POTTERY

"Polish pottery," with distinctive blue-and-white designs, is made in the region of Silesia, west of Kraków (mostly in the town of Bolesławiec). But, assuming you won't be going there, you can browse one of the shops in Kraków. **Ceramika Bolesławiecka,** on a busy urban street between the Old Town and Kazimierz, has a tasteful selection of pottery that's oriented more for locals than tourists, with prices to match (closed Sun, Starowiślna 37). **Dekor Art,** with slightly inflated prices but a convenient, central location, has a nice selection just a couple of blocks north of the Main Market Square (daily, Sławkowska 11).

FOODS, DRINKS, AND COSMETICS

Krakowski Kredens is a handy, well-curated shop for overpriced but good-quality traditional foods from Kraków and the surrounding region, Galicia. While the deli case in the back is a pricey place to shop for a picnic (head for a supermarket instead), this is a good chance to stock up on souvenir-quality Polish foods for the folks back home. They have several locations around Kraków—and elsewhere in Poland—but one handy branch is just steps south of the Main Market Square down Grodzka, at #7 (www. krakowskikredens.pl).

KRAKÓW

Szambelan, a block south of the Main Market Square, is a fun concept for vodka lovers: Peruse the giant casks of three dozen different flavored vodkas, buy an empty bottle, and they'll fill and seal it to take home (Gołębia 2 at the corner with Bracka).

Mydlarnia u Franciszka, with a few locations around Kraków (including a handy one just south of the Main Market Square at Gołębia 2), sells a variety of fragrant local soaps, lotions, shampoos, and other cosmetics, some produced locally.

STOLARSKA STREET

The relatively undiscovered, traffic-free Stolarska street—just a block off of the Main Market Square—is a fine place to stroll day or night, and to browse for gifts. Wander the street from north (Small Market Square) to south (Dominican Church) and window-shop. A few fun places are in the covered arcade on the left, after the Herring Embassy. One of the most interesting is **Galeria Plakatu Kraków,** a print, poster, and postcard shop with a wide variety of engaging images, from commie-retro to contemporary arts to unique Polish variations on American movie posters (closed Sun, Stolarska 8-10). Nearby are an antique bookstore and a pottery art gallery.

DESIGNER SHOPS ALONG ULICA JÓZEFA, IN KAZIMIERZ

As the epicenter of Kraków's low-rent, artsy, hipster scene, Kazimierz is the best place in town to browse one-off galleries—especially designer shops (both decor and fashion). Several good options line up along ulica Józefa, a borderline-drab urban street about a block south of ulica Szeroka and the plac Nowy market square. Begin near the High Synagogue and work your way west down the street; the highest concentration is on the two-block stretch between Estery and Bożego Ciała streets. This is an ever-changing lineup, but keep an eye out for these spots: **Blazko,**

KRAKÓW

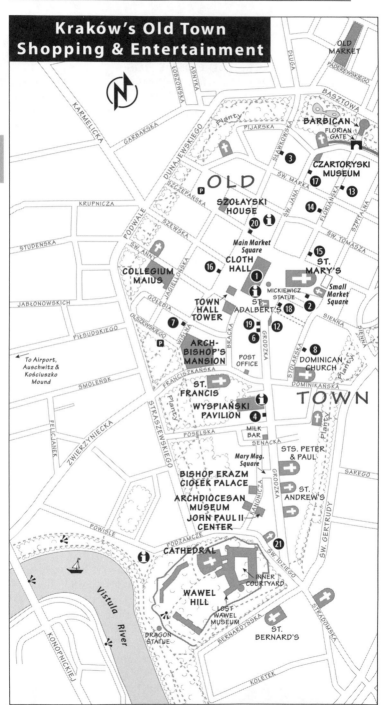

Kraków's Old Town Shopping & Entertainment

KRAKÓW

Shopping
1. Cloth Hall
2. Plac Mariacki 9 Jewelry
3. Galeria Kreko & Dekor Art Pottery
4. Galeria Skarbiec
5. Ceramika Bolesławiecka
6. Krakowski Kredens Gift Store
7. Szambelan Vodkas & Mydlarnia u Franciszka Cosmetics
8. Galeria Plakatu Kraków
9. To Ulica Józefa Design Shops
10. Galeria Krakowska
11. Galeria Kazimierz
12. Pasaż 13 Mall

Entertainment
13. Jama Michalika (Folk Shows)
14. Staropolskie Trunki
15. Jazz Club u Muniaka
16. Harris Piano Jazz Bar
17. Stalowe Magnolie
18. Buddha Nightclub
19. Polonia House/Dom Polonii
20. Bonerowski Palace
21. St. Idziego/Giles Church

KRAKÓW

on the left at #11, has some modern, colorful jewelry, handmade right on the premises. A few doors down (also at #11), **Maly Styl** sells fashion for little kids, and **Galerie d'Art Naïf** features fascinating works by untrained artists. Next door, **Deccoria Galeria** feels like a junk shop, cluttered with handmade jewelry, art, accessories, and vintage clothes. After you pass another vintage shop, **Art Factory** (on the left, at #9) is worth a browse for colorful jewelry, accessories, and housewares by local designers. Across the street, **Mniejwięcej** ("Lessmore," on the right, at #18) highlights art by local designers. **Pracownia** ("Lab"), across the street at #9, sells handmade art, jewelry, and clothes. And more clothes by Polish designers are across the street at **Nuumi Boutique** (#14).

SHOPPING MALLS

Two enormous shopping malls lie just beyond the tourist zone. The gigantic **Galeria Krakowska,** with 270 shops, shares a square with the train station (Mon-Sat 9:00-22:00, Sun 10:00-21:00, has a kids' play area upstairs from the main entry). Only slightly smaller is **Galeria Kazimierz** (Mon-Sat 10:00-22:00, Sun 10:00-20:00, just a few blocks east of the Kazimierz sights, along the river at Podgórska 24). A small but swanky mall called **Pasaż 13** is a few steps off the southeast corner of the Main Market Square, where Grodzka street enters the Square. Enter the mall under the balcony marked *Pasaż 13*. You'll find a cool brick-industrial interior, with upscale international chains...and not much that's Polish (Mon-Sat 9:00-21:00, Sun 11:00-17:00).

Entertainment in Kraków

As a town full of both students and tourists, Kraków has plenty of fun options, especially at night.

IN THE OLD TOWN
Main Market Square

Intoxicating as the Square is by day, it's even better at night... pure enchantment. Have a meal or nurse a drink at an outdoor café, or just grab a bench and enjoy the scene. There's often live, al fresco music coming from somewhere (either at restaurants, at a temporary stage set up near the Town Hall Tower, or from talented buskers). You could spend hours doing slow laps around the Square after dark, and never run out of diversions.

Concerts

You'll find a wide range of musical events, from tourist-oriented Chopin concerts and classical "greatest hits" selections in quaint old ballrooms and churches, to folk-dancing shows, to serious philharmonic performances. While a variety of options exist, two companies typically offer competing shows, often on the same night; to compare both, see www.newculture.pl and www.cracowconcerts.com.

Popular Classical Concerts: Popular venues include churches (such as the churches of Sts. Peter and Paul on ulica Grodzka, St. Adalbert on the Square, or St. Idziego/Giles at the foot of Wawel Hill), various gardens around town (July-Aug only, as part of a festival), and fancy mansions on the Main Market Square (including the Polonia House/Dom Polonii at #14, near ulica Grodzka; and the Bonerowski Palace near the top of the Square at ulica Św. Jana 1; both of these typically offer Chopin concerts). Because Kraków's live-music scene is continually evolving, it's best to inquire locally about what's on during your visit. Hotel lobbies are stocked with fliers for upcoming concerts. But to get all of your options, visit any TI. The TI north of the Square on ulica Św. Jana, which specializes in cultural events, can book tickets for most concerts (no extra fee) and tell you how to get tickets for the others. The free, monthly *Karnet* cultural-events book lists everything (half in Polish and half in English, also online at www.karnet.krakow.pl).

Folk Music: Two different venues present dinner shows in the old center. At both, a small, hardworking ensemble of colorfully costumed Krakovian singers, dancers, and musicians put on a fun little folk show. While the food, the space, and the clientele are all a bit tired, it's a nice taste of Polish folk traditions—and the performers try hard to involve members of the audience in the polkas and circle dances. One option is in the historic **Jama Michalika,** with its dusty old Art Nouveau interior right along Floriańska street (85 zł includes dinner; Wed, Fri, and Sun at 19:00; Floriańska 45, mobile 604-093-570, www.cracowconcerts.com). A similar option is in the more modern **Tradycyja Restaurant,** right on the Main Market Square (next to the famous Wyzierniek Restaurant at #15; 60 zł for just the show, or 120 zł to add dinner; Wed, Fri, and Sat at 19:00; mobile 602-850-900, www.newculture.pl).

Jazz and Other Live Music

For something a little more edgy, delve into Kraków's thriving jazz scene. Several popular clubs hide on the streets surrounding the Main Market Square (open nightly, most shows start around 21:30).

The most famous and best for all-around jazz in a sophisticated cellar environment is **Jazz Club u Muniaka** (10-20-zł cover, open nightly 19:00-1:00 in the morning, live music nightly from

21:30, best music when the owner Janusz plays on Thu-Sat, ulica Floriańska 3, tel. 12-423-1205; described earlier on my self-guided walk).

Harris Piano Jazz Bar, right on the Square (at #28), is more casual and offers a mix of traditional and updated "fusion" jazz, plus blues (free most nights, 15-25-zł cover for more serious shows—typically on Thu-Sat, music nightly from 21:30, tel. 12-421-5741, www.harris.krakow.pl).

Stalowe Magnolie—a former brothel still draped with red lights and waitresses dressing the part—is a bit more youthful, clubby-feeling, and snooty, with jazz about two nights a week and rock or pop the other nights (no cover on weeknights, on weekends 10-zł cover for men and free for women, music nightly from 22:00, 150 yards off Main Market Square at ulica Św. Jana 15, tel. 12-422-8472, www.stalowemagnolie.com).

Nightlife in the Old Town

The entire Old Town is crammed with nightclubs and discos pumping loud music on weekends. On a Saturday, the pedestrian streets can be more crowded at midnight than at noon. However, with the exception of the jazz clubs mentioned earlier, most of the nightspots in the Old Town are garden-variety dance clubs, completely lacking the personality and creativity of the Kazimierz nightspots described next. Worse, to save money, young locals stand out in front of nightclubs to drink their own booze (BYOB), rather than pay high prices for the drinks inside—making the streets that much more crowded and noisy. For low-key hanging out, people choose a café on the Square; otherwise, they head for Kazimierz.

In addition to the Harris Piano Jazz Bar, two places on the Square worth checking out are near the southeast corner. At #6, head into the passage to find the **Buddha** nightclub, with comfy lounge sofas under awnings in an immaculately restored old courtyard. For something funkier and even more local, go down the passage at #12, which runs a surprisingly long distance through the block. Soon you'll start to see tables for the **Herring Embassy;** you'll eventually emerge at **Stolarska street,** a still enjoyable but far less touristy scene.

IN KAZIMIERZ

Aside from the Old Town's gorgeous Square, Kraków's best area to hang out after dark is Kazimierz, the former Jewish quarter. The Jewish Sabbath has nothing to do with the bar scene here.

Klezmer Music

Although there are only about 200 Jews still living in Kraków, you wouldn't know it from the lively klezmer scene. Several restaurants offer traditional Jewish klezmer music most evenings for a steep 25-zł cover charge (plus the cost of food). If you'd rather enjoy a concert separately from dinner, in summer you'll find concerts most evenings at 18:00 or 19:00 in various venues around town: Isaac Synagogue (arguably the most powerful space, in a giant old prayer hall); the Galicia Jewish Museum (a tasteful modern brick space); or at Astoria Hotel (least appealing). The price is typically 60-80 zł; look for posters and fliers around town. The music is evocative, but this is a fairly sedate scene. If you'd like to stay up a bit later, there's no better way to spend your time than exploring the bars of Kazimierz (described next).

KRAKÓW

Bars and Clubs

Squeezed between centuries-old synagogues and cemeteries are wonderful hangouts running the full gamut from sober and taste-ful to wild and clubby. The classic recipe for a Kazimierz bar: Find a dilapidated old storefront, fill the interior with ramshackle fur-niture, turn the lights down low, and pipe in old-timey jazz music from the 1920s. Sprinkle with alcohol. Serves one to two dozen hipsters. After a few clubs of this type caught on, a more diverse cross-section of nightspots began to move in, including some loud dance clubs. The whole area is bursting with life—it's the kind of place where people just spontaneously start dancing—and locals still outnumber tourists. I've listed websites for places that feature periodic live music and other events.

On and near Plac Nowy: The highest concentration of bars ring the plac Nowy market square. While most of these are nondescript, a few stand out. **Alchemia,** one of the first—and still one of the best—bars in Kazimierz, is candlelit, cluttered, and claustrophobic, with cave-like rooms crowded with rickety old furniture, plus a cellar used for live performances (Estery 5, www.alchemia.com.pl). Just around the corner, Alchemia has a sleek, subway-tiled, side restaurant; this space has table ser-vice, but if you'd rather be in the creaky bar, you can order at the counter (20-40-zł meals). Hiding just a half-block down the street is **Miejsce** ("The Place"), which is brighter and more minimalist than the norm, with stripped-down walls and care-fully chosen Scan-design old furniture—it's run by the owners of a design firm specializing in decor from the 50s, 60s, and 70s (Estery 1). Fronting the square, **Kolory** has a pleasant Parisian brasserie ambience (Estery 10), and **Atelier** has a relaxed, mini-malist, art-gallery interior with cushy sofas and a hidden garden deep inside (plac Nowy 7 1/2). **Le Scandale** is all black leather and serves tapas, Italian fare, and cocktails; don't miss the big garden in the back (plac Nowy 9).

Late at night, the little windows in the plac Nowy **market**

hall do a big business selling *zapiekanki* (baguette with toppings) to hungry bar-hoppers.

On Rabina Meiselsa street, just a half-block off plac Nowy, two places share a long courtyard: **Mleczarnia,** a top-notch beer garden with rickety tables squeezed under the trees and its cozy old-fashioned pub across the street (at #20); and **Stajnia,** at the far end of the courtyard, where scenes from *Schindler's List* were filmed (see photos on wall at inner arch). Its interior feels like a Polish village drenched in red light and turned into a dance hall.

Near Isaac Synagogue: A block east of plac Nowy, a few more places cluster on the wide street in front of Isaac Synagogue. The huge **Nova Resto Bar** dominates the scene with a long covered terrace, a vast interior, and seating in their courtyard—all with a cool-color-scheme Las Vegas polka-dot style. This feels upscale and a bit pretentious compared to many of the others, but it's *the* place to be seen (25-40-zł meals, Estery 18). Upstairs is the similarly trendy music club **Taawa** (www.taawa.pl). Facing this double-decker wall of style are some smaller, more accessible options: **Singer** is classy and mellow, with most of its tables made of old namesake sewing machines (Estery 20), while **Warsztat** has an exploding-instruments-factory ambience (Izaaka 3; also recommended later, under "Eating in Kraków").

On Józefa Street: More good bars are just a short block south. Along Józefa, you'll find a pair of classic Kazimierz joints: **Eszeweria,** which wins the "best atmosphere" award, feels like a Polish speakeasy that's been in mothballs for the last 90 years—a low-key, unpretentious, and inviting hangout (Józefa 9). Their less enticing but still enjoyable sister café, **Esze,** is across the street. A block up, look for **Kolanko No. 6,** with a cozy bar up front, a pleasant beer garden in the inner courtyard, and a fun events hall in back (Józefa 17, www.kolanko.net; also recommended later, under "Eating in Kraków").

In Podgórze: If you run out of diversions in the heart of Kazimierz, head south. With the construction of a new pedestrian bridge over the river just south of this area, Kazimierz's nightlife scene is spreading to **Podgórze,** just across the river. Here in this fast-evolving zone, prices are a bit lower.

Sleeping in Kraków

Healthy competition—with new, cleverly run places cropping up all the time—keeps Kraków's accommodation prices reasonable and makes choosing a hotel fun rather than frustrating. Rates are soft; hoteliers don't need much of an excuse to offer you 10 to 20 percent off, especially on weekends or off-season. I've focused my accommodations in two areas: in and near the Old Town; and in

---

Sleep Code

Abbreviations (3 zł = about $1, country code: 48)
S = Single, **D** = Double/Twin, **T** = Triple, **Q** = Quad, **b** = bathroom, **s** = shower only.

Price Rankings

$$$ **Higher Priced**—Most rooms 400 zł or more.

 $$ **Moderately Priced**—Most rooms between 300-400 zł.

  $ **Lower Priced**—Most rooms 300 zł or less.

Unless otherwise noted, credit cards are accepted, breakfast is included, Wi-Fi is generally free, and English is spoken. Prices can change without notice; verify the hotel's current rates online or by email. For the best prices, always book directly with the hotel.

Kazimierz, a local-style, more affordable neighborhood that is home to both the old Jewish quarter and a thriving dining and nightlife zone.

The Old Town is jam-packed with discos that thump loud music on weekend nights to attract roving gangs of rowdy students, backpackers, and obnoxious "stag parties" of drunken louts from the UK in town for a weekend of carousing. The "quiet after 22:00" law is flagrantly ignored. Kazimierz is also home to various hip dance clubs. Because of all these clubs, virtually all of my accommodations come with some risk of noise; to help your odds, always ask for a quiet room when you reserve...and bring earplugs.

IN AND NEAR THE OLD TOWN

Most of my listings are inside (or within a block or two of) the Planty park that rings the Old Town. Sleeping inside the Old Town comes with pros (maximum atmosphere; handy location for sightseeing and dining) and cons (high prices; the potential for noise—especially on weekends—as noted earlier). I've also listed a few in this section that are just outside the Old Town, and are a bit quieter.

Guest Houses

These good-value pensions almost invariably come with lots of stairs (no elevators) and are run by smart, can-do, entrepreneurial owners. They're all located in the heart of the Old Town along busy pedestrian streets, and most don't have air-conditioning—so they can be noisy with the windows open in the summer, especially on weekends. These places book up fast, especially in summer—reserve as far ahead as possible. Don't expect a 24-hour reception

KRAKÓW

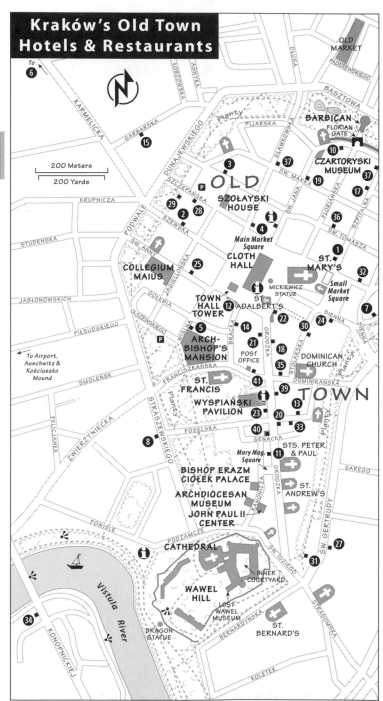

Kraków's Old Town Hotels & Restaurants

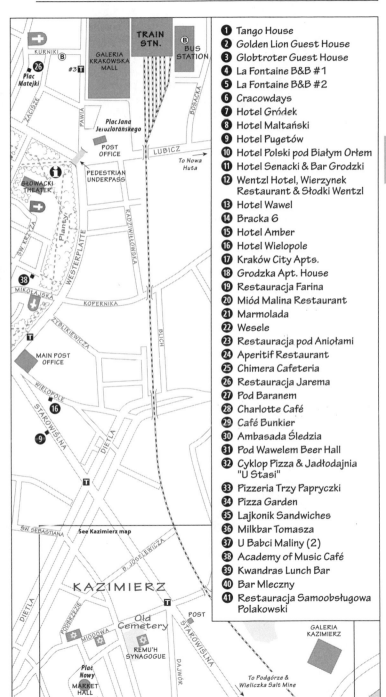

KRAKÓW

1. Tango House
2. Golden Lion Guest House
3. Globtroter Guest House
4. La Fontaine B&B #1
5. La Fontaine B&B #2
6. Cracowdays
7. Hotel Gródek
8. Hotel Maltański
9. Hotel Pugetów
10. Hotel Polski pod Białym Orłem
11. Hotel Senacki & Bar Grodzki
12. Wentzl Hotel, Wierzynek Restaurant & Słodki Wentzl
13. Hotel Wawel
14. Bracka 6
15. Hotel Amber
16. Hotel Wielopole
17. Kraków City Apts.
18. Grodzka Apt. House
19. Restauracja Farina
20. Miód Malina Restaurant
21. Marmolada
22. Wesele
23. Restauracja pod Aniołami
24. Aperitif Restaurant
25. Chimera Cafeteria
26. Restauracja Jarema
27. Pod Baranem
28. Charlotte Café
29. Café Bunkier
30. Ambasada Śledzia
31. Pod Wawelem Beer Hall
32. Cyklop Pizza & Jadłodajnia "U Stasi"
33. Pizzeria Trzy Papryczki
34. Pizza Garden
35. Lajkonik Sandwiches
36. Milkbar Tomasza
37. U Babci Maliny (2)
38. Academy of Music Café
39. Kwandras Lunch Bar
40. Bar Mleczny
41. Restauracja Samoobsługowa Polakowski

desk; it's always smart to tell them your arrival time, especially if it's late in the day.

$ Tango House, run by tango dance instructor Marcin Miszczak, is in a well-located building with an ancient-feeling stairwell decorated with faded Art Nouveau paintings. Its eight long, skinny, stylish rooms have parquet floors (tiny "economy" Sb/Db-260 zł, standard Sb/Db-300 zł, superior Sb/Db-340 zł, prices can be soft in slow times, cheaper Nov-March, Wi-Fi, ask for quieter courtyard room to avoid rowdy street noise on weekends, ulica Szpitalna 4, tel. 12-429-3114, www.tangohouse.pl, info@tangohouse.pl).

$ Golden Lion Guest House has 12 smallish, neat-but-slightly-dated rooms on a bustling pedestrian street a block off the Main Market Square (Sb-180 zł, Db-300 zł, 10 percent cheaper Nov-Feb, ask for quieter room in back, air-con in some rooms, guest computer, Wi-Fi, guest kitchen, no parking, ulica Szewska 19, mobile 501-066-958, tel. 12-422-9323, www.goldenlion.pl, reservation@goldenlion.pl, Łodziński family).

$ Globtroter Guest House offers 18 rustic-feeling rooms with high ceilings and big beams around a serene garden courtyard. Jacek (Jack), who really understands and respects travelers, conscientiously focuses on value—keeping prices as low as possible by not offering needless extras (April-Oct: Sb-180 zł, Db-300 zł; Nov-March: Sb-120 zł, Db-180 zł; ask for 10 percent discount with this book if you reserve direct, 2 people can cram into a single to save money—a little more than the Sb price, larger suites for up to five also available, no breakfast at hotel but you can buy 14-zł breakfast from nearby restaurant, guest computer, Wi-Fi, pay laundry service, fun 700-year-old brick cellar lounge down below, go down passageway at #7 at the square called plac Szczepański, tel. 12-422-4123, www.globtroter-krakow.com, globtroter@globtroter-krakow.com).

$ La Fontaine B&B, run by a French-Polish family, offers 14 rooms and 9 apartments in two different buildings just off the Main Market Square (one of them has lots of stairs and no elevator; the other does have an elevator). Tastefully decorated with French flair, it's cute as a poodle. Each room has a little lounge with a microwave and fridge—most in the hall, some inside the room (Sb-237 zł, Db-253 zł, extra bed-60 zł, apartment for up to four-420 zł, apartment for up to six-493 zł, gigantic apartment-677 zł, 30 percent cheaper Nov-Easter, air-con, low slanted ceilings in some rooms, Wi-Fi, guest kitchen, free self-service laundry machine—or pay them 25 zł to wash clothes for you, ulica Sławkowska 1, tel. 12-422-6564, www.bblafontaine.com, biuro@bblafontaine.com).

Outside of the Old Town: **$$ Cracowdays** is the farthest of my listings from the center of town, about a 15-minute walk away (a tram can cut a few minutes off the trek). But it's also a notch more refined than the guest houses listed previously. It sits in a pleasant residential neighborhood west of the Main Market Square, with six beautifully decorated and thoughtfully tended rooms, all sharing a central kitchen (Db-360 zł, superior Db-405 zł, stand-alone studio Db apartment in another building-425 zł, breakfast-25 zł extra, air-con, on the first floor with no elevator, 24-hour reception, Wi-Fi, Grabowskiego 7, mobile 666-971-478, www.cracowdays.com, reservation@cracowdays.com).

KRAKÓW

Hotels

For this section, I've listed the official, published "rack rates"— which are very soft. Most hotels discount their rates substantially, especially in slow times. Consider asking several hotels for their lowest price during your visit, and take the best deal.

$$$ Donimirski Boutique Hotels, with four different locations in or near Kraków's Old Town, set the bar for splurge hotels in Kraków (website for all: www.donimirski.com). All Donimirski hotels offer my readers a 15 percent discount (I've listed the rates below without the discount, during high season; the base price is cheaper Nov-March and at other slow times). You can expect any of these hotels to have some of the friendliest staff in Kraków and all of the classy little extras that add up to a memorable hotel experience. **Hotel Gródek**—the fanciest of the bunch—offers 23 rooms a three-minute walk behind St. Mary's Church on a quiet dead-end street overlooking the Planty park. This place is easily the best splurge in town, with a handy location, gorgeously decorated rooms, and a top-notch breakfast served in a room surrounded by a mini-museum of artifacts discovered during the recent renovation (Sb-650 zł, Db-850 zł, bigger "deluxe" Db-960 zł, suite-1,300 zł, guest computer, Wi-Fi, good cellar restaurant serves Polish cuisine, parking-50 zł/day, Na Gródku 4, tel. 12-431-9030, grodek@donimirski. com). **Hotel Maltański** has 16 rooms in the beautifully renovated former royal stables, just outside the Planty park and only two blocks from Wawel Castle (Sb-590 zł, Db-650 zł, 80 zł more for "deluxe" room with air-con, no elevator but only 2 floors, Wi-Fi, parking-50 zł/day, ulica Straszewskiego 14, tel. 12-431-0010, maltanski@donimirski.com). **Hotel Pugetów,** with seven small but plush and cozy rooms and a fun breakfast cellar, is on the other side of town, in a more workaday but convenient neighborhood between the Main Market Square and Kazimierz (Sb-390 zł, Db-680 zł, Db suite-950 zł, air-con, cable Internet, parking-50 zł/day, ulica Starowiślna 15A, tel. 12-432-4950, pugetow@ donimirski.com). And the group recently took over **Hotel Polski**

pod Białym Orłem, just inside the north end of the Old Town, near the Florian Gate (rates and amenities may change with planned renovation, but likely Sb-390 zł, Db-590 zł, Tb-630 zł, apartment-850 zł, air-con in a few rooms, elevator, Wi-Fi, ulica Pijarska 17, tel. 12-422-1144, hotel.polski@donimirski.com).

$$$ Hotel Senacki is a business-class place renting 20 comfortable rooms between Wawel Castle and the Main Market Square. The location is handy, but it can be noisy on weekends—ask for a quieter back room. The staff is warm, professional, and conscientious. Top-floor "attic" rooms have low beams, skylight windows, and a flight of stairs after the elevator (prices change constantly with demand, but generally Sb-400 zł, Db-500 zł, deluxe Db-580 zł, extra bed-90 zł, better prices for longer stays, cheaper Nov-March, non-smoking, air-con, elevator—but doesn't go to "attic" rooms, Wi-Fi, ask about nearby parking for 80 zł/day, ulica Grodzka 51, tel. 12-422-7686, www.hotelsenacki.pl, senacki@hotelsenacki.pl).

$$$ Wentzl Hotel is your splurge-right-on-the-Square option, with 18 rooms. The decor is over-the-top-classy Old World with modern touches, like state-of-the-art TVs and bathrooms. When reserving, request a room with a view on the Square—which can be noisy, especially on weekends—or one of the three quieter back rooms (Sb-740 zł, Db-830 zł, bigger "deluxe" rooms cost 50 zł more, air-con, elevator, Wi-Fi, Rynek Główny 19, tel. 12-430-2664, www.wentzl.pl, hotel@wentzl.pl).

$$$ Hotel Wawel has 39 rooms on a well-located street that's quieter than the Old Town norm. It feels plush for the price, though its colorful decor verges on gaudy; above the swanky marble lobby are hallways creatively painted with the history of the building and images from around Kraków. Out back, a fountain gurgles in a cute little courtyard (Sb-340 zł, Db-480 zł, extra bed-100 zł/adult or 50 zł/child, rates are soft so ask for best price, 20 percent less Nov-March, non-smoking, air-con, elevator—but doesn't go to top floor, guest computer, Wi-Fi, ulica Poselska 22, tel. 12-424-1300, www.hotelwawel.pl, hotel@hotelwawel.pl).

$$$ Bracka 6, wonderfully located just one short block off the Main Market Square, is a sort of a hybrid between a hotel and an apartment house: The 16 stylish rooms—with sleek lines, lots of glass, and gentlemen's-hat chandeliers—each have a kitchen, so breakfast is 25 zł extra. It's on the second and third floors with no elevator, and the reception is open limited hours (daily 8:00-22:00 or so), but the lack of full hotel amenities keeps the prices very affordable for this level of modern elegance (standard Db-450 zł, bigger Db-500 zł, biggest Db-600 zł, air-con, Wi-Fi, Bracka 6, tel. 12-341-4011, www.bracka6.pl, info@bracka6.pl).

$$$ Hotel Amber sits on a dull but safe and quiet street just outside the Planty park, less than a 10-minute walk from the Square. The staff is proud of their attentive service (and circulates a handy little informative newsletter daily). The hotel has two parts: 18 perfectly fine, if smallish, rooms in the original building; and 20 slightly more upscale rooms in the newer "design" section. Both parts share a small gym, sauna, and garden in back. It's a good-value alternative to the places inside the Old Town (Sb-350 zł, standard Db-438 zł, bigger "superior" Db-479 zł, "deluxe" Db with fancier touches-499 zł; "design" rooms cost about 50 zł more; cheaper Nov-March, air-con, elevator, Wi-Fi, Garbarska 8-10, tel. 12-421-0606, www.hotel-amber.pl, office@hotel-amber.pl).

$$$ Hotel Wielopole is conveniently located, a block outside of the Planty and on the way to the lively Kazimierz district. Its 35 tight rooms are tucked down a (relatively) quiet side street just past the main post office, facing a big Holiday Inn. Run by the same company as Hotel Amber (described above), it's a similarly good value, with an equally pleasant emphasis on welcoming service (Sb-360 zł, Db-450 zł, 40 zł more for "superior" rooms, 100 zł more for bigger and more ornate "deluxe" rooms, prices can be soft if you book direct, air-con, elevator, Wi-Fi, vegetarian restaurant in cellar, Wielopole 3, tel. 12-422-1475, www.wielopole.pl, office@wielopole.pl).

Apartments

You can save money by staying in your own apartment rather than a hotel. Apartments come with great locations, simple kitchens, and relatively low prices, but no big-hotel services (such as having your room cleaned daily)...in other words, you're on your own. Apartments aren't just for long stays—these places welcome even one-nighters. While the apartments themselves are neat and modern, most are in old buildings with dreary entryways and stairways. As reception times are limited, be sure to clearly communicate your arrival time. A wide variety of apartments are easy to find at online booking sites, but each of these two places has a reception desk that manages several units, making them a bit more hotelesque than the norm.

$ Kraków City Apartments, conscientiously run by Andrzej and Katarzyna, has 14 straightforward but modern and clean apartments tucked away in a quiet courtyard at the corner of the Old Town (small studio Db-240 zł, bigger deluxe Db-320 zł, 2-bedroom apartment-350 zł for 2 or 420 zł for 4, 2-bedroom apartment with view-420 zł for 2 or 650 zł for 4—can also sleep 6, 20 percent cheaper Oct-April, no breakfast but you can pay 30 zł for breakfast at a café on the Square, non-smoking, elevator to all rooms except studios, Wi-Fi, reception open daily 9:00-20:00, ulica Szpitalna

34, reception mobile 507-203-050, Andrzej's mobile 504-235-925, www.krakowapartments.info, info@krakowapartments.info).

$ Grodzka Apartment House offers 12 well-decorated apartments around a courtyard along one of Kraków's most happening streets, just a few steps off the Main Market Square. The studio apartments are as nice as a hotel room and a good value (studio-270 zł, 1-bedroom-360 zł, 2-bedroom-540 zł, prices soft, cheaper Nov-March, no breakfast but can buy 30-zł breakfast at nearby café, reception open daily 10:00-20:00, some apartments have street noise—light sleepers should ask for quieter courtyard room, lots of stairs with no elevator, Wi-Fi, go down the passage at Grodzka 4, tel. 12-421-4835, mobile 660-541-085, www.krakowforyou.com, info@krakowforyou.com, Mikołaj). They also have more apartments (though not quite as nice) in two other Old Town buildings.

IN KAZIMIERZ

Sleep in Kazimierz to be close to Kraków's Jewish heart—or simply to experience a cheaper, less touristy, more local-feeling neighborhood outside the Old Town. With the highest concentration of pubs and nightclubs in town, Kazimierz rivals the Old Town for nightlife—which means that all of these places can be subject to some noise, especially on weekends. Keep in mind that these accommodations put you a 20-minute walk or a 5-minute tram ride from the medieval ambience of Kraków's old center. Some of the klezmer music restaurants listed under "Eating in Kraków" also rent rooms, but they're generally an afterthought to the food and music, and not a good value.

$$$ Rubinstein Residence is your Kazimierz splurge, sitting right in the middle of ulica Szeroka—surrounded by klezmer restaurants and synagogues, in the heart of the neighborhood. It fills a painstakingly restored old townhouse (parts of it dating to the 15th century) with heavy wood beams and 28 swanky rooms—some of them palatial suites that incorporate old features like frescoes and pillars. The rooftop terrace—with views over Kazimierz and to the Old Town—sets this place above...literally (Db-500 zł, suites can be 1,000 zł or more, air-con, elevator, Wi-Fi, Szeroka 12, tel. 12-384-0000, www.rubinstein.pl, recepcja@rubinstein.pl).

$$$ Karmel Hotel, with 11 rooms on a pleasant side street near the heart of Kazimierz, offers elegance at a reasonable price (Sb-275 zł, tight twin Db-298 zł, more spacious "komfort plus" Db with one big bed and air-con-430 zł, pricier suites also available, extra bed-70 zł, about 20 percent less Nov-March, upstairs with no elevator, guest computer, Wi-Fi, some night noise on weekends, ulica Kupa 15, tel. 12-430-6697, www.karmel.com.pl, hotel@karmel.com.pl).

$ Tournet Guest House, well-run by friendly Piotr and Sylwia Działowy, is a great budget option offering 18 clean, colorful rooms near the edge of Kazimierz toward Wawel Hill. While all of the rooms are pretty basic, the ones they call "basic" lack TV sets (basic Sb-120 zł, standard Sb-150 zł, basic twin Db-160 zł, standard Db-200 zł, Tb-250 zł, extra bed-50 zł, 10 zł/person less Nov-March, elevator plus a few stairs, Wi-Fi, reception open 7:00-22:00, ulica Miodowa 7, tel. 12-292-0088, www.nocleg.krakow.pl, tournet@nocleg.krakow.pl).

Hostel: **$ Hostel Momotown** is a smidge more institutional and less party-oriented than your average hostel, but it's still loose and friendly. Run by Paweł Momot, it has 52 dorm beds and a fun garden for hanging out (bunk in 4-bed dorm-60 zł, in 6-bed dorm-55 zł, in 8-bed dorm-55 zł, in 10-bed dorm-45 zł, includes breakfast and sheets, towels-2.50 zł, guest computer, Wi-Fi, kitchen, laundry, lockers, ulica Miodowa 28, tel. 12-429-6929, www.momotownhostel.com, info@momotownhostel.com). Two blocks away, they also rent 14 basic but cheap private rooms that share a kitchenette, overlooking Kazimierz's main square, ulica Szeroka (Sb-140 zł, Db-180 zł).

Eating in Kraków

Kraków has a wide array of great restaurants—for every one I've listed, there are two or three nearly as good. (The downside is a lack of variation; little distinguishes one place from another.) Polish food is rivaled by Italian in popularity. As the restaurant scene changes constantly, I've chosen places that are well-established and have a proven track record for reliably good food.

IN THE OLD TOWN
Kraków's Old Town is loaded with dining options. Prices are reasonable even on the Main Market Square. And a half-block away, they get even better. All of these eateries (except the milk bars) are likely to be booked up on weekends—always reserve ahead.

Restauracja Farina, with a fish-and-bottles theme, features a welcoming atmosphere and Polish and Mediterranean cuisine with an emphasis on fresh fish (30-35-zł pastas, 30-60-zł main dishes). Part of their menu consists of seasonal offerings, and they serve some special seafood dishes (60-100 zł) only on the days that they get their fresh delivery (about twice weekly; open daily 12:00-23:00, 2 blocks north of the Square at ulica Św. Marka 16, at intersection with ulica Św. Jana, tel. 12-422-1680, www.farina.com.pl).

Miód Malina ("Honey Raspberry") is a delightful Polish-Italian fusion restaurant filled with the comforting aroma of its wood-fired oven. The menu is half Polish and half Italian—yet,

KRAKÓW

remarkably, they do both cuisines equally well. For example, you can start with borscht and follow it with lasagna Bolognese. Sit in the cozy, warmly painted interior, or out in the courtyard (19-zł pierogi, 25-30-zł pastas, 40-70-zł main dishes, reservations smart, daily 12:00-23:00, ulica Grodzka 40, tel. 12-430-0411, www.miodmalina.pl). The same people run two other restaurants a bit closer to the Square, with similar atmosphere and equally good food, but are more focused on Polish fare: **Marmolada** (Grodzka 5) and **Wesele** (on the Square at #10).

Restauracja pod Aniołami ("Under Angels") offers a dressy, candlelit atmosphere on a wonderful covered patio, or in a deep, steep, romantic cellar with rough wood and medieval vaults. Peruse the elaborately described menu of medieval noblemen's dishes. The cuisine is traditional Polish, with an emphasis on grilled meats and trout (on a wood-fired grill). Every meal begins with *smalec* (spread made with lard, fried onion, bacon, and apple). Don't go here if you're in a hurry—only if you want to really slow down and enjoy your dinner. Reservations are smart (20-30-zł starters, 45-70-zł main dishes, daily 13:00-24:00, ulica Grodzka 35, tel. 12-421-3999, www.podaniolami.pl).

Aperitif is a cheery, colorful bistro serving tasty international cuisine with Mediterranean flair on the appealing Small Market Square (Mały Rynek) behind St. Mary's Church. It's classy but casual, with a cozy interior and a pleasant garden in back. Their 19- or 25-zł lunch specials are a great deal (30-40-zł pastas, 40-60-zł main dishes, daily 10:00-23:00, ulica Sienna 9, tel. 12-432-3333, www.aperitif.com.pl).

Chimera Cafeteria, just off the Main Market Square, is a handy spot for a quick lunch in the center. It serves fast traditional meals to a steady stream of students. You'll order at the counter—choose a big plate (6 items, 17 zł) or medium plate (4 items, 13 zł), and select from an array of salads and main dishes by pointing to what looks good. Then eat outside on their quiet courtyard (good for vegetarians, daily 9:00-22:00, near university at ulica Św. Anny 3). I'd skip their expensive full-service restaurant (in the basement), which shares an entryway.

Restauracja Jarema (yah-RAY-mah) offers a tasty reminder that Kraków used to rule a large swath of Ukraine and Lithuania. They serve eastern Polish/Ukrainian cuisine (with well-described specialties) amid 19th-century aristocratic elegance—you'll feel like you're dining in an old mansion. It's very sedate and feels a bit tired, but the food satisfies (30-55-zł main dishes, several good vegetarian options, daily 12:00-22:00, usually live music from 19:00, reservations wise, across the street from barbican at plac Matejki 5—facing the Grunwald monument, tel. 12-429-3669, www.jarema.pl).

Pod Baranem ("Under the Ram") is a popular local recommendation for traditional Polish food done very well. It sits just outside of the tourist chaos, quietly facing the Planty near Wawel Castle—keeping the prices reasonable and the passing tourist trade at bay. Several cozy rooms—tasteful but not stuffy—sprawl through an old building (25-30-zł light meals until 19:00, otherwise 25-45-zł main courses, Św. Gertrudy 21, tel. 12-429-4022, www.podbaranem.com).

Youthful Style at Plac Szczepański: While seemingly every corner of the Old Town is jammed with tourists (and businesses catering to them), the pleasant square called plac Szczepański—huddled at the northwest corner of the Old Town—feels like a carefully protected bastion of the local upscale art culture. Come here if you'd like to browse a small array of cafés and galleries that feel more Warsaw-urbane than ye olde Kraków. **Charlotte** is a winner—it's a classy, French-feeling bakery/café/wine bar. They make their own breads and pastries in the basement (with lots of seating—you can watch the bakers work if you come early enough in the morning), cultivate a stay-awhile coffee house ambience upstairs, and throw in a few square-facing sidewalk tables to boot. And it's affordable, serving up 10-20-zł sandwiches, pastries, and salads. While the food is light café fare rather than a filling dinner, after 18:00 they redecorate the borderline-hipster space to give it a more sophisticated flair (Mon-Fri 7:00-24:00, Sat 9:00-24:00, Sun 9:00-22:00, plac Szczepański 2, tel. 12-431-5610). Just around the corner, facing the Planty park, is the delightful **Café Bunkier.** It belongs to the hulking Bunker Sztuki contemporary art gallery, but—in contrast to that building's concrete vibe—the café sits under a delightful glass canopy that faces the lush greenbelt, with well-worn wooden tables and an almost Parisian ambience. While it's not the place for a filling meal, it's worth coming here for some light food and drinks while enjoying Kraków's greenbelt in any weather (light 20-30-zł meals, daily 9:00-24:00, plac Szczepański 3a, tel. 12-431-0585).

On Stolarska Street: Stolarska street, a neatly pedestrianized, oddly untrammeled "embassy row" just a block away from the Main Market Square, is worth exploring for a meal or a drink. Stolarska has a fun variety of more locals-oriented bars and cafés. Begin at the Small Market Square (Mały Rynek) behind St. Mary's Church and head south. On the left, look for the ridiculously long sign that perfectly identifies the business: Pierwszy Lokal Na Stolarskiej Po Lewej Stronie Idąc Od Małego Rynku ("The first pub on the left side of Stolarska coming from the Small Market Square"). Notice that this once-sleepy street is lined with embassies and consulates—it's easy to spot the flags of Germany, the US, and France. On the left, in the stretch of cafés under canopies, you'll see the

Ambasada Śledzia ("Herring Embassy"), with a divey, youthful atmosphere and a "Polish tapas" approach: 10 different types of 8-zł herring, plus a variety of vodka to wash it down, are posted on the menu. You'll order at the bar (there can be a language barrier, but try asking for translation help), then find a table, or take it to go (open long hours daily, Stolarska 8). Across the street, the Pasaż Bielaka (an easy-to-miss passage—look for the low-profile stone doorway and *Rynek Główny* sign at #5) runs through the middle of the block all the way out to the Main Market Square (emerging at Rynek Główny #12); partway along is another sprawling branch of the Herring Embassy.

Beer Hall: Pod Wawelem ("Under Wawel") is a rollicking Austrian-style beer hall right on the Planty park near Wawel Castle. It's packed with locals seeking big, sloppy, greasy portions of meaty fare, with giant mugs of various beers on tap (including Polish and Bavarian). Choose between the bustling interior or the outdoor terrace right on the Planty (20-35-zł main dishes, different specials every day—such as giant schnitzel, pork ribs, or roasted chicken; daily 12:00-24:00, ulica Św. Gertrudy 26-29, tel. 12-421-2336).

Pizza: Two well-established places in the Old Town are reliable choices. **Cyklop,** with 10 tables wrapped around the cook and his busy oven, has good wood-fired pizzas and a cozy, charming ambience (15-25-zł one-person pizzas, 18-30-zł two-person pizzas, daily 11:00-23:00, near St. Mary's Church at Mikołajska 16, tel. 12-421-6603). **Pizzeria Trzy Papryczki** ("Three Peppers"), whose wood-fired pizzas aren't quite as good as Cyklop's, also has inviting ambience, either in the country-cozy interior or out in the welcoming garden (17-25-zł one-person pizzas, 20-29-zł two-person pizzas, daily 11:00-23:00, ulica Poselska 17, tel. 12-292-5532). But the best pizza in town is at **Pizza Garden,** run by Stanisław, who worked at a respected New York City pizzeria for a decade and has brought the art of brick-oven pizza back home. The catch is that his place is well outside the Old Town, about a 10-minute walk across the river from Wawel Hill (the walk is mostly along the pretty riverside parkland and across Dębnicki Bridge, with great views back on the castle). This makes it a good post-Wawel lunch or dinner spot (16-30-zł 1-person pizzas, 20-25-zł 2-person pizzas, Mon-Wed 13:00-22:00, Thu-Sun 13:00-23:00; cross Dębnicki Bridge, then look right to find M. Konopnickiej 11/1; tel. 12-266-7309, www.pizzagarden.pl).

Quick Sandwich: If you need a break from milk bars (described next), but want to grab a sandwich on the go, stop by **Lajkonik,** a modern bakery/coffee shop *(piekarnia i kawiarnia)* that sells fresh 7-10-zł takeout sandwiches (Mon-Fri 7:00-19:00, Sat 8:00-20:00, Sun 8:00-22:00, handy location right in front of the Dominican Church at Dominikański 2, others are just outside of the Old Town).

Milk Bars

Kraków is a good place to try the cheap cafeterias called "milk bars." I've listed them by neighborhoods: north or south of the Main Market Square.

North of the Main Market Square

These options, easy to squeeze in to a busy day of sightseeing, are good for a quick, cheap bite:

Milkbar Tomasza is an updated, upgraded milk bar, popular with local students. Modern and relatively untouristy, it has a hipster ambience and serves big, splittable portions of high-quality food—often with some international flourishes—plus breakfast dishes all day (2-course 18-zł meals, 12-20-zł main dishes, great big salads, daily 8:00-22:00, ulica Tomasza 24, tel. 12-422-1706).

Jadłodajnia "U Stasi" is a throwback that makes you feel like you're in on Kraków's best-kept secret. Its hidden location—tucked at the far end of the passage that leads to, then beyond, the recommended Cyklop pizzeria—attracts a wide range of loyal local clientele, from homeless people to politicians, artists, and actors. They're all here for well-executed, unpretentious, home-style Polish lunch grub. There can be a bit of a language barrier, so go with the flow: Pick up the English menu as you enter, find a table, wait for them to take your order, enjoy your meal, then pay as you leave. This is an excellent value and a real, untouristy Polish experience. The short menu changes every day—and when they're out, they're out (10-15-zł main dishes, Mon-Fri 12:00-17:00, closed Sat-Sun, Mikołajska 16).

U Babci Maliny ("Granny Raspberry"), with a grinning Granny on the sign, is another well-established and popular milk bar (9-23-zł main dishes). One location, frequented almost entirely by Krakovians, is designed for university students and staff and is tucked into an inner courtyard of the Science Academy. Find the door at Sławkowska 17, then follow signs through the stuffy complex to find a rustic cellar where it looks like a kitschy cottage bomb went off (Mon-Fri 11:00-21:00, Sat-Sun 12:00-21:00). Another location is across the street from the National Theater building at Szpitalna 38 (daily 11:00-23:00; self-service upstairs, table service in basement). Both locations have walls of photos of the owner posing with bodybuilders and ultimate fighters...entertaining, if not quite in keeping with the country theme.

The **Academy of Music Café** (a.k.a. Restauracja U Romana) is a no-frills student cafeteria that enjoys a restful, top-floor perch with views over the back of St. Mary's Church and the rooftops of Kraków. It has a short, basic menu of food and drinks; come here not for high cuisine, but for high-up cuisine. You'll enter the Academy of Music at Św. Tomasza 43—using the heavy metal door opposite Hotel Campanile—then angle left inside to find the elevator in the stairwell and ride it to floor 6. Order at the counter, get your food, then head out to the tranquil terrace (12-15-zł grub, Mon-Fri 9:00-18:00, Sat 9:00-16:00, closed Sun).

On Grodzka Street, South of the Main Market Square
Ulica Grodzka, the busy street that cuts south from the Main Market Square, has a convenient little pocket of three milk bars within a few steps of each other (all are open daily for lunch and dinner, but only until 19:00 or 20:00, sometimes later in summer). Survey all three options before you dive in. If they look full, just wait—there's a lot of turnover, so a table should free up soon.

Approaching from the Square, the first one you'll come to is (just after the modern copper-colored Wyspiański Pavilion, on the left) is the most modern and trendy of the three, more popular with students than with their grandparents: **Kwandras Lunch Bar** ("Quarter"—as in, you can eat here in a quarter-hour; pierogi and other dishes for 9-12 zł, full dinner for 14 zł—plus soup for 1 zł more, ulica Grodzka 32, tel. 12-294-2222).

Two blocks down the street and on the right (at the corner with Senacka) is the most basic and traditional milk bar, with a sign reading simply **Bar Mleczny** ("Milk Bar"; a low-profile sign over the door gives the eatery's name, *Restauracja "pod Temidą"*). The next best thing to a time machine to the communist era, this place has grumpy monolingual service, a mostly local clientele, and cheap but good food (12-16-zł main dishes).

A few more steps down, also on the right (just before the two churches), is **Bar Grodzki,** a single tight little room with shared

tables. In addition to the standard milk-bar fare, Bar Grodzki specializes in tasty potato pancake dishes *(placki ziemniaczane)*. Order high on the menu and try the rich and hearty "Hunter's Delight"— potato pancake with sausage, beef, melted cheese, and spicy sauce for 23 zł. The English menu posted by the counter makes ordering easy. Order, sit, and wait to be called to fetch your food (most main dishes 11-23 zł).

Nearby: **Restauracja Samoobsługowa Polakowski** is a glorified milk bar with country-kitchen decor and cheap, tasty

Polish fare. The tongue-twisting *samoobsługowa* simply means "self-service"—as at other milk bars, you'll order at the counter and bus your dishes when done. Curt service...cute hats (10-13-zł main dishes, daily 9:00-22:00, facing St. Francis Basilica at plac Wszystkich Świętych 10).

Splurging on the Main Market Square

You'll find plenty of relatively expensive, tourist-oriented restaurants on the Square. Though all of these places have rich interiors, there's not much point in paying a premium to dine here unless you're sitting outside on the Square. While tourists go for ye olde places, natives hang out at pizza joints (like Sphinx, part of a wildly popular Poland-wide chain). Poles generally afford this zone on their meager incomes by just having a drink on the Square after eating at home.

If any place here is a cut above, it's probably **Wierzynek,** with an elegant upstairs and prime on-the-Square seating. It's famous for the greatest feast in Polish history: In 1364, a royal wedding was celebrated here with 20 days and 20 nights of dining (it's named for the caterer, Nicolas Wierzynek). They pride themselves on their beautifully presented, traditional Polish cuisine (30-40-zł starters, 60-90-zł main dishes, daily 13:00-23:00, consider reserving a window seat upstairs, on corner of Grodzka and Main Market Square—at #15, tel. 12-424-9600, www.wierzynek.com.pl).

And for Dessert: **Słodki Wentzl** ("Sweets") is a local favorite for enjoying dessert on the Square. Consider dining more cheaply elsewhere, then finishing up with coffee, ice cream, or cake here (12-20-zł desserts, daily 11:00-23:00, at #19).

IN KAZIMIERZ

The entire district is bursting with lively cafés and bars—it's a happening night scene. Jewish food is the specialty here, but in general the neighborhood offers more diversity than the Old Town. The non-Jewish places I've listed are fast, cheap, and convenient.

Klezmer Concerts and Jewish Food

Kazimierz is a hub of Jewish restaurants, featuring cuisine and music that honors the neighborhood's Jewish heritage (and caters to its Jewish visitors). On a balmy summer night, the air is filled with the sound of klezmer music—traditional Jewish music from 19th-century Poland, generally with violin, string bass, clarinet, and accordion. Skilled klezmer musicians can make their instruments weep or laugh like human voices. Several places on ulica Szeroka (Kazimierz's main square) offer klezmer concerts. All of these have several rooms, which the musicians move between as the evening goes on. While most places claim to do concerts nightly year-round, in reality they can be canceled anytime it's slow (especially off-season). For this reason—and because these places fill up—it's important to reserve ahead. (If you're in Kazimierz for some daytime sightseeing, visit several places, pick your favorite, and reserve dinner.) Don't expect great cuisine—you're here for the music.

With a Cover Charge: Several well-established, old-fashioned restaurants offer klezmer concerts most nights at around 20:00; you'll pay a cover charge of about 25-30 zł per person. These restaurants have similar menus, with main dishes for 25-60 zł. Sometimes you'll need to order sides and starches separately. At **Klezmer-Hois,** which fills a venerable former Jewish ritual bathhouse, you'll feel like you're dining in a rich grandparent's home. This is probably your best option for the traditional klezmer-concert-during-Jewish-dinner experience (daily 8:00-22:00, at #6, tel. 12-411-1245, www.klezmer.pl). **Ariel,** which dominates the square, was once quite popular but has faded.

No-Cover Alternatives: Two competitive options on the square work great for those wanting only a taste of klezmer music (rather than the full-blown dinner concert). Both of these places generally put their performers outside, facing the square (rather than tucked away inside)—so you can also hear it just fine sitting at other restaurants and bars facing the square, or even just from a bench. **Awiw** is the poor man's option for live klezmer music. Each evening from 18:00 to 23:00, they have live music outside on their patio on ulica Szeroka with no cover charge (Polish and Jewish food, 30-70-zł main dishes, daily 10:00-23:00, Szeroka 13, tel. 12-341-4279). **Hotel Ester**—at the end of the square closest to the Old Synagogue—has outdoor music every day in good weather, generally from about 13:00 to 17:00, and again from 18:00 until 22:00. You can sit and enjoy the music even if you just buy a drink, or stay for a full meal (30-40-zł main dishes, open daily, Szeroka 20, tel. 12-429-1188).

Fast and Cheap

Bagelmama, run by an American named Nava (who has worked as a private chef for US tennis star John McEnroe), is a casual bagel shop that's understandably popular with expats. This place was a Kazimierz pioneer—one of the first innovative eateries to plant its flag in the neighborhood. And today, Nava and his staff still serve up a wide range of sandwiches, soups, salads, burritos, desserts, and good espresso drinks. The bagels come dressed with a wide variety of spreads, from simple cream cheese or peanut butter to lox, tuna, or curried chicken. You can eat in or get it to go (most items 10-17 zł, selection of "bagel tapas" with various toppings for 20 zł/person for 2 people, daily 9:00-18:30, possibly later in summer, ulica Dajwór 10, tel. 12-346-1646).

Polish Fast Food on Plac Nowy: The **plac Nowy market,** around the circular brick slaughterhouse, offers a fully authentic, very cheap, blue-collar Polish experience—join the workers on their lunch break at the little food windows on Kazimierz's market square. This area is particularly known for its *zapiekanki*—the uniquely Polish fast food of a toasted baguette with cheese, ketchup, and other toppings. These are enormous—basically a foot-long baguette sliced lengthwise—splittable, and cheap (7-10 zł, depending on toppings). More recently, a wide range of trendy restaurants and bars has sprung up around the square. Survey your options and choose your favorite.

Food Carts: While food carts haven't quite caught on in Poland, an undiscovered corner of Kazimierz has an inviting little pocket of hipster foodie-mobiles. The parking lot at the corner of Św. Wawrzyńca and Wąska, facing the Museum of Municipal Engineering, is usually filled with a fun little cluster of creative pop-up eateries under dramatic graffiti murals. Although the lineup is always changing, the Big Red Bustaurant (fish-and-chips sold from a double-decker London bus) is a fixture here, along with burgers, Belgian-style fries, milkshakes, and fusion cuisine.

Milk Bar: **Restauracja Samoobsługowa Polakowski,** a good-quality milk bar, has a handy location in Kazimierz—just behind the top of ulica Szeroka at ulica Miodowa 39.

Dining in Kazimierz

For a good-quality sit-down meal, consider these options.

Hamsa, with a prime location at the top of ulica Szeroka, offers "hummus and happiness," with an updated take on Israeli food (that's Middle Eastern, not traditional Jewish fare). Don't come here for matzo balls and klezmer music, but for an enticing menu of 15-20-zł *mezes* (small plates, like hummus and various dips) and 35-60-zł grilled meat dishes in a modern, hip atmosphere (daily 9:00-24:00, ulica Szeorka 2, mobile 515-150-145).

Starka has romantic, dark-red decor and walls hung with sketches from a circa-1910 Berlin cartoonist. In addition to good Polish cuisine, they have 16 types of their own homemade flavored vodkas (25-30-zł starters, 30-45-zł main dishes, daily 12:00-23:00, Józefa 14, tel. 12-430-6538).

Szara is a well-respected Kraków institution (with another location near the Main Market Square). This popular spot—a bit more upscale and dressy than the tired klezmer joints—provides refined food at reasonable prices (20-30-zł starters, 40-70-zł main dishes, 30-zł lunch special includes soup and a main dish, daily 11:00-23:00, Szeroka 39, tel. 12-429-1219, www.szarakazimierz.pl).

Satori is a relaxing eddy of a café/bistro, just outside of the Kazimierz tourist chaos. With an artfully mismatched-furniture atmosphere that encourages lingering, this is a good choice either for a coffee or a full meal (15-25-zł homemade pastas and salads, daily 11:00-22:00, Sun until 21:00, Józefa 25, mobile 660-508-840).

Kazimierz Bars with Food

Three of my favorite atmospheric Kazimierz bars also serve food. It's not high cuisine—the food is an afterthought to the busy bar.

Kolanko No. 6 has a classic Kazimierz atmosphere. The bar up front is filled with old secondhand furniture. Walking toward the back, you discover an inviting garden with tables and, beyond that, a hall where they host events. They serve light meals, specializing in crêpes, toasted sandwiches, and salads (15-20 zł, 25-30-zł main dishes, daily 10:00-24:00, Józefa 17, tel. 12-292-0320).

Warsztat ("Workshop") is littered with musical instruments: The bar is a piano, and the tight interior is crammed with other instruments and rakishly crooked lampshades. The menu is an odd hybrid of Italian, Middle Eastern, and Polish cuisine, and the portions are big (15-25-zł salads, pizzas, and pastas, 30-45-zł meat dishes, daily 9:00-24:00, Izaaka 3, tel. 12-430-1451). They also have two other locations: a small one (focusing on Polish dishes) by the front door of the Tempel Synagogue, and a bigger one on Bożego Ciała street.

Plac Nowy 1 specializes in Polish microbrews, served either at the outdoor tables facing the plac Nowy market square, or in the industrial mod, split-level brick interior. The service can be spotty, and the food is an afterthought, but this is a nice setting to sample a local Polish craft beer (25-40-zł pastas, salads, pizzas, and burgers, 35-60-zł main dishes, open long hours daily, plac Nowy 1, tel. 12-442-7711).

Kazimierz Desserts

Ice Cream: Lody Tradycyjna Receptura has, true to its name, some of the best "ice cream from a traditional recipe" in Kraków—if not in Poland. The straightforward, seasonal flavors—just a few varieties—are made fresh each morning and sold until they run out. Locals line up here—and if you have a sweet tooth, you should, too (daily 9:00-19:00, Starowiślna 83).

Cakes: Ciastkarnia ("Confectionery") is a cute little bakery selling top-quality but still affordable cakes from traditional recipes (daily 9:00-20:00, shorter hours off-season, Brzozowa 13, mobile 602-790-988).

Kraków Connections

To confirm rail journeys, check specific times online (www. rozklad-pkp.pl) or at the main train station.

From Kraków by Train to: Warsaw (hourly, about 2.5 hours, requires seat reservation), **Gdańsk** (6/day direct, 5.5 hours, 1 more with change in Warsaw; plus night train, 11 hours), **Toruń** (1/day direct, 6.5 hours; better to transfer at Warsaw's Zachodnia station: 8/day, 5.5-6 hours), **Prague** (4/day with 1-2 changes, 7-8.25 hours; 1 night train, 8.75 hours), **Berlin** (3/day, 8.25-9.25 hours, transfer in Warsaw; plus 1 direct Deutsche Bahn bus, 8 hours, www. bahn.com), **Budapest** (2/day, 9.5-11 hours, transfer in Katowice, Poland, and Břeclav, Czech Republic; plus 1 night train, 10.5 hours; faster by infrequent Orange Ways bus: 5/week, 7 hours, www.orangeways.com), and **Vienna** (2/day, 6.5 hours, transfer in Katowice; 1 night train, 8 hours).

By Bus: Though train connections are typically faster, buses can be less expensive and make sense for some trips. Polski Bus prides itself on offering buses with Wi-Fi and electrical outlets (www.polskibus.com). However, some of my readers have reported hot, crowded, uncomfortable rides on these buses—you get what you pay for.

AUSCHWITZ-BIRKENAU

The unassuming regional capital of Oświęcim (ohsh-VEENCH-im) was the site of one of humanity's most unspeakably horrifying tragedies: the systematic murder of at least 1.1 million innocent people. From 1941 until 1945, Oświęcim was the home of Auschwitz, the biggest, most notorious concentration camp in the Nazi system. Today, Auschwitz is the most poignant memorial anywhere to the victims of the Holocaust.

A visit here is obligatory for Polish 14-year-olds; students usually come again during their last year of school, as well. You may see Israeli high school groups walking through the grounds wearing Star of David emblems. Many visitors leave flowers and messages. One of the messages—from a German visitor—reads, "Nations who forget their own history are sentenced to live it again."

Orientation to Auschwitz

"Auschwitz" (OWSH-vits) actually refers to a series of several camps in Poland—most importantly Auschwitz I, in the village of Oświęcim (50 miles, or a 1.25-hour drive, west of Kraków), and Auschwitz II, a.k.a. Birkenau (about 2 miles west of Oświęcim). Those visiting Auschwitz generally see both parts, starting with **Auschwitz I,** where public transportation from Kraków arrives. Auschwitz I has the main museum building, the *Arbeit Macht Frei* gate, and indoor museum exhibits in former prison buildings. A brief shuttle-bus ride takes visitors to **Birkenau** (BEER-keh-now)—on a much bigger scale and mostly outdoors, with the infamous guard tower (and another bookshop and more WCs), a

vast field with ruins of barracks, a few tourable rough barracks, the notorious "dividing platform," a giant monument flanked by remains of destroyed crematoria, and a prisoner processing facility called "the Sauna."

Begin at Auschwitz I. The museum's main building has ticket booths (to pay for a tour or to make a donation), bookshops (consider the good 5-zł *Guide-Book* brochure or the bigger laminated map), exchange offices, baggage storage (large bags aren't allowed on site), WCs, and basic eateries. You'll also find maps of the camp (posted on the walls) and a theater that shows a powerful film. A helpful **information desk**—where you can ask questions, buy tickets for the tour (see "Tours at Auschwitz," later), and find out about bus schedules for the return trip to Kraków—is halfway down the main entrance hall on the right, in the back corner.

Cost: Entrance to the grounds is free (though donations are gladly accepted). However, during busy times (April-Oct 10:00-15:00), you'll need to pay 40 zł at Auschwitz I to join a required organized tour, plus 5 zł per person for headphones to hear the guide's commentary (hiring a private guide is another option). At other times, you're allowed to visit Auschwitz I on your own, though the tour is still well worth considering. Any time of year, the grounds at Birkenau can be toured without a guide, though you'll likely need to be accompanied by a guide if you want to climb the guard tower.

Mandatory Reservations: With more than one million visitors each year, Auschwitz struggles with crowd control. Reservations are required, whether visiting on your own or with a tour. Reserving is free and easy at http://visit.auschwitz.org. Select

Why Visit Auschwitz?

Why visit a notorious concentration camp on your vacation? Auschwitz-Birkenau is one of the most moving sights in Europe, and certainly the most important of all the Holocaust memorials. Seeing the camp can be difficult: Many visitors are overwhelmed by a combination of sadness and anger over the tragedy, as well as inspiration at the remarkable stories of survival. Auschwitz survivors and victims' families want tourists to come here and experience the scale  and the monstrosity of the place. In their minds, a steady flow of visitors will ensure that the Holocaust is always remembered—so nothing like it will ever happen again.

Auschwitz isn't for everyone. But I've never met anyone who toured Auschwitz and regretted it. For many, it's a profoundly life-altering experience—at the very least, it will forever affect the way you think about the Holocaust.

"Visit for individuals," then select a date, and finally choose between "General Tour 3,5 h" (for the 40-zł, 3.5-hour guided tour—be sure to select one in English) or "Tour for individuals without an educator" (to visit on your own, for free). After you fill out the form, you'll be emailed an eticket. Print this out and bring it along when you visit the memorial.

Hours: The museum opens every day at 8:00, and closes June-Aug at 19:00, May and Sept at 18:00, April and Oct at 17:00, March and Nov at 16:00, and Dec-Feb at 15:00. These are technically "last entry" times; the grounds at Auschwitz I stay open one hour later (though many buildings—including the national memorials—close promptly at these times). The grounds at Birkenau, where many groups end their visits, may stay open even later. Information: Tel. 33-844-8100, www.auschwitz.org.

Getting There: For details on getting between Kraków and Auschwitz, see "Auschwitz Connections," at the end of this chapter.

Getting from Auschwitz I to Birkenau: Buses shuttle visitors two miles between the camps (free, about 4/hour in peak season, less off-season, times posted at the bus stop outside the main building of each site, timed to correspond with tours). Taxis are also standing by (about 15 zł). Many visitors, rather than wait for the next bus, decide to walk the 20 minutes between the camps, offering a much-needed chance for reflection. Along the way, you'll pass the Judenrampe, an old train car like the ones used to transport prisoners, explained by an informational sign.

Film: The 17-minute movie (too graphic for children) was shot by Ukrainian troops days after the Red Army liberated the camp (4 zł, buy ticket on arrival; schedule for showings in English varies—ask when you arrive).

Photography: Because the philosophy of the camp is to spread the story of Auschwitz, taking photographs of anything outdoors is encouraged. However, to ease the movement of visitors, photography is not allowed inside certain museum buildings (when it *is* allowed, don't use a flash or tripod).

Eating: A café and decent cafeteria (Bar Smak) are at the main Auschwitz building. More options are in the commercial complex across the street.

Etiquette: The camp encourages visitors to remember that Auschwitz is the place where more than a million people lost their lives. Behave and dress here as you would at a cemetery.

Tours at Auschwitz

Visiting Auschwitz on your own works well, given the abundance of English descriptions (and this chapter's self-guided tour). However, due to crowd-control issues, from May through October individual visitors are not allowed to enter the Auschwitz I part of the complex on their own between the peak times of 10:00 and 15:00. Instead, you're required to either join one of the museum's organized tours or reserve your own private museum guide (both options are explained next). Note that even during these busy times, individuals may enter the Auschwitz II/Birkenau part of the complex without a guide.

Organized Museum Tours

The Auschwitz Museum's excellent guides are serious and frank, and they feel a strong sense of responsibility about sharing the story of the camp. Appropriately, these well-trained guides are more historians than entertainers. The regularly scheduled 3.5-hour English tour covers Auschwitz, Birkenau, and the film (40 zł, plus 5 zł to rent headphones to hear the guide). Remember: These tours must be prebooked online at http://visit.auschwitz.org. Most of the year, there are generally at least four English tours scheduled each day. You'll watch the film first; the actual tour begins 30 minutes later (the film usually begins at the top of the hour, while English tours start at :30 past each hour from 9:30-15:30; in winter, tours generally begin at 10:30, 11:30, 12:30, and 13:20).

AUSCHWITZ-BIRKENAU

Auschwitz Renovation

The International Auschwitz Council is planning to renovate the site over the next several years. The museum at Auschwitz I, widely considered the oldest Holocaust exhibit in the world, has remained largely unchanged in the more than 50 years since it opened. Now the museum displays will be modernized and better organized to accommodate the growing number of visitors. The key elements described in this chapter (such as the displays of human hair, eyeglasses, and suitcases) will still be part of the exhibit, but will likely be spread into more buildings (mostly on the ground floor, to avoid congestion on stairways). At Birkenau, restorers will build retaining walls to prevent the remains of the huge crematoria—key evidence of Nazi crimes—from slowly sinking into the ground.

Because of the renovation, be aware that the information in this chapter (especially the locations of exhibits on the self-guided tour) is subject to change. Ask about recent developments when you arrive at the camp.

Private Official Museum Guides

If you have a special interest, a small group, or just want a more personalized visit, it's affordable and worthwhile to hire one of the museum's guides for a private tour. Choose between the basic 3.5-hour tour of the camp (250 zł), or a longer "study tour" (320 zł/4 hours only at Auschwitz I, 400 zł/6 hours at both Auschwitz I and Birkenau in one day, 500 zł/8 hours at Auschwitz I and Birkenau spread over 2 days). For groups larger than 10 people, you'll pay an additional 5 zł per person for headphones to hear the guide's commentary. Because English-speaking guides are limited, try to reserve at least two months in advance (fill out the online form at http://visit.auschwitz.org, or call 33-844-8099 or 33-844-8100). At busy times, individuals might not be able to reserve a private guide between 10:00 and 14:00, when they're needed for bigger groups.

Tours from Kraków

Various Kraków-based companies sell round-trip tours from Kraków to Auschwitz (generally around 130 zł). While these take care of transportation for you and include a guided tour, you'll pay triple and have to adhere to a strict schedule, and the tours tend to be impersonal.

Local Guides and Drivers from Kraków

For hassle-free transportation to the camp, you can hire a Kraków-based guide or driver to bring you to Auschwitz. However, since these people are not officially registered museum guides, they technically aren't allowed to show you around the site. Instead, they will most likely arrange a private museum guide to join you, or time your visit so you can join an organized English tour (both options described earlier). While it's pricey, some travelers consider hiring a driver/guide to be a worthwhile splurge, since you'll have door-to-door service to the camp and three hours in the car with a local expert.

Auschwitz Tour

AUSCHWITZ I

• *From the entrance building, step out and look over the grassy field to get oriented.*

Before World War II, this camp was a base for the Polish army. When Hitler occupied Poland, he took over these barracks and

 turned it into a concentration camp for his Polish political enemies. The location was ideal, with a nearby rail junction and rivers providing natural protective boundaries. An average of 14,000 prisoners were kept at this camp at one time. (Birkenau could hold up to 100,000.) In 1942, Auschwitz became a death camp for the extermination of European Jews and others whom Hitler considered "undesirable." By the time the camp was liberated in 1945, at least 1.1 million people had been murdered here—approximately 960,000 of them Jewish.

• *Go closer to the camp entrance, approaching the notorious...*

"Arbeit Macht Frei" Gate

Although this gate imparts the message "Work Sets You Free," the only way out of the camp for the prisoners was through the crematorium chimneys. Note that the "B" was welded on upside down by belligerent inmates, who were forced to make this sign (and much of the camp). This is actually a replica; the original was stolen one night in December of 2009, then recovered two days later, cut up into several pieces. The original is now safely in the museum's possession, but no longer displayed in public.

Just inside the gate and to the right, the camp orchestra (made up of prisoners) used to play marches; having the prisoners march made them easier to count.

• *From the gate, proceed straight up the "main street" of the camp.*

You'll pass two rows of barracks. The first one holds a variety of national memorials. We'll circle back here later, if you'd like to enter some of them. But these are of less general interest than the second row of barracks, which hold the main museum exhibitions.

AUSCHWITZ-BIRKENAU

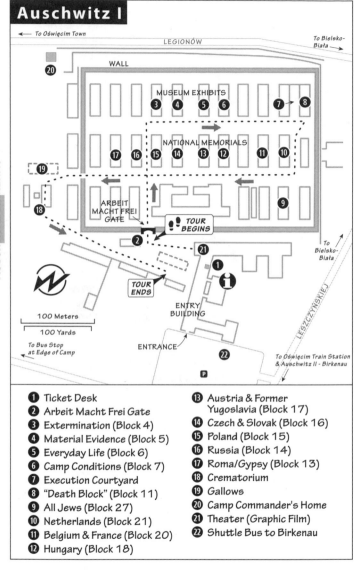

Auschwitz I

← To Oświęcim Town

LEGIONÓW

To Bielsko-Biała →

WALL

MUSEUM EXHIBITS

3 **4** **5** **6** **7** **8**

NATIONAL MEMORIALS

17 **16** **15** **14** **13** **12** **11** **10**

19

18

ARBEIT MACHT FREI GATE

9

2

TOUR BEGINS

21

To Bielsko-Biała

1

TOUR ENDS

100 Meters
100 Yards

To Bus Stop at Edge of Camp ←

ENTRY BUILDING

ENTRANCE

22

To Oświęcim Train Station & Auschwitz II - Birkenau

LESZCZYŃSKIEJ

P

1 Ticket Desk	**13** Austria & Former Yugoslavia (Block 17)
2 Arbeit Macht Frei Gate	**14** Czech & Slovak (Block 16)
3 Extermination (Block 4)	**15** Poland (Block 15)
4 Material Evidence (Block 5)	**16** Russia (Block 14)
5 Everyday Life (Block 6)	**17** Roma/Gypsy (Block 13)
6 Camp Conditions (Block 7)	**18** Crematorium
7 Execution Courtyard	**19** Gallows
8 "Death Block" (Block 11)	**20** Camp Commander's Home
9 All Jews (Block 27)	**21** Theater (Graphic Film)
10 Netherlands (Block 21)	**22** Shuttle Bus to Birkenau
11 Belgium & France (Block 20)	
12 Hungary (Block 18)	

Blocks 4 and 5 focus on how Auschwitz prisoners were killed. Blocks 6, 7, and 11 explore the conditions for prisoners who survived here a little longer than most. In each block, arrows send you on a one-way route from numbered room to numbered room; in many cases, there are also exhibits downstairs and upstairs—don't miss these.

• *Start with...*

Chilling Statistics:
The Holocaust in Poland

The majority of people murdered by the Nazis during the Holocaust were killed right here in Poland. For centuries, Poland was known for its relative tolerance of Jews, and right up until the beginning of World War II, Poland had Europe's largest concentration of Jews: 3,500,000. Throughout the Holocaust, the Nazis murdered 4,500,000 Jews in Poland (many of them brought in from other countries) at camps, including Auschwitz, and in ghettos such as Warsaw's.

By the end of the war, only 300,000 Polish Jews had survived—less than 10 percent of the original population. Many of these survivors were granted "one-way passports" (read: deported) to Israel, Western Europe, and the US by the communist government in 1968 (following a big student demonstration with a strong Jewish presence). Today, only about 10,000 Jews live in all of Poland.

Block 4: Extermination

In Room 1, a map identifies the countries from which Auschwitz prisoners were brought—as far away as the Norwegian fjords and

the Greek Islands. In an alcove along the side of the room is an urn filled with ashes, a symbolic memorial to all of the camp's victims.

Room 2 shows photographs of Jewish ghettos from all over Europe being "liquidated"—that is, its residents assembled and

deported to various concentration camps. Thanks to its massive occupancy, Auschwitz was a common destination for many.

Room 3 displays rare photos of scenes inside the camp, taken by arrogant SS men. To prevent a riot, the Nazis claimed at first that this was only a transition camp for resettlement in Eastern Europe. At the far end of Room 3, a helpful orientation map for visitors shows the town of Oświęcim, Auschwitz I, Auschwitz II (Birkenau), and other parts of the camp network.

Upstairs in Room 4 is a model of a Birkenau crematorium. People entered on the left, then got undressed in the underground rooms (hanging their belongings on numbered hooks and encouraged to remember their numbers to retrieve their clothes later). They then moved into the "showers" and were killed by Zyklon-B gas (hydrogen cyanide), a German-produced cleaning agent that is lethal in high doses. This efficient factory of murder took about 20 minutes to kill 8,000 people in four gas chambers. Elevators brought the bodies up to the crematorium. Members of the *Sonderkommand*—Jewish inmates who were kept isolated and forced by the Nazis to work here—removed the corpses' gold teeth and shaved off their hair (to be sold) before putting the bodies in the ovens. It wasn't unusual for a *Sonderkommand* worker to discover a wife, child, or parent among the dead. A few of these workers committed suicide by throwing themselves at electric fences; those who didn't were systematically executed by the Nazis after a two-month shift. Across from the model of the crematorium are canisters of Zyklon-B.

Across the hall in the dimly lit Room 5 is one of the camp's most powerful exhibits: a wall of actual victims' hair—4,400 pounds of it. Also displayed is cloth made of the hair, used to make Nazi uniforms. The Nazis were nothing if not efficient...nothing, not even human body parts, could be wasted.

Back downstairs in Room 6 is an exhibit on the plunder of victims' personal belongings. People being transported here were encouraged to bring luggage—and some victims had even paid in advance for houses in their new homeland. After they were killed, everything of value was sorted and stored in warehouses that prisoners named "Canada" (after a country they associated with great wealth). Although the Canada warehouses were destroyed, you can see a few of these items in the next building.

• *Head next door.*

Block 5: Material Evidence of the Nazis' Crimes

The exhibits in this block consist mostly of piles of the victims' goods, a tiny fraction of everything the Nazis stole. As you wander through the rooms, you'll see eyeglasses; fine Jewish prayer shawls; crutches and prosthetic limbs (the first people the Nazis exterminated were mentally and physically ill German citizens); and a pile of pots and pans. Then, upstairs, you'll witness a seemingly endless mountain of shoes; children's clothing; and suitcases with names of victims—many marked *Kind*, or "child." Visitors often wonder if the suitcase with the name "Frank" belonged to Anne, one of the Holocaust's most famous victims. After being discovered in Amsterdam by the Nazis, the Frank family was transported here to Auschwitz, where they were split up. Still, it's unlikely this suitcase was theirs. Anne Frank and her sister Margot were sent to the Bergen-Belsen camp in northern Germany, where they died of typhus shortly before the war ended. Their father, Otto Frank, survived Auschwitz and was found barely alive by the Russians, who liberated the camp in January of 1945.

• *Proceed to the next block.*

St. Maksymilian Kolbe (1894-1941)

Among the many inspirational stories of Auschwitz is that of a Polish priest named Maksymilian Kolbe. Before the war, Kolbe traveled as a missionary to Japan, then worked in Poland for a Catholic newspaper. While he was highly regarded for his devotion to the Church, some of his writings had an unsettling anti-Semitic sentiment. But during the Nazi occupation, Kolbe briefly ran an institution that cared for refugees—including Jews.

In 1941, Kolbe was arrested and interned at Auschwitz. When a prisoner from Kolbe's block escaped in July of that year, the Nazis punished the remaining inmates by selecting 10 of them to be put in the Starvation Cell until they died—based on the Nazi "doctrine of collective responsibility." After the selection had been made, Kolbe offered to replace a man who expressed concern about who would care for his family. The Nazis agreed. (The man Kolbe saved is said to have survived the Holocaust.)

All 10 of the men—including Kolbe—were put into Starvation Cell 18. Two weeks later, when the door was opened, only Kolbe had survived. The story spread throughout the camp, and Kolbe became an inspiration to the inmates. To squelch the hope he had given the others, Kolbe was executed by lethal injection.

In 1982, Kolbe was canonized by the Catholic Church. Some critics—mindful of his earlier anti-Semitic rhetoric—still consider Kolbe's sainthood controversial. But most Poles feel he redeemed himself for his earlier missteps through this noble act at the end of his life.

Block 6: Everyday Life

Although the purpose of Auschwitz was to murder its inmates, not all of them were killed immediately. After an initial evaluation, some prisoners were registered and forced to work. (This did not mean they were chosen to live—just to die later.) This block shows various aspects of daily existence at the camp.

The halls are lined with photographs of victims, each one identified with a name, birthdate, occupation, date of arrival at Auschwitz, date of death, and camp registration number. Examining these dates, it's clear that those registered survived here an average of two to three months. (Flowers are poignant reminders that

19472
DĄBROWSKI JAN
ur.8.2.1920 r., robotnik
przybył: 30.7.1941. zginął: wrzesień 1942.

these victims are survived by loved ones.) Similar photographs hang in several other museum buildings, as well; as with the plundered items in the last block, keep in mind that these represent only a tiny fraction of the masses of people murdered at Auschwitz.

Room 1 (on the left as you enter the front door) displays drawings of the arrival process. After the initial selection, those chosen to work were showered, shaved, and photographed. After a while, photographing each prisoner got to be too expensive, so prisoners were tattooed instead (see photographs): on the chest, on the arm, or—for children—on the leg. A display shows the symbols that prisoners had to wear to show their reason for internment—Jew, Roma (Gypsy), homosexual, political prisoner, and so on. At the end of the room, a display case holds actual camp uniforms.

Across the hall, Room 4 shows the starvation that took place here. The 7,500 survivors that the Red Army found when the camp was liberated were essentially living skeletons (the "healthier" inmates had been forced to march to Germany). Of those liberated, 20 percent died soon after of disease and starvation.

In Room 5, you can see scenes from the prisoner's workday (sketched by survivors after liberation). Prisoners worked as long as the sun shone—eight hours in winter, up to twelve hours in summer—mostly on farms or in factories.

Room 6 is about Auschwitz's child inmates, 20 percent of the camp's victims. Blond, blue-eyed children were either "Germanized" in special schools or, if younger, adopted by German families. Dr. Josef Mengele conducted gruesome experiments here on children, especially twins and triplets, ostensibly to find ways to increase fertility for German mothers. Also in this room, look for a display of the prisoners' daily ration (in the glass case): a pan of tea or coffee in the morning; thin vegetable soup in the afternoon; and a piece of bread (often made with sawdust or chestnuts) for dinner. This makes it clear that Auschwitz was never intended to be a "work camp," where people were kept alive, healthy, and efficient to do work. Rather, people were meant to die here—if not in the gas chambers, then through malnutrition and overwork.

• *Block 7 shows living and sanitary conditions at the camp, which you'll see in more detail later at Birkenau. Blocks 8-10 are vacant (medical experiments were carried out in Block 10). And Block 11 was the most notorious of all.*

Block 11: The Death Block
Step into the walled-in **courtyard** between Blocks 10 and 11. The wall at the far end is where the Nazis shot several thousand political prisoners, leaders of camp resistance, and religious leaders. Notice that the windows are covered, so that nobody could

witness the executions. Also take a close look at the memorial—the back of it is made of a material designed by Nazis to catch the bullets without a ricochet. Inmates were shot at short range—about three feet. The pebbles represent prayers from Jewish visitors.

Now head into the **"Death Block"** (#11), from which nobody ever left alive. Death here required a "trial"—but it was never a fair trial. Room 2 (on the left as you enter) is where these sham trials were held, lasting about two minutes each. In Room 5, you can see how prisoners lived in these barracks—three-level bunks, with three prisoners sleeping in each bed (they had to sleep on their sides so they could fit). In Room 6, people undressed before they were executed.

In the **basement,** you'll see several different types of cells. The Starvation Cell (#18) held prisoners selected to starve to death when a fellow prisoner escaped; Maksymilian Kolbe spent two weeks here to save another man's life (see sidebar on Kolbe). In the Dark Cell (#20), which held up to 30, people had only a small window for ventilation—and if it became covered with snow, the prisoners suffocated. In the Standing Cells (#22), four people would be forced to stand together for hours at a time (the bricks went all the way to the ceiling then).

Upstairs, you'll find gallows and a bench used for administering lashes. Filling this floor are exhibits on various forms of punishment, mostly focusing on resistance within the camp, escapees, and local Poles who were executed—either for trying to assist the prisoners, or for fighting with Nazi officers.

• Leaving Block 11, proceed straight ahead, between the buildings, to the other row of barracks. Several of these blocks house...

National Memorials

These exhibits were created not by museum authorities, but by representatives of the home countries of the camps' victims. As these memorials overlap with the general exhibits, and are designed for Europeans to learn more about the victims from their own home countries, most visitors skip this part of the site. On the other hand, while the main museum exhibits await renovation and modernization, the displays in these national memorials tend to be slicker and better-presented than the ones we just saw. (Some of these may be works in progress, as old exhibits are routinely upgraded.) As you walk along this street toward our next stop (the crematorium), consider stepping into the ones that interest you.

AUSCHWITZ-BIRKENAU

The first one you see is the memorial to **Jewish** victims (Block 27). It's compelling and thoughtfully presented, relying heavily on video clips, evocative music, and sound effects.

Most of the other national memorials are on the right side of the street. Across from the Jewish memorial, Block 21 honors **Dutch Jews;** it begins with a quote by perhaps the most famous Dutch victim of the concentration camps, Anne Frank (whose story is also told—among many others'—throughout the exhibit).

Block 20, a former hospital block, is shared by **Belgium** and **France.** A room near the entrance explains how some prisoners were killed by lethal injection, with portraits and biographical sketches of victims. Upstairs is the powerful Belgium exhibit, with a room featuring victims' portraits. Block 18 holds a very modern, conceptual exhibit about **Hungary**'s victims, with an eerie heart-beat sound pervading the space. Block 17, which is likely a work in progress, is intended to memorialize victims from **Austria** and the **former Yugoslavia.** Across from this block, notice the long gallows used for mass hangings. Block 16 contains a new and well-presented exhibit about **Czech** and **Slovak** victims.

Block 15 honors victims from **Poland,** focusing on the 1939 Nazi invasion of the country, which resulted in the immediate internment of Polish political prisoners. Exhibits explain the process of "Germanization"—such as renaming Polish streets with German names—and (upstairs) the underground resistance that fought to re-assert some control over Poland.

Block 14 is the **Russian** national memorial. However, this one's a bit controversial: While Russia claims to have lost "Russian" Jews to the Holocaust, virtually all of them were technically Polish Jews who had been living within Russia. (They spoke Polish, not Russian.) To sidestep the hot topic of how to identify these victims, this memorial focuses not on victims, but on the Russian liberation of the camp.

Block 13 houses the **Roma (Gypsy)** exhibit. You'll learn that the Roma, along with the Jews, were considered no better than "rats, bedbugs, and fleas," and explore elements of the so-called *Zigeunerfrage*—the "Gypsy question" about what to do with this "troublesome" population.

• *At the end of this row of barracks, you reach a guard tower and a barbed-wire fence. Jog a few steps to the right, through the hole in the fence, then angle left toward the earthen mound with the giant, ominous brick chimney. The entrance is at the far end of the building.*

Crematorium

Up to 700 people at a time could be gassed here. People undressed outside, or just inside the door. As you enter, bear right and find your way into the big "shower room." Look for the vents in the ceiling—this is where the SS men dropped the Zyklon-B. In the adjacent room is a replica of the furnace. This facility could burn 340 bodies a day—so it took two days to burn all of the bodies from one round of executions. (The Nazis didn't like this inefficiency, so they built four more huge crematoria at Birkenau.)

• *Turning left as you exit the crematorium takes you back to the entrance building. But first, circle around to the opposite side of the crematorium for the closest thing this story has to a happy ending.*

Shortly after the war, camp commander Rudolf Höss was tried, convicted, and sentenced to death. Survivors requested that he be executed at Auschwitz, and in 1947, he was hanged here. The **gallows** are preserved behind the crematorium (about a hundred yards from his home where his wife—who loved her years here—read stories to their children, very likely by the light of a human-skin lampshade).

• *Take your time with Auschwitz I. When you're ready, continue to the second stage of the camp—Birkenau.*

AUSCHWITZ II—BIRKENAU

In 1941, realizing that the original Auschwitz camp was too small to meet their needs, the Nazis began a second camp in some nearby farm fields. The original plan was for a camp that could hold 200,000 people, but at its peak, Birkenau (Brzezinka) held only about 100,000. They were still adding onto it when the camp was liberated in 1945.

• *Train tracks lead past the main building and into the camp. The first sight that greeted prisoners was the...*

Guard Tower

If you've seen *Schindler's List*, the sight of this icon of the Holocaust—shown in stirring scenes from the movie—may make you queasy.

Climb to the top of the entry building (also houses WCs and bookstore) for an overview of the massive camp. As you look over the camp, you'll see a vast field of chimneys and a few intact wooden and brick barracks. Some of the barracks were destroyed by Germans. Most were dismantled to be used for fuel and building materials shortly after the war. But the first row has been reconstructed (using components from the original structures). The train tracks lead straight back to the dividing platform, and then dead-end at the ruins of the crematorium and camp monument at

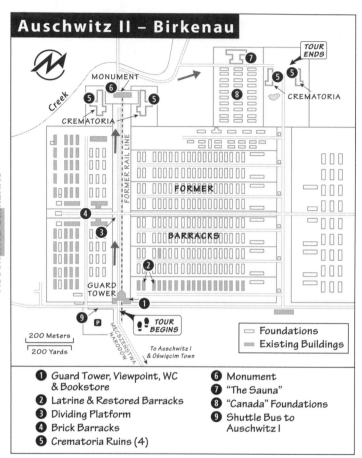

Auschwitz II – Birkenau

MONUMENT

CREMATORIA

Creek

FORMER RAIL LINE

FORMER

BARRACKS

GUARD TOWER

TOUR ENDS

CREMATORIA

"The Sauna"

MĘCZEŃSTWA NARODÓW

P

200 Meters
200 Yards

To Auschwitz I
& Oświęcim Town

TOUR BEGINS

☐ Foundations
■ Existing Buildings

❶ Guard Tower, Viewpoint, WC & Bookstore
❷ Latrine & Restored Barracks
❸ Dividing Platform
❹ Brick Barracks
❺ Crematoria Ruins (4)
❻ Monument
❼ "The Sauna"
❽ "Canada" Foundations
❾ Shuttle Bus to Auschwitz I

AUSCHWITZ-BIRKENAU

the far side.

• *Descend the tower, enter the camp, turn right, and walk through the barbed-wire fence to reach the...*

Wooden Barracks

The first of these barrack buildings was the **latrine:** The front half of the building contained washrooms, and the back was a row of toilets. There was no running water, and prisoners were in charge of keeping the latrine clean. Because of the resulting unsanitary conditions and risk of disease, the Nazis were afraid to come in here—so the latrine became the heart of the black market and the inmates' resistance movement.

The third barrack was a **bunkhouse.** Each inmate had a personal number, a barrack number, and a bed number. Inside, you can see the beds (angled so that more could fit). An aver-

age of 400 prisoners—but up to 1,000—would be housed in each of these buildings. These wooden structures, designed as stables by a German company (look for the horse-tying rings on the wall), came in prefab pieces that made them cheap and convenient. Two chimneys connected by a brick duct provided a little heat. The

bricks were smoothed by inmates who sat here to catch a bit of warmth.

• *Return to the train tracks, and follow them toward the monument about a half-mile away, at the back end of Birkenau. At the intersection of these tracks and the perpendicular gravel road (halfway to the monument)—now marked by a lonely train car—was the gravel pitch known as the...*

Dividing Platform

A Nazi doctor would stand facing the guard tower and evaluate each prisoner. If he pointed to the right, the prisoner was sentenced to death, and trudged—unknowingly—to the gas chamber. If he pointed to the left, the person would be registered and live a little longer. It was here that families from all over Europe were torn apart forever.

• *Photographs near the wooden building—on the left-hand side as you face the back of the camp complex—show the sad scene. Just beyond that building is a field with some...*

Brick Barracks

Enter one of these buildings. The supervisors lived in the two smaller rooms near the door. Farther in, most barracks still have the wooden bunks that held about 700 people per building. Four or five people slept on each bunk, including the floor—reserved for new arrivals. There were chamber pots at either end of the building. After a Nazi doctor died of typhus, sanitation improved, and these barracks got running water.

Now head back to the train tracks. As you walk along the camp's only road, which leads along the tracks to the crematorium, imagine the horror of this place—no grass, only mud, and all the barracks packed with people, with smoke blowing in from the busy crematoria. This was an even worse place to die than Auschwitz I.

• *The train tracks lead to the camp memorial and crematorium. At the end of the tracks, go 50 yards to the left and climb the three concrete steps to view the ruin of the...*

Crematorium

This is one of four crematoria here at Birkenau, each with a capacity to cremate more than 4,400 people per day. At the far-right end of the ruins, see the stairs where people entered the rooms to undress. They were given numbered lockers, conning them into thinking they were coming back. (The Nazis didn't want a panic.) Then they piled into the "shower room"—the underground passage branching away from the memorial—and were killed. Their bodies were burned in the crematorium (on the left), giving off a scent of sweet almonds (from the Zyklon-B). Beyond the remains of the crematorium is a hole—once a gray lake where tons of ashes were dumped. This efficient factory of death was destroyed by the Nazis as the Red Army approached, leaving the haunting ruins you see today.

When the Soviets arrived on January 27, 1945, the nightmare of Auschwitz-Birkenau was over. The Polish parliament voted to turn these grounds into a museum, so that the world would understand, and never forget, the horror of what happened here.

• *At the back of the camp stands the...*

Monument

Built in 1967 by the communist government in its heavy "Socialist Realism" style, this monument represents gravestones and the chimney of a crematorium. The plaques, written in each of the languages spoken by camp victims (including English, far right), explain that the memorial is "a cry of despair and a warning to humanity."

• *With more time, you could continue deeper into...*

The Rest of the Camp

There's much more to see for those who are interested—Birkenau sprawls for a frightening distance. One place worth seeing is the reception and disinfection building that prisoners called **"the Sauna"** (the long building with four tall chimneys). It was here that prisoners would be forced to strip and be deloused; their belongings were seized and taken to the "Canada" warehouses (described earlier) to be sorted. Walking through here (on glass floors designed to protect the

original structure below), you'll see artifacts of the grim efficiency with which prisoners were "processed"—their heads were shaved, they were tattooed with a serial number, and they were assigned uniforms and wooden clogs to wear. Portraits at the end of the building humanize those who passed through here. Look for the cart, which was used to dispose of ashes. In front of the Sauna is a field of foundations of the **"Canada" warehouses.** Nearby are the other two destroyed **crematoria.**

Auschwitz Connections

The Auschwitz Museum is in the town of Oświęcim, about 50 miles west of Kraków. By bus, minibus, or train, the journey takes around an hour and 45 minutes each way; driving shaves off about 10-20 minutes.

FROM KRAKÓW TO AUSCHWITZ

The easiest way to reach Auschwitz is with a **package tour** (figure around 130 zł per person) or **private guide or driver** (300-500 zł for the carload). While the package tours are more convenient than going on your own, three people can hire their own driver for less and have a more intimate experience.

If you're using public transportation, here are your choices:

The most comfortable public-transit option is to take one of the frequent **buses,** mostly run by PKS Oświęcim (14 zł, at least hourly, 1.75 hours, get the most recent schedule at any Kraków TI, buses depart from Kraków's main bus station behind the train station). Buy a one-way ticket from the bus-station ticket office or from the driver to leave your options open for getting home. Look for buses to "Oświęcim" (not necessarily "Auschwitz"). Note that these buses can be full, and because most come from other towns, there's no way to reserve a seat—so line up early (generally about 15 minutes ahead). If you don't get on a bus, you'll have to wait for the next one (or, if there's a minibus leaving sooner, you can take one of those—described next). Once in the town of Oświęcim, buses from Kraków stop first at the train station, then continue on to one of two stops near the museum: About half of the buses go directly into the parking lot at the museum itself, while the rest use a low-profile bus stop on the edge of the Auschwitz camp grounds (you'll see a small *Muzeum Auschwitz* sign on the right just before the stop, and a blue *Oświęcim Muzeum PKS* sign at the stop itself). From this bus stop, follow the sign down the road and into the parking lot; the main museum building is across the lot on your left. Note that since some buses don't actually go into the museum's parking lot, the Auschwitz stop can be easy to miss—don't be shy about

On the Way to Auschwitz: The Polish Countryside

You'll spend about an hour gazing out the window as you drive or ride to Auschwitz. This may be your only real look at the Polish countryside. Ponder these thoughts about what you're passing...

The small houses you see are traditionally inhabited by three generations at the same time. Nineteenth-century houses (the few that survive) often sport blue stripes. Back then, parents announced that their daughters were now eligible by getting out the blue paint. Once they saw these blue lines, local boys were welcome to come a-courtin'.

Big churches mark small villages. Like in the US, tiny roadside memorials and crosses indicate places where fatal accidents have occurred.

Polish farmers traditionally had small lots that were notorious for not being very productive. These farmers somewhat miraculously survived the communist era without having to merge their farms. For years, they were Poland's sacred cows: producing little, paying almost no tax, and draining government resources. But since Poland joined the European Union in 2004, they're being forced to get up to snuff...and, in many cases, collectivize their farms after all.

Since most people don't own cars, bikes are common and public transit is excellent. There are lots of bus stops, as well as minibuses that you can flag down anywhere for a 2-zł ride. The bad roads are a legacy of communist construction, exacerbated by heavy truck use and brutal winters.

Poland has more than 2,000 counties, or districts, each with its own coat of arms; you'll pass several along the way. The forests are state-owned, and locals enjoy the right to pick berries in the summer and mushrooms in the autumn (you may see people—often young kids—selling their day's harvest by the side of the road). The mushrooms are dried and then boiled to make tasty soups in the winter.

letting your driver know where you want to go: *"Muzeum?"*

Several **minibuses** from Kraków head for Auschwitz (10 zł, sporadic departures—generally 1-2/hour, 1.75 hours). Like the buses, some go directly to the museum, while others use the bus stop at the edge of camp. These generally depart from the lower platform of the main bus station (but confirm the departure point at the TI). Some of my readers report that the minibuses are a bit more cramped than the buses and, while intended for local commuters, can be crammed with tourists. But they work fine in a pinch.

You could ride the **train** to Oświęcim, but it's less convenient than the bus because it leaves you at the train station, farther from the museum (15/day, less Sat-Sun, 1.5 hours, 14 zł). If you do wind up at the Oświęcim train station, it's about a 20-minute walk to the camp (turn right out of station, go straight, then turn left at roundabout, camp is several blocks ahead on left). Or you can take a taxi (around 15 zł).

RETURNING FROM AUSCHWITZ TO KRAKÓW

Upon arrival at Auschwitz I, plan your departure by visiting the information window inside the main building (halfway down the main entry hall, on the right, in the back corner behind the tables). They can give you a schedule of departures and explain where the bus or minibus leaves from. (If you'll be staying late into the afternoon, make a point of figuring out the last possible bus or train back to Kraków, and plan accordingly.) Remember to allow enough time to make it from Birkenau back to Auschwitz I to catch your bus.

Although most minibuses and a few buses back to Kraków leave from the camp parking lot itself, if you're taking the bus, you'll most likely catch it from the stop on the edge of the Auschwitz I grounds. To reach this bus stop, leave the Auschwitz I building through the main entry and walk straight along the parking lot, then turn right on the road near the end of the lot. At the T-intersection, cross the street to the little bus stop with the blue *Oświęcim Muzeum PKS* sign. Don't be distracted by the ads for a nearby travel agency—you can buy tickets on board. There's no public transportation back to Kraków from Birkenau, where most people end their tours; you'll have to take the shuttle bus back to Auschwitz I first.

WARSAW

Warszawa

Warsaw (Warszawa, vah-SHAH-vah in Polish) is Poland's capital and biggest city. It's huge, famous, and important...but not particularly romantic. If you're looking for Old World quaintness, head for Kraków. If you're tickled by spires and domes, get to Prague. But if you want to experience a truly 21st-century city, Warsaw's your place.

Stroll down revitalized boulevards that evoke the city's glory days, pausing at an outdoor café to sip coffee and nibble at a *pączek* (the classic Polish jelly doughnut). Stroll through a leafy park to an al fresco Chopin concert, packed with pensive Poles. Commune with the soul of Poland through its artists (at the National Museum), its favorite composer (at the Chopin Museum), its dramatic history (at the Warsaw Historical Museum and Warsaw Uprising Museum), its dedication to the sciences (at the Copernicus Science Center), and its Jewish story (at the Museum of the History of Polish Jews). And ponder the wide range of Warsaw's postwar urban architecture, from dreary communist monstrosities to innovative skyscrapers designed by *the* top names in global architecture.

Varsovians are embracing their role as the capital city of a newly influential nation. The European Union has two universities aimed at educating future political leaders (or "Eurocrats"). One is in Bruges, Belgium, just down the road from the EU capital of Brussels. The other one is right here. You can almost feel Warsaw peeling back the layers of communist grime as it replaces potholed highways with pedestrian-friendly parks. Today's Warsaw has gleaming new office towers and street signs, stylishly dressed locals, cutting-edge shopping malls, swarms of international businesspeople, hipster culture as vivid as anything in Brooklyn, and a gourmet coffee shop on every corner.

Warsaw has good reason to be a city of the future: The past hasn't been very kind. Since becoming Poland's capital in 1596, Warsaw has seen wave after wave of foreign rulers and invasions—especially during the last hundred years. But in this horrific crucible, the enduring spirit of the Polish people was forged. As one proud Varsovian told me, "Warsaw is ugly because its history is so beautiful."

The city's darkest days came during the Nazi occupation of World War II. First, its Jewish residents were forced into a tiny ghetto. They rose up...and were slaughtered. Then, its Polish residents rose up...and were slaughtered. Hitler sent word to systematically demolish this troublesome city. At the war's end, Warsaw was devastated. An estimated 800,000 residents were dead—nearly two out of every three Varsovians.

The Poles almost gave up on what was then a pile of rubble to build a brand-new capital city elsewhere. But ultimately they decided to rebuild, creating a city of contrasts: painstakingly restored medieval lanes, retrofitted communist apartment blocks (*bloki* in Polish), and sleek skyscrapers. Between the buildings you'll find fragments of a complex, sometimes tragic, and often inspiring history.

A product of its complicated past, sprinkled with the big-city style and sophistication of its present, Warsaw remains quintessentially Polish. It is a place worth grappling with to understand the Poland of today...and the Europe of tomorrow. Many tourists here make the mistake of focusing on Warsaw's Old Town. It's pleasant enough, but that's simply not the point of coming to Warsaw. Rather, focus on the urban cityscape, edgy neighborhoods, and high-tech, top-quality museums; it's in these arenas that Warsaw trumps other Polish destinations.

PLANNING YOUR TIME

Warsaw can easily fill two or three days, but if you're pressed for time, one full day is enough. Get your bearings by taking a stroll through Polish history on the Royal Way, using my self-guided walk. Then visit other sights according to your interests: Polish artists, Jewish history, the Warsaw Uprising, royalty, hands-on science gizmos, hipster hangouts, or Chopin. To slow down and take a break from the city, relax in Łazienki Park.

Orientation to Warsaw

Warsaw sprawls with 1.7 million residents. Everything is on a big scale—it seems to take forever to walk just a few "short" blocks. Get comfortable with public transportation and plan your sightseeing wisely to avoid backtracking.

Virtually everything of interest to travelers is on a mild hill on the west bank of the Vistula River. The city's central train station (Warszawa Centralna) is in the shadow of its biggest landmark: the can't-miss-it, skyscraping Palace of Culture and Science. From here, Jerusalem Avenue (aleja Jerozolimskie) runs east toward the river, past the National Museum. It crosses the "Royal Way" boulevard, which connects the sights in the north (Old Town and New Town) with those in the south (Łazienki Park, and at the outskirts of town, Wilanów Palace). Most major sights and recommended hotels and restaurants are along or near these two thoroughfares (Jerusalem Avenue and the Royal Way).

Another tip: You'll hear about two distinct uprisings against the Nazis during World War II. They're easy to confuse, but try to keep them straight: the **Ghetto Uprising** was staged by Warsaw's dwindling Jewish population in the spring of 1943; the **Warsaw Uprising,** a year later, was led by the (mostly non-Jewish) Polish Home Army.

TOURIST INFORMATION

Warsaw's helpful, youthful TI has three branches: on the **Old Town Market Square** (daily May-Sept 9:00-20:00, Oct-April 9:00-18:00), at the **Palace of Culture and Science** (enter on the side facing the train station, on Emilii Plater; daily May-Sept 8:00-20:00, Oct-April 8:00-18:00), and at **Chopin Airport** (daily May-Sept 8:00-20:00, Oct-April 8:00-18:00). The general information number for all TIs is 19431 from inside Warsaw, or 22-19431 from outside Warsaw. All branches offer piles of free, useful materials: a city map and a wide variety of brochures on sights and activities ("city breaks," Jewish heritage, Chopin, mermaids, St. John Paul II, and so on); everything is also available online (www.warsawtour.pl). The TI also has a free room-booking service and can give you advice about live music in town. I'd skip the Warsaw Pass, which covers public transportation and admission to some major sights, and discounts to others; because the shortest pass is good for 72 hours, you'd have to sightsee like mad for three straight days to get your money's worth.

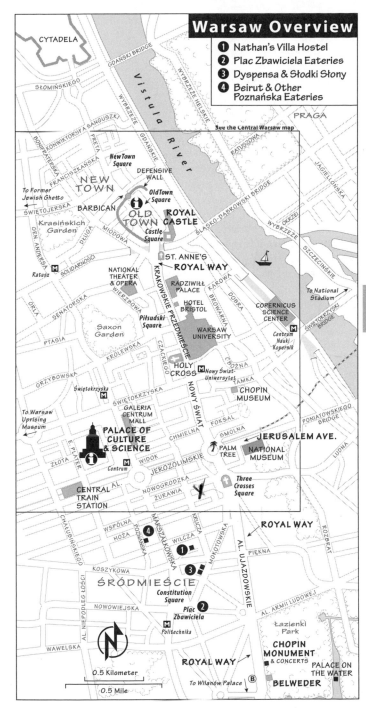

Warsaw Overview

1 Nathan's Villa Hostel
2 Plac Zbawiciela Eateries
3 Dyspensa & Słodki Słony
4 Beirut & Other
   Poznańska Eateries

See the Central Warsaw map

WARSAW

CYTADELA

SŁOMIŃSKIEGO

GDAŃSKI BRIDGE

Vistula River

WYBRZEŻE HELSKIE

PRAGA

PONIATRERSKA

FRANCISZKAŃSKA

KONWIKTORSKA

SANGUSZKI

FRETA

New Town Square

DEFENSIVE WALL

NEW TOWN

Old Town Square

GDAŃSKIE

RATUSZOWA

JAGIELLOŃSKA

To Former Jewish Ghetto

ŚWIĘTOJERSKA

BARBICAN

OLD TOWN

ROYAL CASTLE

OKRZEI

WYBRZEŻE

SZCZECIŃSKIE

Krasiński Garden

GEN. ANDERSA

DŁUGA

MIODOWA

Castle Square

ŚLĄSKO-DĄBROWSKI BRIDGE

St. Anne's

ROYAL WAY

KAROWA

DOBRA

ŚWIĘTOKRZYSKI BRIDGE

To National Stadium

Ratusz M

SOLIDARNOŚCI

ORLA

SENATORSKA

NATIONAL THEATER & OPERA

WIERZBOWA

KRAKOWSKIE PRZEDMIEŚCIE

RADZIWIŁŁ PALACE

HOTEL BRISTOL

COPERNICUS SCIENCE CENTER

BROWARNA

Saxon Garden

Piłsudski Square

WARSAW UNIVERSITY

Centrum Nauki Kopernik M

PTASIA

KRÓLEWSKA

CZACKIEGO

HOLY CROSS

OBOZNA

POZNAŃ

ŚWIĘTOKRZYSKI

GRZYBOWSKA

Nowy Świat-Uniwersytet M

ŚWIĘTOKRZYSKA

Świętokrzyska M

ŚWIĘTOKRZYSKA

GALERIA CENTRUM MALL

NOWY ŚWIAT

TAMKA

CHOPIN MUSEUM

To Warsaw Uprising Museum

PALACE OF CULTURE & SCIENCE

FOKSAL

SMOLNA

PONIATOWSKIEGO BRIDGE

CHMIELNA

JERUSALEM AVE.

E. PLATER

Centrum M

WIDOK

Palm Tree

NATIONAL MUSEUM

LUDNA

ZŁOTA

JEROZOLIMSKIE

AL.

NOWOGRODZKA

ŻURAWIA

Three Crosses Square

CENTRAL TRAIN STATION

CHAŁUBIŃSKIEGO

WSPÓLNA

MARSZAŁKOWSKA

KRUCZA

4 HOŻA

POZNAŃSKA

WILCZA

1

MOKOTOWSKA

ROYAL WAY

AL. UJAZDOWSKIE

PIĘKNA

ROZBRAT

KOSZYKOWA

3

AL. NIEPODLEG. ŁOŚCI

ŚRÓDMIEŚCIE

Constitution Square

NOWOWIEJSKA

Plac Zbawiciela 2

Łazienki Park

CHOPIN MONUMENT & CONCERTS

Politechnika M

PALACE ON THE WATER

WAWELSKA

0.5 Kilometer

ROYAL WAY

AL. ARMII LUDOWEJ

BELWEDER

0.5 Mile

To Wilanów Palace B

ARRIVAL IN WARSAW
By Train

Most trains arrive at the **central train station** (Warszawa Centralna), a renovated communist-era monstrosity next to the Palace of Culture and Science. It can be tricky to get your bearings here: Three parallel concourses run across the tracks, accessed by three different sets of escalators from each platform, creating an underground maze. But be patient: The underground area includes well-signed lockers, ticket windows, and lots of shops and eateries. To get your bearings, try to ride up on your platform's middle escalator, then follow signs to the vast, open **main hall** (follow signs for *main hall/hala główna*). Here you'll find a row of ticket windows, a rail customer service center, and (from outside) views of the adjacent Palace of Culture and Science and Złota 44 skyscrapers. If you have time to kill, you can walk across the street to the super-modern **Złote Tarasy Shopping Mall**.

Getting into Town: To reach the tourist zone and most of my recommended hotels, taxis are the easiest choice, while the bus is more economical (but more challenging to find).

Taxis wait outside the main hall (many are dishonest—look for one with a company logo and telephone number, and ask for an estimate up front; the fare should be no more than about 20-30 zł for most of my recommended hotels).

From the station, **bus #175** or **#128** takes you to the Royal Way and Old Town in about 10 minutes (see "Getting Around Warsaw," later). You can catch this bus—and others going in the same direction—in front of the skyscraper with the Hotel Marriott and big *Bridgestone* sign (across busy Jerusalem Avenue from the station). From the corridors under the main hall, carefully track *Aleje Jerozolimskie* signs. Several different exits are marked this way, but if you hone in on *Hotel Marriott* signs, you'll reach a pedestrian underpass that pops you out next to the bus stop. **Bus #160** also goes to the Old Town (though not via the Royal Way), but it departs from the opposite side of the station: To find its stop from the main hall, go out the side door toward *ul. Emilii Plater.* Before boarding your bus, buy a ticket at the machine near the stop—or get one in the underground zone at any kiosk marked *RUCH*.

Buying Train Tickets: Lining one wall of the main arrival hall *(hala główna)* are 16 **ticket windows.** A much more user-friendly **passenger service center** is in the opposite corner (daily 9:00-20:30). While it can be slower to buy tickets or make reservations here (take a number as you enter), staff members speak English and are generally more patient in helping explain your options. If you're in a hurry and the lines at the ticket windows in the main hall are way too long, you can find more ticket windows in the maze of corridors under the station. Allow yourself plenty of

Warsaw Essentials

English	Polish	Pronounced
Warsaw	Warszawa	vah-SHAH-vah
Central Train Station	Warszawa Centralna	vah-SHAH-vah tsehn-TRAHL-nah
Palace of Culture and Science	Pałac Kultury i Nauki (or simply "Pałac")	PAH-wahts kool-TOO-ree ee nah-OO-kee
New Town	Nowe Miasto	NOH-vay mee-AH-stoh
Old Town	Stare Miasto	STAH-reh mee-AH-stoh
Old Town Market Square	Rynek Starego Miasta	REE-nehk stah-RAY-goh mee-AH-stah
Royal Way	Szłak Królewski	shwock kroh-LEHV-skee
Popular restaurant street on Royal Way	Nowy Świat	NOH-vee SHVEE-aht
Attraction-lined street on Royal Way	Krakowskie Przedmieście	krah-KOHV-skyeh pzhehd-MYESH-cheh
Royal Castle	Zamek Królewski	ZAH-mehk kroh-LEHV-skee
Castle Square	Plac Zamkowy	plahts zahm-KOH-vee
Piłsudski Square	Plac Marszałka Józefa Piłsudskiego	plahts mar-SHAW-kah yoh-ZEH-fah pew-sood-SKYAY-goh
Łazienki Park	Park Łazienkowski	park wah-zhehn KOV-skee
Vistula River	Wisła	VEES-wah

WARSAW

time to wait in line to buy tickets. Some locals bypass these lines altogether and buy their tickets on the train for an extra charge (10 zł extra; find the conductor before he finds you).

Note that even if you have a rail pass, a reservation is still required on certain trains (including express trains to Kraków). If you're not sure, it's worth asking at the service center.

To get to your train, first find your way to the right platform

Warsaw at a Glance

▲▲**Royal Castle** Warsaw's best palace, rebuilt after World War II, but retaining its former opulence and many original furnishings. **Hours:** May-Sept Mon-Sat 10:00-18:00, Thu until 20:00, Sun 11:00-18:00; Oct-April Tue-Sat 10:00-16:00, Sun 11:00-16:00, closed Mon. See page 177.

▲▲**Old Town Market Square** Re-creation of Warsaw's glory days, with lots of colorful architecture. **Hours:** Always open. See page 182.

▲▲**National Museum** Collection of mostly Polish art, with unknown but worth-discovering works by Jan Matejko and the Młoda Polska (Art Nouveau) crew. **Hours:** Tue-Sun 10:00-18:00, Thu until 21:00, closed Mon. See page 185.

▲▲**Museum of the History of Polish Jews** High-tech exhibit on the full Jewish experience through Polish history, displayed in a purpose-built facility. **Hours:** Wed-Mon 10:00-18:00, Sat until 20:00, closed Tue. See page 196.

▲▲**Warsaw Uprising Museum** State-of-the-art space tracing the history of the Uprising and celebrating its heroes. **Hours:** July-Aug Wed-Mon 10:00-18:00, Thu until 20:00; Sept-June Mon and Wed-Fri 8:00-18:00, Thu until 20:00, Sat-Sun 10:00-18:00, closed Tue year-round. See page 199.

▲▲**Copernicus Science Center** Spiffy new science museum with well-explained, hands-on exhibits in English; Warsaw's best family activity. **Hours:** Tue-Fri 9:00-18:00, Sat-Sun 10:00-19:00, closed Mon. See page 190.

(*peron*, as noted on schedules), then keep an eye on both tracks *(tor)* for your train. Train info: Tel. 19436 (22-19436 from outside Warsaw), www.rozklad-pkp.pl.

By Plane

Warsaw's **Fryderyk Chopin International Airport** (Port Lotniczy im. Fryderyk Chopina, airport code: WAW) is about six miles southwest of the center. The airport has just one terminal (Terminal A), which is divided into five check-in areas split between two zones: the southern hall (areas A and B) and the northern hall (areas C, D, E). The airport is small and manageable; outside of the arrivals area, you'll find a TI, ATMs, car-rental offices, and exchange desks *(kantor)*. Airport info: tel. 22-650-4220, www.lotnisko-chopina.pl.

You have two options to get into town, both of which cost the

▲**Castle Square** Colorful spot with whiffs of old Warsaw—Royal Castle, monuments, and a chunk of the city wall—and cafés just off the square. **Hours:** Always open. See page 176.

▲**Łazienki Park** Lovely, sprawling green space with Chopin statue, peacocks, and Neoclassical buildings. **Hours:** Always open; wonderful outdoor Chopin concerts mid-May-late Sept Sun at 12:00 and 16:00. See page 202.

Chopin Museum Elegant old mansion featuring slick exhibits but not much substance about Chopin; occasional piano concerts worthwhile. **Hours:** Tue-Sun 11:00-20:00, closed Mon. See page 189.

Warsaw Museum Glimpse of the city before and after World War II, with excellent movie in English. **Hours:** Museum—Tue-Sun 10:00-20:00, off-season until 18:00, closed Mon year-round; Movie—Tue-Fri at 10:00 and 12:00; Sat-Sun at 12:00 and 14:00. See page 183.

Palace of Culture and Science Huge "Stalin Gothic" skyscraper with a more impressive exterior than interior, housing theaters, multiplex cinema, observation deck, and more. **Hours:** Observation deck—June-Aug daily 9:00-20:00, Fri-Sat until 24:00; Sept-May daily 9:00-18:00. See page 192.

Jewish Ghetto: Path of Remembrance Pilgrimage from Ghetto Heroes Square to the infamous Nazi "transfer spot" where Jews were sent to death camps. **Hours:** Always open. See page 197.

WARSAW

same (a standard 4.40-zł transit ticket, which also covers transfers for up to 75 minutes). The train is faster, while the bus makes more stops in the city center and may get you closer to your hotel. From the arrivals area, just follow signs to either option, and buy your ticket at the red machine before you board.

The **train** departs about every 15 minutes and takes 20-30 minutes. The route is operated by two different companies (SKM and KM)—just take the one that's departing first. Be ready for your stop: Half of the trains make fewer stops and take you to Centralna Station; the others make a few more stops and use the Warszawa Śródmieście station—which feeds into the same underground passages as Centralna (these trains also continue one more stop to the Warszawa Powiśle station, which is a bit closer to Nowy Świat and can be more convenient to some hotels than Śródmieście). Whether arriving at Centralna Station or Warszawa

Śródmieście, see the "By Train" arrival instructions, earlier.

Bus #175 departs every 15-20 minutes and runs into the city center (Centralna Station, the Royal Way, and Old Town, 30-45 minutes depending on traffic).

Only certain **taxi** companies are authorized to pick up arriving travelers at the airport; go to the official taxi stand and avoid random hucksters offering you a ride out front (these creeps are notorious for overcharging). The 30-minute taxi ride to the center shouldn't cost you more than 50 zł. The trip into town can take much longer during rush hour.

Modlin Airport (airport code: WMI), about 21 miles northwest of the city center, primarily serves budget airlines (especially Ryanair). The most direct option for getting to downtown Warsaw is **ModlinBus,** whose shuttle bus goes from the airport terminal to near the Palace of Culture and Science (price depends on how far ahead you buy ticket—can be 10-30 zł, 8-9/day, 1 hour, smart to book well ahead at www.modlinbus.com). A more frequent, well-coordinated **bus-plus-train connection** is operated by Koleje Mazowieckie (KM). You'll take a shuttle bus to Modlin's main train station, then hop on a train to Warsaw's Centralna Station (15 zł, 2-3/hour, 1-1.5 hours total, www.mazowieckie.com.pl). If you want to ride a **taxi** all the way into Warsaw, the maximum legitimate fare is 200 zł (or 250 zł at night). Airport info: www.modlinairport.pl.

GETTING AROUND WARSAW

By Public Transit: In this big city, it's essential to get a handle on public transportation. You'll rely mostly on buses and trams, but the new Metro line can be useful for reaching a few sights (the Warsaw Uprising Museum and the Copernicus Science Center). Everything is covered by the same tickets. A single ticket costs 4.40 zł (called *bilet jednorazowy,* good for one trip up to 75 minutes). But most trips you'll be taking should last no longer than 20 minutes, so you can save a zloty by buying a 3.40-zł "20-minute city travelcard" (*bilet 20-minutowy;* also available in 40- and 60-minute versions). A 24-hour travelcard *(bilet dobowy)*—which pays for itself if you take at least five trips—costs 15 zł. Ticket machines at most major stops and on board some trams are easy to use (English instructions, coins and small bills accepted). Or you can buy tickets at any kiosk with a *RUCH* sign. Be sure to validate your ticket as you board by inserting it in the little yellow box. Transit info: www.ztm.waw.pl.

Most of the city's major attractions line up on a single axis, the Royal Way, which is served by several different buses (but no trams). **Bus #175,** particularly useful on arrival, links Chopin Airport, the central train station, the Royal Way, and Old Town.

Once you're in town, the designed-for-tourists **bus #180** conveniently connects virtually all of the significant sights and neighborhoods: the former Jewish Ghetto, Castle Square/Old Town, the Royal Way, Łazienki Park, and Wilanów Palace (south of the center). This particularly user-friendly bus lists sights in English on the posted schedule inside (other buses don't). Those two buses, as well as buses **#116, #128, #195,** and **#222,** go along the most interesting stretch of the Royal Way (between Jerusalem Avenue and Castle Square in the Old Town). **Bus #178** conveniently connects Castle Square to the Warsaw Uprising Museum. Bus routes beginning with "E" (marked in red on schedules) are express, so they go long distances without stopping; these operate only off-season (Oct-May).

Note that on Saturdays and Sundays in summer (June-Sept), the Nowy Świat section of the Royal Way is closed to traffic, so the above routes detour along a parallel street.

Warsaw's two-line **Metro** system is handy for commuters, but less so for visitors. Still, it can be useful for some trips. Line 1 runs roughly parallel to the Royal Way, several blocks to the west; the most useful stops for tourists are Centrum (near the Palace of Culture and Science) and Świętokrzyska (where it crosses line 2). The new line 2 (which runs deep under the Vistula River) cuts through the city from west to east, making stops near some points of interest: near the Warsaw Uprising Museum (Rondo Daszyńskiego stop); at Świętokrzyska (a transfer station between the two lines); on Nowy Świat (near the Copernicus Monument, Nowy Świat-Uniwersytet stop); near the Copernicus Science Center, by the river (Centrum Nauki Kopernik stop); and at the National Stadium (Stadion Narodowy stop).

By Taxi: As in most big Eastern European cities, it's wise to use only cabs that are clearly marked with a company logo and telephone number (or call your own: Locals like City Taxi, tel. 19459; MPT Radio Taxi, tel. 19191; or Ele taxi, tel. 22-811-1111). All official taxis have similar rates: 8 zł to start, then 3 zł per kilometer (4.50 zł after 22:00 or in the suburbs). The drop fee may be higher if you catch the cab in front of a fancy hotel.

By Bike: The city is trying to be bike-friendly. Because there are few actual bike paths, bikes share the sidewalks with pedestrians. Considering how the city is both level and spread out, biking can be a joy. The TI can direct you to bike-rental offices, and some hotels have loaner bikes.

Tours in Warsaw

Walking Tours

Each year, new companies crop up offering **walking tours** in Warsaw. These tend to have one of two approaches: A "free" tour of the main sights (with generous tipping expected); or communism-themed tours, often with a ride to a gloomy apartment-block area for a taste of the Red old days. None of these companies are firmly established, so survey the latest options, do some homework (check online reviews), and pick one that suits your interests. The TI and most hotels have brochures.

Private Guides

Having a talented local historian as your guide in this city, with such a complex and powerful story to tell, greatly enhances your experience. I've worked with two excellent young guides: the smart and charming **Monika Oleśko** (180 zł/3 hours, 350 zł/6 hours, mobile 784-832-718, warsawteller.wordpress.com, olesko.monika@gmail.com) and the professorial **Hubert Pawlik** (500 zł or €125 for 5 hours on foot or with his car, mobile 502-298-105, www.warsaw-guide.waw.pl). Hubert's big, comfy SUV can fit a small group. Both Monica and Hubert can do theme tours or tailor the time to your interests.

Bus Tours

Two competing companies offer hop-on, hop-off bus tours around Warsaw (60 zł/24 hours, 80 zł/48 hours): CitySightseeing (with red buses) and City-Tour (with yellow buses). While Warsaw's spread-out landscape makes it a natural for a hop-on, hop-off bus, both of these companies have limited frequency (about one bus each hour, and much less than that outside of summer), making them less enticing.

Warsaw's Royal Way Walk

The Royal Way (Szłak Królewski) is the six-mile route that the kings of Poland used to travel from their main residence (at Castle Square in the Old Town) to their summer home (Wilanów Palace, south of the center and not worth visiting). This self-guided walk covers a one-mile section of the Royal Way in the heart of the city—from the Palm Tree Circle to the castle. This is a busy, mostly pedestrian boulevard with two different names: At the south end, hip and vibrant **Nowy Świat** offers lots of shops and restaurants and a good glimpse of urban Warsaw; to the north, and ending at the Old Town, **Krakowskie Przedmieście** is lined with historic landmarks and is better for sightseeing.

Since this spine connects most of my recommended hotels, restaurants, and sights, you'll almost certainly use it—on foot or by bus—sometime during your trip (key buses are noted earlier, under "Getting Around Warsaw"). This walk should make your commute more interesting. Not counting sightseeing stops, figure about 15 minutes to walk along Nowy Świat ("Part 1"), then another 30 minutes along Krakowskie Przedmieście to the Old Town ("Part 2").

PART 1: PALM TREE CIRCLE AND NOWY ŚWIAT

• *Start this walk at the traffic circle officially named for Charles de Gaulle, but colloquially known as...*

Palm Tree Circle

This is one of the city's main intersections, marked by the quirky and now iconic palm tree. Stand near the communist-era monument under the spruce trees, on the curb opposite (kitty-corner) the biggest building.

You're standing at the intersection of two major boulevards: Nowy Świat (where we're heading next) and **Jerusalem Avenue** (**aleja Jerozolimskie,** which leads from the central train station across the river). This street once led to a Jewish settlement called New Jerusalem. Like so much else in Warsaw, it's changed names many times. Between the World Wars, it became "May 3rd Avenue," celebrating Poland's 1791 constitution (Europe's first). But this was too nationalistic for the occupying Nazis, who called it simply Bahnhofstrasse ("Train Station Street"). Then the communists switched it back to "Jerusalem," strangely disregarding the religious connotations of that name. (Come on, guys—what about a good, old-fashioned "Stalin Avenue"?)

The strikingly wide boulevards are part the city's post-WWII Soviet rebuilding. Communist urban planners felt that eight-to twelve-lane roads were ideal for worker pageantry like big May Day parades...and, when the workers aren't happy, for Soviet tanks to thunder around, maintaining order.

You can't miss the giant, out-of-place **palm tree** in the middle of Jerusalem Avenue. When a local artist went to the real Jerusalem, she was struck at how many palm trees she saw there. She decided it was only appropriate that one should grace Warsaw's own little stretch of "Jerusalem." This artificial palm tree went up years ago

as a temporary installation. It was highly controversial, dividing the neighborhood. One snowy winter day, the pro-palm tree faction—who appreciated the way the tree spiced up this otherwise predictable metropolis—camped out here in bikinis and beachwear to show their support. They prevailed, and the tree still continues to bring a little sunshine to gray Warsaw.

The big, blocky building across the street (behind statue of de Gaulle) was the **headquarters of the Communist Party,** built in 1948. *Nowy Świat* translates as "New World," leading to a popular communist-era joke: What do you see when you turn your back on the Communist Party? A "New World." Ironically, when the economy was privatized in 1991, this building became home to Poland's stock exchange. To make matters even worse, the country's only dealership for Ferraris—certainly not an automobile for the proletariat—moved in downstairs.

On the corner, in front of the former Communist Party HQ, a statue of **Charles de Gaulle** strides confidently up the street. A gift from the government of France, this celebrates the military tactician who came to Warsaw's rescue when the Red Army invaded from the USSR after World War I.

To the left of the Communist Party building is the vast **National Museum**—a good place for a Polish art lesson (more interesting than it sounds—see the self-guided tour later, under "Sights in Warsaw").

Before walking down Nowy Świat, notice the small but powerful **monument** 20 yards behind you. In 1956, this was dedicated to the "Poles who fought for People's Poland"—with a strong communist connotation. In a classic example of Socialist Realism, the communists appropriated a religious theme that Poles were inclined to embrace (this *pietà* composition)...and politicized it. But in 2014, the statue was rededicated to the "*partyzantom* who fought for free Poland in World War II." "Partisan" was a bad word in the 1950s, when it was used to describe the soldiers of the Polish Home Army—which fought against both the Nazis and the Soviets.

The little **park** stretching right from the monument is meaningful to older locals who remember when it first opened in 1955. That was a celebratory year as, 10 years after the city's destruction, Warsaw was reawakening and small gestures like this park were making life more livable for its residents.

• *From here, turn your back to the Communist Party building and head into a new world—down Nowy Świat—to the first intersection. As you stroll, notice how massive and intense Warsaw suddenly becomes more intimate and charming.*

Nowy Świat

This charming shopping boulevard is lined with boutiques, cafés, and restaurants—it's the most upscale, elegant-feeling part of the

city. Before World War II, Nowy Świat was Warsaw's most popular neighborhood. And today, once again, rents are higher here than anywhere else in town. While most tourists flock into the Old Town, Varsovians and visiting businesspeople prefer this zone. The city has worked hard to revitalize this strip with broader, pedestrian-friendly sidewalks, flower boxes, and old-time lampposts.

Look down the street and notice the consistent architecture. In the 1920s, this was anything but cohesive: an eclectic and decadent strip of Art Deco facades, full of individualism. Rather than rebuild in that "trouble-causing" style, the communists used an idealized, more conservative (less capitalistic), Neoclassical style, which feels more linked with the 1820s than the 1920s.

Ulica Chmielna, the first street to the left, is an appealing pedestrian boutique street leading to Emil Wedel's chocolate heaven (a five-minute walk away; described later, under "Eating in Warsaw"). Between here and the Palace of Culture and Science stretches one of Warsaw's trendiest shopping neighborhoods (culminating at the Galleria Centrum mall, just across from the Palace).

Across the street from Chmielna (on the right) is the street called **Foksal,** one of Warsaw's most pleasant and trendy dining zones. On a balmy summer evening, this street is filled with chatty al fresco diners, sipping drinks and nibbling at plates of cutting-edge international cuisine.

A few steps farther down Nowy Świat, on the left, don't miss the recommended **A. Blikle** pastry shop and café—*the* place in Poland to buy sweets, especially *pączki* (rose-flavored jelly doughnuts). Step inside for dose of the 1920s: good-life Art Deco decor and historic photos. Or, if you're homesick for Starbucks, drop in to one of the many gourmet coffee shops that line this stretch of Nowy Świat—with American-style lattes "to go" (one of many customs that the Poles have adopted from American culture, which they adore).

A half-block down the street (on the left, at #39) is a rare surviving bit of pre-glitz Nowy Świat: Bar Mleczny Familijny, a classic **milk bar**—a government-subsidized cafeteria filled with locals seeking a cheap meal (an interesting cultural artifact, but not recommended for a meal). Don't be surprised if it's gone by

WARSAW

Central Warsaw

MIĘDZYPARKOWA

Rondo Babka

Z. SŁOMIŃSKIEGO

PARKING LOT WITH FORMER GHETTO WALL

STAWKI

KONWIKTORSKA SANGUSZKI

10

UMSCHLAGPLATZ MONUMENT

MURANÓW
(Former Jewish Ghetto)

FRANCISZKAŃSKA

FORMER SS HQ

NISKA

DUBOIS

BUNKER

OKOPOWA

AL. JANA PAWŁA II

STAWKI

MUSEUM OF THE HISTORY OF POLISH JEWS

MIŁA

ZAMENHOFA

LEWARTOWSKIEGO

GHETTO HEROES SQUARE

Muranów

T

Plac Krasinskich

M. ANIELEWICZA

B Nalewki

Krasińskich Garden

KARMELICKA

GEN. WŁ. ANDERSA

Ratusz **M**

Accommodations
1 Hotel Le Régina
2 Novotel
3 Chopin Boutique B&B
4 Duval Apartments
5 Castle Inn
6 Between Us B&B
7 Royal Route Residence & Old Town Apts. Office
8 Hotel Harenda
9 Zgoda Apartment Hotel
10 Ibis Warszawa Stare Miasto
11 Oki Doki Hostel
12 Szkolne Schronisko Hostel

Eateries
13 Papaya Restaurant
14 Kamanda Lwowska
15 Wiking Milk Bar
16 Mleczarnia Jerozolimska
17 Borpince, Krokiecik & Restauracja Zgoda
18 A. Blikle Bakery
19 E. Wedel Pijalnia Czekolady (Chocolate Shop)
20 Butchery & Wine
21 Warszawa Powiśle Café

Plac Bankowy

SOLIDARNOŚCI

ELEKTORALNA

PTASIA

PL. MIROWSKI

Plac Grzybowski

AL. JANA PAWŁA II

GRZYBOWSKA

WALICÓW

CIEPŁA

TWARDA

ŚWIĘTOKRZYSKA

GRZYBOWSKA

Muzeum Powstania **T** Warszawskiego **B**

ŁUCKA

ŻELAZNA

PROSTA

ZŁOTA

ZŁOTE TARASY MALL

PRZYOKOPOWA

TOWAROWA

WARSAW UPRISING MUSEUM

Rondo Daszynskiego **M**

Rondo Daszyńskiego

WRONIA

SIENNA

PAŃSKA

ZŁOTA

MIEDZIANA

Dworzec Centralny Bus #160 **B**

CENTRAL TRAIN STATION

PROSTA

CHMIELNA

Dw. Centralny **T**

Dworzec Centralny Bus #175 **B**

400 Meters

400 Yards

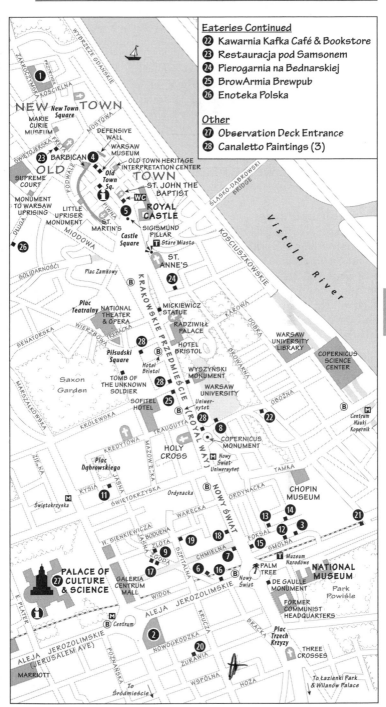

Eateries Continued
22 Kawarnia Kafka Café & Bookstore
23 Restauracja pod Samsonem
24 Pierogarnia na Bednarskiej
25 BrowArmia Brewpub
26 Enoteka Polska

Other
27 Observation Deck Entrance
28 Canaletto Paintings (3)

WARSAW

the time you visit; in this high-rent district, it's unlikely that these few remaining holdovers from the old days will survive for much longer.

Eat and shop your way along Nowy Świat. About one more block down, **Ordynacka street** (on the right) leads downhill to the Chopin Museum, worth considering for musical pilgrims.

• *Continuing along Nowy Świat through a duller stretch, you'll walk alongside a hulking, gloomy building before popping out in a pleasant square with a big Copernicus statue.*

PART 2: KRAKOWSKIE PRZEDMIEŚCIE
• *The street name changes to Krakowskie Przedmieście at the big...*

Copernicus Statue
This statue, by the great Danish sculptor Bertel Thorvaldsen, stands in front of the Polish Academy of Science. Mikołaj Kopernik (1473-1543) was born in Toruń and went to college in Kraków. The Nazis stole his statue and took it to Germany (which, like Poland, claims Copernicus as its own). Now it's back where it belongs. The concentric circles radiating out from the statue represent the course of the planets' orbits, from Mercury to Saturn.

Just to Copernicus' left is a low-profile, black-marble **Chopin bench**—one of many scattered around the center. These benches mark points related to his life (in this case, his sister lived across the street). Each of these benches plays Chopin's music with the push of a button (though because of passing traffic, this one is tough to hear).

In front of the statue, in the glass case, find a replica of a **Canaletto painting** of this same street scene in 1778, and compare it to today's reality. As the national archives were destroyed, city builders referred to historic paintings like these for guidance after WWII. You'll see other Canaletto replicas like this one scattered around the city.

• *Across from Copernicus, the Church of the Holy Cross is worth a look.*

Church of the Holy Cross (Kościół Św. Krzyża)
We'll pass many churches along this route, but the **Church of the Holy Cross** is unique (free entry). Composer Fryderyk Chopin's heart is inside one of the pillars of the nave (first big pillar on the left, look for the marker). After two decades of exile in France, Chopin's final wish was to have his heart brought back to his native

Poland after his death. During World War II, the heart was hidden away in the countryside for safety. Check out the bright gold chapel, located on the left as you face the altar, near the front of the church. It's dedicated to a saint whom Polish Catholics believe helps them with "desperate and hopeless causes." People praying here are likely dealing with some tough issues. The beads draped from the altarpieces help power their prayers, and the many little brass plaques are messages of thanks for prayers answered.

In the back-left corner (as you face the altar) is a chapel dedicated to Poland's favorite son, St. John Paul II. His ghostly image appears out of the wall; beneath him is a rock inscribed with the words *Tu es Petrus* (Latin for "You are Peter"—what Jesus said when he made St. Peter the first-ever pope), embedded with a capsule containing JPII's actual blood. Just opposite, in the back-right corner, behind the giant barbed wire, is a memorial to the 22,000 Polish POWs—mostly officers and prominent civilians—massacred by Soviet soldiers in 1940 near Katyń, a village in today's Russia. Stalin was determined to decapitate Poland's military intelligentsia in a ruthless mass killing, which Poles have never forgotten.

• *Leaving the church, imagine how locals would relate to the 19th-century, bronze-and-granite...*

Statue of Christ Bearing the Cross

In front, a placard reads, "Lift up your hearts." Even as Warsaw bore the burden of Russian occupation, this statue inspired them to be strong and not lose hope. It was one of many crosses they bore: a Catholic nation pinched between Orthodox Russians and Protestant Germans.

• *Cross the street (appreciating how pedestrian-friendly it's become in recent years—this used to be a game of Frogger) and continue left.*

Warsaw University

A long block up the street on the right, you'll see the gates (marked *Uniwersytet*) to the main campus of **Warsaw University,** founded in 1816. This lively student district has plenty of bookstores and cafeterias. Venture in, and you'll find cheap food and English-speaking students who'd love to talk.

The 18th century was a time of great political decline for Poland, as a series of incompetent foreign kings mishandled crises and squandered funds. But ironically, it was also Warsaw's biggest economic boom time. Along this boulevard, aristocratic families of the period built **mansions**—most of them destroyed during World War II and rebuilt since. Some have curious flourishes (just past the university on the right, look for the doorway supported by four bearded brutes admiring their overly defined abs). Over time, many of these families donated their mansions to the university. (Across the street on the corner, look for the recommended BrowArmia brewpub, with some of the best people-watching al fresco tables on the Royal Way.)

• *The bright-yellow church a block up from the university, on the right, is the...*

Church of the Nuns of the Visitation (Kośicół Sióstr Wizytek)

This Rococo confection from 1761 is the only church on this walk that survived World War II, and is notable because Chopin was the organist here in 1825-26.

The monument in front of the church commemorates **Cardinal Stefan Wyszyński,** who was the Polish primate (the head of the Polish Catholic Church) from 1948 to 1981. He took this post soon after the arrival of the communists, who opposed the Church, but also realized it would be risky for them to shut down the churches in such an ardently religious country. The Communist Party and the Catholic Church coexisted tensely in Poland, and when Wyszyński protested a Stalinist crackdown in 1953, he was arrested and imprisoned. Three years later, in a major victory for the Church, Wyszyński was released. He continued to fight the communists, becoming a great hero of the Polish people in their struggle against the regime. Across the street is another then-and-now Canaletto illustration.

• *Farther up (on the right, past the park) is the elegant, venerable...*

Hotel Bristol

A striking building with a round turret on its corner, the Hotel Bristol was used by the Nazis as a VIP hotel and bordello, and survived World War II. If you wander through any fancy Warsaw lobby...make it this one. Step in like you're staying here and explore its fine public spaces, with fresh Art Deco and Art Nouveau flourishes. The café in front retains its Viennese atmosphere, but the *pièce de résistance* is the stunning Column Bar deeper in,

past the dramatically chandeliered lounge.

• *Leave the Royal Way briefly here to reach Piłsudski Square (a block away on the left, up the street opposite Hotel Bristol).*

Piłsudski Square
(plac Marszałka Józefa Piłsudskiego)

The vast, empty-feeling **Piłsudski Square** has been important Warsaw real estate for centuries, constantly changing with the times. In the 1890s, the Russians who controlled this part of Poland began construction of a huge and magnificent Orthodox cathedral on this spot. But soon after it was completed, Poland regained its independence, and anti-Russian sentiments ran hot. So in the 1920s, just over a decade after the cathedral went up, it was torn down. During the Nazi occupation, this square took the name "Adolf-Hitler-Platz." Under the communists, it was Zwycięstwa, meaning "Victory" (of the Soviets over Hitler's fascism). When the regime imposed martial law in 1981, the people of Warsaw silently protested by filling the square with a giant cross made of flowers. The huge **plaque** in the ground near the road (usually marked by flowers) commemorates two monumental communist-era Catholic events on this square: John Paul II's first visit as pope to his homeland on June 2, 1979; and the May 31, 1981 funeral of Cardinal Stefan Wyszyński, whom we met across the street. The cross nearby also honors the 1979 papal visit, with one of his most famous and inspiring quotes to his countrymen: "Let thy spirit descend, let thy spirit descend, and renew the face of the earth—of *this* earth" (meaning Poland, in a just-barely-subtle-enough dig against the communist regime that was tolerating his visit). More recently, on April 17, 2010, more than 100,000 Poles convened on this square for a more solemn occasion: a memorial service for President Lech Kaczyński, who had died in a tragic plane crash in Russia.

Stand in the center, near the giant plaque, with the Royal Way at your back, for this quick spin-tour orientation: Ahead are the Tomb of the Unknown Soldier and Saxon Garden (explained later); 90 degrees to the right is the old National Theater, eclipsed by a modern business center/parking garage; another 90 degrees to the right is a statue of Piłsudski (which you passed to get here—described later); and 90 more degrees to the right is the Sofitel—formerly the Victoria Hotel, the ultimate plush, top-of-the-top hotel where all communist-era VIPs stayed. To the right of the hotel, on the horizon, you can see Warsaw's newly emerging skyline. The imposing Palace of Culture and Science, which once stood alone over the city, is now joined by a cluster of brand-new skyscrapers, giving Warsaw a Berlin-esque vibe befitting its important role as a business center of the "New Europe."

Walk to the fragment of colonnade by the park that marks the **Tomb of the Unknown Soldier** (Grób Nieznanego Żołnierza). The colonnade was once part of a much larger palace built by the Saxon prince electors (Dresden's Augustus the Strong and his son), who became kings of Poland in the 18th century. After the palace was destroyed in World War II, this fragment was kept to memorialize Polish soldiers. The names of key battles over 1,000 years are etched into the columns, the urns contain dirt from major Polish battlefields, and the two soldiers are pretty stiff. Every hour on the hour, they do a crisp Changing of the Guard—which, poignantly, honors those who have perished in this country, so shaped by wars against foreign invaders.

Just behind the Tomb is the stately **Saxon Garden** (Ogród Saski), inhabited by genteel statues, gorgeous flowers, and a spurt-

ing fountain. This park was also built by the Saxon kings of Poland. Like most foreign kings, Augustus the Strong and his son cared little for their Polish territory, building gardens like these for themselves instead of invest- ing in more pressing needs. Poles say that foreign kings such as Augustus did nothing but "eat, drink, and loosen their belts" (it rhymes in Polish). According to Poles, these selfish absentee kings were the culprits in Poland's eventual decline. But they do appreci- ate having such a fine venue for a Sunday stroll.

Walk back out toward the Royal Way, stopping at the statue you passed earlier. In 1995, the square was again renamed—this

time for **Józef Piłsudski** (1867-1935), the guy with the big walrus mous- tache. With the help of a French captain named Charles de Gaulle (whom we met earlier), Piłsudski forced the Russian Bolsheviks out of Poland in 1920 in the so-called Miracle on the Vistula. Piłsudski is credited with creating a once-again-independent Poland after more than a century of foreign oppres- sion, and he essentially ran Poland as a virtual dictator after World War I. Of course, under the communists, Piłsudski was swept under the rug. But since 1989, he has enjoyed a renais- sance as many Poles' favorite prototype anti-communist hero (his name adorns streets, squares, and bushy-mustachioed monuments all over the country).

• *Return to Hotel Bristol, turn left, and continue your Royal Way walk.*

Radziwiłł Palace

Next door to the hotel, you'll see the huge **Radziwiłł Palace.** The Warsaw Pact was signed here in 1955, officially uniting the Soviet satellite states in a military alliance against NATO. This building has also, from time to time, served as the Polish "White House."

• *Beyond Radziwiłł Palace, on the right, you'll reach a park with a...*

Statue of Adam Mickiewicz

Poland's national poet, Adam Mickiewicz spearheaded Poland's cultural survival during more than a century when the country disappeared from maps—absorbed by Austria, Prussia, and Russia. This was an age when underdog nations (and peoples without nations) all over Europe had their own national revival movements. The statue was erected in 1898 with permission from the Russian czar, as long as the people paid for it themselves. It's still an important part of community life: Polish high school students have a big formal ball (like a prom) 100 days before graduation. After the ball, if students come here and hop around the statue on one leg, it's supposed to bring them good luck on their finals. Mickiewicz, for his part, looks like he's suffering from a heart attack—perhaps in response to the impressively ugly National Theater and Opera a block in front of him.

• *Continue to the end of the Royal Way, marked by the big pink palace. Just before the castle, on your right, is...*

St. Anne's Church

This church is Rococo, with playful capitals inside and out and a fine pulpit shaped like the prow of a ship—complete with a big anchor. The richly ornamented apse, behind the altar, survived World War II. This church offers organ concerts nearly daily in summer (see "Entertainment in Warsaw," later).

For a scenic finale to your Royal Way stroll, climb the 150 steps of the **view tower** by the church (5 zł, generally open daily 10:00-18:00, in summer until 22:00, closed in bad winter weather). You'll be rewarded with

WARSAW

excellent views—particularly of Castle Square and the Old Town. From up top, visually retrace your steps along the Royal Way, and notice the emerging skyline surrounding the Palace of Culture and Science. The tower also affords a good look at the Praga district across the river, where the Red Army waited for the Nazis to level Warsaw during the uprising. Help was so close at hand...but stayed right where it was.

• *Just across from the view tower entrance, look for another Chopin bench. From St. Anne's Church, it's just another block—past inviting art galleries and restaurants—to Castle Square, the TI, and the start of the Old Town.*

Sights in Warsaw

THE OLD TOWN

In 1945, not a building remained standing in Warsaw's "Old" Town (Stare Miasto). Everything you see is rebuilt, mostly finished by 1956. Some think the Old Town seems artificial and phony, in a Disney World kind of way. For others, the painstaking postwar reconstruction feels just right, with Old World squares and lanes charming enough to give Kraków a run for its money. Before 1989, stifled by communist repression and choking on smog, the Old Town was an empty husk of its historic self. But now, the outdoor restaurants and market stalls have returned, and Varsovians and tourists are out strolling.

These sights are listed in order from south to north, and linked with walking directions, beginning at Castle Square and ending at the entrance to the New Town. For the best route from the "downtown" at Jerusalem Avenue to the Old Town, see "Warsaw's Royal Way Walk," earlier.

▲Castle Square (Plac Zamkowy)

This lively square is dominated by the big, pink Royal Castle that is the historic heart of Warsaw's political power.

After the second great Polish dynasty—the Jagiellonians—died out in 1572, it was replaced by the Republic of Nobles (about 10 percent of the population), which elected various foreign kings to their throne. The guy on the 72-foot-tall **pillar** is Sigismund III, the first Polish king from the Swedish Waza family. In 1596, he relocated the capital from Kraków to Warsaw. This move made sense, since Warsaw was closer to the center of 16th-century Poland (which had expanded to the east), and because the city had gained political importance over the past 30 years as the meeting point of the Sejm, or parliament of nobles. Along the right side of the castle, notice the two previous versions of this pillar lying on a lawn. The first one, from 1644, was falling apart and had to be replaced in 1887 by a new one made of granite. In 1944, a Nazi tank broke this second pillar—a symbolic piece of Polish heritage—into the four pieces (still pockmarked with bullet holes) that you see here today. As Poland rebuilt, its citizens put Sigismund III back on his pillar. Past the pillars are great views of Warsaw's brand-new, red-and-white National Stadium across the river.

Across the square from the castle, you'll see the partially reconstructed **defensive wall.** This rampart once enclosed the entire Old Town. Like all of Poland, Warsaw has seen invasion from all sides.

Explore the café-lined lanes that branch off Castle Square. Street signs indicate the year that each lane was originally built.

The first street is **ulica Piwna** ("Beer Street"), where you'll find **St. Martin's Church** (Kościół Św. Martina, on the left). Run by Franciscan nuns, this church has a simple, modern interior. Walk up the aisle and find the second pillar on the right. Notice the partly destroyed crucifix—it's the only church artifact that survived World War II. Across the street and closer to Castle Square, admire the carefully carved doorway of the house called *pod Gołębiami* ("Under Doves")—dedicated to the memory of an old woman who fed birds amidst the Old Town rubble after World War II.

Back on Castle Square, find the white **plaque** on the wall (at plac Zamkowy 15/19). It explains that 50 Poles were executed by Nazis on this spot on September 2, 1944. You'll see plaques like this all over the Old Town, each one commemorating victims or opponents of the Nazis. The brick planter under the plaque is often filled with fresh flowers to honor the victims.

• *Turn your attention to the...*

▲▲Royal Castle (Zamek Królewski)

A castle has stood here since the Mazovian dukes built a wooden version in the 14th century. It has grown through the ages, being

rebuilt and remodeled by many different kings. When Warsaw became the capital in 1596, this massive building served a dual purpose: It was both the king's residence and the meeting place of the parliament (Sejm). It reached its peak under Stanisław August Poniatowski—the final Polish king—who imported artists and architects to spiff up the interior, leaving his mark all over the place. Luftwaffe bombs destroyed it in World War II (only one wall remained standing). Rebuilding stalled because Stalin considered it a palace for the high-class elites. It was finally rebuilt in the more moderate 1970s, funded by local donations.

Warsaw's Royal Castle has a gorgeous interior—the most opulent I've seen in Poland. Many of the furnishings are original (hidden away when it became clear the city would be demolished in World War II). A visit to the castle is like perusing a great Polish history textbook. In fact, you'll likely see grade-school classes sitting cross-legged on the floors. Watching the teachers quizzing eager young history buffs, try to imagine what it's like to be a young Pole, with such a tumultuous history.

Cost and Hours: 22 zł, free on Sun; open May-Sept Mon-Sat 10:00-18:00, Thu until 20:00, Sun 11:00-18:00; Oct-April Tue-Sat 10:00-16:00, Sun 11:00-16:00, closed Mon; last entry one hour before closing; plac Zamkowy 4, tel. 22-355-5170, www.zamek-krolewski.pl. A public WC is on the courtyard just around the corner of the castle.

Tours: The castle has a well-produced audioguide (17 zł, worth the extra cost) and good English information posted throughout. For the basics, use my commentary to follow the one-way route through the castle.

❍ Self-Guided Tour: Because the castle visit procedure is always changing, it's possible you won't see these rooms in this exact order; if that happens, match the labels in each room to the corresponding text below.

Entering the courtyard, go to the right to buy tickets, then cross to the opposite side to tour the interior. (If you want an audioguide, go downstairs to rent it first.) Head up the stairs and follow *Castle Route* signs.

Start in the Oval Gallery, then head into the **Council Chamber,** where a "Permanent Council" consisting of the king, 18 senators, and 18 representatives met to chart Poland's course. Next is the **Great Assembly Hall,** heavy with marble and chandeliers. The statues of Apollo and Minerva flanking the main door are modeled after King Stanisław August Poniatowski and Catherine the Great of Russia, respectively. (The king enjoyed a youthful romantic dalliance with Catherine on a trip to Russia, and never quite seemed to get over her...much to his wife's consternation, I'm sure.)

The **Knights' Hall** features the Polish Hall of Fame, with paintings of great events and busts and portraits of VIPs—Very Important Poles. The statue of Chronos—god of time, with the globe on his shoulders—is actually a functioning clock, though now it's stopped at 11:15 to commemorate the exact time in 1944 when the Nazis bombed this palace to bits. Just off this hall is the **Marble Room,** with more portraits of Polish greats ringing the top of the room. Above the fireplace is a portrait of Stanisław August Poniatowski.

Continuing through the Knights' Hall, you'll wind up in the remarkable **Throne Room.** Notice the crowned white eagles, the

symbol of Poland, decorating the banner behind the throne. The Soviets didn't allow anything royal or aristocratic, so postwar restorations came with crown-less eagles. Only after 1989 were these eagles crowned again. Peek into the **Conference Room,** with portraits of other major European monarchs—Russia's Catherine the Great, England's George III, and France's Louis XVI—in whose esteemed royal league Stanisław August Poniatowski liked to consider himself.

After four more grand rooms (including the King's Bedroom, with a gorgeous silk canopy over the bed), you'll enter the **Canaletto Room,** filled with canvases of late-18th-century Warsaw painted in exquisite detail by this talented artist. (This Canaletto, also known for his panoramas of Dresden, was the nephew of another more famous artist with the same nickname, known for painting Venice's canals.) Paintings like these helped post-WWII restorers resurrect the city from its rubble. To the left, on the lower wall, the biggest canvas features the view of Warsaw from the Praga district across the river; pick out the few landmarks that are still standing (or, more precisely, have been resurrected). The castle you're standing in dominates the center of the painting, overlooking the river. Notice the artist's self-portrait in the lower-left. Opposite, on the right side of the room, is Canaletto's depiction of the election of Stanisław August Poniatowski as king, in a field outside Warsaw (notice the empty throne in the middle of the group). Among the assembled crowd, each flag represents a different Polish province.

From here, head left of the big "view of Warsaw" painting into the **side chapel,** reserved for the king. In the box to the left of the altar is the heart of Tadeusz Kościuszko, a hero of both the American Revolution and the Polish struggle against the Partitions.

As you cross over to the other part of the castle, you'll pass through the **Four Seasons Gallery** (with some fine but faded Gobelin tapestries) before entering a few rooms occupied by the houses of parliament—a reminder that this "castle" wasn't just the king's house, but also the meeting place of the legislature. In the

WARSAW

Parliamentary Chambers, notice the maps showing Poland's constantly in-flux borders—a handy visual aid for the many school groups who visit here.

After several rooms, you'll reach the grand **Senators' Chamber,** with the king's throne, surrounded by different coats of arms. Each one represents a region that was part of Poland during its Golden Age, back when it was united with Lithuania and its territory stretched from the Baltic to the Black Sea (see the map on the wall). In this room, Poland adopted its 1791 constitution

(notice the replica in the display case to the left of the throne). It was the first in Europe, written soon after America's and just months before France's. And, like the Constitution of the United States, it was very progressive, based on the ideals of the Enlightenment. But when the final Partitions followed in 1793 and 1795, Poland was divided between neighboring powers and ceased to exist as a country until 1918—so the constitution was never fully put into action.

Next, the **Crown Princes Room** features paintings by Jan Matejko that capture the excitement surrounding the adoption of this ill-fated constitution. The next room has another Matejko painting: King Stefan Batory negotiating with Ivan the Terrible's envoys to break their siege of a Russian town. Notice the hussars—fearsome Polish soldiers wearing winged armor. Finally, you'll wind through more rooms with yet more paintings of great historical events and portraits of famous Poles.

Other Castle Sights: Sharing an entrance lobby with the main castle interiors, the **Gallery of Paintings, Sculpture, and**

Decorative Arts isn't worth the 20-zł extra admission fee for most visitors; save your time and money for the National Museum instead. But art lovers may be interested to see the 36 paintings of the Landkrońoski Collection. These originally belonged to Stanisław August Poniatowski, who sold them to an aristocratic family that eventually presented them to Poland as a gift. The prize of this collection—and this entire gallery—are two canvases by Rembrandt (both from 1641). *Girl in a Picture Frame* is exactly that—except that she's "breaking the frame" by resting her hands on a faux frame that Rembrandt has painted inside the real one...shattering the fourth wall in a way that was unusual for the time. The other, *A Scholar at His Writing Table*, shows the hirsute academic glancing up from his notes. Circle around behind the canvases to see X-rays of the paintings, which have helped experts better understand the master's techniques. The rest of the gallery consists of roomfuls of portraits and a fine cabinet of silver and crystal.

Consider a detour to the **Kubicki Arcades** (Arkady Kubiciego), the impressively excavated arcades deep beneath the castle. From the entrance lobby, head downstairs to the area with the cloakroom, bathrooms, and bookshop, then find the long escalator that takes you down to the arcades. It's free to wander the long, cavernous, and newly clean and gleaming space, made elegant by grand drapes.

The castle has a vast collection, which it organizes into various exhibitions—some permanent (well, as permanent as anything around here) and some temporary. The extensive **oriental carpet collection** in the "Tin-Roofed Palace" (Pałac pod Blachą) is sparsely described and skippable for most; the same building also features seven unimpressive apartments of Prince Józef Poniatowski, the king's brother (14 zł for both, free on Sun, same hours as castle, around the right side of the castle as you face it—past the two fallen columns, buy ticket at main ticket desk). When you're buying your castle ticket, keep an eye out for **temporary exhibits** of interest.

• After you finish touring the castle and are ready to resume exploring the Old Town, turn left at the end of the square onto...

St. John's Street (Świętojańska)

On the plaque under the street name sign, you can guess what the dates mean, even if you don't know Polish: This building was constructed from 1433 to 1478, destroyed in 1944, and rebuilt from 1950 to 1953.

• Partway down the street on the right, you'll come to the big brick...

Cathedral of St. John the Baptist (Katedra Św. Jana Chrzciciela)

This cathedral-basilica is the oldest (1339) and most important church in Warsaw. Superficially unimpressive, the church's own archbishop admitted that it was "modest and poor"—but "the historical events that took place here make it magnificent." Poland's constitution was consecrated here on May 3, 1791. Much later, this church became the final battleground of the 1944 Warsaw Uprising—when a Nazi "tracked mine" (a huge bomb on tank tracks—this one appropriately named *Goliath*) drove into the church and exploded, massacring the rebels. You can still see part of that tank's tread hanging on the outside wall of the church (through the passage on the right side, near the end of the church).

Cost and Hours: Free, crypt-2 zł, good guidebook-5 zł, open to tourists daily 10:00-13:00 & 15:00-17:30, closed during services and organ concerts. The cathedral hosts organ concerts in summer (see "Entertainment in Warsaw," later).

Visiting the Cathedral: Head inside. Typical of brick churches, it has a "hall church" design, with three naves of equal height. Look for the crucifix ornamented with real human hair (chapel left of high altar). The high altar holds a copy of the Black Madonna—proclaimed "everlasting queen of Poland" after a victory over the Swedes in the 17th century. The original Black Madonna is in Częstochowa (125 miles south of Warsaw)—a mecca for Slavic Catholics, who visit in droves in hopes of a miracle. In the back-left corner, find the chapel with the tomb of Cardinal Stefan Wyszyński—the great Polish leader who, as Warsaw's archbishop, morally steered the country through much of the Cold War. (Notice the request to pray for his beatification, as Poles would love to see him become a saint.) The crypt holds graves of several important Poles, including Stanisław August Poniatowski (the last Polish king) and Nobel Prize-winning author Henryk Sienkiewicz.

• *Continue up the street and enter Warsaw's grand...*

▲▲Old Town Market Square (Rynek Starego Miasta)

For two centuries, this was a gritty market square. Sixty-five years ago, it was a pile of bombed-out rubble. And today, like a phoenix from the ashes, it's risen to remind residents and tourists alike of the prewar glory of the Polish capital.

Head to the **mermaid fountain** in the middle of the square. The mermaid is an important symbol in Warsaw—you'll see her everywhere. Legend has it that a mermaid *(syrenka)* lived in the Vistula River and protected the townspeople. While this siren supposedly serenaded the town, Varsovians like her more for her strength (hence the sword). This square seems to declare that life goes on in Warsaw, as it always has. I've often seen children frolicking here, oblivious to the turmoil their forebears withstood. When the fountain gurgles, the kids giggle.

Each of the square's four sides is named for a prominent 18th-century Varsovian: Kołłątaj, Dekert, Barss, and Zakrzewski. These men served as "Presidents" of Warsaw (mayors, more or less), and Kołłątaj was also a framer of Poland's 1791 constitution. Take some time to explore the square. Enjoy the colorful architecture. Notice that many of the buildings were intentionally built to lean out into the square—to simulate the higgledy-piggledy wear and tear of the original buildings.

If you're curious to learn more about the history and restoration of the Old Town, hook around behind the buildings on the river side of the square (behind the mermaid's back), and find the **Old Town Heritage Interpretation Center**—a fine little visitors center with lots of before-and-after photos and videos, glass floors looking down onto original fragments, and thoughtful English explanations (2 zł, daily 10:00-20:00, Nov-April until 18:00, ulica Brzozowa 11/13, www.mhw.pl).

• *On the Dekert (north) side of the square is the...*

WARSAW

Warsaw Museum (Muzeum Warszawy)

When this museum's lengthy restoration is complete, it should provide an insightful look at the history of this city—particularly the Old Town. For now, you can enter the museum to see the network of cellars underneath, and to watch an interesting film.

Cost and Hours: 10 zł, free on Thu, open Tue-Sun 10:00-20:00, off-season until 18:00, closed Mon year-round, last entry 45 minutes before closing, Rynek Starego Miasta 28/42, tel. 22-635-1625, muzeumwarszawy.pl.

Film: Unless you're fascinated by Warsaw's history, skip the museum collection and just buy the separate 10-zł ticket to watch the excellent 20-minute film in English, worth ▲▲; unfortunately, it runs only twice daily (Tue-Fri at 10:00 and 12:00; Sat-Sun at 12:00 and 14:00). With somber narration and black-and-white scenes from before, during, and after the wartime devastation, this film is best appreciated after you've had a chance to see some of today's Warsaw (especially along the Royal Way). The movie ends with, "They say that there are no miracles. Then what is this city on the Vistula?" Emotionally drained, you can only respond, "Amen."

• *Leave the square on Nowomiejska (at the mermaid's 2 o'clock, by the second-story niche sculpture of St. Anne). After a block, you'll reach the...*

Barbican (Barbakan)

This defensive gate of the Old Town, similar to Kraków's, protected the medieval city from invaders.

• *Once you've crossed through the barbican, you're officially in Warsaw's...*

New Town (Nowe Miasto)

This 15th-century neighborhood is "new" in name only: It was the first part of Warsaw to spring up outside of the city walls (and therefore slightly newer than the Old Town). The New Town is a fun place to wander: Only a little less charming than the Old Town, but with a more real-life feel—people live and work here. Its centerpiece is the **New Town Square** (Rynek Nowego Miasta), watched over by the distinctive green dome of St. Kazimierz Church.

Scientists might want to pay homage at the museum (and birthplace) of Warsaw native **Marie Skłodowska-Curie,** a.k.a. Madame Curie (1867-1934); it's along the street between the New Town Square and the Barbican. This Nobel Prize winner was the world's first radiologist—discovering both radium and polonium (named for her native land) with her husband, Pierre Curie. Since she lived at a time when Warsaw was controlled by oppressive Russia, she conducted her studies in France. The museum—with photos, furniture, artifacts, and a paucity of English information—is a bit of a snoozer, best left to true fans (overpriced at 11 zł, Tue-Fri 9:30-16:00, Sat 10:00-16:00, Sun 10:00-15:00, closed Mon, ulica Freta 16, tel. 22-831-8092, http://muzeum-msc.pl).

From the New Town to Castle Square

You can backtrack the way you came, or, to get a look at the Old Town's back streets, consider this route from the big, round barbican gate (where the New Town meets the Old): Go back through the barbican and over the little bridge, turn right, and walk along the houses that line the inside of the wall. You'll pass a leafy garden courtyard on the left—a reminder that people actually live in the tourist zone within the Old Town walls. Just beyond the garden on the right, look for the carpet-beating rack, used to clean rugs (these are common fixtures in people's backyards). Go left into the square called Szeroki Dunaj ("Wide Danube") and look for another mermaid (over the Thai restaurant). Continue through the square and turn right at Wąski Dunaj ("Narrow Danube"). After about 100 yards, you'll pass the city wall. Just to the right (outside the wall), you'll see the monument to the **Little Upriser** of 1944, a child wearing a grown-up's helmet and too-big boots, and carrying a machine gun. Children—especially Scouts (Harcerze)—played a key role in the resistance against the Nazis. Their job was mainly carrying messages and propaganda.

Now continue around the wall (the upper, inner part is more

pleasant). Admire more public art as you head back to Castle Square.

BETWEEN NOWY ŚWIAT AND THE RIVER
▲▲National Museum (Muzeum Narodowe)

While short on big-name pieces, this museum interests art lovers and offers a good, accessible introduction to some talented Polish artists who are largely unknown outside their home country. A modern, state-of-the-art exhibition space allows these unsung canvases to really belt it out. Polish and other European artists are displayed side-by-side, as if to assert Poland's worthiness on the world artistic stage. After seeing a few of the masterpieces here, you won't disagree.

Cost and Hours: 15 zł, more for temporary exhibits, permanent collection free on Tue; open Tue-Sun 10:00-18:00, Thu until 21:00, closed Mon, last entry 45 minutes before closing; one block east of Nowy Świat at aleja Jerozolimskie 3, tel. 22-629-3093, www.mnw.art.pl.

◐ Self-Guided Tour: The collection fills several separate galleries. The museum's strongest point—and the bulk of this tour—is the 19th-century Polish art. But before diving in, consider some of the other collections.

Overview: To get your bearings, pick up a floor plan as you enter. On the ground floor are Ancient Art (from Greek pieces to artifacts left by early Polish tribes); Gallery Faras (highlighting the museum's fine collection of archaeological findings from that ancient Egyptian city); and a good collection of Medieval Art, which gathers altarpieces from churches around Poland—organized both chronologically and geographically—and displays some of the most graphic crucifixes and pietàs I've seen.

Upstairs is the excellent Gallery of 19th-Century Art (described next), which flows into the Old Polish and European Portrait Gallery (as interesting as somebody else's yearbook). Nearby, through the gift shop, is the worthwhile 20th- and 21st-Century Art collection, with an impressive array of Modern and Postmodern Polish artists, including photography and film. The underwhelming Old European Painting collection—pre-19th-century canvases arranged by theme and juxtaposed to highlight the differences between southern and northern European art—is split up among all three floors.

To cut to the chase, focus on the **Gallery of 19th-Century Art.** We'll start with the granddaddy of Polish art, Jan Matejko.

• *From the entrance lobby, head up the left staircase, then do a U-turn left across the mezzanine and enter the collection. Matejko is hiding at the far end of this wing: Entering the collection, angle right, then head all the way to the room at the far end, which is dominated by a gigantic*

Jan Matejko (1838-1893)

Jan Matejko (yawn mah-TAY-koh) is Poland's most important painter, period. In the mid- to late-19th century, the nation of Poland had been dissolved by foreign powers, and Polish artists struggled to make sense of their people's place in the world. Rabble-rousing Romanticism seemed to have failed (inspiring many brutally suppressed uprisings), so Polish artists and writers turned their attention to educating the people about their history, with the goal of keeping their traditions alive.

Matejko was at the forefront of this so-called "positivist" movement. Matejko saw what the tides of history had done to Poland, and was determined to make sure his countrymen learned from it. He painted two types of works: huge, grand-scale epics depicting monumental events in Polish history; and small, intimate portraits of prominent Poles. Polish schoolchildren study history from books with paintings of virtually every single Polish king—all painted by the incredibly prolific Matejko.

Matejko is admired not for his technical mastery (he's an unexceptional painter) or for the literal truth of his works—he was notorious for fudging historical details in order to give his canvases a bit more propagandistic punch. But he is revered for the emotion behind—and inspired by—his works. His paintings are utilitarian, straightforward, and dramatic enough to stir the patriot in any Pole. The intense focus on history by Matejko and other positivists is one big reason why today's Poles are still so in touch with their heritage.

You'll see Matejko's works in Warsaw's National Museum and Royal Castle, as well as in Kraków's Gallery of 19th-Century Polish Art (above the Cloth Hall). You can also visit his former residence in Kraków.

canvas. (If you get lost, ask the attendants, "mah-TAY-koh?")

Jan Matejko: While not the most talented of artists—he's a fairly conventional painter, lacking a distinctive, recognizable style—Matejko more than made up for it with vision and productivity. His works—often on oversized canvases—are steeped in proud Polish history. Matejko's biggest work here—in fact, the biggest canvas in the whole building—is the enormous ***Battle of Grunwald***. This epic painting commemorates one of Poland's high-water marks: the dramatic victory of a Polish-Lithuanian army over the Teutonic Knights, who had been terrorizing northern Poland for decades. On July 15, 1410, some 40,000 Poles and Lithuanians (led by the sword-waving Lithuanian in red, Grand Duke Vytautas) faced off against 27,000 Teutonic Knights (under their Grand Master, in white) in one of the medieval world's bloodiest battles. Matejko plops us right in the thick of the battle's chaos, painting life-size figures and framing off a 32-foot-long slice of the actual two-mile battle line.

In the center of the painting, the Teutonic Grand Master is about to become a shish kebab. Duke Vytautas, in red, leads the final charge. And waaaay up on a hill (in the upper-right corner, on horseback, wearing a silver knight's suit) is Władysław Jagiełło, the first king of the Jagiellonian dynasty...ensuring his bloodline will survive another 150 years.

Matejko spent three years covering this 450-square-foot canvas in paint. The canvas was specially made in a single seamless piece. This was such a popular work that almost as many fans turned out for its unveiling as there are figures in the painting. The TV nearby shows how the vast painting was recently restored.

From Poland's high point in the *Battle of Grunwald*, look on the right wall for another, much smaller Matejko canvas, ***Stańczyk After the Loss of Smolensk***, to see how Poland's fortunes shifted drastically a century later. This more intimate portrait depicts a popular Polish figure: the court jester Stańczyk, who's smarter than the king, but not allowed to say so. This complex character, representing the national conscience, is a favorite symbol of Matejko's. Stańczyk slumps in gloom. He's just read the news (on the table beside him) that the city of Smolensk has fallen to the Russians after a three-year siege (1512-1514). The jester had tried to warn the king to send more troops, but the king was too busy partying (behind the curtain). The painter Matejko—who may have used his own features for Stańczyk's face—also blamed the nobles of his own day for fiddling while Poland was partitioned.

More Matejkos fill this room. Just to the right of Stańczyk is a self-portrait of the gray-bearded artist (compare their features), then a painting of the hoisting of the Sigismund Bell to the cathedral tower in Kraków (it's still there). Farther right, you'll see his portraits of his children and his wife.

On the final wall is a smaller but very dramatic scene, ***The Sermon of Skarga***. In the upper-right corner, a charismatic, early-17th-century Jesuit priest, Piotr Skarga, waves his arms to punctuate his message: Poland's political system is broken. He's addressing fat-cat nobles and the portly King Sigismund II Wasa (seated and wearing a ruffled collar), who were acting in their own self-interests instead of prioritizing what was best for Poland. Notice that Skarga's audience isn't hearing his ravings—they seem bored, or bugged, or both. The king is even taking a nap. They should have listened: Poland's eventual decline is often considered the fault of its unworkable political system. After the Partitions, the ahead-of-his-time Skarga was rehabilitated as a visionary who should have been heeded. Notice that, like Stańczyk, Skarga is a self-portrait of Matejko.

• Leaving Matejko, we'll pass through several more rooms of lesser-known Polish painters to the opposite wing, where we'll meet several of the great artists' students—each of whom developed his own style and left his mark on the Polish art world. But on the way, I'll point out a few canvases that may be worth pausing at.

Other Polish Painters: First, head back down the long corridor the way you came (passing some Matejko copycats), cutting through a corner of the Portrait Gallery. When you reach the door you came in, bear right to stay inside the gallery. At the end of that first, large room, you'll find some battle scenes by **Józef Brandt**—the only painter who rivaled Matejko in capturing epic warfare on canvas. Many of Brandt's scenes focus on confronting an enemy from the east, which was Poland's lot for much of its history. His biggest work here, *Rescue of Tatar Captives,* is typical of his scenes.

Continue straight into the next room, with some fine landscape scenes. This room (the partition in the middle) also has works by the talented **Józef Chełmoński:** *Indian Summer* and (around back) *Storks*—a young boy and his grandfather look to the sky, as a formation of storks flies overhead.

Turn right and go through one more long room (watching, on the right wall, for **Aleksander Gierymski's** small, evocative *Jewish Woman Selling Oranges*).

• You'll emerge into a big room that kicks off the collection of...

Młoda Polska: Matejko's pupils took what he taught them, and incorporated the Art Nouveau styles that were emerging around Europe, to create a new movement called "Young Poland." This room features works by two of the movement's big names. On the left wall are paintings by **Jacek Malczewski,** some of them depicting the goateed, close-cropped artist in a semi-surrealistic, Polish countryside context. Malczewski painted more or less realistically, but enjoyed incorporating one or two subtle, symbolic elements evocative of Polish folkloric tradition—like magical realism on canvas. *The Death of Ellenai* (1907) shows the pivotal scene in Juliusz Słowacki's epic 1838 poem, *Anhelli,* in which a young nobleman exiled from Poland during the Partitions is forced to make his way through the wastelands of Siberia. When his young and idealistic travel companion, Ellenai, perishes, Anhelli kisses her feet and abandons all hope.

Most of the works on the opposite wall are by **Józef Mehoffer,** who paints with brighter colors in a more stylized form, with more abstraction. This creates more dreamlike scenes that are, consequently, somehow less poignant than Malczewski's. Mehoffer's hypnotic *Strange Garden* is a bucolic vision of blue-clad Mary Poppinses, nude cherubs, lots of flowers...and a gigantic, hovering, golden dragonfly that places the otherwise plausible scene in the realm of pure fantasy. In the middle of the room, the small version of Auguste Rodin's *The Kiss* reminds us how this emotion-conveying style, called Symbolism, was also finding expression elsewhere in Europe.

The next room, at the end of the hall, features some lesser-known painters from the age. Among these, **Olga Boznańska**'s works are worth lingering over: gauzy, almost Impressionistic portraits that skillfully capture the humanity of each subject.

Head back into the Malczewski/Mehoffer room and find the small, darkened adjoining rooms. The first one features additional Malczewski paintings; the second is a treasure trove of works by the founder and biggest talent of Młoda Polska, **Stanisław Wyspiański.** The specific items in this room are subject to change—as Kraków, which owns the best collection of hometown boy Wyspiański, is shuffling its works in and out of special exhibitions—but you'll likely see both paintings and pastel works by this Art Nouveau juggernaut. Wyspiański also designed stage sets and redecorated some important churches; some of the large pastel-on-paper works you may see here were used as studies for those projects. And you'll likely see some self-portraits and portraits of his wife and children. Pondering the works here—and throughout the museum—think about how such a talented artist from a small country can be left out of textbooks across the ocean.

Chopin Museum (Muzeum Fryderyka Chopina)

The reconstructed Ostrogski Castle houses this museum honoring Poland's most famous composer. The museum was overhauled

for the "Year of Chopin" in 2010, when all of Poland celebrated the composer's 200th birthday. You'll see manuscripts, letters, and original handwritten compositions by the composer. Unfortunately, the museum's slick and high-tech gadgetry does more to distract from this rich collection of historic artifacts than to bring it to life. While Chopin devotees may find it riveting, those with only a passing familiarity with the composer may leave feeling like they still don't know much about this Polish cultural giant.

Cost and Hours: 22 zł, free on Sun, open Tue-Sun 11:00-20:00, closed Mon, 3 blocks east of Nowy Świat at ulica Okólnik 1, tel. 22-441-6251, www.chopin.museum. Because the museum is highly interactive, only 70 visitors are allowed per hour. But, except for rare occasions, just dropping in should be no problem.

Visiting the Museum: Buy your ticket at the adjacent building, then enter the mansion that houses the exhibit. You'll be given an electronic card; tap it against glowing red dots to access additional information. You'll proceed more or less chronologically through the composer's life, with various opportunities to hear his compositions. You'll see a replica of Chopin's drawing room in Paris, and his last piano, which he used for composing during the final two years of his life (1848-1849). Exhibits here trace themes of the composer's life, such as the women he knew (including his older sister Ludwika, his mother, and George Sand—the French author who took a male pseudonym in order to be published, and who was romantically linked with Chopin). The exhibit ends in the basement, where you can nurture your appreciation of Chopin by listening to his music.

Concerts: Under the palace is a new **concert hall,** which hosts performances by students (call museum to ask for concert schedule; usually Oct-July Thu at 18:00, and typically free).

Other Chopin Sight: The composer's tourable **birth house** is in a park in Żelazowa Wola, 34 miles from Warsaw. While interesting to Chopin devotees, it's not worth the trek for most. On summer weekends, the Chopin Museum sometimes runs a handy bus to the house—ask at the museum (departs from Marszałkowska street, 30 minutes each way; 7 zł for the bus, 7 zł for the park, 23 zł for the park and birth house, 39 zł also includes museum in Warsaw; birth house open Tue-Sun 9:00-19:00, Oct-March until 17:00, closed Mon year-round, tel. 46-863-3300).

▲▲Copernicus Science Center (Centrum Nauki Kopernik)

This facility, a wonderland of completely hands-on scientific doo-dads that thrill kids and adults alike, is a futuristic romper room. Filling two floors of an industrial-mod, purpose-built space, this is Warsaw's best family activity. Exhibits are grouped more or less thematically and described in both Polish and English.

Cost and Hours: 25 zł, 16 zł for kids 19 and under, 66-zł family ticket for up to 4 people; open Tue-Fri 9:00-18:00, Sat-Sun 10:00-19:00, closed Mon, last entry one hour before closing; Wybrzeże Kościuszkowskie 20, tel. 22-596-4100, www.kopernik.org.pl.

Crowd-Beating Tips: As a relatively new attraction, the center can get crowded—especially on weekends and school holidays, when the line can be long. On weekdays, it's generally no problem to walk right in.

Getting There: It's an easy downhill walk from Warsaw's Royal Way, but the hike back up is fairly steep. The nearest bus stop, called Pomnik Syreny, is on a nearby corner, next to the modern bridge; from here, bus #102 goes to Nowy Świat, then up the Royal Way (Uniwersytet and Zachęta stops) before heading south to the central train station. The new Metro line 2 connects the science center to the National Stadium, the Royal Way, and the Warsaw Uprising Museum.

Visiting the Center: Your ticket is a plastic "log-in card" that you can insert into certain interactive exhibits. On the ground floor, the **"Roots of Civilization"** features working models of various tools and machines, demonstrating how humanity has mastered the mechanics of physics. By playing with a model piston, I grasped for the first time how that

technology works. Other exhibits let you play archaeologist in a sandbox, listen to *Ode to Joy* while tuning into different instruments (depending on where you sit), and see a small "fire tornado" (every bit as cool as it sounds). A playroom for toddlers, called **"Buzzz!,"** has a nature theme. Meanwhile, **"RE: Generation"** targets teens and adults with computer touchscreens that investigate the biological underpinnings of emotion—from what makes you laugh to what grosses you out—and examines how cultures around the world are both similar and different.

The **"Heavens of Copernicus" planetarium** requires a separate ticket (18 zł, 13 zł for kids 19 and under, in Polish with English headset, open later than main center, show starts at the top of each hour, ask for schedule at ticket desk).

The fun continues upstairs, where **"Humans and the Environment"** illuminates the human body (find out just how long your intestines are, identify and place the organs, and see how various joints work like hinges). One area focuses on exercise, including the engaging arena, where you can compete with various virtual animals (can you jump as high as a kangaroo or hang like a chimp?). The **"Lightzone"** illustrates how light travels in waves, lets you try out an old-fashioned but still impressive camera obscura, and use prisms and lenses to play a game of "light billiards." **"On the Move"** features fascinating hands-on physics demos, including an earthquake simulator, an air cannon, and a tube that lets you harness sound waves to make water vibrate.

Nearby: The **Discovery Park** surrounding the museum was created when the busy riverfront highway was rerouted into an underground tunnel, creating this delightful people zone. From here you have good views of the modern Holy Cross Bridge (Most Świętokrzyski, from 2000) and the National Stadium, built to host matches for the 2012 Euro Cup and proudly wrapped in the patriotic red and white of the Polish flag.

Two short blocks inland from the science center is the

architecturally innovative **Warsaw University Library** (Biblioteka Uniwersytecka w Warszawie, or BUW), with its distinctive oxidized-copper-colored facade decorated with open books from various cultures. The facade is fun to ogle, and the rooftop holds a huge and inviting garden.

NEAR THE CENTRAL TRAIN STATION

These sights are near Nowy Świat, within a few blocks of the central train station.

Palace of Culture and Science
(Pałac Kultury i Nauki, or PKiN)

This massive skyscraper, dating from the early 1950s, is the tallest building between Frankfurt and Moscow (760 feet with the spire,

though several new buildings are threatening to eclipse that peak). While you can ride the lift to its top for a commanding view, the highlight is simply viewing it up close from ground level.

Viewing the Skyscraper: This building was a "gift" from Stalin that the people of Warsaw couldn't refuse. Varsovians call it "Stalin's Penis"... using cruder terminology than that. (There are seven such "Stalin Gothic" erections in Moscow.) If it feels like an Art Deco Chicago skyscraper, that's because the architect was inspired by the years he spent studying and working in Chicago in the 1930s. Because it was to be "Soviet in substance, Polish in style," Soviet architects toured Poland to absorb local culture before starting the project. Notice the frilly decorative friezes that top each level—evocative of Poland's many Renaissance buildings (such as Kraków's Cloth Hall). The clock was added in 1999 as part of the millennium celebrations. Since the end of communism, the younger generation doesn't mind the structure so much—and some even admit to liking it for the way it enlivens the new, predictable glass-and-steel skyline springing up around it.

Everything about the Pałac is big. Approach it from the east side (facing the busy Marszałkowska street and the slick Galeria Centrum shopping mall). Stand in front of the granite tribune where communist VIPs surveyed massive May Day parades and pageantry on the once-imposing square, which today is a sloppy parking lot. From there, size up the skyscraper—its grand entry flanked by massive statues of Copernicus on the right (science) and the great poet Mickiewicz on the left (culture). It's designed to show off the strong, grand-scale Soviet aesthetic and architectural skill. The Pałac contains various theaters (the culture), museums of evolution and technology (the science), a congress hall, a multiplex (showing current movies), an observation deck, and lots of office space. With all of this Culture and Science under one Roof, it's a shame that only the ground-floor lobby (which feels like stepping into 1950s Moscow and is free to enter) and the 30th-floor observatory deck are open to the public.

Observation Deck: You can zip up to the observation deck (billed as "XXX Floor") in 20 seconds on the retrofitted Soviet elevators—but it's overpriced and the view's a letdown. While you'll get a nice overview of Warsaw's forest of new skyscrapers, you can hardly see the Old Town, and Warsaw's most prominent big building—the Pałac itself—is missing (18 zł, includes Polish-oriented special exhibitions; deck open daily June-Aug 9:00-20:00, Fri-Sat until 24:00; Sept-May 9:00-18:00, enter through main door on east side of Pałac—opposite from central train station, tel. 22-656-7600, www.pkin.pl).

WARSAW

Złote Tarasy Shopping Mall

Tucked behind the central train station, "Golden Terraces" is a super-modern shopping mall with a funky, undulating glass-and-steel roof. Even though you didn't come all the way to Poland to visit a shopping mall, it's worth detouring here to get a taste of Poland's race into the future. In many ways, this—and not humble farmers munching pierogi—is the face of today's Poland.

Hours: Mon-Sat 10:00-22:00, Sun 10:00-20:00, lots of designer shops, good food court on top level, www.zlotetarasy.pl.

Złota 44

This skyscraper, with its dramatic swooping lines rising high from the Złote Tarasy shopping mall, was designed by world-renowned architect Daniel Libeskind (who is also redeveloping the 9/11 site in New York City). Born in Poland, at a very young age Libeskind emigrated with his family to the US, returning only recently to embark on this project. Its shape evokes an eagle (a common symbol for Poland) just beginning to take flight. Of all the shiny new towers popping up in Warsaw's skyline, this is the most architecturally interesting—and offers a striking counterpoint to the Stalinist Palace of Culture and Science nearby. (For more on the building, visit www.zlota44tower.com.)

Warsaw's Jews and the Ghetto Uprising

From the Middle Ages until World War II, Poland was a relatively safe haven for Europe's Jews. While other kings were imprisoning and deporting Jews in the 14th century, the progressive king Kazimierz the Great welcomed Jews into Poland, even granting them special privileges (see page 43).

By the 1930s, there were more than 380,000 Jews in Warsaw—nearly a third of the population (and the largest concentration of Jews in any European city). The Nazis arrived in 1939. Within a year, they had pushed all of Warsaw's Jews into one neighborhood and surrounded it with a wall, creating a miserably overcrowded ghetto (crammed full of half a million people, including many from nearby towns). Over the next year, the Nazis brought in more Jews from throughout Poland, and the number grew by a million.

By the summer of 1942, more than a quarter of the Jews in the ghetto had either died of disease, committed suicide, or been murdered. The Nazis started moving Warsaw's Jews (at the rate of 5,000 a day) into what they claimed were "resettlement camps." Most of these people were actually murdered at Treblinka or Auschwitz. After hundreds of thousands of Jews had been taken away, the waning population—now about 60,000—began to get word from concentration camp escapees about what was actually going on there. Spurred by this knowledge, Warsaw's surviving Jews staged a dramatic uprising.

JEWISH WARSAW

In the early 1600s, an estimated 80 percent of all Jews lived in Poland (which at that time included Lithuania and was the largest country in Europe). But after centuries of dwelling in relative peace in tolerant and pragmatic Poland, Warsaw's Jews suffered terribly at the hands of the Nazis. Several sights in Warsaw commemorate those who were murdered, and those who fought back. Because the Nazis leveled the ghetto, there is literally nothing left except the street plan, some monuments, and the heroic spirit of its former residents. However, the brand-new Museum of the History of Polish Jews is rejuvenating the area, making it even more of a magnet for those interested in this chapter of Polish history.

Getting There: To reach Ghetto Heroes Square and the museum from the Old Town, you can hop a **taxi** (10 zł) or take a **bus** (to the Nalewki-Muzeum stop; bus #180 is particularly useful; bus #111 reaches this stop from farther south—Piłsudski Square, the university, and the National Museum). You can also **walk** there in about 15 minutes: Go through the barbican gate two blocks into the New Town, turn left on Świętojerska, and walk straight 10 minutes—passing the new green-glass Supreme Court building—until you reach a grassy park on Zamenhofa Street. At the corner

On April 19, 1943, the Jews attacked Nazi strongholds and had some initial success. The overwhelming Nazi war machine—which had rolled over much of Europe—imagined they'd be able to put down the rebellion easily. Instead, they struggled for a month to finally crush the Ghetto Uprising. The ghetto's residents and structures were "liquidated." About 300 of Warsaw's Jews survived, thanks in part to a sort of "underground railroad" of courageous Varsovians.

Warsaw's Jewish sights are emotionally moving, but even more so if you know some of their stories. You may have heard of **Władysław Szpilman,** a Jewish concert pianist who survived the war with the help of Jews, Poles, and even a Nazi officer. Szpilman's life story was turned into the highly acclaimed, Oscar-winning 2002 film *The Pianist*, which powerfully depicts events in Warsaw during World War II.

Less familiar to non-Poles—but equally affecting—is the story of Henryk Goldszmit, better known by his pen name, **Janusz Korczak.** Korczak wrote imaginative children's books that are still enormously popular among Poles. He worked at an orphanage in the Warsaw ghetto. When his orphans were sent off to concentration camps, the Nazis offered the famous author a chance at freedom. Korczak turned them down, choosing to die at Treblinka with his children.

of Świętojerska and Nowiniarska, look for the pattern of bricks in the sidewalk, marking *Ghetto Wall 1940-1943*.

▲Ghetto Heroes Square (Plac Bohaterow Getta)

The square is in the heart of what was the Jewish ghetto—now surrounded by bland Soviet-style apartment blocks. After the uprising, the entire ghetto was reduced to dust by the Nazis, leaving the communists to rebuild to their own specifications. The district is called Muranów ("Rebuilt") today.

The **monument** in the middle of the square commemorates those who fought and died "for the dignity and freedom of the Jewish Nation, for a free Poland, and for the liberation of humankind." The statue features heroic Jewish men who knew that an inglorious death at the hands of the Nazis awaited them. Flames in the background show Nazis burning the ghetto. The opposite side features a sad procession of Jews trudging to concentration

camps, with subtle Nazi bayonets and helmets moving things along.

As you face the monument, look through the trees to the right to see a seated statue. **Jan Karski** (1914-2000) was a Catholic Pole and resistance fighter who traveled extensively through Poland during the Nazi occupation, collected evidence, and then reported on the Warsaw Ghetto and the Holocaust to the leaders of the Western Allies (including a personal meeting with FDR). In 1944, while the Holocaust was still going on, Karski published his eyewitness account, *The Story of a Secret State* (which you can see on this statue's armrest), to spread the story of what was happening in Poland. After the war he became a US citizen, and in 2012 President Barack Obama awarded him a posthumous Presidential Medal of Freedom.

• *The huge, glassy building facing the monument from across the square is the...*

▲▲Museum of the History of Polish Jews
(Muzeum Historii Żydów Polskich, a.k.a. POLIN)

Opened in 2014, this powerful, long-overdue museum traces the epic, nearly millennium-long story of Jews in Poland. This is not a "Holocaust museum," but a cel-

ebration of the full and very rich Polish Jewish experience across the centuries. The striking building, designed by Finnish architect Rainer Mahlamäki, is pierced by a dramatically asymmetrical hole (visible from the outside). The building also hosts cultural events and temporary exhibits.

Cost and Hours: Core exhibition-25 zł, more for temporary exhibits, includes audioguide, Wed-Mon 10:00-18:00, Sat until 20:00, closed Tue, 6 Anielewicza, tel. 22-471-0300, www.jewishmuseum.org.pl. It's a modern facility with a cafeteria and children's area.

Visiting the Museum: In the "Core Exhibition," high-tech, interactive exhibits in eight galleries mingle with actual artifacts to bring history to life. You'll pass through a simulated forest—evocative of legends about the Jews' arrival in Poland—to reach the **"First Encounters"** exhibit, focusing on early Jewish settlers during the Middle Ages. You'll learn about Ibrahim ibn Jakub—a Sephardic Jew who penned early travelogues about Europe—and see a prayer book from 1272, with the oldest-known sentence written in Yiddish. Then, **"Paradisus Iudaeorum"** explains the ways Jewish culture flourished in tolerant Poland in the 15th and

16th centuries. An interactive model lets you explore the city of Kraków—and its Jewish quarter, Kazimierz—as it was during the golden age of Polish Jews. But with the Khmelnytsky Uprising in the mid-17th century came pogroms, anti-Semitism, and a more difficult life. "**Into the Country**" traces the spread of Jews throughout the Eastern European countryside, where they forged a unique type of settlement called a *shtetl*. The replica of a roof of a wooden synagogue from the village of Gwoździec illustrates the architecture of the time.

"**Encounters with Modernity**" examines how, after the Partitions (when Polish territory was divided among neighboring powers at the end of the 18th century), Jews struggled to integrate with the respective societies of their new overlords. This was also the time of the Industrial Revolution, when Jewish businessmen were making their mark on the society. As Poland—and its Jewish population—accelerated into the modern age, it brought about changes to Jewish tradition...and saw the emergence of a hateful and aggressive new breed of anti-Semitism.

"**The Street**" re-creates an early 20th-century shopping street from a Jewish community, demonstrating how Jewish culture thrived in the vibrant urban life of Poland between the World Wars. The **Holocaust** section explains the horrific events that claimed the lives of some 9 out of every 10 Polish Jews. This exhibit focuses on the Warsaw ghetto and its residents, whose daily lives and shocking fate are chronicled in a set of contemporaneous diaries and documents remarkably preserved in an underground archive.

Finally, "**The Postwar Years**" follows Holocaust survivors as they navigate an unfriendly, anti-Semitic communist regime. In 1968, the communists launched an "anti-Zionist" campaign; eventually around 15,000 Polish Jews lost their citizenship and left for Israel, Western Europe, and the US. Those who remained had to wait for the fall of communism to finally enter a world of new possibilities.

Ghetto Walking Tour

To see more faint echoes of the ghetto, take this brief, lightly guided walk for a few blocks. Facing the monument with the museum behind you, head left (with the park on your left) and walk along Zamenhofa—which, like many streets in this neighborhood, is named for a hero of the Ghetto Uprising. From the monument, you'll follow a series of three-foot-tall black stone memorials to uprising heroes—the **Path of Remembrance.** Like Stations of the Cross, each recounts an event of the uprising. Every April 19th (the day the uprising began), huge crowds follow this path. In a block, just beyond the corner of Miła (partly obscured by some bushes), you'll find a **bunker** where about 100 organizers of the uprising hid (and where they committed suicide when the Nazis discovered them on May 8, 1943).

Continue following the black stone monuments up Zamenhofa (which becomes Dubois), then turn left at the corner, onto broad and busy Stawki. The ugly gray building on your left (a half-block down at #5/7, near the tram stop) was the **headquarters of the SS** within the ghetto. This is where the transportation of Warsaw's Jews to concentration camps was organized.

Using the crosswalk at the tram stop, cross Stawki and proceed straight ahead into the gap between the two buildings. At the back of this parking lot is a surviving part of the red-brick **ghetto wall,** with a few remaining scraps of 1940s barbed wire.

Farther up Stawki street, on the right, you can stop at the **Umschlagplatz** monument—shaped like a cattle car. That's German for "transfer place," and it marks the spot where the Nazis brought Jewish families to prepare them to be loaded onto trains bound for Treblinka or Auschwitz. This was the actual site of the touching scene in the film *The Pianist* where the grandfather shares bits of chocolate with his family before being forever separated. In the walls of the monument are inscribed the first names of some of the victims.

WARSAW UPRISING SIGHTS

While the 1944 Warsaw Uprising is a recurring theme in virtually all Warsaw sightseeing, two sights in particular—one a monument, the other a museum—are worth a visit for anyone with a special interest. Neither is right on the main tourist trail; the monument is closer to the sightseeing action, while the museum is a subway, tram, or taxi ride away.

Warsaw Uprising Monument

The most central sight relating to the Warsaw Uprising is the monument at plac Krasińskich (intersection of ulica Długa and Miodowa, one long block and about a five-minute walk northwest of the New Town). Larger-than-life soldiers and civilians race for the sewers in a desperate attempt to flee the Nazis. Just behind the monument is the oxidized-copper facade of Poland's Supreme Court.

▲▲Warsaw Uprising Museum
(Muzeum Powstania Warszawskiego)

Thorough, modern, and packed with Polish field-trip groups, the museum celebrates the heroes of the uprising. It's a bit cramped, and finding your way through the exhibits can be confusing, but it helps illuminate this complicated chapter of Warsaw's history. The location is inconvenient (a 10-minute tram or bus ride west of central train station) and, because it eats up several hours to visit, may not be worth the trek for those with a casual interest. But history buffs find it worthwhile.

Cost and Hours: 14 zł, free on Sun (but you'll pay 2 zł for the good *City of Ruins* movie—buy ticket at cashier before entering museum); July-Aug Wed-Mon 10:00-18:00, Thu until 20:00; Sept-June Mon and Wed-Fri 8:00-18:00, Thu until 20:00, Sat-Sun 10:00-18:00, closed Tue year-round; last entry 30 minutes before closing, tel. 22-539-7947, www.1944.pl.

Audioguide: The informative, two-hour audioguide is ideal if you really want to delve into the whole story (10 zł, rent it in the gift shop). But the museum is so well-described, you can just wander aimlessly and be immersed in the hellish events.

Eating: The museum's café is oddly pleasant, serving drinks and light snacks amidst genteel ambience from prewar Warsaw. In summer you can dine on a peaceful terrace.

Getting There: It's on the western edge of downtown—a long, dull walk through urban gloom—at ulica Przyokopowa 28. While it's easiest to reach by taxi (figure about 20 zł from the Royal Way), you can also ride a tram or bus: Tram #22 and #24 come here from near the central train station (from the underground passageways, follow signs for *Ochota* to find the tram tracks) and near the corner of Nowy Świat and Jerusalem Avenue (in the middle of the street in front of the National Museum). You can also get to the museum on bus #109 (departs in front of the central train station—from the main hall, go out the door with the bus icon). From Castle Square in the Old Town, bus #178 goes to the museum. On the Royal Way, catch bus #105 from the Uniwersytet stop (next to the university building) or the Nowy Świat stop. All of these options take you to the Muzeum Powstania Warszawskiego stop. From this stop, cross the tracks and the busy street, walk straight one short block up Grzybowska, and take a left on Przyokopowa. The museum is the big, red-brick building on the left.

If traveling on Metro line 2, you can ride it (from Nowy Świat, among other stops) to Rondo Daszyńskiego—a bit farther away, but still within a few short blocks south of the museum.

◉ Self-Guided Tour: Buy your ticket at the little house on the left (marked *kasa*), then head into the main hall. The high-tech **main exhibit** sprawls across three floors. It chronologically tells

The Warsaw Uprising

By the summer of 1944, it was becoming clear that the Nazis' days in Warsaw were numbered. The Red Army drew near, and by late July, Soviet tanks were within 25 miles of downtown Warsaw.

The Varsovians could simply have waited for the Soviets to cross the river and force the Nazis out. But they knew that Soviet "liberation" would also mean an end to Polish independence. The Polish Home Army numbered 400,000—30,000 of them in Warsaw alone—and was the biggest underground army in military history. The uprisers wanted Poland to control its own fate, and they took matters into their own hands. The resistance's symbol was an anchor made up of a *P* atop a *W* (which stands for *Polska Walcząca*, or "Poland Fighting"—you'll see this icon all around town). Over time, the Home Army had established an extensive network of underground tunnels and sewers, which allowed them to deliver messages and move around the city without drawing the Nazis' attention. These tunnels gave the Home Army the element of surprise.

On August 1, 30,000 Polish resistance fighters launched an attack on their Nazi oppressors. They poured out of the sewers and caught the Nazis off guard. The ferocity of the Polish fighters stunned the Nazis, who thought they'd put down the uprising within hours. But the Nazis regrouped, and within a few days, they had retaken several areas of the city—murdering tens of thousands of innocent civilians as they went. In one notorious incident, some 5,500 Polish soldiers and 6,000 civilians who were surrounded by Nazis in the Old Town were forced to flee through the sewers; many drowned or were shot. (This scene is depicted in the Warsaw Uprising Monument on plac Krasińskich.)

Two months after it had started, the Warsaw Uprising was over. The Home Army called a cease-fire. About 18,000 Polish uprisers had been killed, along with nearly 200,000 innocent civilians. An infuriated Hitler ordered that the city be destroyed—which it was, systematically, block by block, until virtually nothing remained.

Through all of this, the Soviets stood still, watched, and waited. When the smoke cleared and the Nazis left, the Red Army marched in and claimed the wasteland that was once called Warsaw. After the war, General Dwight D. Eisenhower said that the scale of destruction here was the worst he'd ever seen. The communists later tracked down the surviving Home Army leaders, killing or imprisoning them.

Depending on whom you talk to, the desperate uprising of Warsaw was incredibly brave, stupid, or both. As for the Poles, they remain fiercely proud of their struggle for freedom. The city of Warsaw has recently commemorated this act of bravery with the new Warsaw Uprising Museum.

the story of the uprising, with a keen focus on military history. The exhibit covers several topics, but doesn't provide a big-picture narrative; to fully understand the context of what you're seeing, read the sidebar before your visit.

The **ground floor** sets the stage with Germany's invasion and occupation of Poland. The children's area (to the right as you enter) reminds visitors that Varsovian kids played a role in the Warsaw Uprising, too. The Generalgouvernement (Nazi puppet government of occupied Poland, ruled by Hans Frank in Kraków) wasted no time in asserting its control over the Poles; you'll learn how they imprisoned and executed priests, professors, and students. You'll also hear the story of the earlier, smaller uprisings that preceded the Warsaw Uprising, including the Poland-wide Operation Tempest (Burza) in 1943. During those earliest rebellions, Warsaw was intentionally left out of the fray...but the Varsovians' time would come.

To keep with the chronological flow, skip the middle floor for now, and ride the elevator to the **top floor** (#2), which covers the main part of the uprising. You'll meet some of the uprising's heroes and learn about their uniforms, weapons, and methods. The "Kino Palladium" movie screen shows fascinating Home Army newsreel footage from the period (with English subtitles). To the right of the screen, you'll walk through a simulated sewer, reminiscent of the one that many Home Army soldiers and civilians used to evade the Germans. Imagine terrified troops quietly traversing a more than mile-long sewer line like this one (but with lower ceilings)—and doing it while knee-deep in liquid sewage. At the end of the "sewer," stairs lead down to the middle floor.

The **middle floor** focuses on the grueling aftermath of the uprising. The later days of the uprising are outlined, battle by battle. A chilling section describes how Warsaw became a "city of graves," with burial mounds and makeshift crosses scattered everywhere. As you learn about the uprising's aftermath, consider that the Nazis tried to destroy Warsaw four separate times during World War II (at the outbreak of war, to put down the Ghetto Uprising, to put down the Warsaw Uprising, and finally just to be mean). One room honors the Field Postal Service, which, at great personal risk, continued mail delivery of both military communiqués and civilian correspondences. Many of these brave "mailmen" were actually Scouts who were too young to fight. Nearby, another room re-creates a clandestine radio broadcast station set up in a living room.

If you need a break, look for the red corridor leading through the USSR section to the **café** and WC.

End your visit by walking down the stairs into the **main hall,** which is dominated by two large-scale exhibits: a replica of an RAF Liberator B-24 J, used for airborne surveillance of wartime Warsaw; and a giant movie screen showing more fascinating newsreels assembled by the Home Army's own propaganda unit during the uprising. Under the screen, behind the black curtains, an exhibit tells the story of Germans in Warsaw, along

with another, more claustrophobic walk-through sewer. Also in the main hall, look for the entrance to the seven-minute 3-D film *City of Ruins*, with aerial footage of the postwar devastation. This gives you a look at the reality of the thousand people (nicknamed "Robinson Crusoes") who lived in bombed-out Warsaw immediately after the war. It's worth waiting in line to see this powerful film.

The **park** surrounding the building features several thought-provoking sights. A Chevy truck armored by the Home Army is both a people's tank and an example of how outgunned they were. Along the back is the Wall of Memory, a Vietnam War Memorial-type monument to soldiers of the Polish Home Army who were killed in action. You'll see their rank and name, followed by their code name, in quotes. The Home Army observed a strict policy of anonymity, forbidding members from calling each other by anything but their code names. The bell in the middle is dedicated to the commander of the uprising, Antoni Chruściel (code name "Monter").

SOUTH OF THE CENTER
▲Łazienki Park (Park Łazienkowski)

This huge, idyllic park is where Varsovians go to play. The park is sprinkled with fun Neoclassical buildings, strutting peacocks, and young Poles in love. It was built by Poland's very last king (before the final Partition), Stanisław August Poniatowski, to serve as his summer residence and provide a place for his citizens to relax.

On the edge of the park (along Belwederska) is a **monument to Fryderyk Chopin.** The monument, in a rose garden, is flanked by platforms, where free summer piano **concerts** of Chopin's music are given weekly (mid-May-late Sept only, generally Sun at 12:00 and 16:00— confirm at TI). The statue shows Chopin sitting under a wind-blown willow tree. Although he spent his last 20 years and wrote most of his best-known music in France, his inspiration came from wind blowing through the willow trees of his native land, Poland. The Nazis were quick to destroy this statue, which symbolizes Polish culture. They melted the original (from 1926) down for its metal. Today's copy was recast after World War II. Savor this spot; it's great in summer, with roses wildly in bloom, and in autumn, when the trees provide a golden backdrop for the black, romantic statue.

Venture down into the ravine and to the center of the park, where (after a 10-minute hike) you'll find King Poniatowski's strik-

ing **Palace on the Water** (Pałac na Wodzie)—literally built in the middle of a river. Nearby, you'll spot a clever amphitheater with seating on the riverbank and the stage on an island. The king was a real man of the Enlightenment, hosting weekly Thursday dinners here for artists and intellectuals. But Poland's kings are long gone, and proud peacocks now rule this roost.

Łazienki Park is also slated to be the future home of the state-of-the-art **Museum of Polish History,** which is being built along the Łazienkowska highway (near Ujazdów Castle, at the northeastern edge of the park). While it likely won't open until at least 2018, this museum will be yet another big draw for visitors (to check on the progress, see www.en.muzhp.pl).

Getting There: The park is just south of the city center on the Royal Way. Buses #116, #180, and #195 run from Castle Square in the Old Town along the Royal Way directly to the park (get off at the stop called Łazienki Królewskie, by Belweder Palace—you'll see Chopin squinting through the trees on your left). Maps at park entrances locate the Chopin monument, Palace on the Water, and other park attractions.

Entertainment in Warsaw

Warsaw fills the summer with live music options. In addition to more serious options (opera, symphony, etc.), consider these crowd-pleasing choices.

CHOPIN

My favorite Warsaw music option is to enjoy a Chopin performance. There's nothing like hearing Chopin's compositions passionately played by a teary-eyed Pole who really feels the music. The best option is the outdoor concert in front of the big Chopin statue in **Łazienki Park,** but it is held only one day a week in summer (free, mid-May-late-Sept Sun at 12:00 and 16:00, www.lazienki-krolewskie.pl).

If you're not in town on a Sunday, the next best thing is the **Chopin Salon.** Jarek Chołodecki, who runs the recommended Chopin Boutique B&B, hosts an intimate piano concert in his delightful salon nightly at 19:30. The performance can cover a range of musical styles and composers—but generally there are piano pieces featuring Chopin. The concert lasts from 45 minutes to more than an hour and is followed by wine, homemade cakes, and social time. A small group of locals and travelers gathers around Jarek's big shiny Steinway grand to hear great music by talented young artists in a great city (50 zł, ulica Smolna 14/6, reservations required, tel. 22-829-4801, www.bedandbreakfast.pl).

The **Chopin Museum** has a concert series where music academy students recommended by their professors perform an hour-long concert. These are free and typically take place October through July each Thursday at 18:00—but they can be cancelled, so it's smart to confirm (tel. 22-441-6100, http://en.chopin.nifc.pl; no concerts Aug-Sept).

OTHER MUSIC

Two big, opulent churches in and near the Old Town put on 30-minute **organ concerts** most days through the summer. Choose between the Cathedral of St. John the Baptist, with lots of history and a pretty plain brick interior, right in the heart of the Old Town (10 zł, Aug-late Oct Mon-Sat at 14:00, no concerts Sun); or the frilly, Rococo St. Anne's Church, with a more sumptuous interior, just outside of the Old Town (10 zł, May-early Oct Mon-Sat at 12:00, no concerts Sun). Both are run by the same company (mobile 501-158-477, www.kapitula.org).

Free outdoor **jazz concerts** take place each Saturday in summer right on the Old Town Square (July-Aug at 19:00).

Sleeping in Warsaw

Most accommodations in central Warsaw are either overpriced business-class hotels (whose rates can drop dramatically when demand is low—especially on weekends and in summer), or gloomy, impersonal communist-holdover hotels. Thankfully, there are a few happy exceptions—such as the Chopin Boutique B&B and the Duval Apartments, easily the best options in Warsaw. While pricing in most Polish cities is pretty straightforward, most Warsaw hotels employ dynamic pricing, which fluctuates wildly—even from day to day—depending on demand. For comparison's sake, I've listed the average high-season price for a standard double room.

Sleep Code

Abbreviations   (3 zł = about $1, country code: 48)
S = Single, **D** = Double/Twin, **T** = Triple, **Q** = Quad, **b** = bathroom, **s** = shower only.

Price Rankings

$$$ **Higher Priced**—Most rooms 400 zł or more.

  $$ **Moderately Priced**—Most rooms between
                          300-400 zł.

    $ **Lower Priced**—Most rooms 300 zł or less.

Unless otherwise noted, credit cards are accepted, breakfast is included, Wi-Fi is generally free, and English is spoken. Prices can change without notice; verify current rates online or by email. For the best prices, always book directly with the hotel.

$$$ Hotel Le Régina is a tempting splurge buried in the quiet and charming New Town (just beyond the Old Town). From its elegant public spaces to its 61 top-notch rooms, everything here is done with class. Choose between plenty nice "standard" and "classic" rooms, or pay an extra 200 zł for bigger "superior" rooms, with hand-painted frescoes over each bed. While the official rates are ridiculously high, you'll often find amazingly lower promotional prices on their website (for a standard room in summer figure Db-550 zł on weekdays, as low as 350 zł on weekends, prices change constantly—check online for latest deals, more expensive during winter convention season, prices don't include the 110-zł breakfast—skip this very overpriced option, pricier suites, elevator, non-smoking floor, guest computer, Wi-Fi, exercise room, pool, Kościelna 12, tel. 22-531-6000, www.leregina.com, reception. leregina@mamaison.com).

$$$ Novotel, a chain hotel with 733 uninspired cookie-cutter rooms across the street from the Palace of Culture and Science, overlooks Poland's busiest intersection. Recently renovated inside and out, this is a good option for a big, business-class, downtown hotel that's handy to the central train station (rates change daily, in slow times—especially weekends—you might pay 250-450 zł, best deals online, optional breakfast-65 zł, non-smoking rooms, elevator, guest computer, Wi-Fi, Marszałkowska 94/98, tel. 22-596-0000, www.novotel.com, h3383@accor.com).

$$ Chopin Boutique B&B offers more comfort and class than a hotel twice its price, in a beautifully renovated and well-located old building near the National Museum. Jarek Chołodecki, who lived near Chicago for many years, returned to Warsaw and converted apartments into this wonderful bed-and-breakfast with 24 rooms. It's a friendly, casual, stylish place,

WARSAW

creatively decorated and impeccably maintained. You'll feel like you're staying with your Warsaw sophisticate cousin—quirky, charismatic Jarek loves to chat with his guests, many of whom return and become his good friends. Each morning, conversation percolates at the big, family-style breakfast table over  a morning meal made mostly from organic and locally sourced foods. The drawing room plays host to nightly music concerts— see "Entertainment in Warsaw," earlier (Sb-270 zł, standard Db-320 zł, junior suite-360 zł, big suite-500 zł, these special rates for Rick Steves readers who book directly with hotel, elevator, guest computer, Wi-Fi, ulica Smolna 14/6, tel. 22-829-4801, www.bedandbreakfast.pl, office@bedandbreakfast.pl).

$$ Duval Apartments, named for a French woman who supposedly had an affair with the Polish king in this building, offers four beautifully appointed rooms above a restaurant (called Same Fusy) a few steps off the square in the Old Town. Each room has a different theme: traditional Polish, Japanese, glass, or retro (Sb-280 zł, Db-320 zł, Tb-400 zł, includes breakfast, lots of stairs with no elevator, some restaurant noise—light sleepers should request a quiet room, Wi-Fi, Nowomiejska 10, mobile 608-679-346, www.duval.net.pl, duval@duval.net.pl). There's no reception, and the rooms aren't officially affiliated with the restaurant, so arrange a meeting time with Agnieszka (or, if she's busy, Marcin) when you reserve. On arrival, go up the stairs and ring doorbell #5; the restaurant closes at 23:00.

$$ Castle Inn, sitting right on Castle Square at the entrance to the Old Town, is the next rung up the ladder for youth hostelers who've outgrown the grungy backpacker scene. Run by the owners of Oki Doki Hostel (described later), it has 22 creative and colorful rooms, each with completely different but equally artsy decor. Its location in the heart of the tourist zone is handy, but does come with some noise (very slushy rates depending on demand, generally Sb-300 zł, Db-350 zł, "delux" Db-500 zł, 35 zł extra for continental breakfast—have it delivered to your room for the same price, lots of stairs and no elevator, guest computer, Wi-Fi, Świętojańska 2, tel. 22-425-0100, www.castleinn.pl, castleinn@castleinn.pl).

$$ Between Us B&B is an ideal home-away-from-home for hipsters in Warsaw. Beata rents three trendy rooms above a youthful café centrally located in downtown Warsaw. As this place books up early, reserve far ahead (Db-300-525 zł depending on size and length of stay, on second floor, no elevator, Wi-Fi, check in at Miedzy Nami café downstairs, Bracka 20, tel. 22-828-5417, mobile 603-096-701, www.between-us.eu, info@between-us.eu).

$$ Old Town Apartments offers 17 studio, one-bedroom, and two-bedroom apartments inside Warsaw's Old Town. Don't expect romantic Old World ambience—the apartments are modern, practical, and IKEA-furnished. The prices are good and the location is excellent, but you're pretty much on your own (no real reception, no breakfast but all have kitchens). View the apartments on their website, pick the one that looks best, and set up a meeting to get the keys at their Nowy Świat office (prices flex with demand, but figure studio-300 zł, 1-bedroom-350 zł, 2-bedroom-450 zł, some more expensive "featured" apartments on the square also available, slightly cheaper Oct-April and last-minute, Wi-Fi, tel. 22-887-9800, www.apartmentsapart.com, warsaw@bookaa.net). They also rent 15 pricey apartments on Nowy Świat, called **Royal Route Residence** (similar rates, breakfast-25 zł, corner of Nowy Świat and Chmielna). For either place, you'll check in at the office at Nowy Świat 27 (Mon-Fri 10:00-20:00, Sat-Sun 9:00-17:00, at other times arrange a meeting to get the keys). After checking in here, they'll send you in a taxi to your Old Town apartment.

$$ Hotel Harenda, a reliable old standby, has 43 rooms with leather-bound doors on the second and third floors of an office building right in the middle of the Royal Way, by the Copernicus monument. The tired, communist-era rooms are crying out for a renovation, but the location is ideal, and the ground-floor pub is a popular hangout (May-June and Sept-Oct: Sb-340 zł, Db-380 zł; July-Aug and Nov-April: Sb-310 zł, Db-340 zł; breakfast-30 zł, second night is free Fri-Sun, some rowdy street noise—especially on weekends—so request a quiet room, lots of stairs with no elevator, guest computer, Wi-Fi, Krakowskie Przedmieście 4/6, tel. 22-826-0071, www.hotelharenda.com.pl, rezerwacja@ hotelharenda.com.pl).

$ Zgoda Apartment Hotel is conveniently located on an urban street between the Palace of Culture and Science and the Royal Way. With 51 classy-feeling apartments designed for business travelers, it's a comfortable—if impersonal—home base in the city center (small Sb/Db-200 zł, studio Sb/Db-250 zł, bigger "comfort" Sb/Db-300 zł, "superior" Sb/Db-400 zł, fancier rooms also available, rates are soft—especially for longer stays, extra bed-50 zł, breakfast-40 zł or use the kitchenette, air-con, elevator, Wi-Fi, Zgoda 6, tel. 22-553-6200, www.desilva.pl, zgoda@desilva.pl).

$ Ibis Warszawa Stare Miasto, with 333 cookie-cutter rooms, is the place for predictable comfort with zero personality. This hotel, part of the popular European chain, overlooks a WWII memorial in a nondescript, businessy-feeling neighborhood a

10-minute walk north of the Old Town (Sb/Db-289 zł, or 219 zł Fri-Sun, can be higher during conventions, sometimes better deals online, breakfast-33 zł, air-con, non-smoking rooms, elevator, Muranowska 2, tel. 22-310-1000, www.ibishotel.com, h3714@ accor.com).

HOSTELS

$ Nathan's Villa Hostel has 13 dorm rooms (with 95 beds) and 6 private rooms overlooking a cozy courtyard, and plenty of opportunities for backpacker bonding. It's near the Śródmieście dining zone, requiring a 15-minute walk or easy bus ride south of the central train station area (dorm bed in 4-bed room-72 zł, in 6-bed room-60 zł, in 12-bed room-50 zł, D-184 zł, Db-194 zł, all rates about 10 zł/person less on off-season weeknights, includes sheets, lockers, guest computer, Wi-Fi, pay laundry service, guest kitchen, hiding behind a modern glass office building at ulica Piękna 24/26—the nearby square called plac Konstytucji has easy bus connections, tel. 22-622-2946, www.nathansvillahostel.com).

$ Oki Doki Hostel, on a pleasant square a few blocks in front of the Palace of Culture and Science, is colorful, creative, and easygoing. Each of its 37 rooms was designed by a different artist with a special theme—such as Van Gogh, Celtic spirals, heads of state, or Lenin. It's run by Ernest—a Pole whose parents loved Hemingway—and his wife Łucja, with help from their sometimes-jaded staff (complicated pricing structure flexes with demand, approximate high-season prices: dorm bed in 4-bed room-70 zł, in 5- to 6-bed room-60 zł, in 8-bed room-55 zł; S-160 zł, D-180 zł, Db-220 zł, T-220 zł; prices include breakfast except for dorm-dwellers—who pay 15 zł, guest computer, Wi-Fi, laundry service-15 zł, kitchen, lots of stairs with no elevator, plac Dąbrowskiego 3, tel. 22-826-5112, 22-828-0122, www.okidoki.pl, okidoki@okidoki.pl).

$ Szkolne Schronisko, the IYHF hostel, with 110 beds and lots of school groups, is institutional, well-run, bright, and clean. The downside: It's five floors up, with no elevator (nonmembers welcome, all prices per person: dorm beds-40 zł, S-80 zł, twin D-70 zł, T-60 zł, Q-55 zł, towel-3 zł, no breakfast but members' kitchen, 10 percent cheaper for hostel members, all rates 5-10 zł more expensive for guests over age 26, closed 10:00-16:00, curfew at 24:00; email ahead to reserve limited S, D, and T rooms; good location across the street from National Museum at ulica Smolna 30, tel. 22-827-8952, www.hostelsmolna30.pl, info@ hostelsmolna30.pl).

Eating in Warsaw

Tourists are drawn to the Old Town, where you can find decent (if generally overpriced) traditional Polish food. But the best eating options in this city are elsewhere: on or near Nowy Świat or—for a younger take—the emerging Śródmieście zone, to the south. In these neighborhoods, you'll find some traditional (or updated) Polish cuisine mixed in with some more interesting, international options. Wherever you dine, most restaurants are open until the "last guest," which usually means about 23:00 (sometimes later in summer).

ON OR NEAR NOWY ŚWIAT

While most Old Town eateries are traditional and cater to tourists, locals flock to the Nowy Świat neighborhood (near the National Museum and central train station) for a fun night on the town.

Fancy Eateries on Foksal Street: Foksal—the first cross street as you go down Nowy Świat from Jerusalem Avenue—has a thriving assortment of about a half-dozen cafés and restaurants: Mexican, Italian, Asian, international, and more. Most have inviting outdoor seating that's ideal on a balmy summer evening. The clientele is young and sophisticated, and there's not a pierogi in sight. Find the place with the cuisine and ambience you like best. **Papaya** has tasty pan-Asian fare and a trendy, minimalist, black-and-white interior (30-60-zł main dishes plus pricier splurges, daily 12:00-24:00, at #16, tel. 22-826-1199). A block beyond this area is a far more traditional option, **Kamanda Lwowska,** named for the former Polish city that's now in Ukraine. It has a few outdoor seats and a charming, cluttered old cellar; the friendly and fun staff serves up Polish classics (40-55-zł main dishes, daily 10:00-24:00, Foksal 10, tel. 22-828-1031).

Cheap Milk Bars: **Wiking Bar,** a colorful milk bar, serves up Polish grub right on Nowy Świat, with inviting sidewalk seating (10-15-zł main dishes, Mon-Fri 7:30-22:00, Sat 12:00-23:00, Sun 12:00-20:00, Nowy Świat 28). **Mleczarnia Jerozolimska,** just around the corner on busy Jerusalem Avenue, is a more classic milk-bar experience (4-7-zł soups, 9-14-zł main dishes, Mon-Fri 10:00-20:00, Sat-Sun 11:00-19:00, aleja Jerozolimskie 32).

Hungarian and Polish Cuisine on Zgoda Street: **Borpince** ("Wine Cellar") is a cozy cellar serving up very authentic

Hungarian fare a long block off of Nowy Świat (toward the Palace of Culture and Science). As you dive into spicy goulash and *paprikás,* you'll see just how different the cuisine can be on the other side of the Carpathians. If you won't be visiting Hungary on your trip, this is the next best way to sample Hungarian favorites. The restaurant also has a long list of Hungarian wines (40-50-zł main dishes, daily 12:00-23:00, closes earlier when it's slow, ulica Zgoda 1, tel. 22-828-2244). For Magyar flavors at lower prices, try **Krokiecik** ("Croquette"), the simpler self-service restaurant located next door, at street level. Choose from Polish or Hungarian food, order at the counter, then take a seat (10-15-zł main dishes, daily 9:00-21:00, ulica Zgoda 1, tel. 22-827-3037). **Restauracja Zgoda,** across the street and owned by the same people, has affordable, reliable Polish cuisine in an Old World setting; it's popular among traditionalists dining out (9-15-zł soups, 20-zł salads, 20-35-zł fish and meat dishes, Mon-Sat 9:00-23:00, Sun 12:00-23:00, Zgoda 4, tel. 22-827-9934).

Uniquely Polish Treats

These two places are on or close to the busy Nowy Świat boulevard.

A. Blikle, Poland's most famous pastry shop, serves a wide variety of delicious treats. This is where locals shop for cakes when they're having someone special over for coffee. The specialty: *pączki* (PONCH-kee), the quintessential Polish doughnut, filled with rose-flavored jam. You can get your goodies "to go" in the shop (3-zł *pączki,* daily 9:00-21:00), or pay double to enjoy them with coffee in the swanky, classic café with indoor or outdoor seating (7-zł *pączki,* Mon-Sat 9:00-22:00, Sun 10:00-22:00; both at Nowy Świat 35, tel. 22-828-6601). They also have a sit-down restaurant (30-50-zł main dishes), but I come here only for the *pączki.*

E. Wedel Pijalnia Czekolady thrills chocoholics. Emil Wedel made Poland's favorite chocolate, and today, his former residence houses this chocolate shop and genteel café. This is the spot for delicious pastries and a *real* hot chocolate—*czekolada do picia* ("drinking chocolate"), a cup of actual melted chocolate, not just hot chocolate milk (12 zł). The staff describes it as, "True Wedel ecstasy for your mouth that will take you to a world of dreams and desires." Or, if you fancy chocolate mousse, try *pokusa* ("Wedel Temptation"). Wedel's was *the* Christmas treat for locals under communism. Cadbury bought the company when Poland privatized, but they kept the E. Wedel name, which is close to all Poles' hearts...and taste buds (Mon-Fri 8:00-22:00, Sat 10:00-22:00, Sun 10:00-21:00, between Palace of Culture and Science and Nowy Świat at ulica Szpitalna 8, tel. 22-827-2916, www.wedelpijalnie.pl/en).

IN THE ŚRÓDMIEŚCIE DISTRICT

Warsaw's Śródmieście ("Downtown") district, south of Jerusalem Avenue, is emerging as the epicenter of Polish hipster/foodie culture. While this is a bit farther from the main tourist/sightseeing zone, that's sort of the point. And while the Old Town/New Town are for tourists, and the Nowy Świat area is for yuppies and business travelers, in the Śródmieście you'll find young Varsovian foodies digging into affordable dishes at the trendiest new places. This area is a 15-minute walk south of Jerusalem Avenue, and also well-served by public transportation (for example, trams #4, #15, #18, and #35 run frequently along the main north-south Marszałkowska corridor to plac Zbawiciela; of these, tram #4 stops in the middle of the road below Palace Square, where the Royal Way meets the Old Town). Listed next are a few different restaurant-hunting zones, with some specific recommendations for each one. I'd just hop a tram to plac Zbawiciela and explore from there...within a few steps, you'll find more temptations than in the rest of the city combined.

Plac Zbawiciela: Named "Holiest Savior Square" for the looming church, this is a dizzying six-way intersection with a big traffic circle ringed by elegant old colonnades. To get a quick taste of the emerging Śródmieście scene, come here first and just do a slow loop around the circle, surveying your options. Starting to the right of the steeple and moving clockwise, here are a few options you'll see: **Izumi Sushi** and **Karma** coffee shop have their fans, but **Tuk Tuk**—serving quick and delicious Thai street food (order you choice of 20-30-zł dishes at the counter, then take a seat)—is a popular choice. Across the street, **Rumburak** is an inviting café with an impressive menu of 30-40-zł international dishes and atmospheric seating under the colonnade. Just down Mokotowska from the circle, look for the line of people at **Lody Naturalne,** an unpretentious hole-in-the-wall serving all-natural, homemade ice cream. In the next section, **Charlotte** designer bakery and wine bar is another popular choice, with homemade treats and tables spilling out all over the square. Up above, **Plan B** is a hipster dive bar with drinks, snacks, and views down over the square (find the graffiti-slathered staircase up, just past Charlotte). In the unlikely event that you don't find something to your liking around this square, head up Mokotowska (past the ice-cream place, described next).

Mokotowska: This street, stretching north from plac Zbawiciela, has fewer choices—but they're good ones. **Dyspensa** may be the best option in the Śródmieście for a serious sit-down meal in a dressy but not stuffy environment. They serve a thoughtfully selected menu of updated Polish cuisine, plus a few international options, as well as a handwritten list of daily specials.

WARSAW

Reservations are smart (60-85-zł main courses, daily 12:00-23:00, Mokotowska 39, tel. 22-629-9989, www.dyspensa.pl). A half-block up the street is the mellower **Słodki Słony** ("Sweet Salty"), at the casual end of the scale of Polish celebrity chef Magda Gessler's restaurant empire. Up front is a big, tempting display case bursting with over-the-top decadent desserts (10-20 zł); farther in is a cozy dining area where you can dig into 20-35-zł sandwiches, salads, and other light fare (daily 11:00-24:00, Mokotowska 45, tel. 22-622-4934, www.slodkislony.pl).

Poznańska: A few short blocks to the west, this street is also lined with trendy and youthful eateries (particularly between Wilcza and Żurawia). Strolling this strip, you'll find **Kaskrut** (a pun on *casse-croûte*, with 20-25-zł sandwiches); **Leniviec** café and cocktails; **Dwie 3,** offering Mediterranean fusion in a modern and spacious setting; and **Tel Aviv,** with gluten-free and vegan Middle Eastern food. But the foodie anchor in this neighborhood is **Beirut,** a gregariously crowded bar serving up excellent Middle Eastern food. The hummus bar, on the left, has a wide variety of *mezes* (small plates) and grilled meats, while the "Kraken Rum Bar" on the right has fish dishes (15-30 zł dishes on both sides; portions are modest, so plan to share a few). At either side, line up at the bar, ask for the English menu, place your order, try to find a table, then wait for your number to be called. It can be a bit chaotic, but it's delicious and fun (daily 12:00-late, Poznańska 12).

Classy Steakhouse: **Butchery & Wine,** in an unassuming location on a drab urban street, is a pocket of chic international cuisine in the heart of Warsaw. The waiters, smartly dressed in pinstripe aprons, serve upscale comfort food (specializing in steaks) to a small, lively room of business travelers. The wine list is extensive, and reservations are smart (55-85-zł steaks, Mon-Sat 12:00-22:00, closed Sun, across aleja Jerozolimskie from Nowy Świat at Żurawia 22, tel. 22-502-3118, www.butcheryandwine.pl).

HANGOUT CAFÉS NEAR THE RIVER

If you just want to grab a drink (and possibly a light meal) and watch the world go by, Warsaw has two inviting cafés downhill, near the river, that are worth the short trip from the main tourist zone. The first one serves mostly drinks and is a hip hangout by day and by night; the second has a wider menu of food and is open only during the day.

Warszawa Powiśle occupies the old, communist-style ticket office for the suburban train station of the same name. Now it's

been taken over by hipsters and converted into one of the most happening hangouts in town. Tucked along a picturesque bike lane beneath the towering legs of a bridge, its sidewalk is jammed with cool Varsovians and in-the-know visitors living well. The building itself has some indoor seating, but it's quite small—making this a better good-weather option (light sandwiches, daily 9:00 until late, Kruczkowskiego 3B, tel. 22-474-4084). The most direct way to get here from the palm tree at the head of Nowy Świat is to walk down Jerusalem Avenue toward the bridge, enter the rail station, go down the stairs, walk all the way along *peron* (platform) 1 to the end, then go down the stairs at the far end: You'll pop out right at the bar. Alternatively, you can walk partway across the bridge at Jerusalem Avenue, then go down the stairs at the first tower.

Kawarnia Kafka combines a used bookstore (with books sold by weight) with a hip, creative café. You'll find comfy chairs, stay-awhile tables, and checkerboard tiles inside, while outside on the lawn across from the café, guests lounge in slingback chairs (8-18-zł sandwiches and crêpes, 15-25-zł pastas and salads, Wi-Fi, Mon-Fri 9:00-22:00, Sat-Sun 10:00-22:00, Oboźna 3, tel. 22-826-0822).

IN OR NEAR THE OLD TOWN

The restaurants in the Old Town and surrounding streets are 100 percent for tourists. I'd much rather dine at one of the more characteristic areas noted earlier, but if you need to grab a meal near here, the following places are worth considering. Rather than spending too much to eat on the Old Town Market Square, I prefer to venture a few blocks to find a place with good food and much lower prices.

Restauracja pod Samsonem ("Under Samson") is a touristy standby for dining on affordable Jewish and Polish comfort food. The ambience is pleasant—with enjoyable outdoor seating in good weather—the service is playfully opinionated, and the low prices make up for the fact that you have to pay to check your coat and use the bathroom (25-35-zł main courses, daily 10:00-23:00, ulica Freta 3/5, tel. 22-831-1788).

Pierogarnia na Bednarskiej brags, "only our grandmothers make better pierogi." In addition to the classic Polish dumplings, the menu includes soups and a fun variety of drinks (from unusual fruit juices to *kvas*, the nonalcoholic, rye-flavored dark beer). Order at the counter and take a seat—they'll call you when your food's ready. With mellow country decor, wooden menus, and a loyal crowd, this is a handy spot for a quick, cheap meal along the Royal Way (15-zł plates of pierogi, 18-zł combo-plate includes soup and salad, daily 12:00-20:00, hiding down a quiet street behind the statue of Adam Mickiewicz at ulica Bednarska

28/30, tel. 22-828-0392).

BrowArmia is a hit with beer lovers. This sprawling brew-pub makes four different types of beer (plus special seasonal beers) and serves decent pub grub. The dark, mod, long interior fills two levels (including a fun cellar), but in good weather I'd stake out a spot on the terrace—ideal for people-watching along the Royal Way. The food is overpriced, but you're paying for the beer and the location (40-70-zł main dishes, daily 12:00-24:00, live music or DJ in cellar on weekends, right on Krakowskie Przedmieście near Piłsudski Square at ulica Królewska 1, tel. 22-826-5455).

Italian: **Enoteka Polska** is a dressy wine cellar serving Italian food at rustic tables squeezed between crates of wine bottles. Although the location is in the middle of nowhere (about a 10-minute walk through drab sprawl from the Old Town), the decor is nicely modern, and there's a pleasant garden in the summer. Reservations are smart (30-40-zł pastas, 40-60-zł main dishes, daily 12:00-24:00, Sun 13:00-21:00, Długa 23/25, tel. 22-635-5510, www.enotekapolska.pl).

Warsaw Connections

Almost all trains into and out of Warsaw go through the hulking central train station (described earlier, under "Arrival in Warsaw"; pay special attention to the "Buying Train Tickets" section). If you're heading to Gdańsk, note that the red-brick Gothic city of Toruń and the impressive Malbork Castle are on the way (though on separate train lines, so you can't do both en route; see the Gdańsk and Pomerania chapters). Also be aware that express trains to many destinations—including Kraków and Gdańsk—require seat reservations, even if you have a rail pass.

To confirm rail journeys, check specific times online (www.rozklad-pkp.pl) or at the central train station.

From Warsaw's Central Station by Train to: Kraków (hourly, about 2.5 hours, requires seat reservation), **Gdańsk** (hourly, 3 hours), **Toruń** (9/day, 3 hours direct, more with transfer in Kutno or Iława), **Malbork** (hourly, 2.5 hours), **Prague** (2/day direct, including 1 night train, more with changes, 8.5-10.5 hours), **Berlin** (4/day direct, 5.5 hours), **Budapest** (2/day with transfer in Břeclav, Czech Republic, 9.75 hours; 1 direct night train, 11 hours), **Vienna** (2/day direct, 7 hours; plus 1 night train, 8.75 hours).

By Bus: PolskiBus runs bus routes throughout Poland (www.polskibus.com).

GDAŃSK & THE TRI-CITY

Gdańsk (guh-DAYNSK) is a true find on the Baltic Coast of Poland. You may associate Gdańsk with dreary images of striking dockworkers from the nightly news in the 1980s—but there's so much more to this city than shipyards, Solidarity, and smog. It's surprisingly easy to look past the urban sprawl to find one of northern Europe's most historic and picturesque cities. Gdańsk is second only to Kraków as Poland's most appealing destination.

Exploring Gdańsk is a delight. The gem of a Main Town boasts block after block of red-brick churches and narrow, colorful, ornately decorated Hanseatic burghers' mansions. The riverfront embankment, with its trademark medieval crane, oozes salty maritime charm. Gdańsk's history is also fascinating— from its 17th-century Golden Age to the headlines of our own generation, big things happen here. You might even see portly old Lech Wałęsa still wandering the streets. And yet Gdańsk is also looking to its future, steadily repairing some of its WWII damage after a long communist hibernation. Over the past decade, whole swaths of the city have been remade with a bold new modernity...but always with a respect for the past.

Gdańsk and two nearby towns (Sopot and Gdynia) together form an area known as the "Tri-City," offering several day-trip opportunities north along the coast. The once-faded, now-revitalized elegance of the seaside resort of Sopot beckons to tourists, while the modern burg of Gdynia sets the pace for today's Poland. Beyond the Tri-City, the sandy Hel Peninsula is a popular spot for summer sunbathing.

PLANNING YOUR TIME

This region merits two days to make the trip here worthwhile. Gdańsk's major sights can be seen in a day, but a second day allows you to see everything in town at a more relaxing pace, and take your pick from among several possible side-trips.

Gdańsk sightseeing has two major components: the Royal Way (historic main drag with good museums) and the modern shipyard where Solidarity was born (with a fascinating museum). With just one day, do one of these activities in the morning, and the other in the afternoon. With two days, do one each day, and round out your time with other attractions: Art lovers enjoy the National Museum (with a stunning altar painting by Hans Memling), history buffs make the pilgrimage to Westerplatte (where World War II began), and church and pipe organ fans might visit Oliwa Cathedral in Gdańsk's northern suburbs (on the way to Sopot).

If you have more time, consider the wide variety of side-trips. The most popular option is the half-day round-trip to Malbork Castle (30-45 minutes each way by train, plus two or three hours to tour the castle—see next chapter). Closer to Gdańsk, it only takes a quick visit to get a feel for the resort town of Sopot (25 minutes each way by train), but the town's beaches may tempt you to laze around longer. Consider a sprint through Gdynia to round out your take on the Tri-City. If you have a full day and great weather, and you don't mind fighting the crowds for a patch of sandy beach, go to Hel.

Gdańsk gets busy in late June, when school holidays begin, and it's downright crowded with mostly German tourists from July to mid-September—especially during St. Dominic's Fair (Jarmark Św. Dominika, three weeks from late July to mid-Aug), with market stalls, concerts, and other celebrations.

Orientation to Gdańsk

With 460,000 residents, Gdańsk is part of the larger urban area known as the Tri-City (Trójmiasto, total population of 1 million). But the tourist's Gdańsk is compact, welcoming, and walkable—virtually anything you'll want to see is within a 20-minute stroll of everything else.

Focus on the Main Town (Główne Miasto), home to most of the sights described, including the spectacular Royal Way main drag, ulica Długa. The Old Town (Stare Miasto) has a handful of

old brick buildings and faded, tall, skinny houses—but the area is mostly drab and residential, and not worth much time. Just beyond the northern end of the Old Town (about a 20-minute walk from the heart of the Main Town) is the entrance to the Gdańsk Shipyard, with the excellent European Solidarity Center and its top-notch museum. From here, shipyards sprawl for miles.

The second language in this part of Poland is German, not English. As this was a predominantly German city until the end of World War II, German tourists flock here in droves. But you'll win no Polish friends if you call the city by its more familiar German name, Danzig. You'll also find that Gdańsk is becoming an increasingly popular cruise destination, with about 100 ships calling here each year (most dock at the nearby city of Gdynia, and passengers take a bus or train in). During summer daytime hours, the town is filled with little tour groups.

TOURIST INFORMATION

Confusingly, Gdańsk has three different TI organizations. The regional TI occupies the **Upland Gate,** facing the busy road that hems in the Main Town, at the start of my self-guided walk (May-Sept Mon-Fri 9:00-20:00, Sat-Sun 9:00-18:00; Oct-April daily 9:00-18:00; tel. 58-732-7041). The city TI has three branches—one conveniently located at the bottom (river) end of the main drag, at **Długi Targ 28** (just to the left as you face the gate; July-Aug daily 9:00-19:00; Sept-June Mon-Sat 9:00-17:00, Sun 9:00-16:00; tel. 58-301-4355, www.gdansk4u.pl). Satellites TIs are at the **main train station** (in the underpass, same hours, tel. 58-721-3277) and at the **airport** (open 24/7, tel. 58-348-1368). Skip the other TI, which is prominently located (in the red, high-gabled building across ulica Długa from the Town Hall) but sloppily run by the national government.

Sightseeing Card: Busy sightseers should consider the **Tourist Card,** which includes entry to 24 sights in Gdańsk, Gdynia, and Sopot, and discounts at others (such as 20 percent off admission to Malbork Castle). Check the list of what's covered (most of the biggies in town are free with the card, while the European Solidarity Center is 50 percent off), and do the arithmetic. If you'll be seeing several included museums, this card could save you some money (sightseeing-only card: 38 zł/24 hours, 48 zł/72 hours; "max" card also includes local public transit: 58 zł/24 hours, 88 zł/72 hours; sold only at TIs).

ARRIVAL IN GDAŃSK

By Train: Gdańsk's main train station (Gdańsk Główny) is a pretty brick palace on the western edge of the old center. (To save money, architects in Colmar, France, copied this exact design to build their city's station.) Trains to other parts of Poland (marked *PKP*) use platforms 1-3; regional trains with connections to the Tri-City (marked *SKM*) use the shorter platforms 3-5.

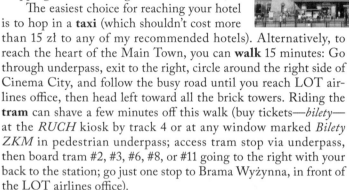

Inside the terminal building, you'll find lockers, ATMs, and ticket windows. Outside, the pedestrian underpass by the McDonald's has a TI and leads you beneath the busy road (first set of exits: tram stop; end of corridor: shopping mall at the edge of the Old Town).

The easiest choice for reaching your hotel is to hop in a **taxi** (which shouldn't cost more than 15 zł to any of my recommended hotels). Alternatively, to reach the heart of the Main Town, you can **walk** 15 minutes: Go through underpass, exit to the right, circle around the right side of Cinema City, and follow the busy road until you reach LOT airlines office, then head left toward all the brick towers. Riding the **tram** can shave a few minutes off this walk (buy tickets—*bilety*—at the *RUCH* kiosk by track 4 or at any window marked *Bilety ZKM* in pedestrian underpass; access tram stop via underpass, then board tram #2, #3, #6, #8, or #11 going to the right with your back to the station; go just one stop to Brama Wyżynna, in front of the LOT airlines office).

By Plane: Gdańsk's newly expanded airport, named for Lech Wałęsa, is about five miles west of the city center (airport code: GDN, tel. 58-348-1163, www.airport.gdansk.pl). In the arrivals area, you'll find a helpful TI and ATMs. You have several ways to get downtown: bus, shuttle, taxi, or (possibly) airport train. Public **bus** #210 connects the airport with downtown, stopping near the main train station and at Brama Wyżynna, near the heart of the Main Town (take it in the direction of Orunia; 3 zł, buy ticket at machine at stop—takes coins, small bills, and credit cards—or buy on board for a bit more; 2/hour on weekdays, 1/hour on weekends, 40 minutes, exit terminal and turn left to find bus stop). The **Airportbus shuttle** zips you directly to various points downtown, though the schedule is sporadic and it must be booked in advance (9-12 zł depending on where you go, various companies including www.mpapoland.pl). The 25-minute **taxi** ride into town will cost you about 50-60 zł. A new **airport train** is expected to start running (likely in late 2015 or early 2016); you'll ride this "metropolitan line" from the terminal to the end of the line at Gdańsk Wrzeszcz; from there you can easily transfer to the regional SKM train line that takes you the rest of the way to the main train station or Gdańsk Śródmieście station (about 30 minutes total; ask for details at the TI in the arrivals area).

HELPFUL HINTS

Blue Monday: Off-season, most of Gdańsk's museums are closed Monday. In the busy summertime, the Gdańsk Historical Museum branches are open—and free—for limited hours on Monday. If museums are closed, Monday is a good day to visit churches or take a side-trip to Sopot (but not to Malbork Castle, which is also closed Mon).

Internet Access: You'll find several free Wi-Fi hotspots in major tourist zones around central Gdańsk.

St. Dominic's Fair: Each summer for three weeks around St. Dominic's Day (last week in July through first half of August), Gdańsk is packed with visitors for its venerable St. Dominic's Fair. You'll find otherwise stately streets jammed with stalls selling crafts and edibles, concert stages (there's a lot of free music), and people from all over Poland milling about. While this is a huge draw, as long as you have a hotel booked (well in advance), the fair has surprisingly little impact on sights or restaurants.

GETTING AROUND GDAŃSK

Everything is within easy walking distance of my recommended hotels. Public transportation is generally unnecessary for sightseers on a short visit, but it's useful for reaching outlying sights such as Oliwa Cathedral, Westerplatte, Sopot, Gdynia, and Hel (specific transportation options for these places are described in each listing).

By Public Transportation: Gdańsk's trams and buses work on the same tickets: Choose between a single-ride ticket (3 zł), one-hour ticket (3.60 zł), and 24-hour ticket (12 zł). Major stops have handy ticket machines, which take coins, small bills, and credit cards. Otherwise, buy tickets *(bilety)* at kiosks marked *RUCH* or *Bilety ZKM,* or pay a little more to buy tickets on board. In the city center, the stops worth knowing about are Plac Solidarności (near the shipyards and European Solidarity Center), Gdańsk Główny (in front of the main train station), and Brama Wyżynna (near the Upland Gate and the new Gdańsk Śródmieście commuter train station). When buying tickets, don't confuse *ZKM* (the company that runs Gdańsk city transit) with *SKM* (the company that runs commuter trains to outlying destinations).

One public bus worth knowing about is Gdańsk's **bus #100.** Every 20 minutes, this made-for-tourists minibus (designed to navigate the twisty streets of the town center) makes a loop through the Old Town and Main Town, with strategic stops near Mariacka street, just south of the Royal Way, at the main train station, and near Solidarity Square. As this is a new service, confirm that it's running and get details at the TI (covered by regular

Gdańsk at a Gdlance

▲▲▲**Royal Way/Ulica Długa Walk** Gdańsk's colorful show-piece main drag, cutting a picturesque swath through the heart of the wealthy burghers' neighborhood. **Hours:** Always open. See page 224.

▲▲▲**Solidarity Sights and Gdańsk Shipyard** Home to the beginning of the end of Eastern European communism, housing a towering monument and an excellent museum. **Hours:** Memorial and shipyard gate—always open. European Solidarity Center exhibit—daily May-Sept 10:00-20:00, Oct-April 10:00-18:00. See page 251.

▲▲**Main Town Hall** Ornately decorated meeting rooms, town artifacts, and climbable tower with sweeping views. **Hours:** Mid-June-mid-Sept Mon-Thu 9:00-16:00, Fri-Sat 10:00-18:00, Sun 10:00-16:00; mid-Sept-mid-June Tue 10:00-13:00, Wed-Sat 10:00-16:00, Thu until 18:00, Sun 11:00-16:00, closed Mon. See page 242.

▲▲**Artus Court** Grand meeting hall for guilds of Golden Age Gdańsk, boasting an over-the-top tiled stove. **Hours:** Same as Main Town Hall. See page 243.

▲▲**St. Mary's Church** Giant red-brick church crammed full of Gdańsk history. **Hours:** June-Sept Mon-Sat 9:00-18:30, Sun 13:00-18:30; closes progressively earlier off-season. See page 233.

▲**Amber Museum** High-tech exhibit of valuable golden globs of petrified tree sap. **Hours:** Same as Main Town Hall, above. See page 240.

▲**Uphagen House** Tourable 18th-century interior, typical of the pretty houses that line ulica Długa. **Hours:** Same as Main Town Hall. See page 241.

---

transit ticket, may run in summer only).

By Taxi: Taxis cost about 8 zł to start, then 2-3 zł per kilometer (a bit more at night). Find a taxi stand, or call a cab (try Neptun, tel. 19686; or Dejan, tel. 58-19628).

Tours in Gdańsk

Private Guides

Hiring a local guide is an exceptional value. **Agnieszka Syroka**—youthful, bubbly, and personable—is a wonderful guide. She has a big SUV for tours of Malbork Castle and the region, too (400

▲**National Maritime Museum** Sprawling exhibit on all aspects of the nautical life, housed in several venues (including the landmark medieval Crane and a permanently moored steamship) connected by a ferry boat. **Hours:** July-Aug daily 10:00-18:00; Sept-Oct and March-June Tue-Sun 10:00-16:00, closed Mon; Nov-Feb Tue-Sun 10:00-15:00, closed Mon. See page 245.

Historical Zone of the Free City of Gdańsk Tiny museum examining Gdańsk's unique status as a "Free City" between the World Wars. **Hours:** Tue-Sun 12:00-17:00, until 18:00 May-Aug, closed Mon year-round. See page 244.

Archaeological Museum Decent collection of artifacts from this region's past. **Hours:** July-Aug Tue-Fri 9:00-17:00, Sat-Sun 10:00-17:00; Sept-June Tue and Thu-Fri 8:00-16:00, Wed 9:00-17:00, Sat-Sun 10:00-16:00; closed Mon year-round. See page 244.

National Museum in Gdańsk Ho-hum art collection with a single blockbuster highlight: Hans Memling's remarkable *Last Judgment* altarpiece. **Hours:** June-Aug Tue-Wed and Fri-Sun 10:00-17:00, Thu 12:00-19:00; May and Sept Tue-Sun 10:00-17:00; Oct-April Tue-Fri 9:00-16:00, Sat-Sun 10:00-17:00, closed Mon year-round. See page 257.

"Blue Lion" Archaeological Education Center Kid-friendly exhibit about medieval Gdańsk. **Hours:** May-Aug Tue-Sun 10:00-18:00, Sept-April Tue-Sun 9:00-17:00, closed Mon year-round. See page 259.

Oliwa Cathedral Suburban church with long, skinny nave and playful organ. **Hours:** Church open long hours daily; frequent organ concerts in summer. See page 259.

GDAŃSK & THE TRI-CITY

zł for up to 4 hours, more for all day, mobile 502-554-584, www.tourguidegdansk.com, asyroka@interia.pl or syroka.agnieszka@gmail.com). **Jacek "Jake" Podhorski,** who teaches economics at the local university, guides in the summer. He's been around long enough to have fascinating personal memories of the communist days (400 zł/3 hours, 100 zł extra with his car, mobile 603-170-761, ekojpp@univ.gda.pl).

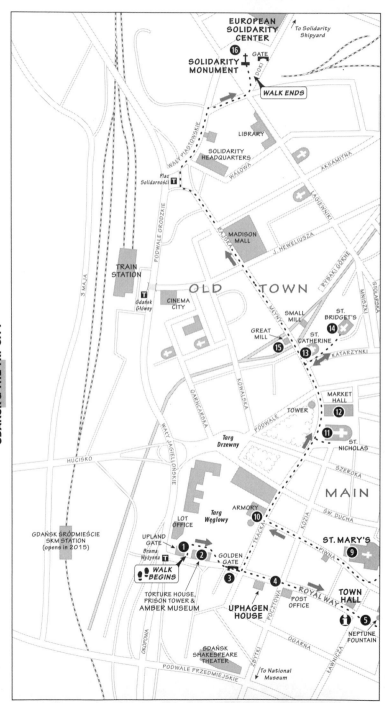

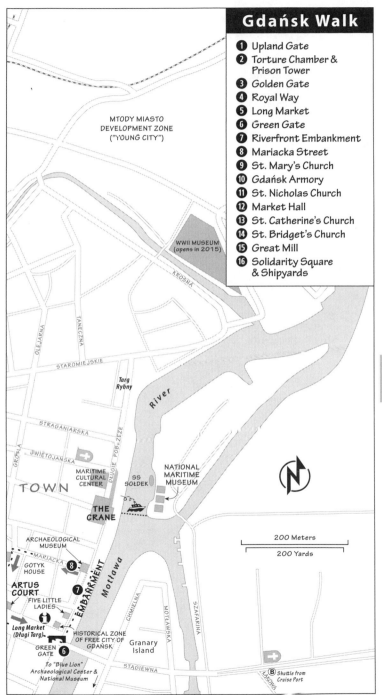

Gdańsk Walk

1. Upland Gate
2. Torture Chamber & Prison Tower
3. Golden Gate
4. Royal Way
5. Long Market
6. Green Gate
7. Riverfront Embankment
8. Mariacka Street
9. St. Mary's Church
10. Gdańsk Armory
11. St. Nicholas Church
12. Market Hall
13. St. Catherine's Church
14. St. Bridget's Church
15. Great Mill
16. Solidarity Square & Shipyards

MŁODY MIASTO DEVELOPMENT ZONE ("YOUNG CITY")

WWII MUSEUM (opens in 2015)

KROSNA

OLEJARNA

TANECZNA

STAROMIEJSKIE

Targ Rybny

River

STRAGANIARSKA

GROLA

ŚWIĘTOJAŃSKA

DŁUGIE POBRZEŻE

MARITIME CULTURAL CENTER

SS SOŁDEK

NATIONAL MARITIME MUSEUM

TOWN

THE CRANE

ARCHAEOLOGICAL MUSEUM

MARIACKA

GOTYK HOUSE

ARTUS COURT

FIVE LITTLE LADIES

Long Market (Długi Targ)

GREEN GATE

To "Blue Lion" Archaeological Center & National Museum

EMBANKMENT

Motława

HISTORICAL ZONE OF FREE CITY OF GDAŃSK

Granary Island

CHMIELNA

MOTŁAWSKA

SZAFARINA

STAGIEWNA

ŁĄSOWA

200 Meters

200 Yards

B Shuttle from Cruise Port

Gdańsk Walk: Royal Way to Solidarity Square and the Shipyards

In the 16th and 17th centuries, Gdańsk was Poland's wealthiest city, with gorgeous architecture (much of it in the Flemish Mannerist style) rivaling that in the two historic capitals, Kraków and Warsaw. During this Golden Age, Polish kings would visit this city of well-to-do Hanseatic League merchants and gawk along the same route trod by tourists today.

The following self-guided walk (rated ▲▲▲) introduces you to the best of Gdańsk. It bridges the two historic centers (the Main Town and the Old Town), dips into St. Mary's Church (the city's most important church), and ends at the famous shipyards and Solidarity Square (where Poland began what ultimately brought down the USSR). I've divided the walk into two parts (making it easier to split up, if you like): The first half focuses on a loop through the Main Town (with most of the high-profile sights), while the second part carries on northward, through the less touristy Old Town to the shipyards.

PART 1: THE MAIN TOWN

• *Begin at the west end of the Main Town, just beyond the last gate at the edge of the busy road (at a road sign that says* Sztokholm...*a reminder that the car ferry to Sweden leaves from near here).*

❶ Upland Gate (Brama Wyżynna)

The Main Town's fortifications were expanded with a Renaissance wall bound by the Upland Gate (built in 1588). "Upland" refers to the hills you see beyond—considered high country in this flat region. Standing with your back to the busy arterial (which traces the old moat), study the gate. Find its three coats of arms (the black eagle for Royal Prussia, the crowned white eagle for Poland, and the two crosses for Gdańsk). Recall that this city has, for almost the entirety of its history before the mid-20th century, been (at least) bicultural—German and Polish, coexisting more or less peacefully. Also notice the little wheels that once hoisted a drawbridge.

• *It's a straight line from here to the river. Walk through the arch (which houses a TI) to the next arch, just a few steps ahead.*

❷ Torture Chamber (Katownia) and Prison Tower (Wieża Więzienna)

The tall, Gothic brick gate before you was part of an earlier protective wall made useless after the Renaissance walls were built in 1588. While today these structures house the Amber Museum (described later), it's free to walk through the evocative passage (except on Mon, when the passage is closed). Inside, find gargoyles (on the left, a town specialty) and the shackles from which prisoners were hung (on the right). Look up at the inside of the high gable to the headless man, identifying this as the torture chamber. This old jail—with its 15-foot-thick walls—was used as a prison even in modern times, under Nazi occupation.

As you leave the Torture Chamber and Prison Tower, look to your left (100 yards away) to see a long, brick building with four fancy, uniform gables. This is the **Armory** (Zbrojownia), one of the finest examples of Dutch Renaissance architecture anywhere. Though this part of the building appears to have the facades of four separate houses, it's a kind of urban camouflage to hide its real purpose from potential attackers. But there's at least one clue to what the building is really for: Notice the exploding cannonballs at the tops of the turrets. (We'll get a better look at the Armory from the other side, later in this walk.)

The round, pointy-topped tower next to the Armory is the **Straw Tower** (Baszta Słomiana). Gunpowder was stored here, and the roof was straw—so if it exploded, it would blow its top without destroying the walls.

• *Straight ahead, the final and fanciest gate between you and the Main Town is the...*

❸ Golden Gate (Złota Brama)

While the other gates were defensive, this one's purely ornamental. The four women up top represent virtues that the people of Gdańsk should exhibit toward outsiders (left to right): Peace, Freedom,

Prosperity, and Fame. The gold-lettered inscription, a psalm in medieval German, compares Gdańsk to Jerusalem: famous and important. Directly above the arch is the Gdańsk coat of arms: two white crosses under a crown on a red shield. We'll see this symbol all over town. Photographers love the view of the Main Town framed in this arch. Inside the arch, study the old photos showing the 1945 bomb damage. On the left is the glorious view you just enjoyed...ravaged by war. And on the right is a heartbreaking aerial view of the city in

1945, when 80 percent of its buildings were in ruins.

• *Passing through the Golden Gate, you reach the Main Town's main drag.*

❹ The Royal Way

Before you stretches ulica Długa (cleverly called the "Long Street"), the main promenade of what, 600 years ago, was the biggest and richest city in Poland (thanks to its profitable ties to the Hanseatic League of merchant cities). This promenade is nicknamed the "Royal Way" because (just as in Warsaw and Kraków) the king would follow this route when visiting town.

Walk half a block, and then look back at the Golden Gate. The women on top of this side represent virtues the people of Gdańsk should cultivate in themselves (left to right): Wisdom, Piety, Justice, and Concord (if an arrow's broken, let's take it out of the quiver and fix it). The inscription—sharing a bit of wisdom as apropos today as it was in 1612—reads, "Concord makes small countries develop, and discord makes big countries fall." Gdańsk was cosmopolitan and exceptionally tolerant in the Middle Ages, attracting a wide range of people, including many who were persecuted elsewhere: Jews, Scots, Dutch, Flemish, Italians, Germans, and more. Members of each group brought with them strands of their culture, which they wove into the tapestry of this city—demonstrated by the eclectic homes along this street. Each facade and each gable were different, as nobles and aristocrats wanted to display their wealth. On my last visit, a traveler seeing this street for the first time gasped to me, "It's like stepping into a Fabergé egg."

During Gdańsk's Golden Age, these houses were taxed based on frontage (like the homes lining Amsterdam's canals)—so they were built skinny and deep. The widest houses belonged to the super-elite. Different as they are from the outside, every house had the same general plan inside. Each had three parts, starting with the front and moving back: First was a fancy drawing room, to show off for visitors. Then came a narrow corridor to the back rooms—often along the side of an inner courtyard. Because the houses had only a few windows facing the outer street, this courtyard provided much-needed sunlight to the rest of the house. The residential quarters were in the back, where the family actually lived: bedroom, kitchen, office. To see the interior of one of these homes, pay a visit to the interesting **Uphagen House** (at #12, on the right, a block and a half in front of the Golden Gate; described later).

This lovely street wasn't always so lively and carefree. At the end of World War II, the Royal Way was in ruins. That epic war actually began here, in what was then the "Free City of Danzig." Following World War I, nobody could decide what to do with this influential and multiethnic city, so rather than assign it to Germany or Poland, it was set apart as its own little autonomous statelet. In 1939, Danzig was 80 percent German-speaking—enough for Hitler to consider it his. And so, on September 1 of that year, the Nazis seized it in one day with relatively minor damage (though the attack on the Polish military garrison on the city's Westerplatte peninsula lasted a week).

But six years later, when the Soviets arrived (March 30, 1945), the city was left devastated. This was the first major, traditionally German city that the Red Army took on their march toward Berlin. And, while it was easy for the Soviets to seize the almost empty city, the commander then insisted that it be leveled, building by building—in retaliation for all the pain the Nazis had caused in Russia. (Soviets didn't destroy nearby Gdynia, which they considered Polish, not German.) Soviet officers turned a blind eye as their soldiers raped and brutalized residents. An entire order of horrified nuns committed suicide by throwing themselves into the river.

It was only thanks to detailed drawings and photographs that these buildings could be so carefully reconstructed. Notice the cheap plaster facades done in the 1950s—rough times under communism, in the decade after World War II. (Most of the town's medieval brick was shipped to Warsaw for a communist-sponsored "rebuild the capital first" campaign.) While the fine facades were restored, the buildings behind the facades were completely rebuilt to modern standards.

Just beyond Uphagen House, the **Cukiernia Sowa** ("The Owl," on the right at #13) is *the* place for cakes and coffee. Directly across the street, **Grycan** (at #73) has been a favorite for ice cream here for generations.

Just a few doors down, on the left, are some of the most strik-

ing **facades** along the Royal Way. The blue-and-white house with the three giant heads is from the 19th century, when the hot style was eclecticism—borrowing bits and pieces from various architectural eras. This was one of the few houses on the street that survived World War II.

At the next corner on the right is the huge, blocky, red **post office,** which doesn't quite fit with the skinny facades lining the rest of the street. Step inside. With doves fluttering under an airy glass atrium, the interior's a class act. Directly across the street, the candy shop **(Ciuciu Cukier Artist)** is often filled with children clamoring to see

GDAŃSK & THE TRI-CITY

Gdańsk History

Visitors to Gdańsk are surprised at how "un-Polish" the city's history is. In this cultural melting pot of German, Dutch, and Flemish merchants (with a smattering of Italians and Scots), Poles were only a small part of the picture until the city became exclusively Polish after World War II. However, in Gdańsk, cultural backgrounds traditionally took a back seat to the bottom line. Wealthy Gdańsk was always known for its economic pragmatism—no matter who was in charge, merchants here made money.

Gdańsk is Poland's gateway to the waters of Europe, where its main river (the Vistula) meets the Baltic Sea. The town was first mentioned in the 10th century, and was seized in 1308 by the Teutonic Knights (who called it "Danzig"; for more on the Teutonic Knights, see page 284). The Knights encouraged other Germans to settle on the Baltic coast, and gradually turned Gdańsk into a wealthy city. In 1361, Gdańsk joined the Hanseatic League, a trade federation of mostly Germanic merchant towns that provided mutual security. By the 15th century, Gdańsk was a leading member of this mighty network, which virtually dominated trade in northern Europe (and also included Toruń, Kraków, Lübeck, Hamburg, Bremen, Bruges, Bergen, Tallinn, Novgorod, and nearly a hundred other cities).

In 1454, the people of Gdańsk rose up against the Teutonic Knights, burning down their castle and forcing them out of the city. Three years later, the Polish king borrowed money from wealthy Gdańsk families to hire Czech mercenaries to take the Teutonic Knights' main castle, Malbork (described in the next chapter). In exchange, the Gdańsk merchants were granted special privileges, including exclusive export rights. Gdańsk now acted as a middleman for much of the trade passing through Polish lands, and paid only a modest annual tribute to the Polish king.

The 16th and 17th centuries were Gdańsk's Golden Age. Now a part of the Polish kingdom, the city had access to an enormous hinterland of natural resources to export—yet it maintained a privileged, semi-independent status. Like Amsterdam, Gdańsk became a progressive and booming merchant city. Its mostly Germanic and Dutch burghers imported Dutch, Flemish, and Italian architects to give their homes an appropriately Hanseatic flourish. At a time of religious upheaval in the rest of Europe, Gdańsk became known for its tolerance—a place that opened

lollipop-making demos. Step in and inhale a universal whiff of childhood.

A few doors farther down, on the left at #62, pop into the **Millennium Gallery** amber shop (which would love to give you an educational amber polishing demo) to see the fascinating collection of old-timey photos, letting you directly compare Gdańsk's cityscape before and after the WWII destruction.

its doors to all visitors (many Mennonites and Scottish religious refugees emigrated here). It was also a haven for great thinkers, including philosopher Arthur Schopenhauer and scientist Daniel Fahrenheit (who invented the mercury thermometer).

Gdańsk declined, along with the rest of Poland, in the late 18th century, and became a part of Prussia (today's northern Germany) during the Partitions. But the people of Gdańsk—even those of German heritage—had taken pride in their independence and weren't enthusiastic about being ruled from Berlin. After World War I, in a unique compromise to appease its complex ethnic makeup, Gdańsk did not fall under German or Polish control, but once again became an independent city-state: the Free City of Danzig (populated by 400,000 ethnic Germans and 15,000 Poles). The city, along with the so-called Polish Corridor connecting it to Polish lands, effectively cut off Germany from its northeastern territory. On September 1, 1939, Adolf Hitler started World War II when he invaded Gdańsk in order to bring it back into the German fold. Later, nearly 80 percent of the city was destroyed when the Soviets "liberated" it from Nazi control.

After World War II, Gdańsk officially became part of Poland, and was painstakingly reconstructed (mostly replicating the buildings of its Golden Age). In 1970, and again in 1980, the shipyard of Gdańsk witnessed strikes and demonstrations that would lead to the fall of European communism. Poland's great anti-communist hero and first post-communist president, Lech Wałęsa, is Gdańsk's most famous resident, and still lives here. When he flies around the world to give talks, he leaves from Gdańsk's "Lech Wałęsa Airport."

A city with a recent past that's both tragic and uplifting, Gdańsk celebrated its 1,000th birthday in 1997. Very roughly, the city has spent about 700 years as an independent entity, and about 300 years under Germanic overlords (the Teutonic Knights, Prussia, and the Nazis). But today, Gdańsk is decidedly its own city. And, as if eager to prove it, Gdańsk is making big improvements at a stunning pace: new museums (the European Solidarity Center), cultural facilities (the Shakespeare Theater), sports venues (a stadium that resembles a blob of amber, built for the 2012 Euro Cup tournament), and an ongoing surge of renovation and refurbishment that has the gables of the atmospheric Hanseatic quarter gleaming once again.

Above the next door, notice the colorful **scenes.** These are slices of life from 17th-century Gdańsk: drinking, talking, buying, playing music. The ship is a *koga*, a typical symbol of Hanseatic ports like Gdańsk.

A couple of doors down—still on the left—is **Neptun Cinema** (marked *KINO*). In the 1980s, this was the only movie theater in the city, and locals lined up for blocks to get in. Old-timers remember coming here with their grandparents to see a full day of cartoons. Now, as with traditional main-street cinemas in the US, this theater is threatened by the rising popularity of multiplexes outside the town center.

Across the street from the theater are the fancy facades of three houses belonging to the very influential medieval **Ferber family,** which produced many burghers, mayors, and even a bishop. On the house with the little dog over the door (#29), look for the heads in the circular medallions. These are Caesars of Rome. At the top of the building is Mr. Ferber's answer to the constant question, "Why build such an elaborate house?"—*PRO INVIDIA,* "For the sake of envy."

A few doors down, on the right, is Gdańsk's most scenically situated milk bar, the recommended **Bar Mleczny Neptun.** Back in communist times, these humble cafeterias were subsidized to give workers an affordable place to eat out. To this day, they offer simple and very cheap grub.

Next door (at #35) is the **Russian Culture Center,** with Russian movies and art exhibits. With the dark past and the Polish support for Ukraine in the recent escalations of tensions there, this is a poignant address.

Before you stands the **Main Town Hall** (Ratusz Głównego Miasta) with its mighty brick clock tower. Consider climbing its observation tower and visiting its superb interior, which features ornately decorated meeting rooms for the city council (described later).

• *Just beyond the Main Town Hall, ulica Długa widens and becomes...*

❺ The Long Market (Długi Targ)

Step from the Long Street into the Long Market, and do a slow, 360-degree spin to appreciate the amazing array of proud architecture here in a city center that rivals the magnificent Grand Place in Brussels. The centerpiece of this square is one of Gdańsk's most important landmarks, the statue of **Neptune**—god of the sea. He's a fitting symbol for a city that dominates the maritime life of Poland. Behind him is another worthwhile museum, the **Artus Court.** Step up to the magnificent door and study the golden relief just above, celebrating the Vistula River (in so many ways the lifeblood of the Polish nation): Lady Vistula is exhausted after her heroic journey, and is finally carried by Neptune to her ultimate destination, the Baltic Sea. (This is just a preview of the ornate art that fills the interior of this fine building—described later.)

Midway down the Long Market (on the right, across from the Hard Rock Café) is a glass case with the **thermometer and barometer of Daniel Fahrenheit.** Although that scientist was born here, he did his groundbreaking work in Amsterdam.
· *At the end of the Long Market is the...*

❻ Green Gate (Zielona Brama)

This huge gate (named for the Green Bridge just beyond) was actually built as a residence for visiting kings...who usually preferred to stay back by Neptune instead (maybe because the river, just on the other side of this gate, stank). It might not have been good enough for kings and queens, but it's plenty fine for a former president: Lech Wałęsa's office is upstairs (see the plaque on the left side, *Biuro Lecha Wałęsy*). His windows, up in the gable, overlook the Long Market. A few steps down the skinny lane to the left is the endearing little **Historical Zone of the Free City of Gdańsk** museum, which explains the interwar period when "Danzig" was an independent and bicultural city-state (described later).
· *Now go through the gate, walk out onto the Green Bridge, anchor yourself in a niche on the left, and look downstream.*

❼ Riverfront Embankment

The Motława River—a side channel of the mighty Vistula—flows into the nearby Baltic Sea. This port was the source of Gdańsk's phenomenal Golden Age wealth. This embankment was jam-packed in its heyday, the 14th and 15th centuries. It was so crowded with boats that you hardly would have been able to see the water, and boats had to pay a time-based moorage fee for tying up to a post.

Look back at the Green Gate and notice that these bricks are much smaller than the locally made ones we saw earlier on this walk. These bricks are Dutch: Boats from Holland would come here empty of cargo, but with a load of bricks for ballast. Traders filled their ships with goods for the return trip, leaving the bricks behind.

The old-fashioned **galleons** and other tour boats moored nearby depart hourly for a fun cruise to Westerplatte (where on September 1, 1939, Germans fired the first shots of World War II) and back. Though kitschy, the galleons are a fun way to get out on the water.

Across the river is **Granary Island** (Spichrze), where grain was stored until it could be taken away by ships. Before World War II, there were some 400 granaries here. Today, much of the island is still in ruins while developers make their plans. Recently, the city ringed the island with an inviting boardwalk, which offers a restful escape from the city and fine views across the narrow river to the embankment. In the summer, sometimes they erect a big Ferris wheel here. And someday there will be several more rebuilt granaries in this area (likely mixed with modern buildings) to match the ones you already see on either side of the bridge. The three rebuilt granaries downstream, in the distance on the next island, house exhibits for the National Maritime Museum (described later).

From your perch on the bridge, look down the embankment (about 500 yards, on the left) and find the huge wooden **Crane (Żuraw)** bulging over the water. This monstrous 15th-century crane—a rare example of medieval port technology—was once used for loading and repairing ships...beginning a shipbuilding tradition that continued to the days of Lech Wałęsa. The crane mechanism was operated by several workers scrambling around in giant hamster wheels. Treading away to engage the gears and pulleys, they could lift 4 tons up 30 feet, or 2 tons up 90 feet.

• *Walk along the embankment about halfway to the Crane, passing the lower embankment, with excursion boats heading to the Westerplatte monument. Pause when you reach the big brick building with green window frames and a tower. This red-brick fort houses the* **Archaeological Museum** *(described later). Its collection includes the five ancient stones in a small garden just outside its door (on the left). These are the* **Prussian Hags**—*mysterious sculptures from the second century A.D. (each described in posted plaques).*

Turn left through the gate in the middle of the brick building. You'll find yourself on the most charming lane in town...

❽ Mariacka Street

The calm, atmospheric "Mary's Street" leads from the embankment to St. Mary's Church. Stroll the length of it, enjoying the most romantic lane in Gdańsk. The **porches** extending out into the street, with access to cellars underneath, were a common feature in Gdańsk's Golden Age. For practical reasons, these were only restored on this street after the war. Notice how the porches are bordered with fine stone relief panels and gargoyles attached to storm drains. If you get stuck there in a hard rainstorm, you'll understand why in Polish these are called "pukers." Enjoy a little amber comparison-shopping. As you stroll up to the towering brick St. Mary's Church, imagine the entire city like this cobbled lane of proud merchants' homes, with street music, delightful facades, and brick church towers high above.

Look up at the church tower viewpoint—filled with people who hiked 409 steps for the view. Our next stop is the church, which you'll enter on the far side under the tower. Walk around the left side of the church, appreciating the handmade 14th-century bricks on the right and the plain post-WWII facades on the left. (Reconstructing the Royal Way was better funded. Here, the priority was simply getting people housed again.) In the distance is the fancy facade of the Armory (where you'll head after visiting the church).

• *But first, go inside...*

❾ St. Mary's Church (Kościół Mariacki)

Of Gdańsk's 13 medieval red-brick churches, St. Mary's (rated ▲▲) is the one you must visit. It's the largest brick church in the world—with a footprint bigger than a football field (350 feet long and 210 feet wide), it can accommodate 20,000 standing worshippers.

Cost and Hours: 4 zł, June-Sept Mon-Sat 9:00-18:30, Sun 13:00-18:30, closes progressively earlier off-season.

Visiting the Church: Inside, sit directly under the fine carved and painted 17th-century Protestant pulpit, midway down the nave, to get oriented.

Overview: Built from 1343 to 1502 by the Teutonic Knights (who wanted a suitable centerpiece for their newly captured main city), St. Mary's remains an important symbol of Gdańsk. The church started out Catholic, became Lutheran in the mid-1500s, and then became Catholic again after World War II. (Remember, Gdańsk was a Germanic city before World War II and part of the big postwar demographic shove, when Germans were sent west, and Poles from the east relocated here. Desperate, cold, and homeless, the new Polish residents moved into what was left of the German homes.) While the church was originally frescoed from top to bottom, the Lutherans whitewashed the entire place. Today, some of the 16th-century whitewash has been peeled back (behind the high altar—we'll see this area soon), revealing a bit of

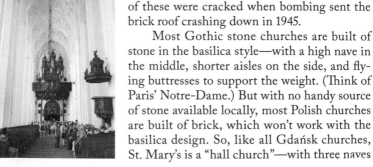

the original frescoes. The floor is paved with 500 gravestones of merchant families. Many of these were cracked when bombing sent the brick roof crashing down in 1945.

Most Gothic stone churches are built of stone in the basilica style—with a high nave in the middle, shorter aisles on the side, and flying buttresses to support the weight. (Think of Paris' Notre-Dame.) But with no handy source of stone available locally, most Polish churches are built of brick, which won't work with the basilica design. So, like all Gdańsk churches, St. Mary's is a "hall church"—with three naves

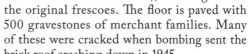

the same height and no exterior buttresses.

Also like other Gdańsk churches, St. Mary's gave refuge to the Polish people after the communist government declared martial law in 1981. When a riot broke out and violence seemed imminent, people flooded into churches, knowing that the ZOMO riot police wouldn't follow them inside.

Most of the church decorations are original. A few days before the Soviets arrived to "liberate" the city in 1945, locals—knowing what was in store—hid precious items in the countryside. Take some time now to see a few of the highlights.

• *From this seat, you can see most of what we'll visit in the church: As you face the altar, the astronomical clock is at 10 o'clock, the Ferber family medallion is at 1 o'clock, the Priests' Chapel is at 3 o'clock (under a tall colorful window), and the magnificent 17th-century organ is directly behind you (it's played at each Mass and during free concerts on Fri in summer).*

Pulpit: For Protestants, the pulpit is important. Designed as an impressive place from which to share the Word of God in the people's language, it's located mid-nave, so all can hear.

• *Opposite the pulpit is the moving...*

Priests' Chapel: The 1965 statue of Christ weeping commemorates 2,779 Polish chaplains executed by the Nazis because they were priests. See the grainy black-and-white photo of one about to be shot, above on the right.

• *Head up the nave to the...*

High Altar: The main altar, beautifully carved in 1517, is a triptych showing the coronation of Mary. She is surrounded by the Trinity: flanked by God and Jesus, with the dove representing the Holy Spirit overhead. The church's medieval stained glass was destroyed in 1945. Poland's biggest stained-glass window, behind the altar, is from 1980.

• *Start circling around the right side of the altar. Look right to find (high on a pillar) the big, opulent family marker.*

Ferber Family Medallion: The falling baby (under the crown) is Constantine Ferber. As a precocious child, li'l Constantine leaned out his window on the Royal Way to see the king's processional come through town. He slipped and fell, but landed in a salesman's barrel of fish. Constantine grew up to become the mayor of Gdańsk.

• *As you continue around behind the altar, search high above you, on the walls to your right, to spot those restored pre-Reformation frescoes. Directly behind the altar, under the big window, is the...*

Empty Glass Case: This case was designed to hold Hans Memling's *Last Judgment* painting, which used to be in this church, but is currently being held hostage by the National Museum. To counter the museum's claim that the church wasn't a good environment for such a precious work, the priest had this display case built—but that still wasn't enough to convince the museum to give the painting back. (You'll see a small replica of the painting in the rear of this church, but the real thing is in the National Museum.)

• *Now circle back the way you came to the area in front of the main altar, and proceed straight ahead into the transept. High on the wall to your right, look for the...*

Astronomical Clock: This 42-foot-tall clock is supposedly the biggest wooden clock in the world. Below it is an elaborate circular calendar that, like a medieval computer, calculates on which day each saint's festival day falls in different years (see the little guy on the left, with the pointer). Above are zodiac signs and the time (back then, the big hand was all you needed). Way up on top, Adam and Eve are naked and ready to ring the bell. Adam's been swinging his clapper at the top of the hour since 1473...but sadly, the clock is broken.

• *A few steps in front of the clock is a modern chapel with the...*

Memorial to the Polish Victims of the 2010 Plane Crash: The gold-shrouded Black Madonna honors the 96 victims of an air disaster that the killed much of Poland's government—including the president and first lady—during a terrible storm over Russia. The main tomb is for Maciej Płażyński, from Gdańsk, who was leader of the parliament. On the left, the jagged statue has bits of the wreckage and lists each victim by name.

• *In a small chapel in the rear corner of the church—on the far right with your back to the high altar—you'll find the...*

***Pietà* and Memling Replica:** The *pietà*, carved of limestone and painted in 1410, is by the Master of Gdańsk. In the same room is a musty old copy of Memling's *Last Judgment*—the exquisite original once graced this very chapel.

• *Next door are stairs leading to the...*

Church Tower: You can climb 409 steps to burn off some pierogi and earn a grand city view (5 zł, Mon-Sat 9:00-17:00, Sun 13:00-17:30). It's a long hike (and you'll know it—every 10th step is numbered). But because the viewpoint is surrounded by a roof, the views are distant and may not be worth the effort. The first third is up a tight, medieval spiral staircase. Then you'll walk through the eerie, cavernous area between the roof and the ceiling, before huffing up steep concrete steps that surround the square tower (as you spiral up, up, up around the bells). Finally you'll climb a little metal ladder and pop out at the viewpoint.

• *Leaving the church, angle left and continue straight up ulica Piwna ("Beer Street") toward the sprightly facade of the Armory.*

❿ The Gdańsk Armory (Zbrojownia)

The 1605 **Armory,** which we saw from a distance at the start of this walk, is one of the best examples of Dutch Renaissance architecture in Europe. Athena, the goddess of war and wisdom, stands in the center, amid motifs of war and ornamental pukers.

• *If you want to make your walk a loop, you're just a block away from where we started (to the left). But there's much more to see. Facing the Armory, turn right and start the second half of this walk.*

PART 2: THROUGH THE OLD TOWN TO THE SHIPYARDS

• *From here we'll work our way out of the Main Town and head into the Old Town, toward Solidarity Square and the shipyards. We'll be walking along this street (which changes names a couple of times) nearly all the way. Keep in mind that this part of the walk ends at the European Solidary Center's fine museum. You'll want plenty of time to tour the museum and linger over its exhibits, so if you're already pooped or it's getting late in the day, consider finishing this walk another time.*

   From the Armory, head down Kołodziejska, which quickly becomes Węglarska. After two blocks (that is, one block before the big market hall), detour to the right down Świętojańska and use the side door to enter the brick church.

⓫ St. Nicholas Church (Kościół Św. Mikołaja)

Near the end of World War II, when the Soviet army reached Gdańsk on its march westward, they were given the order to burn all the churches. Only this one survived—because it happened to be dedicated to Russia's patron saint. As the best-preserved church in town, it has a more impressive interior than the others, with lavish black-and-gold Baroque altars.

• *Backtrack out to the main street and continue to the right, passing a row of seniors selling their grown and foraged edibles. Immediately after the church is Gdańsk's...*

⓬ Market Hall

Built in 1896 and renovated in 2005, Gdańsk's market hall is fun to explore. Appreciate the delicate steel-and-glass canopy overhead. This is a totally untouristy scene: You'll see everything from skintight *Polska* T-shirts, to wedding gowns, to maternity wear. The meat is downstairs, and the veggies are outside on the adjacent square. As this was once the center of a monastic community, the basement has the graves of medieval Dominican monks, which were exposed when the building was refurbished: Peer over the glass railing, and you'll see some of those scant remains.

   Across the street from the Market Hall, a round, red-brick **tower,** part of the city's protective wall back in 1400, marks the

end of the Main Town and the beginning of the Old Town.
• *Another block up the street, on the right, is the huge...*

❸ St. Catherine's Church (Kościół Św. Katarzyny)

"Katy," as locals call it, is the oldest church in Gdańsk. In May of 2006, a carelessly discarded cigarette caused the church roof to burst into flames. Local people ran into the church and pulled everything outside, so nothing valuable was damaged; even the carillon bells were saved. However, the roof and wooden frame were totally destroyed. The people of Gdańsk were determined to rebuild this important symbol of the city. Within days of the fire, fundraising concerts were held to scrape together most of the money needed to raise the roof once more. Step inside. On the left side of the gate leading to the nave, photos show bomb damage. Farther in, on the left, are vivid photos of the more recent conflagration. The interior is evocative, with still-bare-brick walls that almost seem intentional—as if they're trying for an industrial-mod look.

• *The church hiding a block behind Katy—named for Catherine's daughter Bridget—has important ties to Solidarity and is worth a visit. Go around the right side of Katy and skirt the parking lot to find the entrance.*

❹ St. Bridget's Church (Kościół Św. Brygidy)

This was the home church of Lech Wałęsa during the tense days of the 1980s. The church and its priest, Henryk Jankowski, were particularly aggressive in supporting the ideals of Solidarity. Jankowski became a mouthpiece for the movement. In gratitude for the church's support, Wałęsa named his youngest daughter Brygida.

Cost and Hours: 2 zł, daily 10:00-18:00.

Visiting the Church: Head inside. For your visit, start at the high altar, then circle clockwise back to the entry.

The enormous, unfinished **high altar** is made entirely of amber—more than a thousand square feet of it. Features that are already in place include the Black Madonna of Częstochowa, a royal Polish eagle, and the Solidarity symbol (tucked below the Black Madonna). The structure, like a scaffold, holds pieces as they are completed and added to the ensemble. The video you may see playing overhead gives you a close-up look at the amber elements.

The wrought-iron gate of the adjacent **Chapel of Fatima** (right of main altar) recalls great battles and events in Polish history from 966 to 1939, with important dates boldly sparkling in gold. Some say the Polish Church is too political. But it was only through a politically engaged Church that this culture survived the Partitions of Poland over a century and a half, plus the brutal anti-religious policies of the communist period. The national soul of the Polish people—whether religious or not—is tied up in the Catholic faith.

Henryk Jankowski's tomb—a white marble box with red trim—is a bit farther to the right. Jankowski was a key hero during Solidarity times; the tomb pro-

claims him *Kapelan Solidarności* ("Solidarity Chaplain"). But his public standing took a nosedive near the end of his life—thanks to ego-driven projects like his amber altar, as well as accusations of anti-Semitism and corruption. Forced to retire in 2007, Jankowski died in 2010. (An offering box is next to his tomb, if you'd like to donate to the amber altar project.)

In the rear corner, where a figure lies lifeless on the floor under a wall full of wooden crosses, is the tomb of Solidarity martyr **Jerzy Popiełuszko.** A courageous and famously outspoken Warsaw priest, in 1984 Popiełuszko was kidnapped, beaten, and murdered by the communist secret police. Notice that the figure's hands and feet are bound—as his body was found. The crosses are historic—each one was carried at various strikes against the communist regime. The communists believed they could break the spirit of the Poles with brutality—like the murder of Popiełuszko. But it only made the rebels stronger and more resolved to ultimately win their freedom. (Near the exit, on a monitor, a fascinating 12-minute video shows great moments of this church, with commentary by Lech Wałęsa himself.)

• *Return to the main street, turn right, and continue on. The big brick building ahead on the left, with the many windows, is the Great Mill. Walk past that and look down at the canal that once powered it.*

⓰ The Great Mill

This huge brick building dates from the 14th century. Look at the waterfalls and imagine standing here in 1400—with the mill's 18 wheels spinning 24/7, powering grindstones that produced 20 tons of flour a day. Like so much else here, the mill survived until 1945. Today the rebuilt structure houses a modern shopping mall.

The **park** just beyond the mill is worth a look. In the distance is the Old City Town Hall (Dutch Renaissance style, from 1595). The monument in the middle honors the 17th-century astronomer Jan Haweliusz. He's looking up at a giant, rust-colored wall with a map of the heavens. Haweliusz built the biggest telescopes of his era to better appreciate and understand the cosmos. Behind the mill stands the miller's home—its opulence indicates that, back in the Middle Ages, there was a lot of money in grinding. Just steps into the family-friendly park is a fountain that brings shrieks of joy to children on hot summer days. Watching families enjoy this park, I'm struck that these are good times for Poland—stability, one of the EU's healthiest economies, and freedom. But next we walk through a stretch that, if you take away the colors, advertising, and smiles, reminds me of the dark days before 1989. And beyond that are the shipyards, where freedom from communism was born.

• *To get to the **shipyards**, keep heading straight up Rajska. You'll pass the modern Madison shopping mall. After another long block, jog right, passing to the right of the big, ugly, and green 1970s-era skyscraper. On your right, marked by the famous red sign on the roof, is today's **Solidarity headquarters** (which remains the strongest trade union in Poland, with 700,000 members, and is also active in many other countries). Just in front of the Solidarity building, you may see two big chunks of **wall**: a piece of the Berlin Wall and a stretch of the shipyard wall that Lech Wałęsa scaled to get inside and lead the strike. The message: What happened behind one wall eventually led to the fall of the other Wall.*

From here, hike on (about 100 yards) to the finale of this walk.

⑯ Solidarity Square and the Shipyards

Three tall crosses mark Solidarity Square and the rust-colored European Solidarity Center (with an excellent museum).

Sights in Gdańsk

MAIN TOWN (GŁÓWNE MIASTO)

The following sights are all in the Main Town, listed roughly in the order you'll see them on the self-guided walk of the Royal Way.

Gdańsk Historical Museum

The Gdańsk Historical Museum has four excellent branches: the Amber Museum, Uphagen House, Main Town Hall, and Artus Court. Along with St. Mary's Church, these are the four most important interiors in the Main Town. All have the same hours, but you must buy a separate ticket for each.

Cost and Hours: 10 zł apiece—except Main Town Hall, which is 12 zł; hours fluctuate, but typically open mid-June-mid-Sept

Mon-Thu 9:00-16:00, Fri-Sat 10:00-18:00, Sun 10:00-16:00; mid-Sept-mid-June Tue 10:00-13:00, Wed-Sat 10:00-16:00, Thu until 18:00, Sun 11:00-16:00, closed Mon; last entry 30 minutes before closing.

Information: The museums share a phone number and website (central tel. 58-767-9100, www.mhmg.gda.pl).

▲Amber Museum (Muzeum Bursztynu)

Housed in a pair of connected brick towers (the former Prison Tower and Torture Chamber) just outside the Main Town's Golden Gate, this museum has two oddly contradictory parts. One shows off Gdańsk's favorite local resource, amber, while the

other focuses on implements of torture (cost and hours above, overpriced 1.5-hour audioguide—25 zł). You'll follow the one-way route through four exhibits on amber (with lots of stairs), and then walk the rampart to the other tower for a little torture. Exhibits are explained in English. For a primer before you visit, read the "All About Amber" sidebar.

Visiting the Museum: The exhibit has four parts: First, head up to the **second floor** for a scientific look at amber. View inclusions (organic items trapped in resin) through a magnifying glass and microscope, and see dozens of samples showing the full rainbow of amber shades. Interactive video screens explain the creation of amber. The **third-floor** exhibit explains the "Amber Route" (the ancient Celtic trade road connecting Gdańsk to Italy) and medicinal uses of the stuff, and displays a wide range of functional items made from amber—clocks, pipe stems, candlesticks, chandeliers, jewelry boxes, and much more. Take a whiff—what's that smell? It's a cathedral. Amber is an ingredient in incense. The **fourth floor** shows off more artistic items made of amber—sculptures, candelabras, beer steins, chessboards, and a model ship with delicate sails made of amber. At the **top floor,** you'll find a modern gallery showing more recent amber craftsmanship and displays about amber's role in fashion today.

Then, walking along the upper rampart level of the courtyard, you'll enter an exhibit about the building itself and the town's fortifications. This leads to the **Prison Tower** and the torture exhibit—with sound effects, scant artifacts, and mannequins helpfully demonstrating the grisly equipment.

All About Amber

Poland's Baltic seaside is known as the Amber Coast. You can see amber *(bursztyn)* in Gdańsk's Amber Museum, in the collection at Malbork Castle (see the Pomerania chapter), and in shop windows everywhere. This fossilized tree resin originated here on the north coast of Poland 40 million years ago. It comes in as many different colors as Eskimos have words for snow: 300 distinct shades, from yellowish white to yellowish black, from opaque to transparent. (I didn't believe it either, until I toured Gdańsk's museum.) Darker-colored amber is generally mixed with ash and sand—making it more fragile, and generally less desirable. Lighter amber is mixed with gasses and air bubbles.

Amber has been popular since long before there were souvenir stands. Archaeologists have found Roman citizens (and their coins) buried with crosses made of amber. Almost 75 percent of the world's amber is mined in northern Poland, and it often simply washes up on the beaches after a winter storm. Some of the elaborate amber sculptures displayed at the museum are joined with "amber glue"—melted-down amber mixed with an adhesive agent. More recently, amber craftsmen are combining amber with silver to create artwork—a method dubbed the "Polish School."

In addition to being good for the economy, some Poles believe amber is good for their health. A traditional cure for arthritis pain is to pour strong vodka over amber, let it set, and then rub it on sore joints. Other remedies call for mixing amber dust with honey or rose oil. It sounds superstitious, but users claim that it works.

▲Uphagen House (Dom Uphagena)

This interesting place, at ulica Długa 12, is your chance to glimpse what's behind the colorful facades lining this street (see cost and hours above). It's the only grand Gdańsk mansion rebuilt as it was before 1945. The model near the entry shows the three parts: dolled-up visitors' rooms in front, a corridor along the courtyard, and private rooms in the back. The finely decorated salon was used to show off for guests. Most of this furniture is original (saved from WWII bombs by locals who hid it in the countryside). Passing into the dining room, note the knee-high paintings of hunting and celebrations. Along the passage to the back, each room has a theme: butterflies in the smoking room, then flowers in the next room, then birds in the music room. In the private rooms at the back, the decor is simpler. Downstairs, you'll pass through the kitchen, the pantry, and a room with photos of the house before the war, which were used to reconstruct what you see today.

▲▲Main Town Hall (Ratusz Głównego Miasta)

This landmark building contains remarkable decorations from Gdańsk's Golden Age (see cost and hours earlier). You can also climb 293 concrete steps to the top of the **tower** for commanding views (5 zł extra, mid-June-mid-Sept only).

Visiting the Main Town Hall: In the entry room, examine the photos showing this building at the end of World War II and ogle the finely crafted spiral staircase. The ornately carved wooden **door,** which we'll pass through in a minute, is all original, from the 1600s. Above the door are two crosses under a crown. This seal of Gdańsk is being held—as it's often depicted—by a pair of lions. The felines are stubborn and independent, just like the citizens of Gdańsk. The surface of the door is carved with images of crops. Around the frame of the door are mermen, reminding us that this agricultural bounty, like so many of Poland's resources, is transported on the Vistula and out through Gdańsk.

Go through the door into the **Red Hall,** where the Gdańsk city council met in the summertime. (The lavish fireplace, with another pair of lions holding the coat of arms of Gdańsk, was just for show. There's no chimney.) City council members would sit in the seats around the room, debating city policy. Marvel at the 17th-century inlaid wood panels (just above eye level) showing slices of local life. Paintings on the wall above represent the seven virtues that the burghers meeting in this room should possess. And the exquisite ceiling—with 25 paintings in total—is all about theology. Including both Christian and pagan themes, the ceiling was meant to inspire the decision-makers in this room to make good choices. Study the oval painting in the middle (from 1607)—the museum's highlight. It shows the special place Gdańsk occupies between God, Poland, and the rest of the world. In the foreground, the citizens of Gdańsk go about their daily lives. Above them, high atop the arch, God's hand reaches down (from within clouds of Hebrew characters) and grasps the Main Town Hall's steeple. The rainbow arching above also symbolizes God's connection to Gdańsk. Mirroring that is the Vistula River, which begins in the mountains of southern Poland (on the right), runs through the country, and exits at the sea in Gdańsk (on the left, where the rainbow ends).

Continue into the less impressive **Winter Hall,** with another fireplace (this one actually hooked up to a chimney) and another coat of arms held by lions. Keep going through the next room, into a room with photos of **WWII damage.** The twist of wood is all that's left of the main support for the spiral staircase (today reconstructed in the room where you entered). Ponder the inspiring ability of a city to be reborn after the tragedy of war.

Upstairs are some temporary exhibits and several examples of **Gdańsk-style furniture.** These pieces are characterized by three big, round feet along the front, lots of ornamentation, and usually a virtually impossible-to-find lock (sometimes hidden behind a movable decoration). You can also see a coin collection, from the days when Gdańsk had the elite privilege of minting its own currency.

Then head upstairs, to a fascinating exhibit about Gdańsk's time as a **"free city"** between the World Wars—when, because of its delicate ethnic mix of Poles and Germans, it was too precarious to assign it to either country. You'll see border checkpoints, uniforms, signs in German (the predominant language of "Danzig"), and reconstructed rooms (homes and shops) from the era. Near the end of this room, you have the option to climb up to the top of the tower. Otherwise, you'll take stairs down—with huge photos at each landing showing the city in ruins after World War II, then triumphantly being rebuilt—and into the cellars, where you'll wander through some pointless subterranean chambers before emerging back into the courtyard where you started.

▲▲Artus Court (Dwór Artusa)

In the Middle Ages, Gdańsk was home to many brotherhoods and guilds (like businessmen's clubs). For their meetings, the city provided this elaborately decorated hall, named for King Arthur—a medieval symbol for prestige and power. Just as in King Arthur's Court, this was a place where powerful and important people came together. Of many such halls in Baltic Europe, this is the only original one that survives (in tall, white, triple-arched building behind Neptune statue at Długi Targ 43).

Visiting the Artus Court: In the grand hall, various **cupboards** line the walls. Each organization that met here had a place to keep its important documents and office supplies. Suspended from the ceiling are seven giant **model ships** that depict Baltic

vessels, symbolic of the city's connection to the sea.

In the far-back corner is the museum's highlight: a gigantic **stove** decorated with 520 colorful tiles featuring the faces of kings, queens, nobles, mayors, and burghers—a mix of Protestants and Catholics, as a reminder of

Gdańsk's religious tolerance. Almost all of the tiles are original, having survived WWII bombs.

Notice the huge **paintings** on the walls above, with 3-D animals emerging from flat frames. Hunting is a popular theme in local artwork. Like minting coins, hunting was a privilege usually reserved for royalty, but extended in special circumstances to the burghers of special towns...like Gdańsk. These "paintings" are new, digitally generated reproductions of the originals, which were damaged in World War II.

The next room—actually in the next building—is a typical **front room** of the burghers' homes lining ulica Długa. Ogle the gorgeously carved wooden staircase. Upstairs is a hall of knights—once again evoking Arthurian legend. If you've rented an audioguide, take it back up front to return it; otherwise, you can exit through the back.

Other Museums in the Main Town
Historical Zone of the Free City of Gdańsk (Strefa Historyczna Wolne Miasto Gdańsk)

In a city so obsessed with its Golden Age and Solidarity history, this charming little collection illuminates a unique but often-overlooked chapter in the story of Gdańsk: The years between World Wars I and II, when—in an effort to find a workable compromise in this ethnically mixed city—Gdańsk was not part of Germany or Poland, but a self-governing "free city" *(wolne miasto)*. Like a holdover from medieval fiefdoms in modern times, the city-state of Gdańsk even issued its own currency and stamps. This modest museum earnestly shows off artifacts from the time—photos, stamps, maps, flags, promotional tourist leaflets, and other items from the free city, all marked with the Gdańsk symbol of two white crosses under a crown on a red shield. The brochure explains that four out of five people living in the free city identified themselves not as German or Poles, but as "Danzigers." While some might find the subject obscure, this endearing collection is a treat for WWII history buffs. Be sure to borrow the English translations at the entrance.

Cost and Hours: 8 zł, Tue-Sun 12:00-17:00, until 18:00 May-Aug, closed Mon year-round, down the little alley just in front of the Green Gate at Warzywnicza 10A, tel. 58-320-2828, www.tpg. info.pl.

Archaeological Museum (Muzeum Archeologiczne)

This simple museum is worth a quick peek for those interested in archaeology. The ground floor has exhibits on excavated finds from Sudan, where the museum has a branch program. Upstairs, look for the distinctive urns with cute faces, which date from the Hallstatt Period and were discovered in slate graves around Gdańsk. Also upstairs are some Bronze and Iron Age tools; before-and-after photos of WWII Gdańsk; and a reconstructed 12th-century Viking-like Slavonic longboat. You can also climb the building's tower, with good views up Mariacka street toward St. Mary's Church.

Cost and Hours: Museum-8 zł (free on Sat), tower-5 zł; July-Aug Tue-Fri 9:00-17:00, Sat-Sun 10:00-17:00; Sept-June Tue and Thu-Fri 8:00-16:00, Wed 9:00-17:00, Sat-Sun 10:00-16:00; closed Mon year-round; ulica Mariacka 25, tel. 58-322-2100, www.archeologia.pl.

▲National Maritime Museum
(Narodowe Muzeum Morskie)

Gdańsk's history and livelihood are tied to the sea. This collection, spread among several buildings on either side of the river, examines all aspects of this connection. Nautical types may get a thrill out of the creaky, sprawling museum, but most visitors find it little more than a convenient way to pass some time and enjoy a cruise across the river. The museum's lack of English information is frustrating; fortunately, some exhibits have descriptions you can borrow.

Cost and Hours: Each part of the museum has its own admission (6-8 zł). The Maritime Cultural Center is worth neither the time nor the money for grown-ups; I'd consider the 18-zł "karnet" combo-ticket that combines the other, better parts. It's open July-Aug daily 10:00-18:00; Sept-Oct and March-June Tue-Sun 10:00-16:00, closed Mon; Nov-Feb Tue-Sun 10:00-15:00, closed Mon; ulica Ołowianka 9, tel. 58-301-8611, www.cmm.pl.

Visiting the Museum: The exhibit has four parts. The first two parts—the Crane and Maritime Cultural Center—are on the Main Town side of the river. The landmark medieval **Crane** (Żuraw), Gdańsk's most important symbol, houses a humble exhibit on living in the city during its Golden Age (16th-17th centuries).

The **Maritime Cultural Center,** a modern exhibit right next door to the Crane, is not worth the exercise unless you are leading a school group. For adults, the most interesting areas are on the third floor ("Working Boats," with examples of vessels from around the world and English explanations) and the fourth floor (temporary exhibits).

The rest of the museum—the Old Granaries and the *Sołdek* steamship—is across the river on Ołowianka Island, which you can reach via the little **ferry** (named the *Motława*, like the river; 1.50 zł one-way). The ferry runs about every 15 minutes in peak season (during museum hours only) and much less in the off-season.

Once on the island, visit the three rebuilt **Old Granaries** (Spichlerze). These make up the heart of the exhibit, tracing the history of Gdańsk—particularly as it relates to the sea—from prehistoric days to the present.

Models of the town and region help put things into perspective. Other exhibits cover underwater exploration, navigational aids, artifacts of the Polish seafaring tradition, peekaboo cross-sections of multilevel ships, and models of the modern-day shipyard where Solidarity was born. This place is home to more miniature ships than you ever thought you'd see, and the Nautical Gallery upstairs features endless rooms with paintings of boats.

Finally, crawl through the holds and scramble across the deck of a decommissioned steamship docked permanently across from the Crane, called the *Sołdek* (ship generally closed in winter). This was the first postwar vessel built at the Gdańsk shipyard. Below decks, you can see where they shoveled the coal; wander through a maze of pipes, gears, valves, gauges, and ladders; and visit the rooms where the sailors lived, slept, and ate. You can even play captain on the bridge.

SOLIDARITY (SOLIDARNOŚĆ) AND THE GDAŃSK SHIPYARD (STOCZNIA GDAŃSKA)

Gdańsk's single most memorable experience is exploring the shipyard that witnessed the beginning of the end of communism's stranglehold on Eastern Europe. Taken together, the sights in this area are worth ▲▲▲. Here in the former industrial wasteland that Lech Wałęsa called the "cradle of freedom," this evocative site tells the story of the brave Polish shipyard workers who took on—and ultimately defeated—an Evil Empire. A visit to the Solidarity sights has two main parts: Solidarity Square (with the memorial and gate out in front of the shipyard), and the outstanding museum inside the European Solidarity Center.

Getting to the Shipyard: These sights cluster around Solidarity Square (Plac Solidarności), at the north end of the Old Town, about a 20-minute walk from the Royal Way. For the most interesting approach, follow "Part 2" of my self-guided walk (earlier), which ends here.

Background: After the communists took over Eastern Europe at the end of World War II, oppressed peoples throughout the Soviet Bloc rose up in different ways. The most dramatic uprisings—Hungary's 1956 Uprising and Czechoslovakia's 1968 "Prague Spring"—were brutally crushed under the treads of Soviet tanks. The formula for freedom that finally succeeded was a patient, nearly decade-long series of strikes and protests spear-headed by Lech Wałęsa and his trade union, called Solidarność—"Solidarity." (The movement also benefited from good timing, as it coincided with the *perestroika* and *glasnost* policies of Soviet premier Mikhail Gorbachev.) While some American politicians might like to take credit for defeating communism, Wałęsa and his fellow workers were the ones fighting on the front lines, armed with nothing more than guts.

Solidarity Square (Plac Solidarności) and the Monument of the Fallen Shipyard Workers

The seeds of August 1980 were sown a decade before. Since becoming part of the Soviet Bloc, the Poles staged frequent strikes, protests, and uprisings to secure their rights, all of which were put down by the regime. But the bloodiest of these took place in December of 1970—a tragic event memorialized by the **three-crosses monument** that towers over what's now called Solidarity Square.

The 1970 strike was prompted by price hikes. The communist government set the prices for all products. As Poland endured drastic food shortages in the 1960s and 1970s, the regime frequently announced what it called "regulation of prices." Invariably, this meant an increase in the cost of essential foodstuffs. (To be able to claim "regulation" rather than "increase," the regime would symbolically lower prices for a few select items—but these were always nonessential luxuries, such as elevators and TV sets, which nobody could afford anyway.) The regime was usually smart enough to raise prices on January 1, when the people were fat and happy after Christmas, and too hung over to complain. But on December 12, 1970, bolstered by an ego-stoking visit by West German Chancellor Willy Brandt, Polish premier Władysław Gomułka increased prices. The people of Poland—who cared more about the price of Christmas dinner than relations with Germany—struck back.

A wave of strikes and sit-ins spread along the heavily industrialized north coast of Poland, most notably in Gdańsk, Gdynia, and Szczecin. Thousands of angry demonstrators poured through the gate of this shipyard, marched into town, and set fire to the Communist Party Committee building. In an attempt to quell the riots, the government-run radio implored the people to go back to work. On the morning of December 17, workers showed up at shipyard gates across northern Poland, and were greeted by the

Lech Wałęsa

In 1980, the world was turned on its ear by a walrus-mustachioed shipyard electrician. Within three years, this seemingly run-of-the-mill Pole had precipitated the collapse of communism, led a massive 10-million-member trade union with enormous political impact, been named *Time* magazine's Man of the Year, and won a Nobel Peace Prize.

Lech Wałęsa was born in Popowo, Poland, in 1943. After working as a car mechanic and serving two years in the army, he became an electrician at the Gdańsk Shipyard in 1967. Like many Poles, Wałęsa felt stifled by the communist government, and was infuriated that a system that was supposed to be for the workers clearly wasn't serving them.

When the shipyard massacre took place in December of 1970 (see description on page 465), Wałęsa was at the forefront of the protests. He was marked as a dissident, and in 1976, he was fired. Wałęsa hopped from job to job and was occasionally unemployed—under communism, a rock-bottom status reserved for only the most despicable derelicts. But he soldiered on, fighting for the creation of a trade union and building up quite a file with the secret police.

In August of 1980, Wałęsa heard news of the beginnings of the Gdańsk strike and raced to the shipyard. In an act that has since become the stuff of legend, Wałęsa scaled the shipyard wall to get inside.

Before long, Wałęsa's dynamic personality won him the unofficial role of the workers' leader and spokesman. He negotiated with the regime to hash out the August Agreements, becoming a rock star-type hero during the so-called 16 Months of Hope...until martial law came crashing down in December of 1981. Wałęsa was arrested and interned for 11 months in a country

army and police. Without provocation, the Polish army opened fire on the workers. While the official death toll for the massacre stands at 44, others say the true number is much higher. The monument, with a trio of 140-foot-tall crosses, honors those lost to the regime that December.

Go to the middle of the **wall** behind the crosses, to the monument of the worker wearing a flimsy plastic work helmet, attempting to shield himself from bullets. Behind him is a list—pockmarked with symbolic bullet holes—of workers murdered on that day. *Lat* means "years old"—many teenagers were among the dead. The quote at the top of the wall is from St. John Paul house. After being released, he continued to struggle underground, becoming a symbol of anti-communist sentiment.

Finally, the dedication of Wałęsa and Solidarity paid off, and Polish communism dissolved—with Wałęsa rising from the ashes as the country's first post-communist president. But the skills that made Wałęsa a rousing success at leading an uprising didn't translate well to the president's office. Wałęsa proved to be a stubborn, headstrong politician, frequently clashing with the parliament. He squabbled with his own party, declaring a "war at the top" of Solidarity and rotating higher-ups to prevent corruption and keep the party fresh. He also didn't choose his advisors well, enlisting several staffers who wound up immersed in scandal. His overconfidence was his Achilles' heel, and his governing style verged on authoritarian.

Unrefined and none too interested in scripted speeches, Wałęsa was a simple man who preferred playing ping-pong with his buddies to attending formal state functions. Though lacking a formal education, Wałęsa had unsurpassed drive and charisma... but that's not enough to lead a country—especially during an impossibly complicated, fast-changing time.

Wałęsa was defeated at the polls, by the Poles, in 1995, and when he ran again in 2000, he received a humiliating 1 percent of the vote. Since leaving office, Wałęsa has kept a lower profile, but still delivers speeches worldwide. Many poor Poles grumble that Lech, who started life simple like them, has forgotten the little people. But his fans point out that he gives much of his income to charity. And on his lapel, he still always wears a pin featuring the Black Madonna of Częstochowa—the most important symbol of Polish Catholicism.

Poles say there are at least two Lech Wałęsas: the young, bombastic, working-class idealist Lech, at the forefront of the Solidarity strikes, who will always have a special place in their hearts; and the failed President Wałęsa, who got in over his head and tarnished his legacy.

II, who was elected pope eight years after this tragedy. The pope was known for his clever way with words, and this very carefully phrased quote—which served as an inspiration to the Poles during their darkest hours—skewers the regime in a way subtle enough to still be tolerated: "Let thy spirit descend, and renew the face of the earth—of *this* earth" (that is, Poland). Below that is the dedication: "They gave their lives so you can live decently."

Stretching to the left of this center wall are plaques representing labor unions from around Poland—and around the world (look for the Chinese characters)—expressing solidarity with these workers. To the right is an enormous Bible verse: "May the Lord give strength to his people. May the Lord bless his people with the gift of peace" (Psalms 29:11).

Inspired by the brave sacrifice of their true comrades, shipyard workers rose up here in August of 1980, formulating the "21 Points" of a new union called Solidarity. Their demands included the right to strike and form unions, the freeing of political prisoners, and an increase in wages. The 21 Points are listed in Polish on the panel at the far end of the right wall, marked *21 X TAK* ("21 times yes"). An unwritten precondition to any agreement was the right for the workers of 1980 to build a memorial to their comrades slain in 1970. The government agreed, marking the first time a communist regime ever allowed a monument to be built to honor its own victims. Wałęsa called it a harpoon in the heart of the communists. The towering monument, with three crucified anchors on top, was designed, engineered, and built by shipyard workers. The monument was finished just four months after the historic agreement was signed.

• *Now continue to the gate and peer through into the birthplace of Eastern European freedom.*

Gdańsk Shipyard (Stocznia Gdańska) Gate #2

When a Pole named Karol Wojtyła was elected pope in 1978—and visited his homeland in 1979—he inspired his 40 million countrymen to believe that impossible dreams can come true. Prices continued to go up, and the workers continued to rise up. By the summer of 1980, it was clear that the dam was about to break.

In August, Anna Walentynowicz—a Gdańsk crane operator and known dissident—was fired unceremoniously just short of her retirement. This sparked a strike in the Gdańsk Shipyard (then called the Lenin Shipyard) on August 14, 1980. An electrician named Lech Wałęsa had been fired as an agitator years before and wasn't allowed into the yard. But on hearing news of the strike, Wałęsa went to the shipyard and climbed over the wall to get inside. The strike now had a leader.

These were not soldiers, nor were they idealistic flower children. The strike participants were gritty, salt-of-the-earth manual laborers: forklift operators, welders, electricians, machinists. Imagine being one of the 16,000 workers who stayed here for 18 days during the strike—hungry, cold, sleeping on sheets of Styrofoam, inspired by the new Polish pope, excited about finally standing up to the regime...and terrified that at any moment you might be gunned down, like your friends had been a decade before. Workers, afraid to leave the shipyard, communicated with the outside world through this gate—wives and brothers showed up here and asked for a loved one, and those inside spread the word until the striker came forward. Occasionally, a truck pulled up inside the gate, with Lech Wałęsa standing atop its cab with a megaphone. Facing the thousands of people assembled outside the gate, Wałęsa gave progress reports on the negotiations and pleaded for supplies. The people of Gdańsk responded, bringing armfuls of bread and other food to keep the workers going. Solidarity.

During the strike, two items hung on the fence. One of them (which still hangs there today) was a picture of Pope John Paul II—a reminder to believe in your dreams and have faith in God. The other item was a makeshift list of the strikers' 21 Points—demands scrawled in red paint and black pencil on pieces of plywood.

• *Walk around the right end of the gate and enter the former shipyard.*

The shipyard churned out over a thousand ships from 1948 to 1990, employing 16,000 workers. About 60 percent of these ships were exported to the USSR—and so, when the Soviet Bloc broke apart in the 1990s, they lost a huge market. Today the facilities employ closer to 1,200 workers...who now make windmills.

Before entering the museum, take a look around. Let me guess: lots of construction? This part of the shipyard, long abandoned, is being redeveloped into a **"Young City"** (Młode Miasto)—envisioned as a new city center for Gdańsk, with shopping, restaurants, offices, and homes. Rusting shipbuilding equipment has been torn down, and old brick buildings are being converted into gentrified flats. The nearby boulevard called Nowa Wałowa will be the spine connecting this area to the rest of the city. Farther east, the harborfront will also be rejuvenated, creating a glitzy marina and extending the city's delightful waterfront people zone to the north (see www.ycgdansk.com). Fortunately, the shipyard gate, monument, and other important sites from the Solidarity strikes—now considered historical monuments—will remain.

• *The massive, rust-colored European Solidarity Center, which faces Solidarity Square, houses the museum where we'll learn the rest of the story.*

▲▲▲European Solidarity Center (Europejskie Centrum Solidarności)

Europe's single best sight about the end of communism is made even more powerful by its location: in the very heart of the place where those events occurred. Filling just one small corner of a huge, purpose-built educational facility, the permanent exhibition uses larger-than-life photographs, archival footage, actual artifacts,

interactive touchscreens, and a state-of-the-art audioguide to eloquently tell the story of the end of Eastern European communism.

Cost and Hours: 17 zł, includes audioguide, daily May-Sept 10:00-20:00, Oct-April 10:00-18:00, last entry one hour before closing, Plac Solidarności 1, tel. 506-195-673, www.ecs.gda.pl.

◯ Self-Guided Tour: First, appreciate the architecture of the **building** itself. From the outside, it's designed to resemble the rusted hull of a giant ship—seemingly gloomy and depressing. But step inside to find an interior flooded with light, which cultivates a surprising variety of life—in the form of lush gardens that make the place feel like a very expensive greenhouse. You can interpret this symbolism a number of ways: Something that seems dull and dreary from the outside (the Soviet Bloc, the shipyards themselves, what have you) can be full of brightness, life, and optimism inside.

In the lobby, buy your ticket and pick up the essential, included audioguide. The exhibit has much to see, and some of it is arranged in a conceptual way that can be tricky to understand without a full grasp of the history. I've outlined the basics in this self-guided tour, but the audioguide can illuminate more details—including translations of films and eyewitness testimony from participants in the history.

• *The permanent exhibit fills seven lettered rooms—each with its own theme—on two floors. From the lush lobby, head up the escalator and into...*

The Birth of Solidarity (Room A): This room picks up right in the middle of the dynamic story we just learned out on the square. It's August of 1980, and the shipyard workers are rising up. You step straight into a busy shipyard: punch clocks, workers' lockers, and—up on the ceiling—hundreds of plastic helmets. A big **map** in the middle of the room shows the extent of the shipyard in 1980. Inside the cab of the **crane,** you can watch an interview with spunky Anna Walentynowicz, whose firing led to the first round of strikes. Nearby stands a **truck;** Lech Wałęsa would stand on top of the cab of a truck like this one to address the nervous locals who had amassed outside the shipyard gate, awaiting further news.

In the middle of the room, carefully protected under glass, are those original **plywood panels** onto which the strikers scrawled their 21 demands, then lashed to the gate. Just beyond that, a giant wall of photos and a map illustrate how the strikes that began here spread like a virus across Poland. At the far end of the room, behind the partition, stand **two tables** that were used during the talks to end the strikes (each one with several actual items from that era, under glass).

After 18 days of protests, the communist authorities finally agreed to negotiate. On the afternoon of August 31, 1980, the Governmental Commission and the Inter-Factory Strike Committee (MKS) came together and signed the August Agreements, which legalized Solidarity—the first time any communist government permitted a workers' union. As Lech Wałęsa sat at a big table and signed the agreement, other union reps tape-recorded the proceedings and played them later at their own factories to prove that the unthinkable had happened. Take a moment to linger over the rousing **film** that plays on the far wall, which begins with the strike, carries through with the tense negotiations that a brash young Lech Wałęsa held with the authorities, and ends with the triumphant acceptance of the strikers' demands. Lech Wałęsa rides on the shoulders of well-wishers out to the gate to spread the good news.

• *Back by the original 21 demands, enter the next exhibit...*

The Power of the Powerless (Room B): This section traces the roots of the 1980 strikes, which were preceded by several far less successful protests. It all begins with a kiss: a giant photograph of Russian premier Leonid Brezhnev mouth-kissing the Polish premier Edward Gierek, with the caption **"Brotherly Friendship."** Soviet premiers and their satellite leaders really did greet each other "in the French manner," as a symbolic gesture of their communist brotherhood.

Working your way through the exhibit, you'll see the door to a **prison cell**—a reminder of the intimidation tactics used by the Soviets in the 1940s and 50s to deal with their opponents as they exerted their rule over the lands they had liberated from the Nazis.

The typical **communist-era apartment** is painfully humble. After the war, much of Poland had been destroyed, and population shifts led to housing shortages. People had to make do with tiny space and ramshackle furnishings. Communist propaganda blares from both the radio and the TV.

A map shows **"red Europe"** (the USSR plus the satellites of Poland, Czechoslovakia, Hungary, and East Germany), and a **timeline** traces some of the smaller Soviet Bloc protests that led up to Solidarity: in East Germany in 1953, in Budapest and Poznań in 1956, the "Prague Spring" of 1968, and other 1968 protests in Poland.

In the wake of these uprisings, the communist authorities cracked down even harder. Peek into the **interrogation room,** with a wall of file cabinets and a lowly stool illuminated by a bright

GDAŃSK & THE TRI-CITY

spotlight. (Notice that the white Polish eagle on the seal above the desk is missing its golden crown—during communism, the Poles were allowed to keep the eagle, but its crown was removed.)

The next exhibit presents a day-by-day rundown of the **1970 strikes,** from December 14 to 22, which resulted in the massacre of the workers who are honored by the monument in front of this building. A wall of mug shots gives way to exhibits chronicling the steady rise of dissent groups through the 1970s, culminating in the June 1976 protests in the city of Radom (prompted, like so many other uprisings, by unilateral price hikes).

• *Loop back through Room A, and proceed straight ahead into...*

Solidarity and Hope (Room C): While the government didn't take the August Agreements very seriously, the Poles did...and before long, 10 million of them—one out of every four, or effectively half of the nation's workforce—joined Solidarity. So began what's often called the **"16 Months of Hope."** Newly legal, Solidarity continued to stage strikes and make its opposition known. Slick Solidarity posters and children's art convey the childlike enthusiasm with which the Poles seized their hard-won kernels of freedom. The communist authorities' hold on the Polish people began to slip. Support and aid from the outside world poured in, but the rest of the Soviet Bloc looked on nervously, and the Warsaw Pact army assembled at the Polish border and glared at the uprisers. The threat of invasion hung heavy in the air.

• *Exiting this room, head up the staircase and into...*

At War with Society (Room D): You're greeted by a wall of TV screens delivering a stern message. On Sunday morning, December 13, 1981, the Polish head of state, **General Wojciech Jaruzelski**—wearing his trademark dark glasses—appeared on national TV and announced the introduction of **martial law.** Solidarity was outlawed, and its leaders were arrested. Frightened Poles heard the announcement and looked out their windows to see Polish Army tanks rumbling through the snowy streets. (On the opposite wall, see footage of tanks and heavily armed soldiers intimidating their countrymen into compliance.) Jaruzelski claimed that he imposed martial law to prevent the Soviets from invading. Today, many historians question whether martial law was really necessary, though Jaruzelski remained unremorseful through his death in 2014.

Continuing deeper into the exhibit, you come to a **prisoner transport.** Climb up inside to watch chilling scenes of riots, demonstrations, and crackdowns by the ZOMO riot police. In one gruesome scene, a demonstrator is quite intentionally—and practically in slow motion—run over by a truck. From here, pass through a gauntlet of *milicja* riot-gear shields to see the truck crashing through a gate. Overhead are the uniforms of miners from the **Wujek mine** who were massacred on December 16, 1981 (their names are projected on the pile of coal below).

Martial law was a tragic, terrifying, and bleak time for the Polish people. It didn't, however, kill the Solidarity movement, which continued its fight after going underground. Passing prison cells, you'll see a wall plastered with handmade, underground posters and graffiti. Notice how in this era, **Solidarity propaganda** is much more primitive; circle around the other side of the wall to see several presses that were actually used in clandestine Solidarity print shops during this time. The outside world sent messages of support as well as supplies—represented by the big wall of cardboard boxes. This approval also came in the form of a Nobel Peace Prize for Lech Wałęsa in 1983; you'll see video clips of his wife accepting the award on his behalf (Wałęsa feared that if he traveled abroad to claim it, he would not be allowed back into the country).

• *But even in these darkest days, there were glimmers of hope. Enter...*

The Road to Democracy (Room E): By the time the Pope visited his homeland again in 1983, martial law had finally been lifted, and Solidarity—still technically illegal—was gaining momentum, gradually pecking away at the communists. Step into the small inner room with footage of the **Pope's third pilgrimage** to his homeland in 1987, by which time (thanks in no small part to his inspirational role in the ongoing revolution) the tide was turning.

Step into the room with the big, white **roundtable.** With the moral support of the pope and the entire Western world, the brave Poles were the first European country to throw off the shackles of communism when, in the spring of 1989, the "Roundtable Talks" led to the opening up of elections. (If you look through the viewfinders of the TV cameras in the corners, you'll see footage of those meetings.) The government arrogantly called for parliamentary elections, reserving 65 percent of seats for themselves.

In the next room, you can see Solidarity's strategy in those **elections:** On the right wall are posters showing Lech Wałęsa with each candidate. Another popular "get out the vote" measure was the huge poster of Gary Cooper—an icon of America, which the Poles deeply respect and viewed as their friendly cousin across the Atlantic—except that, instead of a pistol, he's packing a ballot. Rousing reminders like this inspired huge voter turnout. The communists' plan backfired, as virtually every open seat went to Solidarity. It was the first time ever that opposition candidates had taken office in the Soviet Bloc. On the wall straight ahead, flashing a V-for-*wiktoria* sign, is a huge photo of Tadeusz Mazowiecki—an early leader of Solidarity, who became prime minister on June 4, 1989.

• *For the glorious aftermath, head into the final room.*

The Triumph of Freedom (Room F): This room is dominated by a gigantic **map of Eastern Europe.** A countdown clock on the right ticks off the departure of each country from communist clutches, as the Soviet Bloc "decomposes." You'll see how the success of Solidarity in Poland—and the ragtag determination of a scruffy band of shipyard workers right here in Gdańsk—inspired people all over Eastern Europe. By the winter of 1989, the Hungarians had opened their borders, the Berlin Wall had crumbled, and the Czechs and Slovaks had staged their Velvet Revolution. (Small viewing stations that circle the room reveal the detailed story for each country's own road to freedom.) Lech Wałęsa—the shipyard electrician who started it all by jumping over a wall—became the first president of post-communist Poland. And a year later, in Poland's first true elections since World War II, 29 different parties won seats in the parliament. It was a free-election free-for-all.

In the middle of the room stands a white wall with **inspirational quotes** from St. John Paul II and Václav Havel—the Czech poet-turned-protester-turned-prisoner-turned-president—which are repeated in several languages. On the huge wall, the **Solidarity "graffiti"** is actually made up of thousands of little notes left behind by visitors to the museum. Feel free to grab a piece of paper and a pen and record your own reflections.

• *Finally, head downstairs and find the...*

John Paul II Room (Room G): Many visitors find that touring this museum—with vivid reminders of a dramatic and pivotal moment in history that took place in our own lifetimes, which was brought about not by armies or presidents, but by everyday people—puts them in an emotional state of mind. Designed for silent reflection, this room overlooks the monument to those workers who were gunned down in 1970.

• *For an epilogue, if you're not already pooped, continue deeper into the former shipyard to see one more important landmark from 1980. The path leads to a low-profile, red-brick building, the...*

Sala BHP

This is the building where the communists sat down across the table from Lech Wałęsa and his team and worked out a compromise (as seen in the videos inside the European Solidarity Center). Entering, turn left to walk through a series of photos—all described in English—that illustrate Solidarity history; these are all the more poignant because they lack the bombastic presentation of the glitzy museum. The images speak for themselves. The other side of the building (right from the entrance) is the actual hall where those fateful meetings took place, with a long table set up on the stage.

Cost and Hours: Free, daily May-Sept 10:00-18:00, Oct-April 10:00-16:00, www.salabhp.pl.

NORTH OF THE MAIN TOWN
World War II Museum
Gdańsk is building this large, state-of-the-art museum just east of the Solidarity shipyard, along the river. When open, it promises high-tech interactive exhibits about Gdańsk's experience during the war that began on its doorstep. It could be open as early as 2015; ask the TI for the latest details (or check www.muzeum 1939.pl).

SOUTH OF THE MAIN TOWN
A 10- to 15-minute walk south of the Main Town, these sights round out your Gdańsk experience. They're most worthwhile to those with a special interest in each one's subject matter: art, theater, and kids who love archaeology.

National Museum in Gdańsk
(Muzeum Narodowe w Gdańsku)
This art collection, housed in what was a 15th-century Franciscan monastery, is worth ▲▲ to art lovers for one reason: Hans Memling's glorious *Last Judgment* triptych altarpiece, one of the two most important pieces of art to be seen in Poland (the other is Leonardo da Vinci's *Lady with an Ermine,* usually in Kraków's Czartoryski Museum). If you're not a purist, you can settle for seeing the much smaller replica in St. Mary's Church. But if medieval art is your bag, make the 10-minute walk here from the Main Town.

Cost and Hours: 10 zł; June-Aug Tue-Wed and Fri-Sun 10:00-17:00, Thu 12:00-19:00; May and Sept Tue-Sun 10:00-17:00; Oct-April Tue-Fri 9:00-16:00, Sat-Sun 10:00-17:00; closed Mon year-round; last entry 45 minutes before closing; walk 10 minutes due south from ulica Długa's Golden Gate, after passing the Shakespeare Theater take the pedestrian underpass beneath the big cross street, then continue down the busy street until you see signs for the museum; ulica Toruńska 1, tel. 58-301-7061, www.muzeum.narodowe.gda.pl.

Visiting the Museum: From the entry, the altarpiece by Hans Memling (c. 1440-1494) is at the top of the stairs and to the right. The history of the painting is as interesting as the work itself. It was commissioned in the mid-15th century by the Medicis' banker in Florence, Angelo di Jacopo Tani. The ship delivering the painting from Belgium to Florence was hijacked by a Gdańsk pirate, who brought the altarpiece to his hometown to be displayed in St. Mary's Church. For centuries, kings, emperors, and czars admired it from afar, until Napoleon seized it in the early 19th century and took it to Paris to hang in the Louvre. Gdańsk finally got the painting back, only to have it exiled again—this time into St. Petersburg's Hermitage Museum—after World War II. On its return to Gdańsk in 1956, this museum claimed it—though St. Mary's wants it back.

Have a close look at Memling's well-traveled work. It's the end of the world, and Christ rides in on a rainbow to judge humankind. Angels blow reveille, waking the dead, who rise from their graves. The winged archangel Michael—dressed for battle and wielding the cross like a weapon—weighs the grace in each person, sending them either to the fires of hell (right panel) or up the sparkling-crystal stairway to heaven (left).

It takes all 70 square feet of paneling to contain this awesome scene. Jam-packed with dozens of bodies, a Bible's worth of symbolism, and executed with astonishing detail, the painting can keep even a non-art lover occupied. Notice the serene, happy expressions of the righteous, as they're greeted by St. Peter (with his giant key) and clothed by angels. And pity the condemned, their faces filled with terror and sorrow as they're tortured by grotesque devils more horrifying than anything Hollywood could devise.

Tune in to the exquisite details: the angels' robes, the devils' genetic-mutant features, the portrait of the man in the scale (a Medici banker), Michael's peacock wings. Get as close as you can to the globe at Christ's feet and Michael's shining breastplate: You can just make out the whole scene in mirror reflection. Then back up and take it all in—three panels connected by a necklace of bodies that curves downward through hell, crosses the earth, then rises up to the towers of the New Jerusalem. On the back side of the triptych are reverent portraits of the painting's patron, Angelo Tani, and his new bride, Catarina.

Beyond the Memling, the remainder of the collection isn't too thrilling. The rest of the upstairs has more Flemish and Dutch art, as well as paintings from Gdańsk's Golden Age and various works by Polish artists. The ground floor features a cavernous, all-white cloister filled with Gothic altarpiece sculptures, gold and silver wares, majolica and Delft porcelain, and characteristic Gdańsk-style furniture.

Gdańsk Shakespeare Theater (Teatr Szekspirowski)

Gdańsk has a long and proud tradition of staging plays by Shakespeare. As early as the 17th century, theater troupes from England were coming to this cosmopolitan trading city to perform. In 1993, local actors revived the tradition with an annual Gdańsk Shakespeare Festival. And in 2014, the city built the state-of-the-art Gdańsk Shakespeare Theater to honor its connection to the Bard.

The building's minimalist, black-brick, blocky architecture—with a few symbolic faux-buttresses to echo the gables of the surrounding buildings—was criticized for not blending in very well with its surroundings. But the celebration of theater that takes place inside is welcomed by all. The main theater can be modified to create three different types of performance spaces (proscenium, thrust stage, and theater in the round)—and even has a retractable roof to wash the actors with direct sunlight. There's not much to see—unless you're attending a play, you can only get as far as the box office. But if you want to take a peek, the building is on ulica Zbytki—just follow Pcztowa street south from the middle of ulica Długa.

Shakespeare contributes only a tiny piece of the theater's full lineup—it plays host to a wide variety of performances and festivals throughout the year. You're most likely to find Shakespeare performed in English during the annual Shakespeare Festival, which is typically in late summer or early fall (www.shakespearefestival.pl). For details on all upcoming performances, see www.teatrszekspirowski.pl (box office open daily 13:00-18:00).

"Blue Lion" Archaeological Education Center (Centrum Edukacji Archeologicznej "Błękitny Lew")

Hiding far from the Main Town on Granary Island, this kid-friendly exhibit re-creates the atmosphere of medieval Gdańsk. Occupying a rebuilt granary called the "Blue Lion," its highlight is a full-scale replica of an atmospheric medieval street, populated by mannequins whose features are based on actual human remains. Also telling the tale are artifacts from the period, a selection of films (subtitled in English), and touchscreens that provide some background. Though information is a bit sparse (especially along the medieval street), the collection tries hard not to be just another fuddy-duddy, dusty old museum, making it popular with kids on field trips.

Cost and Hours: 10 zł, May-Aug Tue-Sun 10:00-18:00, Sept-April Tue-Sun 9:00-17:00, closed Mon year-round, ulica Chmielna 53, tel. 58-320-3188, www.archeologia.pl.

OUTER GDAŃSK

These two sights—worthwhile only to those with a particular interest in them—are each within the city limits of Gdańsk, but they take some serious time to see round-trip.

Oliwa Cathedral (Katedra Oliwska)

The suburb of Oliwa, at the northern edge of Gdańsk, is home to this visually striking church. The quirky, elongated façade hides a surprisingly long and skinny nave. The ornately decorated 18th-century organ over the main entrance features angels and stars that move around when the organ is played. While locals are proud of this place, it's hard to justify the effort it takes to get out here. Skip it unless you just love Polish churches or you're going to a concert.

Concerts: The animated organ performs its 20-minute show frequently, especially in summer (concerts at the top of each hour: July-Aug Mon-Fri 10:00-13:00 & 15:00-17:00, Sat 10:00-15:00, Sun 15:00-17:00; June Mon-Sat 10:00-13:00, Sun 15:00-17:00; May and Sept Mon-Sat 10:00-13:00, Sun at 15:00 and 16:00; 1-2/day off-season, www.archikatedraoliwa.pl). Confirm the schedule at the TI before making the trip. Note that on Sundays and holidays, there are no concerts before 15:00.

Getting There: Oliwa is about six miles northwest of central Gdańsk, on the way to Sopot and Gdynia. To get to Oliwa, you have two options: The tram is slower (30 minutes) but gets you closer, while the SKM commuter train is faster (15 minutes) but requires a longer walk. **Tram #6** or **#12** from Gdańsk's main train station lets you off right at the entrance to Oliwski Park. Go straight through to the back of the park; near the end, you can see the copper roof and two skinny, pointy spires of the cathedral on your right. Exit through the back of the park, bear right, and go one block to find the entrance to the church. **SKM commuter trains** from Gdańsk's main train station zip to the "Gdańsk Oliwa" stop in 15 minutes. From the Oliwa train station, it's a 15-minute walk or 10-zł taxi ride to the cathedral. Walk straight ahead out of the station and turn right when you get to the busy road. Cross the road at the light and enter the tree-filled Park Oliwski at the corner, then follow the directions above.

Westerplatte ✓

World War II began on September 1, 1939, when Adolf Hitler sent the warship *Schleswig-Holstein* to attack this Polish munitions depot, which was guarding Gdańsk's harbor. Though it may interest serious WWII history buffs, most visitors will find little to see here aside from a modest museum, a towering monument, and some old bunkers. As it's surrounded by shipyard sprawl, it's not a particularly scenic trip, either.

Getting There: The most enjoyable approach is on a cruise—either on a modern boat, or on the fun old-fashioned galleons (45-50 minutes each way). You can also take **bus #138** from the main train station (about 30 minutes).

Shopping in Gdańsk

The big story in Gdańsk is amber *(bursztyn)*, a fossil resin available in all shades, shapes, and sizes (see the "All About Amber" sidebar, earlier). While you'll see amber sold all over town, the best place to browse and buy is along the atmospheric ulica Mariacka (between the Motława River and St. Mary's Church). This pretty street, with old-fashioned balconies and dozens of display cases, is fun to wander even if you're not a shopper. Other good places to buy amber are along the riverfront embankment and on ulica Długa. To avoid rip-offs—such as amber that's been melted and reshaped—always buy it from a shop, not from someone standing on the street. (But note that most shops also have a display case and salesperson out front, which are perfectly legit.) Prices everywhere are about the same, so rather than seeking out a specific place, just window-shop until you see what you want. Styles range from gaudy necklaces with huge globs of amber, to tasteful smaller pendants in silver settings, to cheap trinkets. All shades of amber—from near-white to dark brown—cost about the same, but you'll pay more for inclusions (bugs or other objects stuck in the amber).

Gdańsk also has several modern shopping malls, most of them in the Old Town or near the main train station. The walk between the Main Town and the Solidarity shipyard goes past some of the best malls.

Sleeping in Gdańsk

I've listed rates here for the high season, generally May through September; at all of these places, you'll pay a bit less in the off-season (Oct-April). Many hotels are booked up (mostly with German tourists) in peak season (mid-June-mid-Sept)—reserve ahead.

ACROSS THE RIVER

These hotels are across the river from the Main Town. That puts you a bit farther from the sightseeing action, but it's a relatively short walk (no more than 10 minutes from any of these), and the rooms are a better value.

$$$ Hotel Podewils is the top choice for a friendly splurge. Filling a storybook-cute house from 1728, overlooking the marina and across the river from a fine panorama of the Gdańsk embankment, it's classy. The public spaces and 10 rooms have all the modern amenities, but with plush, almost Baroque, decor (Db-600-800 zł depending on size of room—each one is different—and demand, air-con, Wi-Fi, Szafarnia 2, tel. 58-300-9560, www.podewils.pl, gdansk@podewils.pl).

Sleep Code

Abbreviations (3 zł = about $1, country code: 48)
S = Single, **D** = Double/Twin, **T** = Triple, **Q** = Quad, **b** = bathroom, **s** = shower only.

Price Rankings

   $$$ **Higher Priced**—Most rooms 400 zł or more.
   $$ **Moderately Priced**—Most rooms between 300-400 zł.
   $ **Lower Priced**—Most rooms 300 zł or less.

Unless otherwise noted, breakfast is included, credit cards are accepted, Wi-Fi is generally free, and English is spoken. Prices can change without notice; verify the hotel's current rates online or by email. For the best prices, always book directly with the hotel.

$$$ Hotel Królewski, a classy hotel in a beautifully renovated red-brick granary, offers 30 stylish rooms sitting right along the river, facing classic Gdańsk embankment views. It's just beyond the three granaries of the National Maritime Museum, across the river from the Crane. The Polish Baltic Philharmonic is right next door, so you may be serenaded by a rehearsal or performance (Sb-400 zł, Db-450 zł, fancier suite-like Db "plus"-500 zł, pricier apartments, lower rates mid-Oct-April, 50 zł to reserve a view room—or try asking for one when you check in for no extra charge, non-smoking rooms, elevator, Wi-Fi, good restaurant, ulica Ołowianka 1, tel. 58-326-1111, www.hotelkrolewski.pl, office@hotelkrolewski.pl). You can commute to your sightseeing by ferry (take the 1.50-zł boat trip across the river offered by the Maritime Museum). But the ferry runs only during the museum's opening hours and is sporadic off-season. If the ferry isn't running, it's a scenic 15-minute walk along the river, past the marina, and over the bridge into the Main Town.

$$ Willa Litarion, run by the eager Owsikowski family, sits on the back side of a charmingly restored row of colorful houses on the island just across the river from the main drag. It's tall and skinny, with no elevator, and faces a gloomy parking lot, but it's a handy location at a decent price. Each of the 13 small rooms has a totally different design, but all are artsy and mod (Sb-255 zł, Db-330 zł, bigger "deluxe" Db-360 zł, 20-25 percent cheaper Oct-April, extra bed-60 zł, Wi-Fi, parking garage-30 zł/day, ulica Spichrzowa 18, tel. 58-320-2553, www.litarion.pl, recepcja@litarion.pl). Several other, similar (but less appealing) "villas" line this same street—if you're in a pinch for a room, this is a handy place to go ringing doorbells.

At the Academy of Music: **$$ Dom Muzyka** rents 87 simple, tidy rooms in a nondescript residential neighborhood. The catch:

It's very difficult to find, hiding in the back of the big Academy of Music building (Akademia Muzyczna). But the prices are worth the hunt, and once you're set up, it's an easy 10-minute walk to the sights. Their "deluxe" rooms, mostly twins, are bigger and overlook the quiet courtyard; most of the standard rooms face a busy street but have good windows and air-conditioning (Sb-250 zł, standard Db-340 zł, deluxe Db-360 zł, apartment-500 zł, extra bed-100 zł, cheaper Oct-April, elevator, guest computer, Wi-Fi, popular with tour groups, good restaurant, free and easy parking, ulica Łąkowa 1, tel. 58-326-0600, www.dommuzyka.pl, biuro@ dommuzyka.pl).

In the same complex, **$ Dom Sonata** is a tempting budget option. Its 60 rooms—nearly as nice as the Dom Muzyka's, but with fewer hotelesque amenities—house students for most of the year, but are rented out to tourists from July through September. Given the good quality of the rooms, the price is right (Db-150 zł, breakfast-19 zł extra, air-con, elevator, Wi-Fi, ulica Łąkowa 1, tel. 58-300-9260, www.domsonata.com.pl, domsonata@amuz. gda.pl). From the Main Town's Green Gate, cross the two bridges, then walk a long block along the modern commercial building and turn right just before the park (on Łąkowa, across from the big brick church). Walk to the end of this block; before the busy road, go through the gate just before the big yellow-brick building on the right. Once inside the gate checkpoint, the hotel is around the back of the yellow building, the farthest door down. If you get lost, just ask people, "Hotel?"

IN THE MAIN TOWN

With a recent increase in midrange accommodations inside the Main Town, this prime location has become more affordable. However, the Main Town can come with more nighttime noise, particularly in summer, when loud bars and discos keep things lively. Request a quiet room...and pack earplugs.

$$$ Hotel Wolne Miasto ("Free City") offers rich, wood-carved public spaces with photos of old Gdańsk and 68 elegant rooms on the edge of the Main Town, just two blocks from the main drag. It's above a popular disco that gets noisy on weekends (Thu-Sat nights), so it's especially important to request a quieter room when you reserve (Sb-390 zł, Db-470 zł, bigger "deluxe" Db-570 zł, all rooms 20 zł less Fri-Sun, even cheaper Oct-March, elevator, guest computer, Wi-Fi, ulica Świętego Ducha 2, tel. 58-322-2442, www.hotelwm.pl, rezerwacja@hotelwm.pl).

$$$ Hotel Admirał is simply practical: a big, impersonal, business-class place with 44 nicely decorated rooms tucked in a quiet residential alley at the north end of the embankment, just a few steps off the old fish market. This is especially worth

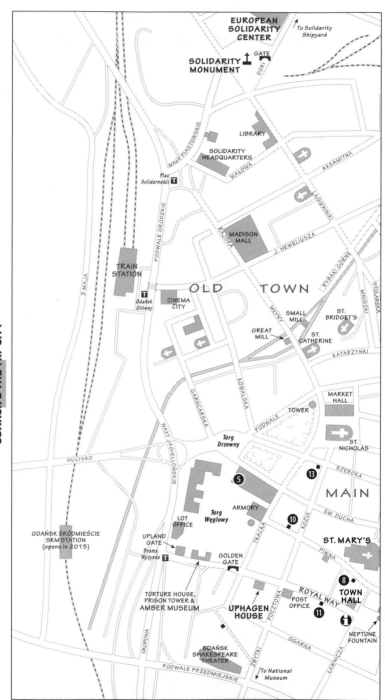

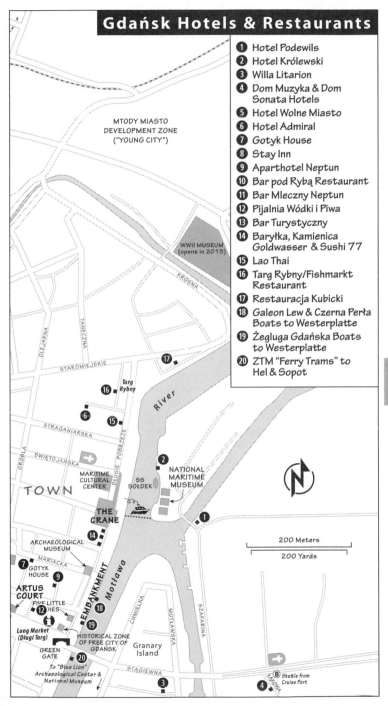

Gdańsk Hotels & Restaurants

1 Hotel Podewils
2 Hotel Królewski
3 Willa Litarion
4 Dom Muzyka & Dom Sonata Hotels
5 Hotel Wolne Miasto
6 Hotel Admiral
7 Gotyk House
8 Stay Inn
9 Aparthotel Neptun
10 Bar pod Rybą Restaurant
11 Bar Mleczny Neptun
12 Pijalnia Wódki i Piwa
13 Bar Turystyczny
14 Baryłka, Kamienica Goldwasser & Sushi 77
15 Lao Thai
16 Targ Rybny/Fishmarkt Restaurant
17 Restauracja Kubicki
18 Galeon Lew & Czerna Perła Boats to Westerplatte
19 Żegluga Gdańska Boats to Westerplatte
20 ZTM "Ferry Trams" to Hel & Sopot

MŁODY MIASTO DEVELOPMENT ZONE ("YOUNG CITY")

WWII MUSEUM (opens in 2015)

GDAŃSK & THE TRI-CITY

KŁOSNA

TANECZNA

OLEJARNA

STAROMIEJSKIE

Targ Rybny

STRAGANIARSKA

GROBLA

ŚWIĘTOJAŃSKA

DŁUGIE PORZEZE

River

National MARITIME MUSEUM

MARITIME CULTURAL CENTER

SS SOŁDEK

TOWN

THE CRANE

ARCHAEOLOGICAL MUSEUM

MARIACKA

GOTYK HOUSE

ARTUS COURT

FIVE LITTLE LADIES

Long Market (Długi Targ)

EMBANKMENT

Motława

GREEN GATE

To "Blue Lion" Archaeological Center & National Museum

HISTORICAL ZONE OF FREE CITY OF GDAŃSK

Granary Island

CHMIELNA

MOTŁAWSKA

STĄGIEWNA

SZAFARNIA

B Shuttle from Cruise Port

200 Meters
200 Yards

N

considering if you can get a good deal (rates fluctuate but generally around Db-400 zł in high season, air-con, elevator, Wi-Fi, Tobiasza 9, tel. 58-320-0320, www.admiralhotel.pl, recepcja@admiralhotel.pl).

$$ Gotyk House, a good value, is run with warmth and pride by the Rybicki family. Owner Andrzej is an energetic armchair historian who works hard to make his little hotel comfortable while still respecting the sanctity of what's supposedly Gdańsk's oldest house. The chimes from St. Mary's Church, next door, provide a pleasant soundtrack. The cellar houses a minuscule gingerbread museum and small shrine to Copernicus (whose longtime lover may have lived here). The seven straightforward rooms share a tiny breakfast room, so you'll have to tell them what time you'd like to eat (Sb-280 zł, Db-310 zł, cheaper Oct-April, Wi-Fi in most rooms, tight public spaces, ulica Mariacka 1, tel. 58-301-8567, mobile 516-141-133, www.gotykhouse.eu, reservation@gotykhouse.eu).

$-$$ Stay Inn, a self-declared "hostel with vibe," is fresh and young, but still feels practical. The location couldn't be more central—facing the side of St. Mary's Church, right in the heart of the Main Town—and, while the street it's on is quieter than most, a downstairs pub can be noisy on weekends. It combines 29 beds in small 5- to 8-bed dorms with 10 private rooms that are as hotel-like as any in this price range. The dorm dwellers and fancier folks alike share the same kitchen/lounge/breakfast room. Everything feels tidy and well-designed; as it lacks the grungy party personality of some hostels, it's well worth considering even for non-hostelers (dorm bed-60 zł, tiny Db with cozy platform double bed-300 zł, more spacious twin Db-350 zł, includes breakfast, elevator, guest computer, Wi-Fi, bike rental, Piwna 28, tel. 58-354-1543, www.stayinngdansk.com, booking@stayinngdansk.com).

$$ Aparthotel Neptun lacks personality, but owns a great location—on a slightly dreary side-street between delightful Mariacka and bustling Długi Targ ("Long Square"). While it's just a few steps to most of the town's big sights, it's just far enough away to avoid the crowds and the weekend noise. The 30 rooms and apartments are modern, efficient, well-equipped, and forgettable...but well-priced for the central location (Db-350 zł, apartments start at 450 zł, breakfast-25 zł extra, elevator, Wi-Fi, Grzaska 1, mobile 604-466-466, www.aparthotelgdansk.com, info@aparthotelgdansk.com).

Eating in Gdańsk

In addition to traditional Polish fare, Gdańsk has some excellent Baltic seafood. Herring *(śledź)* is popular here, as is cod *(dorsz)*. Natives brag that their salmon *(łosoś)* is better than Norway's. For a stiff drink, sample *Goldwasser* (similar to Goldschlager). This sweet and strong liqueur, flecked with actual gold, was supposedly invented here in Gdańsk. The following options are all in the Main Town, within three blocks of the Royal Way.

BUDGET RESTAURANTS IN THE CITY CENTER

These places are affordable, tasty, quick, and wonderfully convenient—on or very near the Royal Way (ulica Długa). They're worth considering even if you're not on a tight budget.

Bar pod Rybą ("Under the Fish") is nirvana for fans of baked potatoes *(pieczony ziemniak)*. They offer more than 20 varieties, piled high with a wide variety of toppings and sauces, from Mexican beef to herring to Polish cheeses. They also serve fish dishes with salad and potatoes, making this a cheap place to sample local seafood. The tasteful decor—walls lined with old bottles, antique wooden hangers, and old street signs—is squeezed into a single cozy room packed with happy eaters. In the summer, order inside, and they'll bring your food to you at an outdoor table (potatoes and fish dishes are each about 20-30 zł, daily 10:00-22:00, ulica Piwna 61, tel. 58-305-1307).

Bar Mleczny Neptun is your handiest milk-bar option in the Main Town. A hearty meal, including a drink, runs about 15-20 zł. This popular place has more charm than your typical institutional milk bar, including outdoor seating along the most scenic stretch of the main drag, and an upstairs dining room overlooking it all. The items on the counter are for display—point to what you want and they'll dish it up fresh (Mon-Fri 7:30-19:30, Sat-Sun 10:00-19:00, may have shorter hours off-season, free Wi-Fi, ulica Długa 33, tel. 58-301-4988).

Pijalnia Wódki i Piwa, part of a popular Polish chain, hides half a block behind the Hard Rock Café (on Kuśnierska). This little vodka-and-herring bar takes you back to the 1970s. Pop in to study the retro decor—ads from the 1970s and photos of the lines people routinely endured. The place is literally wallpapered with pages from the "Tribune of the Masses" newspaper infamous for its propaganda that passed for news. They play pop hits from the last years of communism. The menu is fun, accessible, and simple: 4 zł for vodka or other drinks, and 8 zł for herring or other bar nibbles (open daily 9:00-late).

Bar Turystyczny is misnamed—while it seems to harbor the illusion that it's for tourists, it has become beloved by locals as the central area's favorite milk bar. Easy to miss on the way between the Main Town and the Solidarity sights, it's always jammed (9-13-zł main dishes, Mon-Fri 8:00-18:00, Sat-Sun 9:00-17:00, Szeroka 8, tel. 58/301-6013).

ON THE RIVERFRONT EMBANKMENT

Perhaps the most appealing dining zone in Gdańsk stretches along the riverfront embankment near the Crane. On a balmy summer evening, the outdoor tables here are

enticing. As it's a popular area, consider scouting a table during your sightseeing, and reserve your choice for dinner later that night. While these places are mostly interchangeable, I've listed a few to consider, in the order you'll reach them as you walk north along the embankment.

Baryłka ("Barrel") is a simpler, more affordable alternative to some of the pricier places along here. While the outdoor seating is enticing, the elegant upstairs dining room, with windows overlooking the river, is also appealing (35-45-zł main dishes, daily 9:00-24:00, Długie Pobrzeże 24, tel. 58-301-4938).

Kamienica Goldwasser offers high-quality Polish and international cuisine. Choose between cozy, romantic indoor seating on several levels, or scenic outdoor seating (most main dishes 60-75 zł, daily 10:00-24:00, occasional live music, Długie Pobrzeże 22, tel. 58-301-8878).

Sushi 77, serving up a wide selection of surprisingly good sushi right next to the Crane, is a refreshing break from ye olde Polish food. Choose between the outdoor tables bathed in red light, or the mod interior (30-50-zł sushi sets, daily 12:00-23:00, Długie Pobrzeże 30, tel. 58-682-1823).

Past the Crane

About 100 yards past the Crane, near the old fish market (Targ Rybny), cluster several more options.

Lao Thai is a modern space right along the embankment selling surprisingly high-quality, yet still affordable, Thai cuisine (35-50-zł dishes, daily 12:00-22:00, ulica Targ Rybny 11, tel. 58/305-2525).

Targ Rybny/Fishmarkt ("The Fish Market") has less appealing outdoor seating that overlooks a park and parking lot. But the warm, mellow-yellow nautical ambience inside is pleasant, making this a good bad-weather option. It features classy but not stuffy service, and an emphasis on fish (most main dishes 40-55 zł, plus pricier seafood splurges, daily 10:00-23:00, ulica Targ Rybny 6C, tel. 58-320-9011).

Restauracja Kubicki, along the water just past the Hilton, has a long history (since 1918), but a recent remodel has kept the atmosphere—and its food—feeling fresh. This is a good choice for high-quality Polish and international food in a fun, sophisticated-but-not-stuffy interior that's a clever mix of old and new elements (30-55 zł main dishes, daily 12:00-23:00, Wartka 5, tel. 58-301-0050).

Gdańsk Connections

BY TRAIN

Gdańsk is well-connected to the Tri-City via the commuter SKM trains (explained later, under "Getting Around the Tri-City"). It's also connected to Warsaw and Kraków by the new, high-speed EIC line (which requires reservations). Given the distance between Gdańsk and other Polish destinations, also consider domestic flights; Eurolot often has easy flights between Gdańsk and Kraków for about the same price as a train ticket, while LOT and others connect Gdańsk to Warsaw.

From Gdańsk by Train to: Hel (town on Hel Peninsula, 3/day direct July-Aug only, 2-3 hours; otherwise about hourly with transfer in Gdynia), **Malbork** (2/hour, about half are express EIC trains that take 30 minutes, the rest are slower regional trains that take around 45 minutes), **Toruń** (5/day, about 3 hours; more with a transfer in Bydgoszcz, 3.5 hours), **Warsaw** (hourly, 3 hours), **Kraków** (6/day direct, 5.5 hours, 1 more with change in Warsaw; plus 11-hour night train), **Berlin** (1/day direct, 5.75 hours; 2/day, 6-8 hours, transfer in Poznań).

BY BOAT

Various boats depart from Gdańsk's embankment to nearby destinations, including **Westerplatte** (the monument marking where World War II started) and **Hel** (the beachy peninsula, described below). While boats also run sporadically to Sopot and Gdynia, the train is better for those trips (described under "Getting Around the Tri-City," later). As these boat schedules tend to change from year to year, confirm your plans carefully at the TI. All boat trips are weather permitting, especially the faster hydrofoils. In shoulder season (April-June and Sept-Oct), even though most boats stop running from Gdańsk, several routes still run between Sopot, Gdynia, and Hel. Boats generally don't run in winter (Nov-March).

To Westerplatte: To travel by boat to the monument at Westerplatte, you have three options. The most enjoyable one is to ride the replica **17th-century galleons,** either the *Galeon Lew* ("Lion Galleon") or the *Czarna Perła* ("Black Pearl"). These over-the-top, touristy boats depart hourly from the embankment just outside the Green Gate for a lazy 1.5-hour round-trip cruise to Westerplatte and back. (You can choose to get off at Westerplatte

after 45 minutes and take a later boat back.) Both of them have English commentary on the way there and live nautical music on the return trip (if you've ever wanted to hear "What Shall We Do with a Drunken Sailor?" in Polish, here's your chance). It's not exactly pretty—you'll see more industry than scenery—but it's a fun excuse to set sail, even if you don't care about Westerplatte (40 zł round-trip, 30 zł one-way, the two boats take turns departing at the top of each hour 10:00-19:00 in July-Aug, fewer departures May-June and Sept, from the embankment near the Crane, mobile 601-629-191, www.galeony.pl). Two other, duller alternatives leave from right nearby: big, modern **Żegluga Gdańska** boats (40 zł round-trip, 30 zł one-way, 50 minutes each way, daily April-Oct, 3-6/day in each direction, www.zegluga.pl); or much cheaper but less frequent city-run **ZTM "ferry trams"** *(tramwaj wodny),* which depart from the embankment on the south side of the bridge (10 zł each way, line #F5, 3/day).

To Hel: Various boats zip out to Hel in two hours during the summer. Though the specifics change from year to year, this route is most likely run by Żegluga Gdańska (May-June weekends only, July-Aug 3/day, 35 zł each way, www.zegluga.pl).

BY CRUISE SHIP
While many cruises advertise a stop in "Gdańsk," most actually dock in the nearby town of Gdynia.

The Tri-City (Trójmiasto)

Gdańsk is the anchor of the three-part metropolitan region known as the Tri-City (Trójmiasto). The other two parts are as different as night and day: Sopot, a once-swanky resort town; and Gdynia, a practical, nose-to-the-grindstone business center. The Tri-City as a whole is home to bustling industry and a sprawling university, with several campuses and plenty of well-dressed, English-speaking students. Beyond the Tri-City, the long, skinny Hel Peninsula—a sparsely populated strip of fishing villages and fun-loving beaches—arches dramatically into the Baltic Sea.

Sopot—boasting sandy beaches, tons of tourists, and a certain elegance—is clearly the most appealing day-trip option. Gdynia offers a glimpse into workaday Poland, but leaves most visitors cold. Hel, which requires the better part of a day to visit, is worthwhile only if you've got perfect summer weather and a desire to lie on the beach.

GETTING AROUND THE TRI-CITY

Gdańsk, Sopot, and Gdynia are connected by regional commuter trains (*kolejka*, operated by SKM) as well as by trains of Poland's

GDAŃSK & THE TRI-CITY

national railway (operated by PKP). Tickets for one system can't be used on the other. While trains for the two systems chug along the same tracks, they use different (but nearby) platforms/stations. For example, at Gdańsk's main train station, national PKP trains use platforms 1-3, while regional SKM trains use platforms 3-5. And in Sopot, the SKM station is a few hundred feet before the PKP station. Regional SKM trains are much more frequent than long-distance PKP trains—they go in each direction about every 10-15 minutes (less frequently after 19:30).

Traditionally, the easiest place to catch the SKM trains is at Gdańsk's main train station. However, the new Gdańsk's Śródmieście station (which may open in late 2015) is a bit closer to the tourist zone, just across the street from the Upland Gate. At either place, buy tickets at the machine marked *SKM Bilety* (English instructions). Some likely trip durations and prices: 3.80 zł and 15 minutes to Oliwa, 3.80 zł and 25 minutes to Sopot, or 5.70 zł and 35 minutes to Gdynia. Tickets purchased from a machine come already validated. But if you buy one from a kiosk, you'll need to stamp it in the easy-to-miss yellow slots under the boards with SKM information.

Each city has multiple stops. In Gdańsk, use "Gdańsk Główny" (the main station) or—if it's open—"Gdańsk Śródmieście" (closer to the Main Town); for Sopot, use the stop called simply "Sopot"; and for Gdynia, it's "Gdynia Główna" (the main station).

The bigger PKP trains are faster, but less frequent—unless you notice one that happens to be leaving at a convenient time, I'd skip them and stick with the easy SKM trains. But note that trains to Hel are always operated by PKP.

For a more romantic—and much slower—approach, consider the boat (see "Gdańsk Connections," earlier).

Sopot

Sopot (SOH-poht), dubbed the "Nice of the North," was a celebrated haunt of beautiful people during the 1920s and 1930s, and remains a popular beach getaway to this day.

Sopot was created in the early 19th century by Napoleon's doctor, Jean Georges Haffner, who believed Baltic Sea water to be therapeutic. By the 1890s, it had become a fashionable seaside resort. This gambling center boasted enough high-roller casinos to garner comparisons to Monte Carlo.

The casinos are gone, but the health resorts remain, and you'll still see more well-dressed people here per capita than just about anywhere else in the country. While it's not quite Cannes, Sopot feels relatively high class, which is unusual in otherwise unpretentious Poland. But even so, a childlike spirit of summer-vacation fun pervades this St-Tropez-on-the-Baltic, making it an all-around enjoyable place.

PLANNING YOUR TIME

You can get the gist of Sopot in just a couple of hours. Zip in on the train, follow the main drag to the sea, wander the pier, get your feet wet at the beach, then head back to Gdańsk. Why not come here in the late afternoon, enjoy those last few rays of sunshine, stay for dinner, then take a twilight stroll on the pier?

Orientation to Sopot

The main pedestrian drag, Monte Cassino Heroes street (ulica Bohaterów Monte Cassino), leads to the Molo, the longest pleasure pier in Europe. From the Molo, a broad, sandy beach stretches in each direction. Running parallel to the surf is a tree-lined, people-filled path made for strolling.

TOURIST INFORMATION

Sopot's helpful TI is near the base of the Molo at Plac Zdrojowy 2 (look for blue *it* sign). Pick up the free map, info booklet, and events schedule. They also offer a free room-booking service (daily June-mid-Sept 9:00-20:00, mid-Sept-May 10:00-18:00, ulica Dworcowa 4, tel. 58-550-3783, www.sopot.pl).

ARRIVAL IN SOPOT

From the SKM station, exit to the left and walk down the street. After a block, you'll see the PKP train station on your left. Continue on to the can't-miss-it main drag, ulica Bohaterów Monte Cassino (marked by the big red-brick church steeple). Follow it to the right, down to the seaside.

Sights in Sopot

▲Monte Cassino Heroes Street
(Ulica Bohaterów Monte Cassino)

Nicknamed "Monciak" (MOHN-chak) by locals, this in-love-with-life promenade may well be Poland's most manicured street (and is named in honor of the Polish soldiers who helped the

Allies pry Italy's Monte Cassino monastery from Nazi forces during World War II). Especially after all the suburban and industrial dreck you passed through to get here, it's easy to be charmed by this pretty drag. The street is lined with happy tourists, trendy cafés, al fresco restaurants, movie theaters, and late-19th-century facades (known for their wooden balconies).

The most popular building along here (on the left, about halfway down) is the so-called **Crooked House** (Krzywy Domek), a trippy, Gaudí-inspired building that looks like it's melting. Hard-partying Poles prefer to call it the "Drunken House," and say that when it looks straight, it's time to stop drinking.

Molo (Pier)

At more than 1,600 feet long, this is Europe's longest wooden entertainment pier. While you won't find any amusement-park rides, you will be surrounded by vendors, artists, and Poles having the time of their lives. Buy a *gofry* (Belgian waffle topped with whipped cream and fruit) or an oversized cloud of *wata cukrowa* (cotton candy), grab your partner's hand, and stroll with gusto (7.50 zł, free Oct-April, open long hours daily, www.molo.sopot.pl).

Climb to the top of the Art Nouveau lighthouse for a water-front panorama. Scan the horizon for sailboats and tankers. Any pirate ships? For a jarring reality check, look over to Gdańsk. Barely visible from the Molo are two of the most important sites in 20th-century history: the towering monument at Westerplatte, where World War II started, and the cranes rising up from the Gdańsk Shipyard, where Solidarity was born and European communism began its long goodbye.

In spring and fall, the Molo is a favorite venue for pole vaulting—or is that Pole vaulting?

The Beach

Yes, Poland has beaches. Nice ones. When I heard Sopot compared to places like Nice, I'll admit that I scoffed. But when I saw those stretches of inviting sand as far as the eye can see, I wished I'd packed my swim trunks. (You could walk from Gdańsk to Gdynia on beaches like this.) The sand is finer than anything I've seen in Croatia...though the water's not exactly crystal-clear. Most of the beach is public, except for a small private stretch in front of the Grand Hotel Sopot. Year-round, it's crammed with locals. At these northern latitudes, the season for bathing is brief and crowded.

Overlooking the beach next to the Molo is the **Grand Hotel Sopot.** It was renovated to top-class status just recently, but its history goes way back. They could charge admission for room #226, a multiroom suite that has hosted the likes of Adolf Hitler,

Marlene Dietrich, and Fidel Castro (but not all at the same time). With all the trappings of Sopot's belle époque—dark wood, plush upholstery, antique furniture—this room had me imagining Hitler sitting at the desk, looking out to sea, and plotting the course of World War II.

Gdynia

Compared to its flashier sister cities, straightforward Gdynia (guh-DIN-yah) has retained a more working-class vibe, still in touch with its salty, fishing-village roots. Gdynia is less historic than Gdańsk or Sopot, as it was mostly built in the 1920s to be Poland's main harbor after Gdańsk became a free city. Although nowhere as attractive as Gdańsk or Sopot, Gdynia has an authentic feel and a lovely waterfront promenade (www.gdynia.pl).

Gdynia is a major business center, and—thanks to its youthful, progressive city government—has edged ahead of the rest of Poland in transitioning from communism. It enjoys one of the highest income levels in the country. Many of the crumbling downtown buildings have been renovated, and Gdynia is becoming known for its top-tier shopping—all the big designers have boutiques here. If a local woman has been shopping on Świętojańska street in Gdynia, it means that she's got some serious złoty.

Because Gdańsk's port is relatively shallow, the biggest cruise ships must put in at Gdynia...leaving confused tourists to poke around town looking for some medieval quaintness, before coming to their senses and heading for Gdańsk. Gdynia is also home to a major military harbor and an important NATO base.

To get a taste of Gdynia, take the SKM train to the "Gdynia Główna" station, follow signs to *wyjście do miasta,* cross the busy street, and walk 15 minutes down Starowiejska. When you come to the intersection with the broad Świętojańska street, turn right (in the direction the big statue is looking) and walk two blocks to the tree-lined park on the left. Head through the park to the Southern Pier (Molo Południowe). This concrete slab—nowhere near as charming as Sopot's wooden-boardwalk version—features a modern shopping mall and a smattering of sights, including an aquarium and a pair of permanently moored museum boats.

Plans are afoot to convert the big warehouse at the Nabrzeże Francuskie pier into an emigration museum, possibly as early as mid-2015; when this opens, it will offer a handy sightseeing opportunity for cruisers arriving here (for the latest, see www.muzeumemigracji.pl).

ARRIVING BY CRUISE IN GDYNIA

Many Northern European cruises include a stop at "Gdańsk"; most of these actually put in at Gdynia's sprawling port. And, while Gydnia's town center is relatively manicured and pleasant, its port area is the opposite—like a Soviet Bloc bodybuilder, it's muscular and hairy. Cruise ships are shuffled among hardworking industrial piers that make the area feel uninviting. Three of the port's many piers are used for cruises: **Nabrzeże Francuskie** (French Quay), where most large ships dock; **Nabrzeże Stanów Zjednoczonych** (United States Quay), farther out, a secondary option for large ships; and convenient **Nabrzeże Pomorskie** (Pomeranian Quay, part of the Southern Pier), used by small ships and located alongside Gdynia's one "fun" pier, with museums and pleasure craft (from here, it's easy to simply walk into downtown Gdynia). Port information: www.port.gdynia.pl.

Unfortunately, there are no **ATMs** or money-exchange options at or near the cruise-ship berths; but cash machines are plentiful in downtown Gdynia.

To get from your cruise ship to Gdańsk, the best option is a **shuttle bus-plus-train connection.** First, ride your cruise line's shuttle bus into downtown Gdynia (5-minute trip; price depends on the cruise line). The shuttle drops you off at Skwer Kościuski; from here, it's a 10-minute walk (gradually uphill) to the train station. Start by walking away from the water on the broad, parklike boulevard. After the street becomes ulica 10 Lutego (you'll pass the TI on your right), it curves to the right; once you're around the corner, use the crosswalk to reach the train station (marked *Dworzec Podmiejski*). From here you can ride the handy *kolejka* commuter train into Gdańsk (runs every 10-15 minutes, 35 minutes; for details on this train, see "Getting Around the Tri-City," earlier). Arrive at the Gdańsk train station ("Gdańsk Główny" stop). If the new "Gdańsk Śródmieście" stop—one stop beyond Gdańsk Główny—is open, get off there instead, and simply cross the busy street to the Upland Gate and the start of my self-guided walk. Returning on the train, you want the "Gdynia Główna" stop.

Taxi drivers line up to meet arriving cruise ships. Cabbies here tend to overcharge, but if they use the meter, these are the legitimate rates: 20 zł to Gdynia's train station (*Dworzec*, DVOH-zhets); 125 zł to Gdańsk's Main Town; and 60-80 zł to Sopot. Taxi drivers generally take euros, though their off-the-cuff exchange rate may not be favorable.

For more details on Gdynia's port—and several others on the Baltic, North Sea, and beyond—pick up the *Rick Steves Northern European Cruise Ports* guidebook.

Hel Peninsula (Mierzeja Helska)

Out on the edge of things, this slender peninsula juts 20 miles into the ocean, providing a sunny retreat from the big cities—even as it shelters them from Baltic winds. Trees line the peninsula, and the northern edge is one long, sandy, ever-shifting beach.

On hot summer days, Hel is a great place to frolic in the sun with Poles. Sunbathing and windsurfing are practically religions here. Small resort villages line Hel Peninsula: Władysławowo (at the base), Chałupy, Kuźnica, Jastarnia, Jurata, and—at the tip—a town also called Hel. Beaches right near the towns can be crowded in peak season, but you're never more than a short walk away from your own stretch of sand. There are few permanent residents, and the waterfront is shared by budget campgrounds, hotels hosting middle-class families, and mansions of Poland's rich and famous (former president Aleksander Kwaśniewski has a summer home here).

The easiest way to go to Hel—aside from coveting thy neighbor's wife—is by boat (see "Gdańsk Connections," earlier). Trains from Gdańsk also reach Hel (summer only), and from Gdynia, you can take a train, bus, or minibus. But overland transit is crowded and slow—especially in summer, when Hel is notorious for its hellish traffic jams.

POMERANIA

Malbork Castle • Toruń

The northwestern part of Poland—known as Pomerania (Pomorze)—has nothing to do with excitable little dogs, but it does offer two attractions worth singling out, both conveniently located between Gdańsk and Warsaw. Malbork, the biggest Gothic castle in Europe, is one of the most interesting castles in Eastern Europe. Farther south, the Gothic town of Toruń—the birthplace of Copernicus, and a favorite spot of every proud Pole—holds hundreds of red-brick buildings...and, it seems, even more varieties of tasty gingerbread.

PLANNING YOUR TIME

Malbork works well as a side-trip from Gdańsk (frequent trains, 30-45 minutes each way), and it's also on the main train line from

Gdańsk to Warsaw. While Toruń doesn't merit a long detour, it's worth a stroll or an overnight if you want to sample a smaller Polish city. Unfortunately, Toruń is on a different train line than Malbork—if you visit both in one day, it'll be a very long one. Ideally, if traveling round-trip from Warsaw, see one of these destinations coming to Gdańsk, and visit the other on the way back. Or do Malbork as a side-trip from Gdańsk, then visit Toruń on the way to or from Warsaw.

Malbork Castle

Malbork Castle is soaked in history. The biggest brick castle in the world, the largest castle of the Gothic period, and one of Europe's most imposing fortresses, it sits smugly on a marshy plain at the edge of the town of Malbork, 35 miles southeast of Gdańsk. This was the headquarters of the notorious Teutonic Knights, a Germanic band of ex-Crusaders who dominated northern Poland in the Middle Ages.

GETTING THERE
Malbork is on the train line between Gdańsk and Warsaw. Coming by train from Gdańsk, you'll enjoy views of the castle on your right as you cross the Nogat River. Store your luggage at the station's lockers and head into town.

To get from the station to the castle, consider taking a **taxi** (shouldn't cost more than 10 zł, though many corrupt cabbies charge twice that—keep asking until someone agrees to 10 zł). Or you can **walk** 15 minutes to the castle: Leave the station to the right, walk straight, and go through the pedestrian underpass beneath the busy road (by the red staircase). When you emerge on the other side, follow the busy road (noticing peek-a-boo views on your right of the castle's main tower) and take your first right turn (onto Kościuszki, the main shopping street). On Kościuszki, you'll pass the fancy pink building housing the TI on the right. Near the bottom of Kościuszki, at the fountain and the McDonald's, jog right, then bear left over two moats to find the ticket office (marked *kasa*).

Orientation to Malbork Castle

Cost and Hours: Mid-April-mid-Sept—40 zł, open Tue-Sun 9:00-19:00; mid-Sept-mid-April—30 zł, open Tue-Sun 10:00-15:00; closed Mon year-round; grounds stay open an hour later than the castle, ticket office opens 30 minutes before the castle; tel. 55-647-0978, www.zamek.malbork.pl.

Tours: You are technically required to enter the castle with a three-hour **guided tour** or an audioguide, but this is rarely enforced—you can usually just walk in. (If they do enforce this rule, simply enter with a Polish group—tours leave from the ticket booth every 15 minutes—and split off on your own once inside.) My self-guided tour covers the basics.

Your ticket includes a good **audioguide,** but supply is limited—they're generally available only before 11:00 and after 15:00. Ideally, try to get an audioguide, which lets you

POMERANIA

wander aimlessly through this fascinating place, keying in *audio-tour stop* numbers as you explore.

In July and August, **English tours** run three times a day (likely at 11:00, 14:00, and 15:30; 8 zł extra). Otherwise, year-round, you can pay 210 zł for a private English tour (English guides are easy to arrange in summer—even on short notice—but more difficult in winter). Ideally, contact the castle a few days ahead to reserve a guide (tel. 55-647-0978, kasa@zamek.malbork.pl), or hire your own guide in Gdańsk (such as Agnieszka Syroka).

If you show up and there's no scheduled English tour, ask whether an English-speaking guide is available. Then take the initiative, play "tour organizer," and get together a group of frustrated English speakers by the cashier. On a recent visit, it took me only a few minutes to gather a dozen strangers eager for some English information—bringing the per-person cost of the private tour down to less than 20 zł.

Best Views: The views of massive Malbork are stunning—especially at sunset, when its red brick glows. Be sure to walk out across the bridge over the Nogat River. The most scenic part of the castle is probably the twin-turreted, riverside Bridge Gate, which used to be connected by a bridge to the opposite bank.

BACKGROUND

When the Teutonic Knights were invited to Polish lands to convert neighboring pagans in the 13th century, they found the perfect site for their new capital here, on the bank of the Nogat River. Construction began in 1274. After the Teutonic Knights conquered Gdańsk in 1308, the order moved its official headquarters from Venice to Malbork, where they remained for nearly 150 years. They called the castle Marienburg, the "Castle of Mary," in honor of the order's patron saint.

At its peak in the early 1400s, Malbork was both the imposing home of a seemingly unstoppable army and Europe's final bastion of chivalric ideals. Surrounded by swamplands, with only one gate in need of defense, it was a tough nut to crack. Malbork Castle was never taken by force in the Middle Ages, though it had to withstand various sieges by the Poles during the Thirteen Years' War (1454-1466)—including a campaign that lasted over three years. Finally, in 1457, the Polish king gained control of Malbork by buying off Czech mercenaries guarding the castle. Malbork became a Polish royal residence for 300 years. But when Poland was partitioned in the late 18th century, this region went back into German hands. The castle became a barracks, windows were sealed up, delicate vaulting was damaged, bricks were quarried for new buildings, and Malbork deteriorated.

In the late 19th century, Romantic German artists and poets rediscovered the place. An architect named Konrad Steinbrecht devoted 40 years of his life to Malbork, painstakingly restoring the palace to its medieval splendor. A half-century later, the Nazis used the castle to house POWs. Hitler—who, like many Germans, had a soft spot for Malbork's history—gave the order to defend it to the last man. About half of it was destroyed by the Soviet army, who saw it as a symbol of long-standing German domination. But it was restored once again, and today Malbork has been returned to its Teutonic glory.

Malbork Castle Tour

The official tour of Malbork lasts about three hours. And, while there's plenty to see, this self-guided tour allows you to see the highlights at your own pace. Use the map on the next page to navigate and jump around as needed. The castle complex is a bit of a maze, with various entrances and exits for each room, often behind closed (but unlocked) doors. Don't be shy about grabbing a medieval doorknob and letting yourself in.

LOWER CASTLE AND ENTRANCE GATE

Just past the ticket taker, step through the front gate and stand on the castle's drawbridge. Look up at one of Europe's most intimidating fortresses—home to the Grand Master, monks, and knights of the Teutonic Order.

Above the door to the brick gate is a sculpture of the Virgin Mary with Baby Jesus...next to a shield and helmet. The two messages to visitors: This castle is protected by Mary, and the Teutonic Knights are here to convert pagans—by force, if necessary.

From the drawbridge, look right to observe the formidable fortifications. The rooster-capped tower (which contains a toilet) is connected by a sky bridge to the fancy Gothic 14th-century facade of the brick infirmary—kept at a distance for disease control.

Pass through the gate, into the entry area. Imagine the gate behind you closing. Look up to see wooden chutes where archers are preparing to rain arrows down on you. Your last thought: Maybe we should have left the Teutonic Knights alone, after all.

Before you're pierced by arrows, read the castle's history in its walls: The foundation is made of huge stones brought from

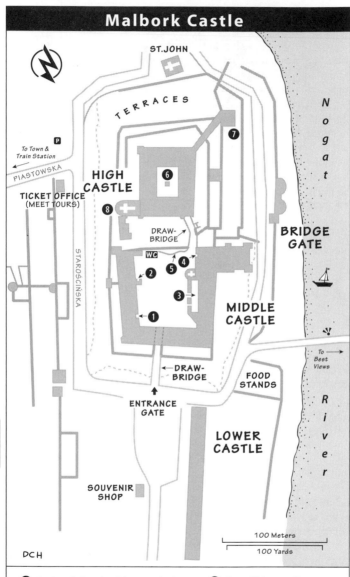

Malbork Castle

ST. JOHN

TERRACES

To Town & Train Station

PIASTOWSKA

P

HIGH CASTLE

TICKET OFFICE (MEET TOURS)

STAROŚCIŃSKA

DRAW-BRIDGE

WC

DRAW-BRIDGE

ENTRANCE GATE

FOOD STANDS

MIDDLE CASTLE

BRIDGE GATE

Nogat

To Best Views

LOWER CASTLE

River

SOUVENIR SHOP

POMERANIA

100 Meters
100 Yards

DCH

1 Amber Collection (downstairs)
2 Armory (upstairs) & Gothic Café (downstairs)
3 "Boiler Room" (downstairs) & Grand Refectory (upstairs)
4 Grand Master's Palace
5 Grand Master Statues
6 Well
7 Dansker Tower
8 St. Mary's Church (temp. closed)

Sweden, which are rare in these marshy lands. But most of the castle, like so many other buildings in northern Poland, was built with handmade red brick. Throughout the castle, the darker-colored, rougher brick is original, and the lighter-colored, smoother brick was used during later restorations (in the 19th century, and again after World War II). Marvel at the ironclad doors and the heavy portcullis.

Venture through two more enclosed spaces, watching for the holes in the wall (for more guards and soldiers). The Teutonic Knights connected nearby lakes to create a system of canals, forming a moat around the castle that could be crossed only by this drawbridge. Ponder the fact that you have to go through five separate, well-defended gates to reach the...

MIDDLE CASTLE (ZAMEK ŚREDNI)

This part of Malbork, built at an uphill incline to make it even more imposing, was designed to impress. Knights and monks lived here.

Let's get oriented: To your left is the east wing, where visiting monks would sleep. Today this houses the Amber Collection

(ground floor) and the armory (upstairs). To the right (west) as you enter the main courtyard is the Grand Refectory (closer to the entrance) and the Grand Master's Palace (the taller, squarer building at the far end).

• *Before we move on, this is a good time to read up on the history of the Teutonic Knights (see sidebar). When*

POMERANIA

you're ready to continue, enter the ground floor of the building on the left (at audiotour stop #15; remember, don't be shy about opening closed doors), and visit the...

Amber Collection

This exhibit will make jewelry shoppers salivate. You'll start 42 million years ago and follow the story of amber. Begin at the huge chunks of raw amber and the illuminated display of inclusions (bugs and other organic objects stuck in the amber, à la *Jurassic Park*). Some of the ancient amber artifacts displayed here are up to 3,000 years old. These were found in graves, put there by people who thought amber would help the deceased enter a better world. Wandering the hall, you'll see all manner of amber creations: boxes, brooches, necklaces, chess sets, pipes, miniature ships, wine glasses, and belts for skinny-waisted, fashion-conscious women. Look for two truly exquisite pieces: a small casket and an altar.

The Teutonic Knights

Historically, Germans in Poland have had a volatile track record. And that goes all the way back (at least) to the arrival of the Teutonic Knights in the northern Polish lands in the 13th century.

The Order of the Teutonic Knights began in the Holy Land in 1191, during the Third Crusade. These German militarized monks, who took vows of poverty, chastity, and obedience, built hospitals, and cared for injured knights. When the Crusades ended in the 12th century, the order returned to Europe and reorganized as a chivalric order of Christian mercenaries—pagan-killers for hire.

In 1226, a northern Polish duke was struggling to subdue a tribe of pagans who had been attacking his lands, so he called in the Teutonic Knights. Clad in their white cloaks with skinny black crosses, and claiming to be "missionaries," the Teutonic Knights spent 60 years "saving" the pagans by turning them into serfs or brutally massacring them.

Job done, the Teutonic Knights decided they enjoyed northern Poland—and stuck around. With the support of the pope and the Holy Roman Emperor (who were swayed by their religious zeal), the Knights built one of Europe's biggest and most imposing fortresses: Malbork. In 1308, they seized large parts of northern Poland, including Gdańsk—cutting off Polish access to the Baltic Sea. Other Germans flocked to join the Knights, further developing a Germanic city-state—the Teutonic Grand Master's own mini-empire. The Knights grew rich from Hanseatic trade, specializing in amber, grain, and timber. By the late 14th century, the Teutonic Knights had conquered Estonia and Latvia,

Many of the finely decorated jewelry boxes and chests have ivory, silver, or shell inlays—better for contrast than gold. The portable religious shrines and altars allowed travelers to remain reverent on the road and still pack light. Find the amber crucifix. This is a small replica of a six-foot-tall amber and silver cross, presented to St. John Paul II by the people of Gdańsk. Another exhibit case contains necklaces displaying the full range of amber colors, from opaque white at the top, to transparent yellow in the middle, to virtually black at the bottom.

• *Go back outside and turn left, to the wooden staircase above the recommended Gothic Café (described later). Go up that staircase, and several more inside, to the top-floor...*

creating Europe's largest-ever monastic state, and were threatening Poles' pagan neighbor to the east, Lithuania.

Inspired by a mutual desire to fight back against the Teutonic Knights, the Poles and the Lithuanians merged their two realms. In 1386, Polish Princess Jadwiga married Lithuanian Prince Władysław Jagiełło (who converted to Christianity for the occasion), uniting Poland and Lithuania and kick-starting a grand new dynasty, the Jagiellonians.

Just as every American knows the date July 4, 1776, every Pole knows the date July 15, 1410—the Battle of Grunwald. King Władysław Jagiełło and Lithuanian Grand Duke Vytautas the Great led a ragtag army of some 40,000 soldiers—Lithuanians, Poles, other Slavs, and even speedy Tatar horsemen—against 27,000 Teutonic Knights. At the end of the day, some 18,000 Poles and Lithuanians were dead—but so were half of the Teutonic Knights, and the other half had been captured. Poland and Lithuania were victorious.

The Battle of Grunwald marked a turning point. The Teutonic Knights' political power waned, they pulled out of Lithuania, and they once again allowed free trade on the Vistula. A generation later, the Thirteen Years' War (1454-1466) finally put an end to the Teutonic Knights' domination of northern Poland. The order officially dissolved in 1575, when they converted to Protestantism (though some conspiracy theorists claim the Teutonic Knights are still very much active). Much of their land eventually became part of Prussia.

The 19th-century Romantics who fanned the flames of Polish patriotism reimagined the Teutonic Knights as a symbol of Germanic oppression, which resonated among Poles throughout the troubled 20th century. Even today, Poles—and all Slavs—think of the Teutonic Knights as murderous invaders whereas Germans see them as a mere footnote in their history.

POMERANIA

Armory

This is a small armory for such a massive castle. In its two rooms you'll see an impressive array of swords, armor, and other armaments (English descriptions). Look for the 600-year-old "hand-and-a-half" swords—too big to be held in one hand. At the end, in the display of cannons, pikes, and spears, find the giant shield. These shields could be lined up to form a portable "wall" to protect the knights. Downstairs, the suit of armor from the Hussars—Polish horseback knights—came with wings, which created a terrifying sound when galloping.

• *Head back outside (noticing the handy and rare WC straight ahead). Cross the main courtyard going downhill and enter the smaller courtyard through the passage next to the stubby, dark-wood-topped tower. Find the dark, steep, and unlabeled steps down into the...*

"Boiler Room"

The Teutonic Knights had a surprisingly sophisticated method for heating this huge complex. You see a furnace down below and a holding area for hot rocks above. The radiant heat given off by the rocks spread through the vents without also filling them with smoke (illustrated by a chart on the wall). This is one of 11 such "boiler rooms" in the castle complex. As you tour the rest of the castle, keep an eye out for little saucer-sized heating vents in the floor.

• *Climb back up the stairs, take an immediate left through a tiny arch, and then go left again, up through the door labeled #5 (not down, which takes you out of castle). This leads into the...*

Grand Master's Palace

This was one of the grandest royal residences in medieval Europe, used in later times by Polish kings and German Kaisers. (Today it's sometimes used for special exhibitions.)

• *Walk through the kitchen into the big and bright...*

Grand Refectory: With remarkable palm vaulting and grand frescoes, this dining hall hosted feasts for up to 400 people to celebrate a military victory or to impress visiting dignitaries. Notice the 36 heating vents—which are directly above the boiler room you just visited—designed to keep the VIPs warm.

• *From here, climb the stairs into the...*

Private Rooms of the Grand Master: Though the Teutonic Order dictated that the monks sleep in dormitories, the Grand Master made an exception for himself—with a suite of private rooms that came with his own toilet (with a river view) and his own chapel, dedicated to St. Catherine. Exploring the Top Knight's residence, appreciate the show-off decor (including some 15th-century original frescoes of wine leaves and grapes). His private bedroom was decorated with frescoes of four virgins—female martyrs. The passage outside the private rooms came with a washbasin, as anyone wanting an audience with the Grand Master had to wash both his hands and his feet.

Next, enter the private dining room, the **Winter Refectory,** with fewer windows (better insulation) and little manhole-like openings in the floor where the "central heating" entered the room. The adjacent **Summer Refectory** had big stained-glass windows. With all the delicate vaulting supported by a single pillar in the middle, this room was clearly not designed with defense in mind. In fact, medieval Polish armies focused their attacks on this room. On one legendary occasion, the attackers—tipped off by a spy—knew that an important meeting was going on here and fired a cannonball into the room. It just missed the pillar. (You can see where the cannonball hit the wall, just above the fireplace.) The ceiling eventually did collapse during World War II.

• *Back out in the courtyard, look for the four...*

Grand Master Statues

Though this was a religious order, these powerful guys look more like kings than monks. From left to right, shake hands with Hermann von Salza (who was Grand Master when the Teutonic Knights came to Poland); Siegfried von Feuchtwangen (who actually moved the T. K. capital from Venice to Malbork, and who conquered Gdańsk for the Knights—oops, can't shake his hand, which was supposedly chopped off by Soviet troops); Winrich von Kniprode (who oversaw Malbork's Golden Age and turned it into a castle fit for a king); and Markgraf Albrecht von Hohenzollern (the last Grand Master before the order dissolved and converted to Protestantism).

• *To the right of the statues, continue into the High Castle by passing over the...*

Drawbridge

As you cross, notice the extensive system of fortifications and moats protecting the innermost part of the castle just ahead. Check out the cracks in the walls (on right)—an increasing threat to this ever-settling castle set on marshy, unstable terrain. On the left is a collection of stone catapult balls that were actually fired at this castle when it was under siege. (Look high above to see the dents such stones can make.) The passage ahead is lined with holes (for surveillance) and with chutes up above (to pour scalding water or pitch on unwanted visitors). It's not quite straight—so a cannon fired here would hit the side wall of the passage, rather than entering the High Castle and its central courtyard. Which is what you're about to do now.

HIGH CASTLE (ZAMEK WYSOKI)

This is the heart of the castle, and its oldest section. From this spot, the Teutonic Knights governed their vast realm—the largest monk-ruled territory in European history. As much a monastery as a fortress, the High Castle was off-limits to all but 60 monks of the Teutonic Order and their servants. (The knights stayed in the Middle Castle.) Here you'll find the monks' dormitories, chapels, church, and refectory. As this was the nerve center of the Teutonic Knights—the T. K. HQ—it was also their last line of defense. They stored enormous amounts of food here in case of a siege.

In the middle of the High Castle courtyard is a **well**—an

essential part of any inner castle, especially one as prone to sieges as Malbork. At the top is a sculpture of a pelican. Because this noble bird was believed to kill itself to feed its young (notice that it's piercing its own chest with its beak), it was often used in the Middle Ages as a symbol for the self-sacrifice of Jesus.

• *Take some time to explore the...*

High Castle—Ground Floor

Work clockwise around the courtyard from where you entered. A door leads to the prison (with small "solitary confinement" cells near the entrance). Along the next wall of the cloister is a post-WWII photo of bombed-out Malbork. Just adjacent, hiding in the far corner, is an exhibit on stained-glass windows from the castle church. Somewhere around here, you should see a demonstration of how medieval money was made. The Teutonic Knights minted their own coins—and you can buy your very own freshly minted replica today.

• *Continuing around the courtyard, you'll find the...*

Kitchen: This exhibit—with a long table piled with typical ingredients from that time—really gives you a feel for medieval monastery life. The monks who lived here ate three meals a day, along with lots of beer (made here) and wine (imported from France, Italy, and Hungary). A cellar under the kitchen was used as a primitive refrigerator—big chunks of ice were cut from the frozen river in winter, stored in the basement, and used to keep food cool in summer. Behind the long table, see the big dumbwaiter (with five shelves for hot dishes), which connects this kitchen with the refectory upstairs. Step into the giant stove and look up the biggest chimney in the castle.

• *Now go back out into the courtyard and climb up the stairs near where you first entered.*

High Castle—Middle Floor

• *From the top of the stairs, the first door on the left (with the colorfully painted arch) leads to the most important room of the High Castle, the...*

Chapter Room: Monks gathered here after Mass, and it was also the site for meetings of Teutonic Knights from around the countryside. If a Grand Master was killed in battle, the new one would be elected here. Carvings above each chair indicated the status of the man who sat there. The big chair belonged to the Grand Master. Notice the little windows above his chair, connecting this room to the church next door. Ecclesiastical music would filter in through these windows; imagine the voices of 60 monks bouncing around with these acoustics.

While monks are usually thought to pursue simple lives, the elegant vaulting in this room is anything but plain. The

POMERANIA

14th-century frescoes (restored in the 19th century) depict Grand Masters. In the floor are more vents for the central heating.

• *Leave the Chapter House and walk straight ahead, imagining the monk-filled corridors of Teutonic times. The first door on the right is the...*

Treasury: As you explore the five rooms of the tax collector and the house administrator, notice the wide variety of safes and other lock boxes. Documents, amber, and coins were kept behind heavily armored and well-locked doors.

• *Continue around the cloister. At the end of the corridor, spot the little devil at the bottom of the vaulting (on the right, about eye level). He's pulling his beard and crossing his legs—pointing you down the long corridor leading about 50 yards away from the cloister to the...*

Dansker Tower: From the devil's grimace, you might have guessed that this tower houses the latrine. Four wooden toilet stalls filled this big room. Where one is missing, you can look down to see how the "toilets" simply dropped the waste into the moat. For obvious sanitary (and olfactory) reasons, this potty tower is set apart from the main part of the castle. The bins above the toilets were filled with cabbage leaves, to be used by the T. K. as TP (and as an organic form of Preparation H). This tower could also serve as a final measure of defense—it's easier to defend than the entire castle. Food was stored above, just in case. More info on this grand castle WC is on the wall.

• *Return down the long corridor. Before the end, on the right-hand side of the long passage, a door leads into the...*

Church Exhibition: Once dormitories for the monks, these three rooms today display a wide range of relics from the church (with English descriptions). In the last room, on the far wall, is the artistic highlight of the castle: a finely carved and painted three-panel altarpiece from about 1500 featuring the coronation of Mary. Mary's face is mesmerizing. Characteristic of the late Gothic period, the robes seem to fly unrealistically (as if they were bent metal).

• *Back out in the main cloister, turn right, and continue to the end, arriving at the...*

Golden Gate: This elaborate doorway—covered in protective glass—marks the entrance to St. Mary's Church (which is closed for a multi-year renovation). This is a rare original door in the castle. Ringed with detailed carvings from the Old Testament,

POMERANIA

and symbolic messages about how monks of the Teutonic Order should live their lives, it's a marvelous example of late-13th-century art. At the bottom-left end of the arch, find the five wise virgins who, having filled their lamps with oil and conserved it wisely, are headed to heaven. On the right, the five foolish virgins who overslept and used up all their oil are damned, much to their dismay.

• *Go through the narrow door next to the Golden Gate (on the right) and hike up the tight spiral staircase to the final set of exhibits.*

High Castle—Top Floor

Walk through an exhibit about the illustrious guests of the castle. At the end, descend into the monks' common room (left at the bottom of the stairs). Over the fireplace is a relief depicting the Teutonic Knights fighting the pagans. To the left and above (see the stone windows) is a balcony where musicians entertained the monks after a meal. The next, very long room, with seven pillars, is the refectory, where the monks ate in silence. Along the right-hand wall are lockable storage boxes for tableware. At the end of this room, just beyond another ornate fireplace, notice the grated hole in the wall. This is where the dumbwaiter comes up from the kitchen (which we saw below). Beyond this room is an exhibit about the architectural renovation of the castle.

• *Your Malbork tour ends here. You leave the way you came. En route, you can walk around terraces lining the inner moat, between the castle walls (stairs lead down off of the drawbridge, by the catapult balls). It's hardly a must-see, but it's pleasant enough, with the Grand Master's garden, a cemetery for monks, and the remains of the small St. Anne's Chapel (with Grand Master tombs).*

Eating at Malbork Castle

Several cheap food stands cluster outside the castle (by the river). For a meal inside the castle complex, the **Gothic Café,** under the stairs to the armory in the Middle Castle, is good. Dishing up traditional Polish food inspired by old dishes once served here, it's handy for its 39-zł lunch deal that includes a main dish and soup.

POMERANIA

You can eat in the busy cellar or out in the garden (30-50-zł main dishes, open same hours as castle, tel. 55-647-0889, www.gothic.com.pl, Chef Bogdan is passionate and welcoming).

Malbork Connections

From Malbork by Train to: Gdańsk (2/hour, about half are express EIC trains that take 30 minutes, the rest are slower regional trains that take around 45 minutes), **Toruń** (about every 2 hours, 3 hours, transfer in Tczew or Iława), **Warsaw** (hourly, 2.5 hours on express EIC train).

Toruń

Toruń (TOH-roon) is a pretty, lazy Gothic town conveniently located about halfway between Warsaw and Gdańsk. It's worth a

couple of hours to stroll the lively streets, ogle the huge red-brick buildings, and savor the flavor of perhaps Poland's most livable city.

With about 210,000 residents and 30,000 students (at Copernicus University), Toruń is a thriving burg. Like Kraków (and unlike most other Polish cities), Toruń escaped destruction during World War II and remains well-preserved today. Locals brag that their city is a "mini-Kraków." But that sells both cities short. Toruń lacks Kraków's over-the-top romanticism, and its sights are quickly exhausted. On the other hand, Toruń may well be Poland's most user-friendly city: tidy streets with a sensible grid plan (and English signposts to keep you on track), wide pedestrian boulevards crammed with locals who greet each other like they're long-lost friends, and an easygoing ambience that seems to say, "Hey—relax." And, while it has its share of tourists, Toruń feels more off-the-beaten-path than the other Polish destinations in this book.

Toruń clings fiercely to its two claims to fame: It's the proud birthplace of the astronomer Copernicus (Mikołaj Kopernik), and home to a dizzying variety of gingerbread treats (*piernika;* pyer-NEE-kah).

POMERANIA

Orientation to Toruń

Everything in Toruń worth seeing is in the walled Old Town, climbing up a gentle hill from the Vistula River. The broad, traffic-free main drag, ulica Szeroka (called Różana at the entrance of town) bisects the Old Town, running parallel to the river.

ARRIVAL IN TORUŃ

Toruń's main train station (called Toruń Główny) is across the river from the Old Town, about a mile away. The main hall has ticket windows, an ATM, and lockers.

To reach the Old Town, you have two options: If you go out the door from the main hall, you'll spot **taxis** waiting to take you into town (the trip costs around 15-20 zł). To take the **bus,** buy a 2.80-zł ticket from the *RUCH* kiosk overlooking the tracks near the main hall. Then follow the pedestrian underpass beneath track 4 (entrance to underpass marked with low-profile *wyjście do miasta* sign and bus icon, outside main hall and to the left). When you emerge on the other side, the bus stop for bus #22, #25, or #27 into the center is ahead and on your right. Take the bus to Plac Rapackiego, the first stop after the long bridge. To return to the station, catch bus #22, #25, or #27 across the busy road from where you got off.

TOURIST INFORMATION

The TI is on the main square, behind the Old Town Hall. Pick up the free map and get information about hotels in town and city tours (Tue-Fri 9:00-18:00, Mon and Sat 9:00-16:00; closed Sun except May-Sept, when it's open 9:00-16:00; Rynek Staromiejski 25, tel. 56-621-0930, www.it.torun.pl).

Toruń Walk

This brief self-guided walk takes you through the heart of Toruń. With no stops, you could do it in 20 minutes.

• *From the Plac Rapackiego bus stop, head into town through the passageways under the colorful buildings. Within a block, you're at the bustling...*

Old Town Market Square (Rynek Staromiejski): This square is surrounded by huge brick buildings and outdoor restaurants buzzing with lively locals. The **Old Town Hall** (Ratusz Staromiejski) fills the middle of the square, as was often the case in medieval Hanseatic towns. Its fine museum and climbable tower are Toruń's main sights worth visiting (described later, under "Sights in Toruń"). The building with the pointy spires on the right (across from the Old Town Hall) is the **Artus Court,** where

POMERANIA

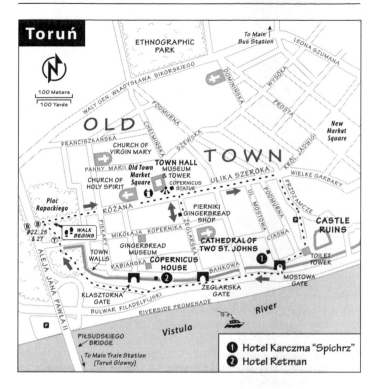

Toruń

ETHNOGRAPHIC PARK

To Main Bus Station

LEONA SZUMANA

100 Meters
100 Yards

WAŁY GEN. WŁADYSŁAWA SIKORSKIEGO

PODMURNA

CHEŁMIŃSKA

DOMINIŃSKA

WYSOKA

PROSTA

O L D

New Market Square

FRANCISZKAŃSKA

CHURCH OF VIRGIN MARY

SZEWSKA

T O W N

PANNY MARII

CHURCH OF HOLY SPIRIT

Old Town Market Square

TOWN HALL MUSEUM & TOWER

COPERNICUS STATUE

ULIKA SZEROKA

KRÓL. JADWIGI

WIELKE GARBARY

PRZEDZAMCZE

Plac Rapackiego

RÓŻANA

PIERNIKI GINGERBREAD SHOP

UL. MOSTOWA

CIASNA

CASTLE RUINS

B B
#22, 25 & 27
T

WALK BEGINS

MIKOŁAJA KOPERNIKA

ŻEGLARSKA

CATHEDRAL OF TWO ST. JOHNS

TOILET TOWER

PIEKARY

GINGERBREAD MUSEUM

TOWN WALLS

ALEJA JANA PAWŁA II

KLASZTORNA GATE

 KABIAŃSKA

COPERNICUS HOUSE

BANKOWA

ŻEGLARSKA GATE

MOSTOWA GATE

BULWAR FILADELFIJSKI

RIVERSIDE PROMENADE

River

P

PIŁSUDSKIEGO BRIDGE

Vistula

To Main Train Station (Toruń Glowny)

❶ Hotel Karczma "Spichrz"
❷ Hotel Retman

the medieval town council and merchants' guilds met. While the town was founded in 1231, the current building is Neo-Gothic, dating from the 19th century.

The guy playing his violin in front of the Old Town Hall is a **rafter** *(retman)*—one of the medieval lumberjacks who lashed tree trunks together and floated them down the Vistula to Gdańsk. This particular rafter came to Toruń when the town was infested with frogs. He wooed them with his violin and marched them out of town. (Hmm...sounds like a certain pied piper....)

The bigger statue, at the other end of the Old Town Hall, depicts **Mikołaj Kopernik,** better known as Nicholas Copernicus (1473-1543). This Toruń-born son of aristocrats turned the world on its ear when he suggested that the sun, not the earth, is the center of the universe (the "heliocentric theory"). Toruń is serious about this local boy done good—he's the town mascot, as well as the namesake of the local university. Among its fields of study, Copernicus U. has a healthy astronomy program. There's a planetarium in the Old Town (just past the far corner of the square) and a giant radio telescope on the town outskirts. Despite all the local fuss over Copernicus, there's some dispute about his ethnicity; he was born in Toruń, all right, but at a time when it was the predominantly German town of "Thorn." So is he Polish or German? (For more on Copernicus, visit his birth house—now a modest museum on the astronomer—just two blocks away and described later, under "Sights in Toruń").

Copernicus faces a shiny donkey at the corner of **Szeroka** and Żeglarska streets. We'll venture down Żeglarska first, and then return to walk down Szeroka. By the way, that shiny donkey with a sharp ridge on his back, while happy today, recalls a humiliating punishment. Centuries ago, delinquents and petty criminals needing to be set straight would be forced to straddle this donkey— after townspeople had tied heavy stones to their feet, weighing them down painfully.

• *But you're on vacation and, rather than humiliation, you get gingerbread. Head down Żeglarska to #25 (on the right).*

Pierniki **(Gingerbread) Shop:** For Poles, Toruń is synonymous with **gingerbread** *(piernika)*—you'll smell its sweet scent all over town. This Toruń treat can be topped with different kinds of jams or glazes, and/or dipped in chocolate. This shop has a fun system: All of the varieties cost the same, so you can create just the mix you like by pointing. *Róża* is rose, *malina* is raspberry, *czarna porzeczka* is black currant, *morela* is apricot, and—of course—*czekolada* is chocolate.

• *A few steps down and across the street is the...*

Cathedral of Two Saint Johns (Katedra Św. Jana Chrzciciela i Jana Ewangelisty): Dedicated in the 12th century to John the Baptist and John the Evangelist, this is the parish church of the Old Town. From the street, notice the architectural heaviness: This marshy land lacked big stones, so instead of flying buttresses, they designed a bulky and sturdy brick structure so they could build big. Stepping inside, you find pure Gothic architecture (free, open daily until last Mass at 18:00). The gravestones of big shots pave the floor. Each trade guild had its own chapel. To the left of the altar, notice the finely restored 13th-century *Last Judgment*. In the rear of the church (on the right) is the baptismal font where, in 1473, Copernicus was baptized.

• *Having satisfied your ginger tooth and seen the town's most important church, head back to the square and that painful donkey, turn right, and join the human stream down the appropriately named...*

Ulica Szeroka ("Wide Street"): This enjoyable pedestrian promenade leads through the heart of town. Embedded in the paving bricks are the coats of arms of Toruń's medieval trading partners. And on each side of the street is an eclectic commotion of fun facades.

About 30 yards before the road forks at the stately, white Empik building, look down narrow Przedzamcze street to the right to see fragments of the town wall. This marks the border between the Old Town and the New Town (chartered only about 30 years later—both in the 13th century). While these areas are both collectively known today as the unified "Old Town," they were quite different in the Middle Ages—each with its own market square, and separated by a wall. (If you're curious to see the New Town Square and Town Hall, take the left fork at the Empik building and walk two blocks up ulica Królowej Jadwigi.)

• *Turn right down Przedzamcze, bear left at the parking lot, and continue under the stubby, stand-alone brick gate to the...*

Toruń Castle Ruins: This castle, built by the Teutonic Knights who were so influential in northern Poland in the Middle Ages, was destroyed in the 15th century by the locals—who, aside from a heap of bricks, left only the tower that housed the Teutonic toilets. The ruins have nothing much to offer, but what survives is one of the better toilet towers in Europe—which was connected to the castle by an elevated walkway and located far enough away to keep things hygienic. The old mill next to the toilet is now a hotel named 1231, for the date the Teutonic Order arrived here.

• *Our walk is over. You can backtrack the way you came and explore more of the city (including the sights listed next). Or you can take a quick riverside stroll: Go under the toilet tower and down to the Vistula River, turn right, and stroll along the castle and 14th-century city walls back to your starting point. The road is called Bulwar Filadelfijski—for Toruń's sister city in Pennsylvania.*

Sights in Toruń

Toruń is more about strolling than it is about sightseeing—the town's museums are underwhelming. Aside from its half-dozen red-brick churches (any of which are worth dropping into), the following attractions are worth considering on a rainy day.

▲City Hall Museum and Tower

Like Kraków's Cloth Hall, this building, dominating the town square, was a general market. It served as the heart of the city. Today it offers the only chance to see historic artifacts in town, all well-described in English. It gives a good history of the Teutonic Knights, who first came to Toruń in 1231. You'll see intimate bits and pieces of history, from pewter tankards to old gingerbread molds, that show the richness of this traders' city. Another wing of the ground floor is filled with medieval church art saved from the region's churches. Much of it is pre-Reformation Catholic art, with lots of Marys (as she was the patron of the Teutonic Order) and a close-up look at some 14th-century stained glass. The royal halls upstairs feature portraits and fine 17th-century inlaid wooden doors. The 130-foot-tall tower can be climbed (on narrow wooden steps) for great views over the city center.

Cost and Hours: 11 zł apiece for museum and tower, 17-zł combo-ticket for both; May-Sept Tue-Sun 10:00-18:00, Oct-April Tue-Sun 10:00-16:00, tower may be open later, closed Mon year-round; Rynek Staromiejski 1, tel. 56-660-5612, www.muzeum. torun.pl.

Gingerbread Museum (Muzeum Piernika)

This fun attraction—by far Toruń's liveliest—is an actual working gingerbread bakery of yore. Barefoot, costumed medieval bakers walk you through the traditional process of rolling, cutting out, baking, and tasting your own batch of gingerbread cookies (30-40 minutes, start to finish). After aging for 12 weeks to achieve the proper consistency, the dough bakes for only 12 minutes—or, according to the medieval bakers, about 50 Hail Marys.

Cost and Hours: 12 zł, daily 10:00-18:00, Polish tours start at the top of each hour, English demonstrations most likely at 13:00 and 16:00, can be crowded in peak times—call ahead to confirm schedule and reserve a spot, 2 blocks toward the river from Old Town Market Square at Rabiańska 9, tel. 56-663-6617, www. muzeumpiernika.pl.

Copernicus House (Dom Kopernika)

Filling a pair of beautiful, gabled brick buildings, this dull, overpriced little museum celebrates the hero of Toruń. As much about medieval Toruń as about the famous astronomer, and sprawling over several floors in the two buildings, the exhibits loosely explain Nicolaus Copernicus' life and achievements. The displays are copies of important documents and paintings, and models of his instruments—all with English descriptions. The second part of the exhibit is an 18-minute slideshow with recorded commentary about medieval Toruń, with a model of the city that lights up dramatically at appropriate moments (plays on the half-hour, in English by request).

Cost and Hours: Museum only-11 zł, model/slideshow only-20 zł, 22-zł combo-ticket for both; May-Sept Tue-Sun 10:00-18:00, Oct-April Tue-Sun 10:00-16:00, closed Mon year-round; Kopernika 15, tel. 56-662-7038, www.muzeum.torun.pl. To get to the museum, head down Żeglarska and take the first right—on Kopernika, of course.

Ethnographic Park (Park Etnograficzny)

This open-air folk museum, while not ranking with Europe's best, is at least your most convenient opportunity to stroll through some traditional buildings from the region. It's in the middle of a pleasant park just outside the Old Town. Even if you're not interested in the museum, the park is a fine place to pass some time.

Cost and Hours: 14 zł; mid-April-June Tue and Thu 9:00-17:00, Wed and Fri 9:00-16:00, Sat-Sun 10:00-18:00; July-Sept Tue, Thu, and Sat-Sun 10:00-18:00, Wed and Fri 9:00-16:00; shorter hours off-season; closed Mon year-round; Wały Gen. Sikorskiego 19, www.etnomuzeum.pl. To get there from the Old Town Market Square, walk up Chełmińska with the river at your back and the Old Town Hall on your left. Cross the busy road, and you're in the park.

Sleeping in Toruń

Toruń's Old Town has more than its share of good-value hotels. The TI has a brochure listing the options and can help you find a room for no extra charge.

$$ Hotel Karczma "Spichrz" ("Granary") is a fresh, atmospheric hotel in a renovated old granary. Its 23 rooms and public spaces are a fun blend of old and new—with huge wooden beams around every corner and the scent of the restaurant's wood-fired grill wafting through the halls. It's comfortable, central, well-priced, and a little kitschy (Sb-230 zł, Db-290 zł, 10-20 percent cheaper on weekends, tall people may not appreciate low ceilings and beams, elevator, a block off the main drag toward the river at ulica Mostowa 1, tel. 56-657-1140, www.spichrz.pl, hotel@spichrz.pl). The restaurant is also good (30-55-zł grilled meat dishes, daily 12:00-23:00).

$ Hotel Retman ("Rafter") has 29 older but nicely appointed rooms over a restaurant just down the street from the Gingerbread Museum (Sb-190 zł, Db-250 zł; Fri-Sun prices drop to Sb-160 zł, Db-200 zł; ulica Rabiańska 15, tel. 56-657-4460, www.hotel-retman.pl, recepcja@hotelretman.pl).

POMERANIA

Sleep Code

Abbreviations   (3 zł = about $1, country code: 48)

S = Single, **D** = Double/Twin, **T** = Triple, **Q** = Quad, **b** = bathroom, **s** = shower only.

Price Rankings

  $$ Higher Priced—Most rooms more than 250 zł.

  $ Lower Priced—Most rooms 250 zł or less.

Unless otherwise noted, credit cards are accepted, breakfast is included, Wi-Fi is generally free, and English is spoken. Prices change; verify current rates online or by email. For the best prices, always book directly with the hotel.

Toruń Connections

Toruń is a handy stopover on the way between Warsaw and Gdańsk. It's on a different train line than Malbork—so visiting both Toruń and the mighty Teutonic castle in the same day is surprisingly time-consuming.

From Toruń by Train to: Warsaw (9/day, 3 hours direct, longer with a transfer in Kutno or Iława), **Gdańsk** (5/day, about 3 hours; additional options with a transfer in Bydgoszcz, 3.5 hours), **Malbork** (about every 2 hours, 3 hours, transfer in Tczew or Iława), **Kraków** (1/day direct, 6.5 hours; better to transfer at Warsaw's Zachodnia station: 8/day, 5.5-6 hours), **Berlin** (4/day, 5.75-6 hours, transfer in Poznań).

POMERANIA

PRACTICALITIES

This section covers just the basics on traveling in Poland (for much more information, see *Rick Steves Eastern Europe*). You can find free advice on specific topics at www.ricksteves.com/tips.

Money

Poland uses a currency called the złoty: 3 Polish złoty (zł) = about $1. To roughly convert Polish złoty into dollars, divide by three (e.g., 30 zł = about $10, 85 zł = about $30, 150 zł = about $50).

The standard way for travelers to get złoty is to withdraw money from ATMs (called a *bankomat* in Poland) using a debit or credit card, ideally with a Visa or MasterCard logo. Before departing, call your bank or credit-card company: Confirm that your card(s) will work overseas, ask about international transaction fees, and alert them that you'll be making withdrawals in Europe. Also ask for the PIN number for your credit card in case it'll help you use the "chip-and-PIN" payment machines (see below); allow time for your bank to mail your PIN to you. Memorizing your credit card's PIN lets you use it at some chip-and-PIN machines—just enter your PIN when prompted. To keep your valuables safe, wear a money belt.

Dealing with "Chip and PIN": While much of Europe has shifted to a "chip-and-PIN" security system for credit and debit cards, Poland still uses the old magnetic-stripe technology. (European chip-and-PIN cards are embedded with an electronic security chip, and require the purchaser to punch in a PIN rather than sign a receipt.) If you happen to encounter chip and PIN, it will probably be at payment machines, such as those at train stations, toll roads, or self-serve gas pumps. On the outside chance that a machine won't take your card, don't panic. Find a cashier who can make your card work (they can print a receipt for you to sign), or find a machine that takes cash. You can always use an ATM to withdraw cash with your magnetic-stripe card, even in countries where people predominantly use chip-and-PIN cards.

Phoning

Smart travelers use the telephone to reserve or reconfirm rooms, reserve restaurants, get directions, research transportation connections, confirm tour times, phone home, and lots more.

To call Poland from the US or Canada: Dial 011-48 and then the phone number, minus its initial zero. (The 011 is our international access code, and 48 is Poland's country code.)

To call Poland from a European country: Dial 00-48 followed by the phone number, minus its initial zero. (The 00 is Europe's international access code.)

To call within Poland: Just dial the whole number, including the initial zero.

To call from Poland to another country: Dial 00 followed by the country code (for example, 1 for the US or Canada), then the area code and number. If you're calling European countries whose phone numbers begin with 0, you'll usually have to omit that 0 when you dial.

Tips on Phoning: A mobile phone—whether an American one that works in Poland, or a European one you buy when you arrive—is handy, but can be pricey. If traveling with a smartphone, consider getting an international plan from your provider and try to switch off data-roaming until you have free Wi-Fi. With Wi-Fi, you can use your smartphone to make free or inexpensive domestic and international calls by taking advantage of a calling app such as Skype, FaceTime, or Google+ Hangouts.

To make calls without a mobile phone, your best bet is to buy a prepaid phone card to insert into public phone booths. Sold locally at newsstands, these are reasonable for calls within Poland; they work for international calls as well, but can be expensive. (Cheap international phone cards that work with a PIN code, which are common in many European countries, generally aren't available in Poland.)

Calling from your hotel-room phone is usually expensive—ask the rates before you dial. For more on phoning, see www.ricksteves.com/phoning.

Making Hotel Reservations

To ensure the best value, I recommend reserving rooms in advance, particularly during peak season. Email the hotelier with the following key pieces of information: number and type of rooms; number of nights; date of arrival; date of departure; and any special requests. (For a sample form, see the sidebar.) Use the European style for writing dates: day/month/year. Hoteliers typically ask for your credit-card number as a deposit.

Given the economic downturn, hoteliers may be willing to make a deal—try emailing several hotels to ask for their best price.

PRACTICALITIES

From: rick@ricksteves.com
Sent: Today
To: info@hotelcentral.com
Subject: Reservation request for 19-22 July

Dear Hotel Central,

I would like to reserve a room for 2 people for 3 nights, arriving 19 July and departing 22 July. If possible, I would like a quiet room with a double bed and a bathroom inside the room.

Please let me know if you have a room available and the price.

Thank you!
Rick Steves

In general, hotel prices can soften if you do any of the following: offer to pay cash, stay at least three nights, or travel off-season.

Eating

Poland offers good food for relatively little money. Polish cuisine has a reputation for being heavy and hearty, with lots of pork, potatoes, and cabbage...which is true. But the food here is also delicious, with more variety than you might expect. For all the details about Polish food, see page 17. Ethnic restaurants provide a welcome change of pace. Seek out Italian, Indian, sushi, and other alternatives (I've recommended several in this book).

Service: Good service is relaxed (slow to an American). You won't get the bill until you ask for it: *"Rachunek?"* (rah-KHOO-nehk). To tip at restaurants that have a waitstaff, round up the bill 5 to 10 percent if you're happy with the service.

Transportation

Public transportation is the best way to connect the cities in this book.

By Train: Poland has an extensive, if dated, rail network; you can reach most towns and cities by train. Since point-to-point tickets are affordable, a rail pass won't likely save you money (but to review your options, see www.ricksteves.com/rail). To research train schedules and fares, visit the Polish rail site, www.rozklad-pkp.pl, or Germany's excellent online timetable, www.bahn.com. While most short-haul journeys do not require a seat reservation, you must reserve on some high-speed trains (such as the Kraków-Warsaw or Warsaw-Gdańsk express). It's also smart to reserve a sleeping berth if you're taking a night train. For more tips, see "Train Station Lingo" on page 6.

By Bus: PolskiBus runs bus routes throughout Poland (www.polskibus.com).

By Car: It's cheaper to arrange most car rentals from the US. For tips on your insurance options, see www.ricksteves.com/cdw. Bring your driver's license. It's also required to carry an International Driving Permit (IDP), available at your local AAA office ($15 plus two passport-type photos, www.aaa.com). For route planning, consult www.viamichelin.com. Poland is building a network of new expressways, but they're far from complete (you'll pay tolls to take completed segments). Instead, locals travel long distances on two-lane country roads. Since each lane is about a lane and a half wide, passing is commonplace. Slower drivers should keep to the far-right of their lane, and not be surprised when faster cars zip past them. A car is a worthless headache in cities—park it safely (get tips from your hotel).

You are required to have your headlights on whenever you're driving—even in broad daylight, and it's mandatory to wear seat belts. Local road etiquette is similar to that in the US. Ask your car-rental company for details, or check the US State Department website (www.travel.state.gov, click on "International Travel," then specify your country of choice and click "Traffic Safety and Road Conditions").

By Plane: Consider covering long distances on a budget flight, which can be cheaper (and much faster) than a train. Poland's national carrier, LOT Airlines (www.lot.com), generally charges reasonable fares for short-distance trips. Or try some no-frills carriers, such as www.wizzair.com, www.easyjet.com, and www.ryanair.com. To compare several budget airlines, see www.skyscanner.com.

Helpful Hints

Emergency Help: For any emergency—whether **medical or police**—dial 112. For passport problems, call the **US Embassy** in Warsaw (tel. 022-504-2784, after-hours emergency tel. 022-504-2000) or the **US Consulate** in Kraków (tel. 012-424-5100); or the **Canadian Embassy** in Warsaw (tel. 022-584-3100).

If you have a minor illness, do as the locals do and go to a pharmacist for advice. Or ask at your hotel for help—they'll know of the nearest medical and emergency services. For other concerns, get advice from your hotelier.

Theft or Loss: To replace a passport, you'll need to go in person to an embassy or consulate (see above). Cancel and replace your credit and debit cards by calling these 24-hour US numbers collect: Visa—tel. 303/967-1096, MasterCard—tel. 636/722-7111, American Express—tel. 336/393-1111. In Poland, to make a collect call to the US, dial 00-800-111-1111; press zero or stay on the line for an operator. File a police report either on the spot or within a day or two; it's required if you submit an insurance claim for lost or stolen rail passes or electronics, and can help with replacing your passport or credit and debit cards. Precautionary measures can minimize the effects of loss—back up your digital photos and other files frequently. For more information, see www.ricksteves.com/help.

Time: Poland uses the 24-hour clock. It's the same through 12:00 noon, then keep going: 13:00, 14:00, and so on. Poland, like most of continental Europe, is six/nine hours ahead of the East/West Coasts of the US.

Dress Code: At churches, a modest dress code (no bare shoulders or shorts) is encouraged.

Holidays and Festivals: Poland celebrates many holidays, which can close sights and attract crowds (book hotel rooms ahead). For information on holidays and festivals, check Poland's website: www.poland.travel. For a simple list showing major—though not all—events, see www.ricksteves.com/festivals.

Numbers and Stumblers: What Americans call the second floor of a building is the first floor in Europe. Europeans write dates as day/month/year, so Christmas 2016 is 25/12/16. Commas are decimal points and vice versa—a dollar and a half is 1,50, and there are 5.280 feet in a mile. Poland uses the metric system: A kilogram is 2.2 pounds; a liter is about a quart; and a kilometer is six-tenths of a mile.

Resources from Rick Steves

This Snapshot guide is excerpted from the latest edition of *Rick Steves Eastern Europe*, which is one of more than 30 titles in my series of guidebooks on European travel. I also produce a public television series, *Rick Steves' Europe*, and a public radio show, *Travel with Rick Steves*. My website, www.ricksteves.com, offers free travel information, a forum for travelers' comments, guidebook updates, my travel blog, an online travel store, and information on European rail passes and our tours of Europe. If you're bringing a mobile device on your trip, you can download free information from Rick Steves Audio Europe, featuring podcasts of my radio shows, free audio tours of major sights in Europe, and travel interviews about Poland (via www.ricksteves.com/audioeurope, iTunes, Google Play, or the Rick Steves Audio Europe free smartphone app). You can also follow me on Facebook and Twitter.

Additional Resources

Tourist Information: www.poland.travel
Passports and Red Tape: www.travel.state.gov
Packing List: www.ricksteves.com/packing
Travel Insurance: www.ricksteves.com/insurance
Cheap Flights: www.kayak.com

Airplane Carry-on Restrictions: www.tsa.gov
Updates for This Book: www.ricksteves.com/update

How Was Your Trip?

If you'd like to share your tips, concerns, and discoveries after using this book, please fill out the survey at www.ricksteves.com/feedback. Thanks in advance—it helps a lot.

INDEX

Start your trip at

Our website enhances this book and turns

Explore Europe

At ricksteves.com you can browse through thousands of articles, videos, photos and radio interviews, plus find a wealth of money-saving travel tips for planning your dream trip. And with our mobile-friendly website, you can easily access all this great travel information anywhere you go.

TV Shows

Preview the places you'll visit by watching entire half-hour episodes of Rick Steves' Europe (choose from all 100 shows) on-demand, for free.

Radio Interviews

Enjoy ready access to Rick's vast library of radio interviews covering travel

tips and cultural insights that relate specifically to your Europe travel plans.

Travel Forums

Learn, ask, share! Our online community of savvy travelers is a great resource for first-time travelers to Europe, as well as seasoned pros. You'll find forums on each country, plus travel tips and restaurant/hotel reviews. You can even ask one of our well-traveled staff to chime in with an opinion.

Travel News

Subscribe to our free Travel News e-newsletter, and get monthly updates from Rick on what's happening in Europe.

Audio Europe™

Pack Light and Right

Gear up for your next adventure at rick steves.com

Light Luggage

Pack light and right with Rick Steves' affordable, custom-designed rolling carry-on bags, backpacks, day packs and shoulder bags.

Accessories

From packing cubes to moneybelts and beyond, Rick has personally selected the travel goodies that will help your trip go smoother.

Rick Steves has

Experience maximum Europe

Save time and energy

This guidebook is your independent-travel toolkit. But for all it delivers, it's still up to you to devote the time and energy it takes to manage the preparation and logistics that are essential for a happy trip. If that's a hassle, there's a solution.

Rick Steves Tours

A Rick Steves tour takes you to Europe's most interesting places with great

great tours, too!

with minimum stress

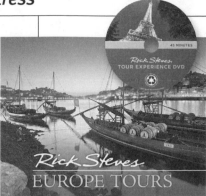

guides and small groups of 28 or less. We follow Rick's favorite itineraries, ride in comfy buses, stay in family-run hotels, and bring you intimately close to the Europe you've traveled so far to see. Most importantly, we take away the logistical headaches so you can focus on the fun.

customers—along with us on 40 different itineraries, from Ireland to Italy to Istanbul. Is a Rick Steves tour the right fit for your travel dreams? Find out at ricksteves.com, where you can also get Rick's latest tour catalog and free Tour Experience DVD.

Join the fun

This year we'll take 18,000 free-spirited travelers— nearly half of them repeat

Europe is best experienced with happy travel partners. We hope you can join us.

See our itineraries at ricksteves.com

EUROPE GUIDES

Best of Europe
Eastern Europe
Europe Through the Back Door
Mediterranean Cruise Ports
Northern European Cruise Ports

COUNTRY GUIDES

Croatia & Slovenia
England
France
Germany
Great Britain
Ireland
Italy
Portugal
Scandinavia
Spain
Switzerland

CITY & REGIONAL GUIDES

Amsterdam, Bruges & Brussels
Barcelona
Budapest
Florence & Tuscany
Greece: Athens & the Peloponnese
Istanbul
London
Paris
Prague & the Czech Republic
Provence & the French Riviera
Rome
Venice
Vienna, Salzburg & Tirol

SNAPSHOT GUIDES

Basque Country: Spain & France
Berlin
Bruges & Brussels
Copenhagen & the Best of
    Denmark
Dublin
Dubrovnik
Hill Towns of Central Italy
Italy's Cinque Terre
Krakow, Warsaw & Gdansk
Lisbon
Madrid & Toledo
Milan & the Italian Lakes District
Munich, Bavaria & Salzburg
Naples & the Amalfi Coast
Northern Ireland
Norway
Scotland
Sevilla, Granada & Southern Spain
Stockholm

POCKET GUIDES

Amsterdam
Athens
Barcelona
Florence
London
Paris
Rome
Venice

Rick Steves guidebooks are published by Avalon Travel,
a member of the Perseus Books Group.

NOW AVAILABLE:
eBOOKS, DVD & BLU-RAY

TRAVEL CULTURE

Europe 101
European Christmas
Postcards from Europe
Travel as a Political Act

eBOOKS

*Nearly all Rick Steves guides are
available as ebooks. Check with
your favorite bookseller.*

RICK STEVES' EUROPE DVDs

11 New Shows 2013–2014
Austria & the Alps
Eastern Europe
England & Wales
European Christmas
European Travel Skills & Specials
France
Germany, BeNeLux & More
Greece, Turkey & Portugal
Iran
Ireland & Scotland
Italy's Cities
Italy's Countryside
Scandinavia
Spain
Travel Extras

BLU-RAY

Celtic Charms
Eastern Europe Favorites
European Christmas
Italy Through the Back Door
Mediterranean Mosaic
Surprising Cities of Europe

PHRASE BOOKS & DICTIONARIES

French
French, Italian & German
German
Italian
Portuguese
Spanish

JOURNALS

Rick Steves Pocket Travel Journal
Rick Steves Travel Journal

PLANNING MAPS

Britain, Ireland & London
Europe
France & Paris
Germany, Austria & Switzerland
Ireland
Italy
Spain & Portugal

RickSteves.com @RickSteves

Rick Steves books and DVDs are available at bookstores
and through online booksellers.

Photo © Patricia Feaster

ABOUT THE AUTHORS

RICK STEVES

Since 1973, Rick Steves has spent 100 days every year exploring Europe. Along with writing and researching a best-selling series of guidebooks, Rick produces a public television series *(Rick Steves' Europe)*, a public radio show *(Travel with Rick Steves)*, a blog (on Facebook), and an app and podcast (Rick Steves Audio Europe); writes a nationally syndicated newspaper column; organizes guided tours that take over 20,000 travelers to Europe annually; and offers an information-packed website (www.ricksteves.com). With the help of his hardworking staff of 100 at Rick Steves' Europe—in Edmonds, Washington, just north of Seattle—Rick's mission is to make European travel fun, affordable, and culturally enlightening for Americans.

Connect with Rick:

facebook.com/RickSteves

twitter: @RickSteves

instagram: ricksteveseurope

CAMERON HEWITT

Cameron was born in Denver and grew up in central Ohio. The Polish nursery rhymes and gentle spirit of his grandfather, Jan Paweł Dąbrowski, instilled in him a deep affection for the Slavic world. After college, a backpacking trip reignited Cameron's interest in Eastern (ahem, "Central") Europe, and he's enjoyed annual trips to the region ever since. Since moving to Seattle and joining Rick Steves' Europe (where he serves as content manager) in 2000, Cameron has traveled to more than 35 European countries, contributing to guidebooks, tours, radio and television shows, and other media. Cameron married his high school sweetheart (and favorite travel partner), Shawna, and enjoys taking pictures, trying new restaurants, and planning his next trip.

Avalon Travel
a member of the Perseus Books Group
1700 Fourth Street
Berkeley, CA 94710

For the latest on Rick's lectures, guidebooks, tours, public radio show, and public television
series, contact Rick Steves' Europe, 130 Fourth Avenue North, Edmonds, WA 98020,
425/771-8303, www.ricksteves.com, rick@ricksteves.com.

ISBN 978-1-63121-075-4

Rick Steves' Europe
Managing Editor: Risa Laib
Editorial & Production Manager: Jennifer Madison Davis
Editors: Glenn Eriksen, Tom Griffin, Suzanne Kotz, Cathy Lu, Carrie Shepherd
Editorial & Production Assistant: Jessica Shaw
Editorial Intern: Stacie Larsen
Maps & Graphics: David C. Hoerlein, Sandra Hundacker, Lauren Mills, Mary Rostad

Avalon Travel
Senior Editor & Series Manager: Madhu Prasher
Editor: Jamie Andrade
Associate Editor: Maggie Ryan
Copy Editor: Jennifer Malnick
Proofreader: Gayle Hart
Indexer: Stephen Callahan
Production & Typesetting: McGuire Barber Design
Cover Design: Kimberly Glyder Design
Maps & Graphics: Kat Bennett, Mike Morgenfeld

Cover Photo: St. Andrew's Church At Grodzka Street, Poland © Chris Bradley/
Design Pics/Getty Images
Additional Photography: Dominic Arizona Bonuccelli, Cameron Hewitt, David C.
Hoerlein, Sandra Hundacker, Debi Jo Michael, Gene Openshaw, Rhonda Pelikan,
Rick Steves, Gretchen Strauch, Honza Vihan (photos are used by permission and are
the property of the original copyright owners).

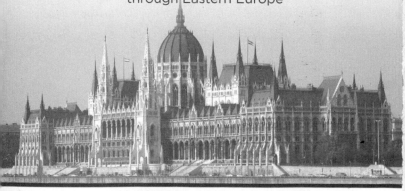